CW00518565

The Last Haul

The Last Haul

Recollections of the Days before English Fishing Died

David Butcher

POPPYLAND
PUBLISHING

Copyright © David Butcher.
This edition 2020 published by Poppyland Publishing, Lowestoft, NR32 3BB.

www.poppyland.co.uk

ISBN 978 1 909796 48 5

All rights reserved. No part of this publication may be reproduced, stored in a retrieval system or transmitted by any means, mechanical, photocopying, recording or otherwise, without the written permission of the publishers.

Designed and typeset in 10.5 on 13.5 pt Times New Roman.

Printed by Ashford Colour Press.

Picture credits:
Author's collection front cover, 91, 93, 98 (all three, courtesy of the late Jack Rose), 190
Banham, B. 10, 138
Brown, S. 12, 31, 32, 35, 48, 73, 74, 88, 118, 120, 130, 150, 163, 197
Bunn, I.A.W. 13, 215
Earl, S. 76
JB Archive 177
Poppyland Collection 165
Port of Lowestoft Research Society 10, 36, 49, 55, 127, 136, 153, 170, 212.

Front Cover: Lowestoft Harbour Entrance.

A late 1930s pencil drawing by local artist, Cyril Walker (entitled "Returning to harbour: Lowestoft"), showing the steam trawler "Croton" (LT 84) entering the port. Built at Govan in 1898 and formerly registered as GY 1344, this vessel was one member of a fleet of former Grimsby steam trawlers operated out of the Suffolk port by Consolidated Fisheries Ltd.

Contents

Illustrations

Plates

Figures

Maps

Preface & Acknowledgements

This book is the last, in a series of five, recording the oral history of commercial fishing in the Lowestoft area during the first half of the twentieth century. The previous four (*The Driftermen, The Trawlermen, Living From the Sea* and *Following the Fishing*) were all published between 1979 and 1987 and, while this particular volume was both intended and planned, the opportunity to bring it to completion did not arise until the writer had retired from teaching. Such were the demands of working in a comprehensive high school during the last ten to fifteen years of his career (far outweighing what had gone before), to say nothing of various other commitments outside of compulsory education—especially the time spent on a part-time research degree at the University of East Anglia. The programme of tape-recording itself, with all the various respondents (male and female), was carried out between 1976 and 1983, with the recordings and their transcripts now forming part of the Suffolk County Oral History Collection. A photo-copied set of the transcripts is lodged at the University of Freiburg, Germany, where it forms part of the material used for the advanced study of linguistics appertaining to English regional dialects.

Much has changed in the British fishing industry since the earlier books were produced and, generally, the story has been one of consistent and continued decline (particularly in the case of English ports)—a process that was already under way at the time of writing. In Lowestoft, the decline has been drastic, and for some twenty years or so there have been no mid-water trawlers working. The fish market continues to function, but as a much-reduced operation relying on fish brought in from outside sources (the current number of inshore vessels not being capable of supplying the needs of the merchants) and with its future far from certain. Even thirty years ago, few people living in the town would have foreseen such a situation or believed that it was possible. Such is the fragility of fishing economies in the face of over-exploitation of stocks, pollution of the oceans, rises in sea temperature and too much reliance on certain key species in the convenience-food market.

Some optimism has been expressed, in certain quarters, regarding a revival in the fishing industry as a whole now that the UK has left the European Union. It is difficult to see this happening on any significant scale because of all the complex factors involved in negotiating a catching policy (acceptable to all parties) which can be made to work to everyone's satisfaction. In Lowestoft's case, its substantial mid-water fleet will never return, simply because the operation became increasingly difficult to make profitable in its latter years. There was not enough fish close to home and the voyages made to distant, more northerly sectors of the North Sea were rarely fully cost-effective. The sale of the catches did not make enough money to cover the expenses of wages, fuel, maintenance and replacement of gear, and investment in new craft. The best that can be hoped for is an increase in smaller vessels working close to home, engaged in a local, sustainable fishery underpinned by strict supervision and enforcement of the old three- and twelve-mile limit-lines, equitable catch-quotas for the small operator, and the banning of harmful ways of fishing—particularly electrical "pulsing" for soles and other valuable flatfish.

Given all that has happened in recent years regarding fishing activity in the town of Lowestoft, much of what is contained within the covers of this book will seem to reflect not only another age, but perhaps even another world! And, in a sense, the experiences recorded and presented do indeed belong to an era very different from our own. The earlier books dealt with drift-netting and the herring industry, with trawling, with the social life of shore-side communities and with land-based industries associated with fishing. This particular volume will consider various types of fishing not previously covered, interesting and dangerous experiences connected with a life at sea, fisheries research, the role of the railway-system in serving fishing, life on board Trinity House lightships, and (strangest of all) a treasure-hunting expedition to Cocos Island in a converted Lowestoft, diesel-powered herring drifter.

The presentation of material will be similar to that previously used: substantial passages of personal recollection, prefaced and linked by commentary needed to create a framework within which the narrative can function. The oral testimony is presented so as to reflect the East Anglian dialect, but full phonetic treatment is not adopted because of the difficulties this presents to the reader. People from East Anglia will recognise both usage and tone; those not familiar with the dialect will develop a sense of it. Some of the men to be heard were among my most regular informants; others were recorded for a single session only. All of them had long retired from the sea when the interviews took place and all are now long deceased. The book will serve as a posthumous tribute to them. As an aid to the reader, italic font has been used to highlight specialist vocabulary and key-words, as well as dialect forms, and there is a glossary at the end to explain meanings of most of the terms thus noted. A final vestige of the past is to be found in the line-drawings of the late Syd Brown—an older teaching colleague of the writer, whose artistic skills and knowledge of fishing contributed greatly to both *The Driftermen* and *The Trawlermen*.

Apart from the demise of the respondents themselves, the other notable departure from the project of collecting and making available the oral history of the Lowestoft-Great Yarmouth fishing industry (especially the former town) is that of Colin Elliott, who died many years ago. Colin was publisher of the first three volumes under his Tops'l Books imprint and editor of the fourth as a member of staff at David & Charles. His knowledge of the British fishing industry was extensive, his interest in the writer's work genuine and the working relationship developed between the two something of great value. The house-style of the earlier works will not be adhered to in this final volume. A different publisher inevitably means a different format and I am very happy to have worked, first of all, with Peter Stibbons (a valued acquaintance of many years) and then with his successor at Poppyland Publishing, Gareth Davies.

Other acknowledgements also need to be made. First of all, is Stanley Earl, Chairman of the Port of Lowestoft Research Society, who has supplied photographs of vessels mentioned in text from that organisation's archive and found port registration numbers for smaller longshore craft which do not appear either in local directories (such as Huke's or Flood's) or in Olsen's Fisherman's Nautical Almanack—as well as checking port registration numbers for the many fishing vessels referred to. Another member, Barry Banham, has kindly provided back-up from his own extensive records. Ivan Bunn created the excellent image of the seine-netting technique featured in Chapter One and the map of Cocos Island reproduced in Chapter Eleven. Finally, my friend, and leading member of the Suffolk local history establishment, Bob Malster, kindly read through the text and exercised his corrective and informed scrutiny. Any errors which remain, therefore, are the fault of the author—and no one else.

David Butcher, 2020.

Plate 1:   Boy Ben (LT 212)

The steam drifter "Boy Ben" (LT 212), shown on her trial trip, with a multitude of people on board (no Health & Safety constraints in those days!). Built at Lowestoft in 1906, she was later renamed "Girl Phyllis".

Plate 2:   Faithful Friend (LT 33)

The steam drifter "Faithful Friend" (LT 33): built at Lowestoft in 1913: shown under way, at sea, with the foremast typically secured to its resting-place on top of the wheelhouse. Its main use when erected (in tandem with the steam capstan) was to have the boom serve as derrick to run catches ashore when landing.

CHAPTER ONE

The Danish Seine

Thou shalt have a fish,
Thou shalt have a fin.
Thou shalt have a haddock
When the boat comes in.
(Traditional folksong: *Dance to Your Daddy*)

A major consideration in any kind of commercial fishing is the expense of financing a vessel relative to its earning capacity, as the latter has to outweigh the former in order for a profit to be made. The capital cost of purchasing the craft has to be allowed for, as well as the annual depreciation on the initial sum spent. Thus, the assessment of a boat's performance in economic terms is not simply a matter of calculating whether the catches sold at market add up to a greater value than the money committed to the day-to-day running costs (fuel, gear, wages, provisions and repairs). However, these latter are a useful indicator of financial viability, or lack of it, and if earnings generally exceed expenses then a vessel may be termed a success in operational terms.

Among the ways of keeping costs down is minimising the amount of of fuel used and ensuring that the gear employed works to best advantage—preferably with the least amount of wear and tear. This was (and still is) the attraction of the *Danish seine-net* for operators, as it is cost-effective in both areas. F.M. Davis, in what is still probably the classic work on fishing gear, says that English fishermen began to use this type of equipment during the 1930s,[1] but it had actually been in operation during the previous decade. The particular attractions for certain of the Lowestoft fishing-vessel owners who adopted it were not only lower fuel costs (in this case, coal) and less expenditure on the repair of gear, but also the overall catching capacity and the relative ease of converting steam drifters and drifter-trawlers to a different method of fishing. Such conversion enabled a vessel to extend its working practice, making it more versatile and (potentially) more profitable.

An explanation of the Danish seine and the way it functioned is best kept brief. The net itself was a tapering bag about eighty to 100 feet in length by 150 to 170 feet wide across the mouth (depending on the way it was rigged and the species sought). Each extremity of the mouth was fixed to a wooden post, about two feet in length, known as a *dan leno*, which served to separate the *ground-*

---

1   F.M. Davis, *An Account of the Fishing Gear of England and Wales*, 4th ed. (London, 1958), p. 72. This HMSO publication, which was originally published in 1923 as Vol. V in Series II of *Fisheries Investigations*, underwent three updates.

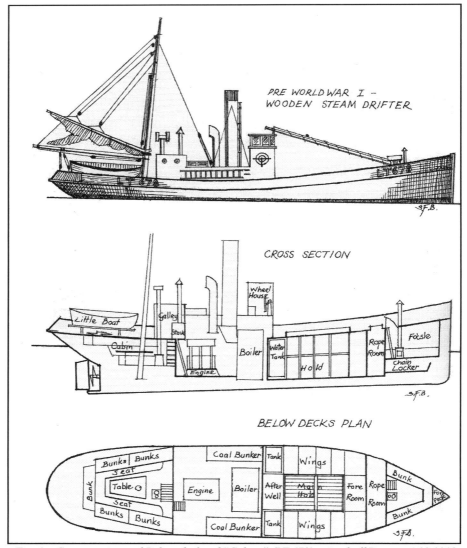

Fig. 1: Cross-section and Below-decks of "Coleus" (LT 678), mined off Dover—4.10.1918.

Cross-section of and below-decks views of a typical wooden steam drifter built before the First World War. This type of vessel was, in many ways, the life-blood of Lowestoft right up until the outbreak of the Second World War.

rope from the *head-line* and to help keep the mouth open when hauling began.[2] The dan lenos were then secured to the two *warps* or towing ropes (one either side), each of which consisted of eight to ten individual lengths, known as *coils*

---

2 The term *dan leno* was a corruption of the French word *guindineaux* and named after a popular, late Victorian, English music hall performer.

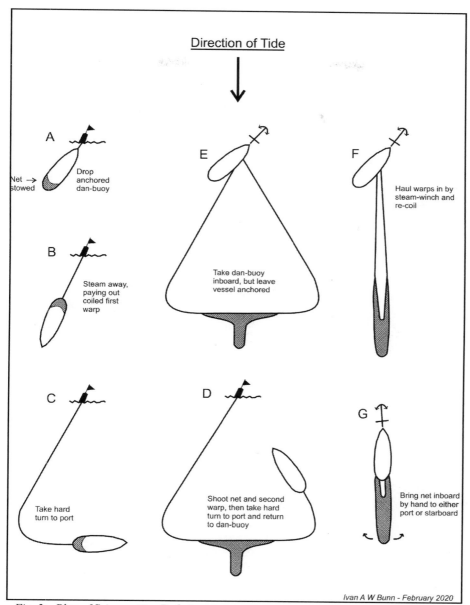

Fig. 2: Plan of Seine-netting Technique

The diagram shows the seven stages of the seine-netting process, as described by Ned Mullender in this chapter. Its overall success had a serious effect on North Sea haddock stocks during the 1920s.

and measuring 120 fathoms (720 feet). These were *spliced* together, to give an unbroken, continuous run. Spherical glass *floats*, each encased in a net bag, were set along the head-line to create buoyancy and the ground-rope was weighted down with lead weights or short lengths of light chain.

The gear was originally intended for *flatfish* (especially plaice), but it caught species such as cod and haddock equally well, with appropriate adjustments made to the net. Basically speaking, the haddock net had broader *wings*, smaller meshes and a longer *bag* (or *cod-end*) than the plaice variety, and it was made of finer *cotton* twine. The cod net was the same gauge twine as that used for plaice, but it was longer and wider. All of them were either treated against the rotting effect of salt water with a wood-preserving agent, such as Cuprinol, or not treated at all. The ropes themselves were periodically dressed with creosote, in order to give them a longer working-life.

The fishing method itself may be termed "stationary trawling" (because there was no towing of the gear) and it worked in the following manner. An *anchor* was dropped to the seabed from the bow of the vessel, with a *mooring-line* (made up of varying lengths of chain, *bass* rope and wire cable) leading up to a *buoy* floating on the surface. A *dan* [al. dhan] was fixed to this buoy by a wire link and a further length of wire cable, supported by three *buffs*, then completed the mooring-line, having its terminating *eye* slipped over a double *bollard* in the foredeck and secured. Both *warps*—of two and a half inch circumference *manila*—lay coiled in the *kids* on either side of the boat, the first one to be shot (either to port or starboard, depending on what the skipper wished to accomplish) being fixed to the mooring-line and the second one having its end secured to the winch's *drum*.

A *clip-link* was used to join the first warp to be shot to the *mooring-line*, after which the latter was freed from the deck bollard, the helm brought hard over and the boat steamed off down tide, paying out the warp with its momentum (one of the crew watched this operation to ensure no fouling of the rope). Once the required amount of warp had been released, the vessel then slowed and turned at a right-angle across the tide to allow the net to be pulled from a specially constructed platform on the stern, where it had been laid ready for use. The *cod-end* was cast by hand (usually by the mate), to ensure that it cleared the propeller and, as soon as the whole net was overboard, the boat again turned through a right-angle and gathered speed once more—this time on its return leg back towards the mooring, against the tide, with the second warp running freely overboard. As soon as the marker dan was reached, about twenty to twenty-five minutes after *shooting* had begun, the second warp was secured to a deck bollard and the dan itself picked up, brought inboard and made fast.

The vessel itself was now secured to the anchor and the configuration of the net roughly resembled an equilateral triangle, with the boat at the apex and the net in the middle of the base. The whole shooting operation usually took something like thirty to forty minutes and, as soon as it was over, *hauling* could begin. The end of the first warp was unclipped from the mooring-line and put on to the *winch*, the second warp (already on the winch) freed from the deck bollard, and the machinery set in motion. There were only about two turns of the warp around the winch's *drum*, on either side of the machine, and each rope ran off it through a coiling device, which re-coiled the ropes and pushed them back into the *kids* ready for the next shoot.[3] The drum speeds were variable and each drum could be operated independently of the other. Thus, adjustments could be made to the rate of haul on each warp, should this be needed.

The net was hauled in against the tide and the winch ran quickly at first, until both warps were taut. The speed of haul was then slowed for a period of time, until the distance between the warps had narrowed down, when the speed was increased again in order to get the net inboard as soon as possible.[4] After the *wings* had been hauled in over the rail, the *cod-end* was hoisted overhead by a *derrick* bolted on to the side of the galley, or fixed to the mizzen mast, and emptied into a deck *pound*. Sometimes, the weight of fish caught was too great for the cod-end to be safely lifted inboard, so it was left partly in the water, the securing knot released and the catch brought on board by means of a large *didall* manipulated by two of the crew. In order to help with the operation, the didall was joined to the mizzen mast's derrick (or *boom*) by a rope, thereby creating extra lifting capacity if required.

Shooting and hauling usually took about an hour, which made this particular method of fishing generally more effective and profitable than conventional trawling, whereby a vessel towed its gear for the length of a tide (up to six hours) before the net was hauled. However, there were limitations as to its use. It was mainly effective during daylight hours and relied upon relatively fine weather in order to be successful. The less robust nature of the gear, when compared with a conventional trawl, also meant that it was unsuited to rough grounds and to those areas of the sea where strong tides ran. However, in the right kind of environment, its fishing capacity and its earning power were unmatched. The calculation has been made that in one haul alone, using warps of ten coils a side, 140 acres of seabed were covered.[5] Edward ("Ned") Mullender (1896-1981) was a fisherman of vast experience, who went seining during the early 1920s—both as fill-in between other fishing voyages (when men were often laid off) and as a means of broadening his experience. His comments (recorded, 19 October 1976 and 3 December 1979) are illuminating.

---

3   Some of the coilers were made by Elliott & Garrood Ltd., of Beccles—a firm which produced many of the steam-capstans used in the British fishing industry, as well as steam-reciprocating marine engines—the most notable of which was the famed *Monkey-triple*. This space-saving machinery had the high-pressure cylinder set above the intermediate one, with the low-pressure one to the side—the layout supposedly resembling a monkey sitting on top of a barrel-organ.

4   As soon as the warps had narrowed, the net was no longer sweeping the seabed and catching fish.

5   Davis, *Fishing Gear*, p. 75.

"Seine nettin' wuz a big thing here once. Cor, bless me, yis! 1921, '22, '23. I think the *Indomitable* (LT 196) an' the *Brackendale* (LT 695) were the first two to go. That wuz Tommy Doddington, what used to live up here [in Florence Road, Pakefield]—he wuz skipper o' the *Indomitable*—an' George Killington wuz in the *Brackendale*. I come out o' Joe Colby's boat, the *Silver Herrin'* (LT 1145), in 1922, because the skipper got finished an' she wuz laid up.[6] An' I wuz a-walkin' about, an' this seine-nettin' business had started the year before, see? An' I had set an' got my *mate's ticket* an' my *skipper's ticket* the year before, an' the seine net business come on an' I could see it wuz a payin' thing. See? An' I thought to myself, 'I dun't know. I'd like to have a go at that.' Well, my brother-in-law's brother wuz goin' skipper o' the *Victoria* (LT 1056), which belonged to Bob Sillett, an' I asked Bob Sillett if I could go out as they were goin' to have a Dane show 'em how to work. See? An' I says, 'Can I go out? You know, as a spare hand. *Pleasure trip*. I'll pay for my food.' Which they were goin' to charge me £1 for. And, o' course, I agreed to that.

"Well now, when they started to git her ready, I went down to see how things were bein' organised. You know, gettin' the nets an' what they were doin' about the ropes an' all this, that an' the other. And the owner come up an' say to me, 'One o' the crew hent turned up. Will you go *deckie*?' I say, 'Yes, I'll go deckie—on one condition.' He say, 'What's that?' I say, 'If I can better myself by goin' mate somewhere, I'll go. And you let me go, whether I can give forty-eight hours notice or no.' So he say, 'All right. Agreed on.' And I say, 'You know it's a verbal agreement, but stick to it. Because,' I say, 'I'm not goin' to keep deckie.'

"So, anyway, we goes. An' when we goes to sea, the Dane wuz occupied on the *Vesper Star* (LT 94)—one o' the Star Company's boats.[7] They'd got him, yuh see. Whether they paid him more money, I dun't know. Well, I can say, but I can't prove it. Anyway, we went out and we didn't really know what to do—though the third hand, Dilly Flowers, had done a little bit and I'd done some trawlin'. None o' the others knew anything about it—includin' the skipper. Well, I dun't know what trouble we had! Everything bar the right thing! And we come in and I think we made about £60.[8] Well, we'd done six trips and I give my notice in. And when we went out agin for the last time, some o' the blokes say to me, 'What, have you give your notice in?' I say, 'Yis. I'm goin' mate in a ship when we come come in.' I say, 'I'm goin' to better myself.'

"Well, we goes out and that wuz a flop again. We were all amongst the other boats. Yeah, we were workin' with other boats, but we couldn't fish with 'em! And I kept on sayin' what the trouble was: we were draggin' the anchor all over the North Sea! Well, consequences was we were goin' down to the net, instead o'

---

6 This was in the spring of 1922, after the *mackerel voyage* to Newlyn had finished.

7 The Star Drift Fishing Co. Ltd.

8 This amount was not sufficient to make a profitable trip.

the net comin' to us. We hadn't got enough anchor down. And that's just what had happened. That wuz shined up just like a bit o' silver, on the *flukes*. They wouldn't have it, though. They say, 'Oh, that'd hold a man o' war!' So I just say, 'All right.'

"Next boat I went in wuz the *Girl Phyllis* (LT 212) and the first thing I say wuz, 'I want plenty o' chain.' The owner say, 'How much?' I say, 'Forty-five fathom.' 'Good God!' he say. 'You dun't want that!' I say, 'Oh yes, I do.' That wuz to go on the anchor, see. Yeah. Well, o' course, he give us some old chain what he could git hold of, because everybody wanted chain just about then! Everyone wuz seine-nettin', see. So, consequences was, we got old chain. But, anyway, that looked all right and out we goes. Well, first haul, we didn't git a lot o' fish, because the ropes wun't *sanded*. But after we'd used the ropes a couple o' days, that got better. We went to sea on the Monday and we did the first shoot on Tuesday, round about midday. Then we worked all Wednesday and the ol' ropes were fishin' a little better every time. Well, on the Thursday afternoon and the Friday mornin' we got some damn good hauls, so the skipper, Darkie Green, say to me, 'How much fish, boy?' I say, 'Oh, I dun't know- about a hundred *kit*.' I say, 'That might even be a little better. You know me.' He say, 'Yis, I know. There's a good hundred kit down there because I've bin countin' 'em.'

"We'd had one haul on the Friday mornin' and, after the second one, he say, 'All right. Stow your ropes up.' So we *stewed* the ropes up and I thought to myself, 'Well, we must be goin' hoom.' We gutted the fish up and, after we'd done that, we put the *log* over—so I knew we wuz headin' south an' I thought to myself.'Oh, we're a-goin' hoom.' You always put a log over when you were *a-steamin'*. Oh yeah. I mean, I'm goin' back afore *Decca* an' all that sort o' stuff. If, say, you were about 140 mile down from the Knoll, you'd measure that on your *log*. I mean, you didn't want to run 160 mile on the way back, because you'd got to turn in from the Knoll to make Low'stoft. If you run too far, you'd find yourself up the Shipwash. There wun't no buoys down there. No buoys, nor nothin'. No, not then![9]

"Anyway, we got in and landed on the Saturday mornin'. Then we went to sea agin on Monday and shot away on Tuesday. Friday mornin', the skipper say to me, 'What fish have we got, Mr. Mate?' Calls me 'Mr. Mate' this time! Ha, ha.' I say, 'Well, we're got more'n what we had last week.' 'Righto,' he say. 'Stow up.' And we stew up an' hoom we come. I forgit exactly how much we made, but that wuz £40 or £50 more'n we did the first trip. That wuz mixed stuff—haddick, codlin' and that sort o' thing. And, consequences was, out we go again o' Monday.

---

9   Fishing on the Dogger Bank is being referred to in this paragraph. *The Knoll* was Smith's Knoll, a fishing ground about twenty-five miles north-east of Great Yarmouth. The Shipwash was an area of the North Sea about six miles east by south off Orford Ness—acquiring its name because of a supposed similarity between the white waves breaking over it and sheep going through a dip (*ship* being the old Suffolk dialect pronunciation of "sheep", as in the village of Shipmeadow, near Bungay).

Well, Friday mornin' we wuz haulin' an' the net went clean out o' the *frame*.[10] And we shot away agin in a hurry an' the same thing happened. That went just as it wuz comin' out o' the water. The net went clean out o' the frame! So we let go o' the anchor, and I had a pair o' *creepers*, and I threw it in amongst this net an' that kept it afloat. We brought it up to the top, but there wuz a lot o' haddicks went out, so we turned the net an' then got started, *didallin'*. A-didallin' on 'em in. Then, when we'd done that, we got back to the dan an' picked that up. 'Right,' say the skipper. 'Hoom we go!' 'Yis,' I say. 'I dun't know as I'd had no more ice after that haul. If we'd got them two hauls,' I say, 'I shouldn't have had a ha'porth o' ice left!' We made £248 that trip! We went to sea on the Monday an' got in the harbour here about half-past five Saturday mornin'."

These remarks serve well to demonstrate the effectiveness of seine-netting, when correctly carried out, and also to create some feeling for the period in which it was being pioneered in Lowestoft. The 1920s were not the buoyant times hoped for in the whole of the British fishing industry once the First World War had run its course. Landings had been at record levels in 1913 in the herring sector, but catches were never to return to those quantities and export markets in continental Europe were disabled by the currency crisis in Germany and by the Communist regime in Russia cancelling all debts incurred under the Tsarist regime. Trawling continued to flourish, and Lowestoft operated both sailing smacks and steam trawlers, but its herring fleet was the largest part of its total fishing effort and anything which took up spare capacity in terms of vessels was welcome. Seine-netting did not develop into anything significant in the long term in the port of Lowestoft, but it provided a profitable activity while it lasted and taught new skills to the men involved. Ned Mullender was high in his praise of it.

"That wuz a marvellous way o' fishin'! Far superior to trawlin'. Yes. If I wuz about forty or fifty year younger now and anyone started seine-nettin' up, I would go. I would go! See, when you go seine-nettin', you anchor. You could have what you call a *fly-shoot*, but in them days we used to anchor. You used to steam away about seven ropes from your *moorings* and then you'd turn the boat square and shoot about a rope an' a half, to make about eight ropes, say, or nine. Then, after the net had gone, you'd shoot about another rope an' a half the other side o' the net and turn back to your moorings. When you got back there, you'd pick the moorings up and fix them on your *pollards* [bollards] and then bring the rope to the *winch*. See, you'd alriddy got one rope aboard and the one you'd picked up from the mooring. Well, you'd put that one on the winch and you'd level the two warps orf. Then you'd turn the winch and gradually bring the net to yuh. You only steamed with the net if you had a fly-shoot.

"The net wuz about 170 foot wide, I spose, by about eighty to ninety long,

---

10 This means that the weight of fish in the net caused the meshes to tear away from the cords that formed the overall shape of the gear and gave it its dimensions.

and you had glass *bottles* all along the *head-line*, like the ones I've got hangin' up here.[11] That wuz hellishly deep as well, and all along the bottom [i.e. on the *ground-rope*] you had little round leads threaded through the rope. That went on the ground and if you wanted to dig in more, you cut up little bits o' thin chain and put that on. And then you'd bottle up more. The ropes travel along the bottom and make a sand [i.e. stir the sand up], and as you hauled they gradually closed and forced the fish to go to the only openin' they could see—which wuz the net. See? That wuz bein' floated well up on the head-line, so the fish would go in. There wun't hardly no sand where the net wuz. The ropes were makin' the sand and the fish wouldn't go through that; they'd go where that wuz clear—inta the net. That wuz the method. The net didn't catch the fish; the ropes did. On a good day, say from four o' clock in the mornin' till eleven o'clock at night, if you had a smart crew and were workin' only eight ropes, you could git in about fourteen to fifteen hauls!

"The ropes were 120 fathoms long and you *spliced* 'em together. And, in each end, you had a hook—a *hook-link*—and you'd hook that onto your net. There wuz one on one end o' the net and one on the other.[12] The net wuz a kind of twine, a very thin kind o' twine, and that had very big *mashes* [meshes] in places. And that wuz more complicated than what a trawl wuz. Oh, that wuz a lot more complicated than what a trawl wuz! The net had quite a big *poke* on it and all, on the cod-end and in the wings. There wuz nothin' on the cod end itself, no *false bellies* or nothin', and you didn't tie it like the cod-end on a trawler. You had a special lashin' on, which you could undo to open the cod-end, because if there wuz a lot o' fish in there you couldn't git 'em aboard because the net wouldn't hold. So, therefore, you had to *didall* 'em out. See? You'd hold that cod end open from the boat for didallin' in.

"I went mainly for haddick, but I used to go a-plaicin' sometimes as well. Yis. And we used to git cod an' all. We got thirty odd kit in one haul once—mostly good-sized codlin'. You'd git the odd sole or two, if you were more or less in the Pits, or if you were orf the Bank [Dogger Bank]—you know, in what we used to call the *scruff ground*.[13] Yeah, you'd git an odd sole then. The most soles I ever had would be, roughly, hardly a box full. You used to sort them out from the rest. You didn't put them on the market.[14] You'd git turbots as well sometimes. Yeah. An' whitins, dabs, lemons. If you were workin' the Hospital Ground, you'd git

---

11 Ned Mullender had glass seine-net floats hanging up in his living room as a form of decoration. They are still popular with some people as a form of interior décor.

12 The hook-links, or *clip-links*, engaged the dan leno posts on either side of the net's mouth.

13 The Great Silver Pit and Little Silver Pit were fishing grounds on the Dogger Bank, famed for catches of sole. The Upper Scruff and the Lower Scruff were grounds on the eastern side of the Dogger, about midway between the coasts of England and Denmark.

14 Soles were one of the most valuable species landed, but because they were only taken in very small quantities by seine-nets they were usually shared out amongst the crew.

a lot o' dabs on there wi' sores on 'em. Yeah, that used to be called the Hospital Ground.[15] You'd git *dorgs* [dogfish] if you were anywhere where they were. Not so much *nurses*, but yeah, you'd git the odd dorg or two. But we never got bags o' dorgs or anything like that.[16]

"The nets varied as well. See, you had a *plaice net* and you had a *haddick net*. They used to call 'em plaice nets and haddick nets. The haddick net had a lot more flow in it, and if you were haddickin' you shot about eight ropes [per side]. But if you went after plaice, you put on two more ropes or what you fancied. If you fancied you wanted four more ropes, well, you put four more on—and you had twelve ropes then. I have known somebody to say that they had fifteen ropes on, but I've never had fifteen. You hauled slower for plaice. Yeah, that took a lot longer. Your *foot-rope* [ground-rope] wuz weighted down, on the bottom. You were on the bottom with a haddick net, o' course, but you were just trimmin' the bottom and you had a lot more bottles on. Now, if you deepen the water—. Say if you're workin' in about twenty fathom, you'd have about twenty-five, thirty, thirty-five bottles on. They were in *single nets*, just the single nets, so you put 'em on singly. You didn't put 'em on like you did on a trawl. No, you had 'em on singly.[17] You'd have them in the *little boat*, which wuz aft. Yeah, you'd have spare ones in there for when they got broke comin' over the rail. Now, if you wuz workin' deeper water—say forty to forty-five fathom, or deeper—you'd put more bottles on. You'd have forty-five to fifty then, to keep the headline up because o' the pressure.

"Like I said before, that wuz the ropes what done the fishin', because as you hauled so the ropes stirred the sand up. Now, if you didn't have ropes what were doin' that work, they wouldn't fish. And the more they were sanded up, the better. That wuz a good way o' fishin' for the owners [boatowners] too. I tell yuh, we never bunkered only about nine and a half ton o' coal in the little ol' *Girl Phyllis*. Cor, bless me, yes! The biggest money spent wuz for ropes. Your ropes didn't last long. You know, specially if you got a poor quality o' ropes, what some of 'em tried. They wouldn't fish like the good quality. If you had a good quality o' ropes, so they were heavy when they got wet an' sanded up, they were the boys what fished. When I wuz in the *Girl Phyllis*, after we'd done three or four trips in her, they decided to take the ropes ashore an' dress 'em. I dun't know what with, but they were goin' to dress 'em. An', anyway, they give us some new ropes. Do yuh know what?—that wuz the worst trip we had. Yeah, the ropes wun't no good! They wun't fish.

---

15 This particular area was on the Dogger Bank, about 100 miles east of Scarborough.

16 The dogfish referred to here were Spur-dogs (*Squalus acanthias*), not the Larger-spotted Dogfish, or Nursehound (*Scyliorhinus stellaris*).

17 Glass seine-net floats were housed singly in a net pouch. Glass floats used on trawls (in cases where they were preferred to metal ones) were secured in lengths of net known as *sausages.*

"You soon knew when you struck fish, though! Like that time I told you about on the *Girl Phyllis*, when the net broke. You knew when fish were in the net, because the warps would close together. Yeah, after you'd got about five ropes in, if you kept a good look out, you could see whether you were goin' to git fish. As soon as you'd got any quantity, if you'd got a big bag, they'd come to the surface—so all your ropes were comin' along the top o' the water. Oh, you'd soon know! We'd shot that mornin' an' I went down an' had my breakfast. That wuz the second shoot an' the skipper wuz in charge—little ol' Darkie Green. Now, you had some *brakes* on the winch, which you could stop the ropes comin' in with. That wuz like a handle which you worked up and down. And if you didn't have them warps square, level—if one wuz up like that [indicating the respective levels with his hands]—well, you'd have to slack that away until you brought it down level with the other one.

"Well, when I come up from my breakfast, I come round the side where the warps were an' one wuz up like this an' one wuz down like that [again, using the hands as indicators]. Well, o' course, my language wun't too good! See? And when I got there, that wuz the skipper who wuz responsible. He say, 'I can't *blue-pencil* keep 'em right! Have you a go!' [The term *blue-pencil*, as used here indicates strong language.[18]] Well, o' course, I got on the winch an' I couldn't do it! Then up come the fish an', afore I could ease the winch up, the whole net went right clean out o' the frame with the weight o' fish. An' we lorst 'em. We didn't think about goin' after 'em to see whether they'd float. We made haste and got another net riddy and shot away agin. Now, the same thing happened, only we'd got the net closer this time when that went out o' the frame. So we let go o' our *moorins* right quick and went down to the net, and I threw a pair o' *graplins* [i.e. a double-headed grapnel] inta the net and pulled it up to the surface. Well, I hadn't got the openin' properly hooked, so the haddicks were goin' out wholesale. God know how many went out! But, anyway, we got the cod end twizzled round so we held the rest in an' that took us two hours to didall 'em out. An' that filled all our *kids* down one side [of the vessel], an' two o' the boys got what they called *roarin' shovels* an' were puttin 'em round the other side. An' we were full up both sides wi' that one bag!

"Oh yeah, plenty o' times we hadn't gutted one lot afore the next lot come in. That'd pile up. You'd be full up both sides. Well, then you'd hafta stop up half the night an' gut 'em. You didn't stop fishin'. And unless you'd got over a *lump* [i.e. finished gutting one particular haul], you'd pile 'em one on top o' the other while the fish were there to be caught. It wuz very rare you left orf. I tell yuh, that time we got that bag o' cod in the little ol' *Girl Phyllis*—God know how many it wuz! Well, I know how many it wuz. That one haul, there wuz thirty-odd *kit*! An' we wuz guttin' them till we nearly got hoom. Well, till we got to the Knoll, anyway.

---

18 It presumably derives from editorial practice concerning material to be published, whereby unnecessary or offending passages were once crossed out in blue crayon.

We ought to ha' made more money wi' that trip."

There is a great deal of technical detail in the paragraphs above and most of it (if not all) is broadly in line with that given in the introduction to this chapter. The actual dimensions of fishing gear could, and did, vary according to the type of grounds worked, the species sought and the whims and beliefs of individual skippers. Given the length of time between Ned Mullender being involved in seine-netting and having his reminiscences recorded (fifty years or more later), there is impressive accuracy in what he divulged. His last remark may be taken as a summative comment regarding the lot of fishermen generally, whereby the rewards for many of them were not always commensurate with their labours. That was particularly true of herring-catching and also, at times, of trawling—though the security of a *weekly wage* in the latter occupation made it a better option than the former, where crew members were paid a *share of the profits* at the end of a voyage (if a profit had been made).[19]

Seine-netting, however, for the first few years that it was carried out by Lowestoft vessels, proved to have a greater earning potential than the two main forms of fishing in the port. This was because it had lower operating costs (especially where the consumption of coal was concerned), it was an extremely effective method of fishing, it did not suffer from the inconsistency of prices at market as herring-fishing tended to, and it benefited from a country-wide demand for *white fish*. Once the techniques had been mastered, and as long as a boatowner did not attempt to keep costs down by skimping on gear, good money for all parties could be made.

"That wuz a life I liked, seine-nettin'. Yeah, I took to that. You got paid on what you earnt. You were on a *share*. All of yuh. All on the share, yeah, like on a drifter, only you got more because you only had eight in the crew, see.[20] A skipper's money would be about—. What would he be about? I dun't know, about six or seven *quid* [£6-£7] on the hundred. Yeah, and the mate would be about £5 odd.[21] Yeah, I tell yuh, I accumulated a good bit o' money when I wuz single in the little ol' *Girl Phyllis*. Yeah. And we used to git £1 a week *stockie* an' all. And, that's what we got when I started in the *Faithful Friend* (LT 33) for ol' Gilbert [Arthur Gilbert, the vessel's owner]. We saved all the small fish for *stockie bait*. Well, we come in one trip and that made twenty odd quid. So that wuz £2 a man, or more, yuh see. That wuz too much! So he decided to give us a pound each. An' then, o' course, I kicked up about it. He say, 'That's a lot o' money!' I say, 'Yis. So is 300 quid for the trip!

---

19 Herring fishermen were also advanced a weekly subsistence payment, known as an *allotment*, which could be drawn by wives (or other designated family members) for the duration of a *voyage*. This was deducted from the final payout.

20 There were usually ten crew members on a herring drifter.

21 In other words, the skipper would receive about £6 or £7 for every £100 worth of fish sold at market and the mate about £5.

"I went in the *Faithful Friend* in 1923, after I'd bin in the *Girl Phyllis*. I wuz mate along o' Darkie Green until we finished in about the middle o' October, '22, then I went in the *Plumer* (LT 596) a week afterwards for trawlin'. We went out o' here first of all and then we went round to *West'ard*.[22] When we come hoom, she [the *Girl Phyllis*] wuz havin' a new skipper and crew go in her, so that left me out o' a job. Anyway, as I wuz walkin' along the market one day, Harry Parker come along. An' Harry an' me were pals durin' the war; we'd both bin out in Italy together.[23] He say to me, 'What're you doin', Neddy?' I say, 'Nothin'. I've just finished.' 'Well,' he say. 'Will yuh come wi' me?' I say, 'I dun't know. That all depend where you're goin' and how quick you want to go.' He say, 'Well, we wun't be goin' for a day or two. I'll let yuh know.' This wuz the Friday. Saturday, he come up to my house and told me he wuz goin' skipper o' the *Faithful Friend* and said would I go mate with him, seine-nettin'?

"That'd be about the middle o' May when I went out seine-nettin' with Harry. And we got haddicks, plaice, whitins, a few turbots an' a few cod—but moostly haddicks. We went to sea on the Thursday and we'd gotta go inta dry dock in Grimsby. He wanted a clean boat, and they couldn't git us in dock, not here, so we went to Grimsby. Well, we landed in Grimsby and all, to start with. And she'd done six trips and she'd only made £340! An' that wuz the same complaint [as in the *Victoria*]. The anchor wuz shined up every time we hauled. That wuz like a bit o' silver every time we got it aboard, where you'd bin pullin' it through the sand and mud. Afore we went to sea, I wanted some more chain, and they give me some, but that wun't enough. So I knew we wuz draggin' the anchor, see, and I kept tryin' to impress that on the skipper. Once we got it sorted out, we did out and out well.

"That first time when I asked for chain, I say to Arthur Gilbert, who wuz the owner, 'That chain ent man enough, guvnor.' 'What!' he say. 'That'll hold a man o' war.' 'All right,' I say. 'That'll hold a man o' war. But I dun't think it's any good.' See, I'd heard it all before in the *Victoria*, the year before. Well, bor, he bit! He say, 'I'll let you know that everything aboard here is good!' See? So I thought to myself, 'I'd better shut up.' The nexta mornin' he set on the *rail*, watchin' me splice a bad part in the *warp*. He say, 'I dunt know, Mr. Mate. I think you're wastin' a lot o' rope. I've seen you cut them two warps four times alriddy!' I say, 'Well, they want splicin', guvnor.' And I tried to explain to him that they wouldn't pass through the *coiler* unless they were done properly. Then I say, 'Look here,

---

22 This refers to the annual migration from Lowestoft of *drifter-trawlers* to take part in the Cornish sole-fishing voyage. The boats left in either January or February and based themselves at Padstow, either returning to the home port in May or going on to Fleetwood to fish in Morecambe Bay.

23 Both men, like many British fishermen in the two world wars, had belonged to the Royal Naval Patrol Service during the first great conflict and both had been involved in patrolling duties and in working on the anti-submarine barrage across the Straits of Otranto, in the Adriatic.

guvnor. Betwixt you an' me,' I say, 'You're bin at me ever since I come aboard this ship.' I say, 'Have you ever bin seine-nettin'?' He say, 'No.' 'Well,' I say, 'you know nothin' about it. An' that's that. Now, leave me alone,' I say, 'and we'll do our best.' Well, o' course, when I come ashore, he stood there talkin' to the skipper. And Harry told me about it afterwards. 'Who's that you're got mate wi' you?' he say. 'No one can't speak to him.' Harry say, 'Can't speak to him. What do yuh mean?' 'Well,' he say, 'I've said one or two things to him and he say to me that I dun't know nothin' about it! Where's he bin?' Harry say, 'He wuz mate o' that little ol' *Girl Phyllis* last year, what earnt all that money!' 'Wuz he?' he say. 'I dint know that. Better not say much to him, then!' Well, when I come down in the mornin', he stood there, see. And he say, 'Mr. Mate,' he say, 'I dint know you wuz in the *Girl Phyllis*.' 'No,' I say. 'I dun't'spect you did!'

"We used to fish the east side o' The Dogger, mostly. In *the Deeps*. You know, workin' in there. Yeah, the Clay Deeps and away down to the Tail End, and all round about there. More or less in that vicinity. Now and agin, you'd come onta the bank, see, and that's when you wanted a good anchorage because the ground wuz hard. See, that wuz hard sand and if you dint have enough chain, you'd drag your anchor. I have known these little Danish and Swedish ships have a *peg anchor*.[24] Yeah, they'd have another little anchor on the big one, so that'd hold the bigun down. Yeah. You'd gotta gauge which way the tide wuz runnin' an' my method wuz savin' the potater peelins from the cook. Then, afore we shot, I'd chuck some o' them over an' see which way they would *drive*, so I knew which way the tide wuz runnin'. You hauled inta the tide [i.e. against it] an' if you dint, you wun't git no fish! Yeah, you wun't git no fish!

"In regards to the grounds, I wuz in one boat seine-nettin', and we went to the North-West Rough. An' while we were down there, we worked on what they called "the Patches". There wuz patches o' little stones about the size o' peas and little nuts, and the ol' haddicks used to git on there and git their feed. Now, that wuz down on the nor'-west side o' the Dogger, right down at the bottom. Well, say nor'-nor'-west side o' the Dogger. You were well below Scarborough. Yeah, below that. Orf Newcastle. Yis. Cor blimey, you'd be down nearly as far as Aberdeen sometimes, afore yuh finished! When I wuz in the *Scadaun* (LT 1183), wi' plenty o' coal, we went down to what they called the Monkey Bank [off the coast of Denmark], and we fished down there for three or four trips.[25] And the fish we were gittin' were good. We were a-gittin' some good plaice. See? And we'd have about twenty kit o' good plaice, along o' the rest o' the catch. So when we

---

24 The Scandanavian vessels were almost certainly specialist seining craft, not converted drifters or trawlers.

25 The terms *down* and *below*, which appear in this paragraph, are fishermen's terms that indicate a northerly direction. In the North Sea, the ebb tide runs north and this fact created the sense of locations being lower than ones further to the south. Conversely, with the flood tide running south, the words *up* and *above* were chosen to describe movement in that direction.

come hoom, though we dint have so much fish as other people what just caught haddicks, we were makin' more money 'cause our plaice wuz such good quality stuff.

You dint go seine-nettin' out here, 'cause there wuz too much tide. When I wuz along o' Darkie Green, he say t' me, 'There's slack tides, Mr. Mate. What say let's have a go on the lower part o' the Long Shoal?'[26] I say, 'That's good enough for me, if you think we can git the net back.' I say, 'I have my doubts, even though it's slack tide.' Anyway, we shot, an' that took us a long while to git back to the dan. And, when we eventually got back to the dan and started to haul, we had to let go or we were goin' to part the ropes. Yeah, we were goin' to lose all the gear. We had to let go o' the moorins and go down to the net and haul that way. Yeah. So we never tried that no more. No. But we did go in the upper part o' the Botney Gut—though we never got a lot o' fish outa there.[27] O' course, whether that wuz the right time o' year or not, I dun't know. See, with seine-nettin' you'd fish from about March through to October.[28]

"You usually carried about three haddick nets an' a couple o' plaice nets. The haddick nets were bigger and had more spread. Oh yeah. When I wuz skipper o' the *Scadaun*, I went down to where some o' these trawlers are workin' now—about 200 or 300 mile down.[29] You had a crew o' eight when you were seinin'. You had the *skipper*, the *mate*, the *third hand*, two *deckhands*, the *cook* and two *engineers*. Now, the *Glow* (LT 668), she went practically all one year, seinin'. After she'd finished trawlin', she went seine-nettin' an' wuz a-workin' up till nearly Christmas. That wuz the year I wuz in the *Scadaun*, 1924, and if I'd kept in her I should have bin a lot better orf, as things turned out. The only reason I left is because my crew left to go herrin' catchin'. They didn't want to go seine-nettin' no more and I couldn't git a new crew. But the *Glow* kept a-goin' and that wuz a fine season, that hoom fishin', so he could git his time in. See, you can't shoot in bad weather wi' seine-nettin' because your ropes are only about, I spose, two and a half inches circumference, and they wouldn't stand too much strain. Nor would the net.

"I wuz in the *Scadaun* in 1924, like I said. Yeah. Now, I dint have no trouble wi'

---

26 This was a fishing-ground about thirty miles north-east of Cromer.

27 The Botney Cut (not "Gut") was a fishing-ground at the southern end of the Dogger Bank, about forty miles north-east of the Long Shoal.

28 Most of the drifters and drifter-trawlers involved in seine-netting would convert to *drift-netting* at the beginning of October, in order to participate in the local autumn herring voyage. This was known as *the Home Fishing*.

29 This would mean working grounds such as the Monkey Bank and Little Fisher Bank (off the coast of Denmark) and the English Klondyke (off the south-western coast of Norway). This last-named area was a favourite fishing-ground with Lowestoft vessels during the 1970s and 80s (Mr. Mullender was recorded in 1976 and 1979 concerning his seine-netting experiences).

the *haddick rash*, but a lot o' my crew did. But I dint—not even when I wuz mate. I allus used to keep my hands clean. See, if there wuz shells in the gut (which a good lot of 'em had shells), I'd have a bucket o' water, an' every now and agin I'd dip this hand in the water—'cause that wuz moostly your right hand, unless you were left-handed.[30] Now, the *Dogger Bank itch*, that wuz caused through weed, but I can't remember any o' my crowd gittin' that. That wuz hard work, yuh know, seine-nettin'. I mean, if you were after haddicks, you'd be shot and hauled in an hour! If you were after plaice, you'd be an hour and a half, two hours. The haul wuz slower there. That all depended on what fish there wuz, but you usually worked all daylight. All daylight. Yeah, when I wuz with Harry Parker [in the *Faithful Friend*], we used to git on the move at half-past three in the mornin' in the summer and we wun't knock orf till midnight! You wun't git down below afore midnight. You were tired enough when you'd bin there a week! You dint want to worry about you couldn't sleep! You could sleep all right! Yeah, you dint want to worry about you couldn't sleep. When I used to come hoom, I used to flop inta bed as soon as I got in."

Up until now, Ned Mullender has talked almost exclusively about fishing in the North Sea, on or near the Dogger Bank. But while this was the main area where seine-netting was carried out, it was not the only one. Such was the earning capacity demonstrated by some of the craft involved that a few of the Lowestoft vessel owners operated their craft on voyages in western waters also. Links with Cornwall were already long-established with the annual migration of East Anglian drifters (especially Lowestoft ones) to catch *mackerel* at Newlyn, in the early months of the year, going back to the 1860s, and with the Padstow *sole-fishing* a regular activity for some craft well before 1900.[31] During the 1920s and 30s, further contacts were made with ports on the other side of the country, notably Milford Haven and Fleetwood (especially the latter), as trawling activity spread further and further from the East Anglian home base. Like many other fishermen of his generation, Ned Mullender was well acquainted with fishing grounds in the Atlantic Ocean and the Irish Sea, and with the ports which served them.

"In 1931, I wuz mate along o' Tom Cook, in the *Swiftwing* (LT 675), and we were trawlin' out o' Fleetwood when they [the owners, J.V. Breach Ltd.] decided to send her seine-nettin'. O' course, they'd got the seine-net gear, so they rigged us up and we went an' had a go in the Firth o' Clyde. Well, we couldn't git any fish, so we shifted. I recollect fishin' one place in Jura Sound and that looked like

---

30 Haddocks' guts often contained debris from small bivalves and crustaceans, which formed part of the diet. Prolonged contact with this material (particularly on the hand which held the gutting knife) could cause a painful irritation.

31 Mackerel fishing was conducted from Newlyn and Penzance and lasted from about the end of February through until May. The sole voyage was of similar duration. During the steam era, especially during the 1920s and 30s, some vessels found it possible to participate in both activities (mackerel first, then sole) by sending their drift-netting gear back to Lowestoft on the railway and receiving trawling gear in return by the same means of transport.

a distillery, and we went in there and had a haul. Well, you could nearly see people walkin' about on the land! Yeah. And we got three baskets o' lovely plaice. So we shot in towards the land next time and we got five baskets o' lovely plaice.[32] Next haul we dint git so many. Then, when we tried to shoot the net on the other side, we couldn't git it back. No, we had to go back after it. That wuz some lot o' big ol' weed wi' stalks on and we couldn't git the ropes through it, so that wuz a flop.[33] But we wuz just in the right place for them other two hauls.

"Anyway, we come back round inta the Clyde agin, but we still wun't gittin' a lot o' stuff. That wuz a mixture o' thornyback rooker and God know what! There wuz a lot'o' trouble wi' them a-shakin' down in the net, 'cause a seine-net is very fine and dun't take a lot o' damagin'. We went inta Ayr on that trip and put the rough stuff ashore—dorgs, rooker, flatfish, whitins and that like. We were goin' to save all the hake, but we never got enough to make it pay. I can't remember what we made, but that wun't very much.

"The next trip we went out, we went somewhere up the north end o' Morecambe Bay, and we were gittin' a nice bit o' fish there, till they took orf. So I say to Cookie, 'Why not go orf *Bee's Hid* and try for some plaice.' I say, 'A boatload o' plaice would be all right.' He say, 'Righto! We'll go.' So we fished orf St. Bee's Hid [St. Bee's Head] and we got about ninety kit o' plaice. Little ol' tiddlers, they were. God know how many we dint throw back—apart from the ones we kept! The first haul, you never saw anything like it! Some o' the fish we got wun't any bigger'n that [indicating the size with forefinger and thumb]. Only four inches long! Well, o' course, you had to git the ordinary size if yuh could—though there wuz no measurements then, yuh know [i.e. no official minimum sizes for species]. Anyway, we got 'em and we sorted 'em out, and when we went in, they made about ten bob a kit! I dun't know who bought 'em, but they made ten bob. And I say to Cookie, 'There you are, Cookie. If we'd had a lot more o' them, we'd ha' pulled out nicely.' We made £90 as it wuz! That wuz a payin' trip, on the mixture what we got from the other plaice. Then, o' course, Jack Breach come along. He wuz there. And he say, 'I dun't know,' he say, 'I think you'd better go hoom and have a go at herrin' catchin'.

"There wun't many Low'stoft boats seine-netted round the west side. No, no. That wuz an experiment. But, o' course, there used to be the Danes. They worked The Clyde. Oh yis, they used to work it! They'd be after hake.[34] Yeah, yeah, you could catch hake all right, if they were about. We never got none, though! Well, a kit or two, but nothin' special. We went summertime round there. Then, o' course, poor ol' Tom Cook, he got the *shift* [sack] when we come back, after we'd done the hoom fishin'. And I *walked about* a bit myself, then I went in *The*

---

32 A basket held just over three stones of fish. There were three baskets to the *kit*.

33 The sea weed described was probably Oarweed (*Laminaria digitata*).

34 Hake was a highly regarded fish in Fleetwood and other west-side ports.

Consalidated.[35]

"I think only about one Low'stoft boat went seine-nettin' after the last war [the Second World War]. Lewis Keable, he went in his *Ex Fortis* (LT 350). But he dint make a go of it, I dun't think. He dint go long, anyway. If I had the money and I wuz forty or fifty year younger, I'd buy a seine-net boat. They're makin' £10,000 out o' Grimsby now on a fourteen, fifteen, day trip. And there's only about five in the crew! There wuz eight when we were a-goin'. Yeah, eight. But these here seine-net boats out o' Grimsby, they have a crew o' five and a cook, and they pay the cook.[36] I dun't know where they're fishin', but they're makin' a lot o' money out o' Shields [North Shields] as well. Yeah, some o' them are makin' £3,000 for a couple o' nights sometimes! If I wuz a younger fella and I had the money, I'd have a go at it, 'cause I think I could make a livin' out of it. Providin' I could git the crew. That's half the battle."

Ned Mullender's closing comment about getting suitable crew is pertinent. It was important to get men who had had some experience of seining, if possible, or who would at least prove adaptable in learning a new method of fishing if it were not. And this was not the only constraint. Seine-netting was extremely tiring for those who practised it, because of the number of shoots and hauls made in a working day. Thus, the physical exertion incurred made it more suited to younger men—who were not always prepared to tolerate the demands made upon them.

The remarks made above about Grimsby are interesting, too—especially in the light of what has happened in the forty years since they were made. Grimsby has a much reduced fishing fleet these days, while its neighbour, Hull, no longer functions as a trawling base. Elsewhere, among other, one-time, major ports (in England), Fleetwood has long ceased to operate and so has Lowestoft—at least, as far as the larger, mid-water vessels are concerned. Brixham and Newlyn are left as ports of significant size—though this is not to diminish the importance (especially in their home-areas) of a number of smaller fishing stations which continue to send boats to sea and handle the catches landed. If the days of industrial-scale fishing in England are over (at least, for the forseeable future), it may not be an entirely bad development—especially if a less environmentally destructive regime replaces it and the general public becomes influenced to see the worth of a good quality whole-fish trade rather than processed convenience foods, which sometimes give no sense of having begun life in the oceans at all. Whatever happens, though, the state of the industry bears no comparison with what Ned Mullender remembered from his working days—especially those in the earlier part of his long career at sea.

35 Ned Mullender joined the Consolidated Steam Fishing & Ice Co. Ltd., of Grimsby, which had a fleet of steam trawlers based in Lowestoft, and worked on its boats for a number of years.

36 This suggests that the cook was paid an agreed, fixed wage, irrespective of what the boat earned. His duties were probably solely concerned with the galley.

"Seine-nettin' wuz very popular here in the 1920s, 'cause things were a bit slack otherwise. I mean, Lugs Seago, he went in it. Pod Catchpole, he went in it.The *Norfolk County* (LT 103), the *Sussex County* (LT 63), they went in it. See? And you can mention some o' the *Star* boats what went into it.[37] There wuz quite a big fleet out o' here. An' there wuz some out o' Yarmouth an' all. The *Frons Olivae* (YH 217) an' them there, an' the *Wydale* (YH 105) and them, they were a-seinin' Yeah. An' two or three o' Westmacott's [Westmacott Ltd.]. There used to be quite a lot o' boats where the fish were. Oh yeah. But you always used to give each other room. You know, that wuz very rare that you shot over one another's ground. See, you'd be roughly—say, what?—a mile, mile an' a half each side, to give one another room. See? Well, that meant to say that you'd be two mile, three mile, away from one another so you had room to go round [i.e. steam the triangular course required]. If not, you'd interfere with one another's fishin'. We dint used to like the trawlers. I mean, if you'd got four or five trawlers together, they could soon frighten a seine-net boat out of it. Oh yeah! Where you wanted to shoot, you could be just where they wanted to shoot, an' you couldn't go aginst 'em. So you had to move.[38]

"Sometimes things used to work out funny. When I wuz in the *Scadaun* there once, we were gittin' fish the two hauls round about daylight, so we used to git on the move so we shot at twilight. The first haul, we got about thirty baskets; an' the next haul, at daylight we got about ten. Then, the next haul, we wun't gittin' above two! Well, that wun't payin'. But, evenin' time, on the last two hauls, we were gittin' twenty to thirty baskets agin, in the dark. So I say to the mate, 'That's a *dark fishin'* here. We'll put a light on our dan an' we'll work all night.' So, anyway, we put the bigger dan, which we had—we put that on the moorins and put a light on that. And we were workin' in the dark, but we wun't gittin' enough fish to justify it. We were gittin' a few baskets, but not enough to do it justice. Well, when that come the mornin', I'd gotta let my men have some sleep. So we all went and laid down. See? And when we turned out agin, we had a haul and we never got anything partic'lar. And I say, 'Look. There's plenty o' ol' gulls around the *Achievable* (YH 92) down there.' I say, 'I think we'll go and have a look at him." Well, when we got down there, God, his decks were full o' haddicks. 'Cor!' I say. "We've lorst somethin' by workin' all night.'

"Anyway, we went the other side o' him. And, o' course, when we got to the

---

37 The first two vessels named belonged to the County Fishing Co. Ltd. The *Star* boats referred belonged to the Star Drift Fishing Co. Ltd. and all had the word "star" as part of their names (e.g. *Beacon Star* and *Guiding Star*).

38 Trawling gear was much heavier and more robust than seine-netting equipment and would have caused serious damage if dragged across it.

other side, we began to fish like billy-o![39] But then, yuh see, we'd lorst nearly all that day. Well, the nexta day, hoom he come [i.e. the *Achievable* returned to port], but we'd gotta fish that day. And we got a nice lot o' fish and, o' course, we fished the nexta day as well. Well, that wuz the day he landed. We come hoom the nexta day and he wuz then a-comin' out. We met him in the *roads*, down aginst Yarmouth there.[40] And, o' course, he come alongside an' wanted to know what fish we'd got. So I told him: we'd got 300 odd kit. 'Cor!' he say. 'You'll be all right.' He say, 'We made £400 for about the same amount.' I say, 'Cor blimey! That's a nice trip.'

"So, anyway, when we got inta the harbour, about eleven o' clock, Walter Podd (a big buyer here at Low'stoft in them days) come alongside and say, 'What're yuh got, skipper?' I say, 'About 300 kit. Praps a little better.' He say, 'I'll give yuh £400 for your trip.' I say, 'Thass nothin' to do wi' me.' I say, 'You'll hefta see the boss. Colonel Lucas wuz the owner, but we had a manager to run things. See? So Walter Podd say to me, 'What do yuh think to it?' I say, 'Well, if they're worth £400 today, they'll be worth at least £400 tomorrer mornin', 'cause you'll have some opposition then [in the fish auction]. So he say, 'Yeah. I'm like you. We'll hefta see what the salesman say.' Anyway, the salesman say, 'I think we'll risk tomorrer, 'cause there'll be more buyers.' Well, anyway, the nexta day, o' course, we landed. An' I wuz down there, weighin' up what we made. An' we made £360! An' I say, 'We should ha' made more'n that!' And there wuz a little bit o' dispute about it and I went in the orffice. And the manager say, 'Give the skipper five quid [£5].' I thought to myself, 'Oh dear, oh dear! I've gotta keep my mouth shut.' I couldn't prove there wuz a fiddle goin' on, betwin the salesman and the orffice, so I could't say nothin' about it. See, they'd sling the books at yuh and say, 'There you are! Finish!' And you were out o' a job."[41]

---

39 This particular trip took place in April, 1924, on a fishing gound called the Elbow Spit, which was situated on the north-eastern part of the Dogger Bank about 175 miles east of Newcastle.

40 *Roads* was an East Anglian term for inshore reaches of the sea situated between outlying sandbanks and the shore. Although the *Achievable* was a Great Yarmouth vessel, it had not landed in the home-port, but sold its catch on the Lowestoft market. This was because Yarmouth was almost exclusively geared to the autumn herring trade and had very little to do with trawlfish. The trip described here took place in April, 1924.

41 The catch had been sold at a lower price than it had realised at auction, with the salesman and the fishing company's manager being given a generous commission (or *backhander*) by the buyer. The manager had then given Ned Mullender a £5 gratuity as a "sweetener". The *Scadaun's* owner would not have been aware of the deception practised.

The "Home Fishing" – Lowestoft drifters off to sea again in the 1930's.

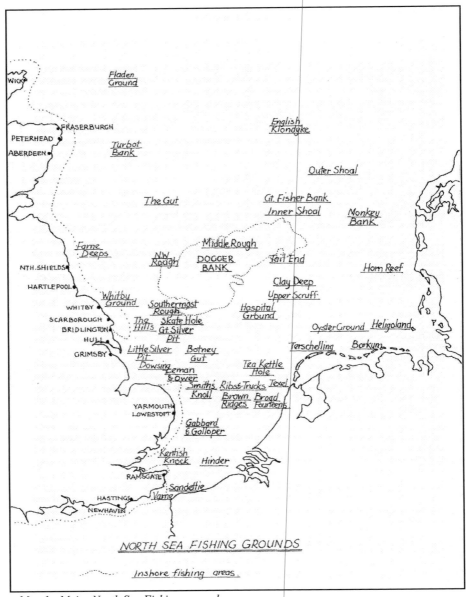

Map 1: Major North Sea Fishing-grounds

The main fishing-grounds of the southern North Sea (not to scale). The three-mile limit (or exclusion) area for larger vessels is indicated by a dotted line, as is the famed Dogger Bank area itself.

CHAPTER TWO

Hook, Line and Anchor

Come, come, my lads, and listen here.
A fisherman's tale you soon shall hear.
What I didn't undergo
When first I went a-cod-banging- o!
To my la-fol-di-day, riddle-all-day.
This is a smacksman's life at sea.
(Traditional Essex folksong: *Cod Banging*)

Using hook and line is probably one of the most ancient methods of catching fish, with precedents in Europe certainly dating back to Neolithic times. The concern here is not to investigate an ancient, subsistence mode of fishing, but to look at a much later development of it. Commercial hand-lining voyages to Iceland and the Faeroe Islands for cod and other demersal species—notably, ling—were carried out periodically from various East Coast ports (especially ones in Suffolk, Norfolk and Yorkshire) from the first half of the fifteenth century onwards and were continued with, in one form or other, for the next three hundred years. There were a number of reasons for the development of this fishery, which took place during the spring and summer months. One was the ever-increasing demand for fish in Roman Catholic Europe as its population recovered from the ravages of The Black Death, another the relatively imperishable nature of cod and its versatility with regard to both curing and cooking.[1] Account also has to be taken of the improvement in vessel design which made journeys to northern waters possible. And, finally, there was the importance of an alternative fishery to Newfoundland (especially from the sixteenth century onwards), which was dominated largely by Basques and Frenchmen and which was only exploited effectively in England by craft based in ports on the west side of the country.

The gear mainly used on the cod-fishing voyages, whether to Newfoundland or to Iceland, was known as the *great-line*—a ninety fathom length of stout hempen twine, with an iron *cross-piece* fixed to one end, which acted as a weight and which also supported a *hook* tied on at either extremity [i.e. four hooks in all]. This was operated, by hand, over the side of the vessel, and the cod (or whatever other species took the bait) drawn up through the water and landed on the deck. The bait used was probably a pelagic species such as herring and mackerel to

---

1 Even after the Reformation, the consumption of fish remained important in Protestant countries –especially those like England and Holland, which saw the strategic significance of having a strong fishing industry to act as a back-up to conventional naval forces, both in terms of vessels and suitably trained men. The consumption of cod in its many dried and salted forms remained important over the whole of Europe.

begin with; but, as the fishing got under way, waste from the decapitation and gutting process was probably employed, as well as any lesser or unwanted species that were caught.[2] Once a vessel had taken a sufficient amount of fish on board (the catches were salted down and stored in compartments in the hold), it returned to its home-part and the cargo was re-processed, as required, into the different forms of dried and salted fish which were eaten at the time, such as *stockfish* and *haberdines* etc. All the cod livers, which had been carefully stored in small wooden casks, were rendered down for *train oil*—which was used, in turn, to dress leather and provide the fuel for household lamps.

Lowestoft, among other East Coast ports, participated in this distant-water fishery and, even as late as the 1730s, was still sending a handful of vessels down to Iceland on an occasional basis.[3] However, long before this, it had begun a less risky and expensive lining voyage closer to home in the central and southern sectors of the North Sea and was content to devote the majority of its larger fishing craft to this activity. The parish tithe accounts show that this fishery was well established by the end of the seventeenth century and also reveal that many of the small, off-the-beach vessels (crewed by about three or four men as opposed to ten or twelve on board the larger boats) had adopted a lining technique of their own. This involved laying a continuous length of baited lines on the seabed, with small anchors at periodic intervals to weight everything down, and leaving them there for a period of time in order for various demersal species to become hooked. These lines were more slender than *great-lines* (and were, in fact, known as *small-lines*) and they had the hooks fixed to them at regular intervals on lengths of twine known as *snoods*. It was a way of fishing that was to prove more effective than the single, hand-held line, and it gradually replaced the older method, not only in East Anglia but in many other parts of the country as well—eventually becoming as much used in deep water as it was in the shallower, inshore reaches.[4]

As things turned out, Lowestoft never developed into a lining port of any significance. Its nineteenth century development, especially during the second half, was very much geared to herring and mackerel catching and to trawling. However, the smaller, *longshore* vessels continued to work *longlines*, as they had now become known, and during the 1920s and 30s it was not unknown for

---

2   Iceland vessels from East Anglia always carried a *bait-net*, which was either some kind of *seine* or a type of *drift-net*. This was obviously used to catch fish with which to bait the hooks. There is a good description of the lining gear used in a late seventeenth century publication: John Collins, *Salt and Fishery: a Discourse Thereof* (London, 1682), pp. 106-7.

3   According to the parish tithe accounts (Norfolk Record Office, PD 589/80), the last recorded voyage took place in 1743, when a single craft ventured north.

4   There is a detailed explanation of longlining methods and the different types of gear used in Davis, *Fishing Gear*, pp. 140-4. Some of the larger English vessels working Iceland also used longlines as early as the sixteenth century, leading to complaints from the Icelanders themselves that the gear fished too effectively and reduced cod stocks.

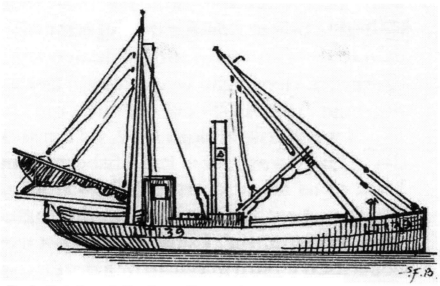

Fig. 3: Early Steam Drifter Cameo: Narcissus (LT 139)

A line-drawing of the early Lowestoft steam drifter "Narcissus" (LT 139). Built in the town in 1901, she was typical of the first generation of vessels constructed, with funnel for'ad of the wheelhouse.

some of the herring drifters to be equipped for lining voyages.[5] This was done to keep the vessels working at times when they might otherwise have been laid up, especially between the end of the *Home Fishing* in December and the start of the summer herring voyage to Shetland, in June. Again, as with *seine-netting*, it was a relatively easy matter to convert a steam drifter to lining, and it also involved less expense.

Ned Mullender went on a lining voyage during the winter and spring of 1919, after his discharge from the Royal Naval Patrol Service in the First World War and it is his experience which is recounted here. His recollections will run in an unbroken sequence, mainly because there is very little need for interpolated comments. The quality of the oral testimony is of a high order and, though some re-sequencing has had to be done in a number of places, in order to create a more logical structure, the commentary is solely that of the man himself. He was an excellent respondent to work with, having an extremely good memory concerning his working life and a very clear mode of delivery—both in terms of voice projection and the recounting of detail in an ordered way. Some of the information included in this chapter comes from the first tape-recording made

---

5 This was especially true of vessels which had been built in the earliest years of the twentieth century and which usually had *compound* steam engines of less capacity (often no more than fifteen horse-power) than the later *triple-expansion* models.

Plate 3:   Excelsior (LT 698)

The steam drifter "Excelsior" (LT 698), seen leaving her home port, where she was constructed in the year 1904. The "Woodbine funnel" is a prominent feature of her appearance, as she heads out into the North Sea. .

(21 September 1976), which was intended as an introductory session and which covered a number of his early fishing experiences, but most of the narration derives from a later, follow-up tape which dealt specifically with longlining (4 January 1979). Such had been the interest generated by the first interview that it was necessary to elicit further information, in order to build up a more detailed picture of the activity. What follows is an in-depth account of a mode of fishing that dated back over centuries and is still in regular use today on inshore craft all around the British Isles.

"I come hoom in 1918, just afore Christmas, and I'd gotta find a job.[6] I got inta Low'stoft on the Saturday afore Christmas and, over the weekend, I see a friend o' mine and he say, 'George Rushmore want a crew for *linin'*. And, o' course, I accepted the job and went and got demobbed. There wun't right a lot o' linin' done out o' Low'stoft, not to my knowledge, and this wuz 1919, but anyway I got a *berth* in the the little ol' *Excelsior* (LT 698). She wuz one o' them little ol' drifters with the wheelhouse aft and she belonged to about five people.[7] I wuz the *whilk-cracker*, as well as bein' *second engineer*. Yeah, I used to go on deck and help bait the lines and haul the lines and put the fish away.

6 Ned Mullender had been serving abroad, in the Mediterranean and the Adriatic Sea, with the Royal Naval Patrol Service.

7 This vessel was a wooden steam drifter, built at Lowestoft in 1904 and having a fifteen horse-power compound engine made by Elliott & Garrood Ltd. of Beccles. The wheelhouse was situated aft-side of the funnel, as it was in a number of the early steam drifters, but it was much more common in such vessels to have these positions reversed.

"Now, we started orf in the Hamilton Dock, gittin' riddy, and we took an old man for a *pilot* 'cause none of us had been before. But this ol' pilot had been durin' the war or some other time. His name wuz Billy Peak and he wuz mate wi' my father in 1911 and 1912. He wuz a Pakefield man and he wuz the one who wuz goin' to show us how it wuz goin' to be done. He wuz goin' to have a month with us, see, and then he wuz goin' to finish. Well, after we got started, we found that instead o' havin' a crew o' seven, we wanted eight. We wanted nine really, if we coulda had 'em because we were all strangers to it. The baitin' took us a lot longer, see, and o' course wi' me crackin' the whilks—well, that wuz a job on its own, when we first started. Anyway, we kept the pilot on so he wuz with us all the time, and he wuz the man who used to *shoot* the lines.

"When we started, we *coiled* the lines on wooden *hoops* about that much round [indicating about a fifteen inch diameter with the hands]. They had a canvas bottom sewn onto 'em and they dint have no sides—just *lashins* [lashings] to keep the lines in place, until you unlashed 'em to use. And you coiled your lines round and round, and as you come up you laid your hooks to the front, all down one side. So, when you shot, all your hooks were on that side. Well, we had so many foul lines with the hoops that we packed 'em in. Yeah, we started usin' a box thing, a *chute*, which wuz tapered orf at an angle, with nothin' in front of it but built up at the sides and the back. That wuz about eighteen inches acrorss at the front, and the back would be about twenty-four, and that wuz what you used to coil yuh lines in.[8] But instead o' coilin' 'em like you did on the hoops, where yuh hooks were all in rows, on one side, as you went up the coils, you coiled the lines so yuh hooks were all in rows facin' outwards at the front o' the chute.

"Each hoop or chute had seven *shanks* o' line in it to make up what wuz called a *peck*. See, a shank wuz sixty fathom long, so you had 420 fathoms each peck, and you allus baited thirty-two pecks up—which meant that you shot fifteen mile o' line, with hooks every twelve foot on *snoods* about two and a half to three foot long. So that meant you'd hev 210 hooks in a chute. They were an ordinary cod hook, not as big as the big lines had—the *deep-water lines*.[9] No. These were more of a half-size hook. I dun't know the actual number [i.e. the official, specified size], but if you had a good-sized whilk that wuz all you put on one hook. But, o' course, if they were smaller ones, you baited up with more on.

"We used to shoot the whilks down below onta *coca mattin'* [i.e. coconut fibre]. See, in the *fore-room*, on the bottom, wuz coca mattin', and we used to put the whilks onta this, all wet, so they could suck orf that and keep alive. That wuz if you were in port and couldn't git out to fish. But, normally, you'd start to bait up

---

8 Both the pieces of equipment described here are well illustrated in Davis, *Fishing Gear*, p. 141.

9 The lines referred to here were the ones used on the lining voyages to Milford Haven, to catch conger eels and other species.

as soon as you got 'em. We used to hafta order 'em, and they used to come down from The Wash or somewhere.[10] There wuz what they called three *washins* in a bag, and you'd git about a dozen or fourteen bags each trip. I dunt know how much a bag weighed, but that wun't a hundredweight. I mean, I wuz pretty strong at the time and I could smack a hundredweight about as easy as kissin' yuh hand. No, that wun't a hundredweight. More like half a hundredweight, I should say.

"You allus used to bait up afore yuh *shot*, and you'd coil the line in the chutes and lay the hooks down in like a rotation, so they looked like piano keys. You went right aft when you shot, right aginst the *small boat*, an' you allus shot orf the *lee side*. You had a table there, and you set the chute on the table so the edge wuz on the *taffrail*. On the bulwerks, see. And you used to hev one man shootin' the lines with a stick—what you called a *shootin' stick*.[11] That wuz a pointed stick, as smooth as anything and about three foot long, with a loop in it, so that wuz over the man's wrist, and he used to stand aft side o' the chute an' just keep flickin' the hooks out. The *pilot* done that; he wuz the one what shot the hooks.

"The boat wuz a-goin' about five mile an hour on the engine when you shot, and you allus shot *acrorss the tide*—not with it. Whatever way that wuz runnin', you shot acrorss it.[12] You allus put a *dan* over to start with, with an anchor on, and the line wuz attached to that.[13] Now then, you hed a man bringin' the chutes aft and he'd tie the end o' the line what wuz bein' shot onta the next one to be shot. And when four pecks o' line had been shot, I used to throw an anchor and a dan over. They wun't very heavy anchors, and that wuz my job. I wuz the dan man when we shot and the whilk man when we hauled. I used to crack the whilks and clear orf the shells, then give 'em to the man who wuz baitin' up.

"Now, that took yuh three hours to shoot, so we used to hev a nap afore that. And then we used to turn out and start to shoot at about nine o' clock at night and finish about midnight. Now then, we'd set the watch and we'd drop anchor so we were alongside the dan. See? The last one. Yeah, we'd anchor there, if the weather permitted—and if that dint, well, we used to hafta lay and *dodge* her up.

---

10 The whelks probably came from Boston, in Lincolnshire. They were often the preferred bait for use on longlines because they held onto the hook better than some other types of bait.

11 This stick prevented hooks from becoming caught in the hand of the man who was shooting the lines.

12 Shooting across the tide ensured that the current carried the lines clear of the boat and stretched them out.

13 The anchors were secured to the longlines by lashings of about five to six feet length, which were tied at one end to a ring in the top of the anchor and to a loop in the longline at the other. The dan-tow (made from thicker twine) was also tied to the anchor ring and ran up from thence to the dan itself, on the surface. Nine anchors and dans were used altogether, set at four-peck intervals (3,360 yards). The dans at either end of the lines were larger than those spaced between.

But whichever you did, you allus had a watch, in case anything happened.[14] You only shot and hauled twice on each trip, 'cause you'd use up all yuh bait. An' sometimes you dint allus hev enough bait to do the full shoot second time. Praps starfish or somethin' else had taken the bait orf on the first shoot, so you had to use more bait to make it up. And then you wouldn't git yuh full shoot in.[15] We used to put *acetylene lights* on the two end dans when we first went. Then, o' course, we said, 'Well, what's the good o' puttin' a light on the far end!' You couldn't see it!

"When we hauled, we steamed. We started about four in the mornin'. The skipper wuz in the wheelhouse and the chief [engineer] wuz down below, and the rest of us would be haulin' the lines by hand or baitin' up for the next shoot. That used to take us roughly twelve hours to haul. And you'd stand for'ad, in the midships—you know, between the foremast and the wheelhouse. And that's where you hauled from. You'd have one man a-haulin' the lines with his hands, with mittens on. You'd have another one aft side o' him, with a *garft* [gaff], a-garftin' the fish in, and he would pay the line overboard agin when he'd got the fish orf. Yeah, he'd pay that overboard and then another man would be *backin' it in* an' puttin' it on the chute. You'd have it all over the deck otherwise. You had yuh hatch covers on while you hauled and you had two men acrorss the other side o' the boat baitin' up for the next shoot, on top o' the hatch.[16]

"That wuz hard work, haulin'. Yuh hands swole at the back, with the grip. Yeah, we all had swollen hands. Nobody what hauled the lines wuz any different. We all had this swellin' at the back o' the hands. An' we used to work mittens [woollen ones] and a pair o' mittens would only go about, oh, four or five hauls. The middle, where you gripped the lines, that'd wear away, yuh see. Sometimes, if you hed a little bit o' *heft* on the bottom, you'd put the line down on the bulwerk and nip it with yuh knee so that'd pull clear. You'd bring the line over the rail and push it underneath and press it with yuh knee to bring it up clear o' the heft. And sometimes you'd *part* the line doin' that, so then you had to go to the next dan an' haul that line back to where you parted.[17] Then you'd go back to that next dan and carry on haulin' from there. So that wun't all pleasure at times!

---

14 The usual watch system employed was to have one man on deck and one below, when at anchor, and two men on deck and one below, when dodging. The watch period usually lasted about four hours and the duties worked on a rota basis.

15 Any bait that wasn't taken, and was left intact on the hooks, was used second time round.

16 The crew members did not work continuously at the same task for the duration of the haul. They changed round periodically, so as to relieve each other from repetition and physical strain. Even the skipper took his turn at hauling the lines and the cook would also assist with various on-deck duties.

17 The sudden jamming of the line beneath the rail, combined with the vessel's forward momentum, was usually sufficient to free the gear from minor obstructions. However, a more resistant obstacle might well have caused the line to break—as would any weakness in the line itself.

"Sometimes, when you got *parted* (specially when you'd just hauled a dan), you had a job findin' the next one. See, wi' that bein' so low, if there wuz a little bit o' motion in the water, you couldn't see it—unless you went right on top of it! Well then, if you couldn't find it, you used the *creepers* an' creeped it up to yuh.[18] We dint lose many fish, though! No, no. You'd garf 'em outboard an' bring 'em inboard. And the man who wuz haulin' had nothin' to do with garfin'. Like I said, you had three of yuh on the line: one a-haulin', one a-garfin' and one a-backin' in. And the man who wuz a-backin' in, he wuz also a-coilin' the line onta the chute. And when he come to the knot where that joined, he'd untie that an' start on another chute. Yeah, he just loosely coiled the line and passed the chute acrorss the hatch to them what wuz baitin'. And you baited the lines an' coiled 'em up neatly agin. The hooks used to be lined acrorss the chute, so you'd start on one side an' come acrorss, then you'd go back the other way and carry on like that till you finished the chute and all the hooks were facin' outwards.

"With the garftin' in, you'd gotta learn the knack o' gittin' the fish orf the hook and you got so you could do it easy. Unless he'd swallered it! If he'd swallered the hook, you broke the *snude* [snood] and left the hook in till you put him away. But if he wuz only hooked by his jaw, you could git him orf as easy as kissin' yuh hand. You used to git hold o' the snude, pass it under the hook an give it a jerk. That'd turn the hook upside-down, so the *berb* [barb] would be right for pullin' out. The fish would land on the deck and you'd drop him inta the *kid*.

"As soon as you'd done haulin', you'd start *guttin'*. Well, you'd hev somethin' to eat first. Yeah, yuh meals had to work round what you were doin'. Most o' the crew would be a-guttin' and washin' on 'em up. And then there'd be a man down below *icin'* 'em away and *shelfin'* 'em. See, that wuz cod we were after mainly and we allus shelfed them. We hed the *pounds* all fixed up so we could shelf 'em all.[19] You know, the bigger ones. Yeah. The same wi' haddicks or flat stuff. The small ones, you dint lay them out . No, they just went inta the pounds. An' we hed a *liver-jar* for the cod livers.[20] Oh, definitely. You were a long while gittin' a jar o' livers and all. I forgit who used to take 'em orf us now, but there wuz one

---

18 In other words a grapnel was used to locate the anchor and dan-tow and draw the whole assemblage to the side of the vessel. It was possible to do this because, with a distance of nearly two miles between each dan, the approximate position of each marker was able to be calculated.

19 Shelfing was a particular way of storing cod (or other species) on board ship so as to keep them in top condition. Boards were laid across the bottom of the fish-hold's pounds and a layer of ice put on. The cod were then laid on this, belly down or sideways, but no more ice was applied. Another set of boards was then placed above and another layer of fish put down. The process continued until the pound was full, to the height required, and everything held in place by the front boards, which slotted in between the stanchions.

20 A liver-jar was a standard wooden barrel, of thirty-six gallons capacity, which was placed lengthways on the foredeck and lashed to the mast. The livers were put into the barrel through the bung-hole, which was then sealed when the container was full.

firm used to buy 'em orf us loose, not in jars, so we used to bring 'em in on ice, in *peds*, and they used to buy 'em like that. I mean, we used to eat 'em, raw. You'd be sick, if you tried it! We saved the *rows* [roes] an' all. Yis, definitely. I mean, that wuz a bit of our *stockie bait*.

"You only did two *shoots and hauls* in forty-eight hours, then you went in to land. When we first went, we started on the first o' January and were fishin' down orf Grimsby. And when we first went there, we were twenty-four hours shootin' and haulin', so we never had no sleep at all. But the ol' chief, down below, he could have cat-naps 'cause she wuz just tickin' over slow while we wuz haulin'. Like I said, we had so many foul lines with the hoops that we packed 'em in. Yeah, we got to know about the chutes in Grimsby and o' course we hed some made and that wuz a bigger success. This *shannockin'*, as they call it, this linin', wuz done a lot out o' Grimsby, an' Scarborough as well. But I dun't know why that wuz called shannockin'—unless that originated from Sheringham.[21]

"Like I said, when we first started, that took us all the time to git baited up. We were novices at the first and that took us a long while. We were messin' about there twenty-four hours! I don't think we slept at all the first two days we were out! But, o' course, after we'd bin at it about a month, we began to git experts. I mean, we knew everything we'd gotta do and what we hent gotta do. Yeah, when we got so we'd had a little practice, by the time we'd hauled, we could practically git moost o' the lines baited up agin. That used to take us, say, about another couple o' hours or three hours to finish orf baitin', so we could git a nice sleep in. I mean, we'd git from four o'clock [in the afternoon] till nine o' clock, which wuz a good lot when you were at sea. When we first went, about the first three weeks or a month, that took me all the time to crack the whilks for the others to bait. I used a hammer, a wooden mallet. Well, I used so many up that they put tin on each end so that wuz solider. Yeah, and after I'd bin goin' about four or five weeks, I got so I could bait a couple o' lines up besides crackin' the whilks.

"When we first went, we landed in at Grimsby. Yeah we run a couple or three *trips* in there, till the skipper got suspended—suspended from goin' up the Humber. The Humber wuz still under the Gover'ment, see, and you hed a *pilot* come to yuh and tell yuh what flag to hoist up so you could go up the river. This wuz wartime regulations, see, 'cause this wuz early in January, 1919. The first time, we waited for a group o' trawlers. The pilot went aboard the leadin' ship, but by the time they were up the river we were only halfway. See, we weren't very fast, so they were in dock long afore us.[22] Well, consequences wuz, comin' in next trip, there wun't no pilot waitin' and I say to the skipper, George Rushmore, 'What flag hev

---

21 Shannock was the traditional nickname given to an inhabitant of the town of Sheringham on the North Norfolk coast. It may be a variant of *shammock*, a dialect word for a horse of unsteady gait.

22 The *Excelsior's* engine was only fifteen horse-power.

yuh gotta put up, skipper?' He say, 'Same as last time.' I say, 'What about if that's altered?' 'Oh,' he say, 'Never mind. If that's the wrong one, that's the wrong one.' So, o' course, we hoisted M up an' away we come. Went straight inta the piers and moored up.

"Well, along come one o' the officials. I wuz on deck at the time. I believe I wuz cleanin' the breakfast fish. And he say to me, 'What flag have you got up there?' I say, 'M. Letter M.' He say, 'Who told yuh to hoist that up?' I say, 'The skipper.' I dint say the pilot; I said the skipper. He say, 'Where is the skipper?' I say, 'Turned in. Havin' a little nap.' He say, 'Call him up.' So I called him up, and up he come. And this official say, 'What do yuh mean by hevin' that flag up?' See? So George Rushmore say, 'Well, that's the one we hed last time.' He say, 'Yis, but that's bin changed.' Anyway, George hetta go afore a court o' inquiry at Immingham. And, to top the lot, Sam Chapman, who wuz our agent at Grimsby, he hetta go an' all.[23] And the bloke what wuz in charge o' this conference, he said to our George Rushmore, 'Do you know we coulda had you shot, skipper?' See? Well, George dint care a heck! An' he say, 'What are you goin' to do wi' Kaiser William when yuh git him?' Well, o' course that wuz enough! And, consequences wuz, they suspended him for about eight weeks—from goin' up the Humber. So hoom we come. The mate hetta bring us hoom and George hetta come by train.

"When we got back, we come inta the Hamilton Dock. I think we wuz the only drifter what wuz linin' out o' here. We'd got our whilks aboard and George went to the Gover'ment, up in the Customs House, and asked how far we could come up to the south.[24] Well, after we found out how far we were allowed up there, we goes out. And I think we were allowed—oh, I dun't know, just up somewhere by *Sowle*.[25] Well, I mean, a little bit further out, but orf Southwold. That might even ha' bin as far up as the Shipwash. We shot seven pecks o' lines, just for a trial. This wuz just afore dark, an' we hauled 'em just as that come in dark. All we hed wuz two little ol' *sprags* an' one blind cod with a rotten eye in it. 'Oh!' George say. 'I've seen all I want!' So back we come inta port. Well, instead o' comin' right in, we lay on the lifeboat pier, outside o' the main harbour; and when I turned out to clean these fish the nexta mornin' for breakfast, we were bumpin' inta the jetty. So we come inta the trawl dock, an' that come on a gale o' wind, so we went back

---

23 Sam Chapman was the fish salesman, acting on behalf of the *Excelsior* on the Grimsby market. He would also have been responsible for provisioning the vessel and generally seeing that things ran smoothly on shore.

24 Lowestoft, like Grimsby, was still under Naval authority, following on from the end of the war. Advice was required on where to fish because of minefields that had not yet been cleared.

25 Sowle was an old local name for Southwold—possibly the result of slurred pronunciation.

inta the Hamilton Dock.[26] We laid there nearly a week afore we went out. Yeah, an every mornin' I used to go down an' give these here whilks some sea water. I took 'em out o' the bags and laid 'em on hessian, on top o' the coca mattin'. And I used to go down every mornin' and give 'em some fresh sea water and wash 'em down, 'cause they used to climb up the sides o' the ship like *dodnums* [snails]. Yeah, I used to soak 'em well to keep 'em alive.

"We went down orf Flamborough Head, when we got out. We shot the lines and went to work about four o' clock the nexta mornin', and we were haulin' and gittin a *cop*—oh, a nice livin', lovely cod! Well, we come to part o' the lines and they were clean and the baits wun't touched and they were comin' along on the top o' the water. And the skipper wuz a-haulin' and the cook wuz in the wheelhouse a-steerin' on her. He wuz givin' the skipper a *spell*; you know, they hed long hours in the wheelhouse. Well, I wuz *garfin' in* and I say to George, I say to him, 'I dun't know whass up wi' these lines.' I say, 'They're comin' on top o' the water. They hent bin down on the bottom. Well, bor, just as the line got to the boat, that started to go down, an' George give it a pull and a mine come on top o' the water. No further orf the boat than that [indicating an arm's length distance]. A moored mine wi' spikes on! A live un! Then that went down agin and, as we went ahead, that went under the bottom o' the boat and come up the other side 'cause George had let go o' the line. Well, the mate, Iptip Barber, he flew aft an' got hold of a *hook*, a garft, and hooked up the line and cut it so we could git hold o' the line from the other side and let the mine go. Yeah, he hed the presence o' mind to do that and then, o' course, we were clear. And we never see no more mines. There wuz one boat got lorst down there. I can't think o' her name now. That mighta bin the *Au Revoir* (LT 505) or somethin' like that. She wuz an ol' Low'stoft drifter, workin' down there out o' Grimsby or Scarborough, and she went out where we got this here mine, and all the other boats knew wuz that they heared an explosion. And she never returned. So I spose she got one o' the mines on her line.

"That wuz one o' our own mines, though they were deep enough so you could git over 'em. That wuz a minefield, see, and that wuz when we first went down there. I dun't think the skipper knew we were in a minefield. I think he thought we were inside of it.[27] Anyway, we got forty-eight score o' big cod that night, without other fish, and the next night we got forty score. So we hed more'n eighty score altogether. We iced the fish an' shelfed them. Yeah, an' we dint hev enough shelfs in the *pounds*, so we shelfed 'em on the *perks*—underneath the perks and on top

---

26 The Hamilton Dock had been constructed during the early years of the twentieth century to accommodate the fleet of Scottish drifters (especially steam vessels) which came to Lowestoft each autumn to participate in the local herring voyage. It was named after Lord Claud Hamilton, Chairman of the Great Eastern Railway Co. Ltd., which owned the Lowestoft harbour complex.

27 In other words, between the coastline and the minefield.

o' the perks, so they'd git nice an' shiny.[28] When we landed 'em at Low'stoft, we made about £250 or £260 just for two nights' work. But that took us a day to git down there an' a day to git home on top o' the time we spent fishin'.

"You varied the grounds where you worked. That wun't very successful up this way, but we used to go somewhere round about sixty mile north from the Haisborough light vessel. Yeah, we used to go about sixty mile north by east an' work down there. That wuz roughish ground, but we used to go down there. Might go a little further one time an' a little shorter another. We used to work down round about the Sole Bank, the Sole Pits an' the [Little] Silver Pits, an' that way.[29] Yeah, we used to work down there. That wuz reasonable, too. We used to make £120 to £130 a trip down there, an' were gittin' about £3 or £4 each o' *stockie bait*. See, linin' wuz a cod fishin' and all the rest o' the fish we were promised for stockie bait. Yeah, and o' course, we got haddicks and skate, and sometimes plaice and turbots. You used to git a brill or two and, chance time, a gurnet [gurnard]. Yeah, we orften used to git a couple or three boxes o' turbots and a couple or three boxes o' plaice, and that wuz all *perks*. I know we went out once and tried out at the Knoll [Smith's Knoll]. Now, we got £60 worth o' haddicks and about £60 worth o' cod. Well, o' course, the owners dint agree with us havin' £60 odd worth o' stockie bait! But, anyway, we got £3 each, which wuz fair enough.[30]

"Once, outside The Knoll there, Smith's Knoll, we got a lot o' *dogs* [Spur dogfish]. Yeah, we got about three ton o' dogs and, o' course, we hed a job gittin 'em orf the hooks.[31] We dint use to git a lot o' trouble, though. The ol' whilks used to stay on the hooks well—unless you had *five-fingers* or somethin' like that. You know, starfish. They'd eat the baits orf. We once hed some trawlers give us a bit o' trouble. They used to work in groups just after the war and we had a group tow over our lines. But, a funny thing—they never parted 'em, though they took a lot o' the hooks orf. They were workin' light gear, 'cause they were Grimsby ships and they dint work heavy gear like they did out o' Low'stoft. They probably hed a *corkscrew rope* or somethin' like that[32]. That wuz just an ordinary, thin rope. Yeah, wire with a rope wrapped round it, like a corkscrew. Anyway, they never parted us. We were surprised, 'cause we went after the lines thinkin' they had played *Ol'*

28 Shelfing cod kept the fish in better condition than just placing them in the hold's pounds and icing them in the usual way. When they were landed on the Lowestoft market, cod were always laid out in neat rows and tallied up in twenties (hence the term *scores*).

29 These fishing grounds were located in the southern sector of the Dogger Bank.

30 Vessel owners sometimes tried to make the stockie bait agreement null and void, if landings of cod were small and there were substantial quantities of other species.

31 This was partly because of difficulty of handling caused by the robust nature of this fish and partly because of the sharp spine in front of the dorsal fin, which could cause a painful puncture to the hand.

32 This is a reference to the type of ground-rope used, which was a light variety and not one that was weighted down with bobbins and lengths of chain.

Harry [the Devil] up with 'em, and they hent. A lot o' hooks were orf, but that wuz all.

"We dint work in really big rough weather. No, we only got caught in one gale. That's all I know. And that wuz the second haul. So, as we hauled, we put the lines right down below, out o' the way. Yeah, you put yuh lines down below, out o' the way, if there wuz any weather—put 'em down on the perks, same as herrin' nets. If that wuz really bad weather, we dint used to go. See, they were ordinary cod-lines what we used. The size [gauge] of 'em wuz just like a *ripper* line, like a bit o' cord. That wun't very thick. [33] O' course, we were workin' out o' Low'stoft the moost o' the time, so you'd wait till yuh whilks arrived and then bait up as many lines as you could and go to sea the nexta mornin'. You wun't work only up to about dinner-time, or lunch-time, and then you'd go hoom. [34] See? An' then, the nexta mornin', you'd be a- baitin' as you were a-goin' away down.

"The depth you fished at varied. When you were in the Pits, I mean, that varied. And if you were up on the Long Shoal, or any shoal o' water, that varied. [35] That varied yuh *dans*, yeah [i.e. the length of mooring-line used]. Oh definitely, yeah. The bait dint vary, though. We allus used whilks—except for one time at Grimsby there, when we got four boxes o' herrin' from Norway. The whilks were in short supply and we used these herrin'. We did it so there wuz seven baits in each one and these Grimsby men reckoned we were goin' to lose the lines wi' skate. They were goin' to take 'em away. You know, so many skate that they were goin' to swim away wi' the lines! Well, anyway, we went out, but the price o' the fish we got dint pay for gittin' that class o' bait. So we never had no more herrin'. Yeah, we dint lose the lines wi' skate, I'll tell yuh that!

"Some o' the Low'stoft boats used to go long-linin' round to *Westward*, but they were a different type o' line. They used to hev the lines in baskets and they were goin' after conger. My father went round there in the *Confier* (LT 658), afore the First World War, but he dint do a lot o' good. That carried on after the war and all. Oh yes, some o' the Low'stoft boats did that quite a lot. I never went there, but I know they used to. I mean, the *Couronne* (LT 21), ol' Jack Clarke, he used to go quite a lot. Every year. They used to go, like on the *Westward* [mackerel] *voyage*, after Chris'mas. Now, one man I can tell yuh who used to go with him wuz George Kent, who live down at the end o' the road here [Florence Road,

---

33 The long-lines used were probably two-pound ones (i.e. a 240 feet length of line weighed two pounds). The ripper referred to was a hand-held line, which crew members on steam drifters sometimes used to catch fish as the vessel hung to its nets (a period of several hours' duration). These would then be sold on return to port to boost individual earnings.

34 In the parlance of the time, dinner was the meal in the middle of the day, or early afternoon, and lunch was the mid-morning *elevenses*.

35 The fishing-grounds referred to here are the Little Silver Pit and the Great Silver Pit, on the Dogger Bank, and the area of sandbanks off the north-east coast of Norfolk known generally as the Shoals.

Pakefield].[36] He wuz with him. And I think Billy London went in the *Forerunner* (LT 1160) one year, a-linin'. Like I say, they went after conger and they used to hev a winch to haul the line with. I dun't know exactly where they used to go— praps orf the Irish coast or outside the Fastnet, or anywhere that way. That wuz heavier gear than what we used, thicker line, and they hed baskets to shoot out of an' coil 'em in, with cork round it where they used to put the hooks in. See? But I never went there. No. The Scotchmen used to do a fair bit o' deep-sea linin', too. There's still some what go. They go out west'ard, out in the Atlantic, for cod and ollabuts [halibut]. I see in the *Fishing News* where one liner hed a really big trip o' ollabuts, and she'd bin linin'. But, o' course, they're got a different method o' doin' things now. I mean, they keep improvin' with everything.

"Like I said, we only went that one voyage, linin'. Yeah. Then the skipper, he bought a share in a boat, the *Hope* (LT 1075), and we all went herrin' catchin' wi' him—well, all bar poor ol' Billy Peak, the pilot. We were about sixteen weeks on that voyage and I dun't think we were more'n eight weeks at sea altogether on account o' bad weather. We got £90 a share when we paid orf. The owners took half an' we took half—clear o' the *expenses*, the runnin' expenses. What you got paid wuz worked out accordin' to yuh rank on the boat.[37] Yeah, yeah. That wuz on the *Excelsior*. She wuz a little ol' boat with a *woodbine funnel* an' the wheelhouse aft side. An' she hed an *Elliott pot* engine in her with a little ol' *stand-up boiler*.[38] That wuz all right, too!

"I know we were comin' hoom there once an' George Rushmore come to me an' say, 'Neddy.' I say, 'What?' He say, 'If you dun't turn an' stir this boat up,' he say, 'you wun't see your young woman tonight!' I say, 'Oh. Is it like that?' He say, 'Yis.' Well, I went down below an' say to the chief, 'All right, chief, I'll give yuh a spell.' See, I wuz second engineer, as well as whilk-cracker. He say, 'Oh, I dun't want no spell.' I say, 'Yis, you do. I'll give yuh one.' An' after he wuz gone out o' the engine-room, I turned the *whiffler* on. They hed what wuz called a whiffler to make a draught to draw the fire up. Well, he never hed that on; he wuz afraid o' the boiler goin' to bust. He wuz an oldish man, see. An' I turned the whiffler on and I wun't long afore I'd got a full head o' steam. Yeah, I turned that ol' engine round an' that wun't long afore the *thrush* wuz dancin' about like anything![39] That wuz quite laughable, you know. But, anyhow, we got hoom. Yeah, we got hoom all right!"

---

36 The vessel that George Kent worked in under Jack Clarke's captaincy was the *Contrive* (LT 1123).

37 For a full explanation of the share system of payment, see D. Butcher, *The Driftermen* (Reading, 1979), Chapter Six. Ned Mullender was on a *seven-eighths share*, so his end-of-voyage payment would have been £78 15s 0d [£78.75]—a good pay-off for the time, especially with the *stocker-bait* payments added to it.

38 The so-called *pot* engine, made by Elliott & Garrood Ltd. of Beccles, was a small, two-cylinder, compound, with a vertical boiler. Its funnel was tall and slender and supposedly like a Wills Woodbine cigarette in shape.

39 The thrush was a coupling that connected the engine to the crankshaft.

CHAPTER THREE

Go West, Young Man

Away, haul away; oh, haul and sing together.
Away, haul away. Haul away, Joe!
Away, haul away; we'll haul for better weather.
Away, haul away. Haul away, Joe!
(Traditional capstan song: *Haul Away, Joe*)

Towards the end of the previous chapter, Ned Mullender made reference to the line-fishing carried out by Lowestoft vessels in western waters, mentioning (among other things) how his own father had had experience of it before the First World War. In essence, the basic method did not differ greatly from the long-lining for cod that Ned himself had done for a season, following his discharge from wartime duties. The main differences lay in the dimensions of the two types of gear and the respective depths of water fished[1]—plus, to a certain degree, the different species sought. The basic reason for craft being committed to the western *lining voyage* was exactly the same as that which influenced the owners of the *Excelsior* to send her *longlining*. It was done to keep boats and men employed for as much of the year as possible, so as to maximise earning potential and create profit (or, if this latter could not be achieved, to at least break even).

Two voices will be heard in this chapter discussing various aspects of longlining in waters off the coasts of Wales, Cornwall and Ireland, and both belong to men who went on this particular voyage during the 1930s. One is that of George Kent (1907-98), the man referred to by Ned Mullender in the closing paragraphs of the previous chapter; the other belongs to Tom Outlaw (1915-97) who, during the course of a long career at sea, had experience of both fishing and working on Trinity House lightships. Between them, they produce an extremely interesting and informative account of the specific type of lining practised by Lowestoft drifters far from the home-port—each serving to corroborate the other's testimony in a number of places, while at the same time creating an individual statement concerning the work done. George Kent (recorded, 19 January 1981) speaks first.

"The boat I wuz on wuz called the *Contrive* (LT 1123) [not the *Couronne*] and I first went round to the West'ard in 1931, and I wuz there till 1936. Yes, yes. 1931 to 1936. There wuz a lot o' boats went before ever we started workin' the lines, but there wuz only roughly about six or seven when I wuz goin'. I think that, as people got older, they gradually finished and what have you. The *Forerunner* (LT 1160) and all them lot used to go before ever we started. We were one o'

---

1 In general terms, the Western fishery often entailed working in deeper water than was customary in the North Sea.

Map 2: Major Western Fishing-grounds

The Western fishing-grounds of Great Britain (not to scale). The three-mile exclusion limit is partially represented by a dotted line, but not shown at all around Ireland. From what Harry Colby says in the next chapter, it seems not to have existed for Skipper "Oscar" Pipe, who regularly trawled close inshore during the hours of darkness in the Waterford-Wexford area.

Plate 4: Contrive (LT 1123)

A fine view of the steam drifter "Contrive" (LT 1123) heading out to sea, as a Scottish boat (Banff-registered) is returning to port. Four crew members are visible (hard to see) at work on the starboard side, dressed in oilskins, and herring drift-nets are stacked ready for use on top of the hatch-covers. The vessel was built in Lowestoft in 1911.

the last to start, I believe. Jack Clarke wuz our skipper and he wuz part-owner of the *Contrive* with George Mitchell. When he first went, he knew no more, I think, than the rest o' the crew. No, he'd never had any experience, but he asked several of the old skippers what had been linin' an' he went himself. See, there wuz money to be earnt then in linin' because, I mean, yuh coal wuz cheap, and ice wuz cheap, and yuh bait wuz reasonable. Mind you, we were a long while before we learnt the art, because everybody wuz strange to the job.

"We used to *make up* the boat first, after the *Home Fishin'* had finished. Then we would go up on the *store* here and turn round an' get the gear ready.[2] The gear consisted of forty-five *baskets* of lines, which had got to be made up—but we didn't use forty-five baskets, o' course, when we first went. There wuz six lengths of line in a basket an' about 110 hooks. The lines were three-stranded *manila* an' about half an inch thick; they were tanned in *cutch* every year, after you'd finished the voyage. There wuz an *eye* in one end and you used that to tie 'em together when you were at sea. There wuz a fathom and a half from hook to hook and a three-quarters of a fathom *snud*, where the hook wuz on. The hooks were what we

---

2 The Mitchell family had a net-store in Florence Road, Pakefield, not far from where Mr. Kent lived.

used to call a *swivel-hook*, and they were a *number nine*. Thass a fair size hook, that is. Yes, yes. Yes, they were all swivel-hooks. And the idea of a swivel-hook was that, when you got the fish comin' up, when you were haulin', the fish would swim up with the line. And the swivel, that would help the fish and take the weight orf yuh line.[3] We tried out *cotton* snuds and we tried out *hemp*. But we found that the cotton snuds, after the first year, used to what we call *chittle up* on the line. They used to go windin' round and round and round, so we used hemp and you got very little turn from that.

"We also had *anchors* and *dans* [dhan-buoys] to see to, and o' course we'd already got the *linin' winch* on the boat. That wuz one o' the old-fashioned ones what we had—a tall one, roughly about five foot in length, and it had two wheels. And we used to pass the line over the top o' the large wheel, and then onto the small wheel, and coil the lines into the baskets. The winch wuz steam driven and that wuz on the right-hand side o' the ship—right up front an' fixed onto the *rail*.[4] You know, in the *kid*. Yes, yes, in the kid. I wuz *fireman* on the boat to start with, then I went *chief* [engineer].

"Once we'd got all the gear rigged up, we used to leave here roughly about the third week in January and go to Milford Haven. Mitchell Brothers were our salesmen, and a member o' the fam'ly used to be down there and he would order us bait for the lines. We used to bait for a full trip on about twelve kits of *squid* an' seven boxes of *Norwegian herrin'*, and once we'd got our coal and ice and everything we were ready to go to sea. We used to take in roughly about twenty-three tons of coal—seventeen tons under the deck and the rest on top, loose. Three tons each side. *Welsh nuts*. And then all our work, when we first went out, was on the starboard side o' the ship—to burn all that coal as we were going our distance to have a clear deck for shooting and hauling. We carried about ten tons o' ice as well, but that wuz down in the *hold*, in the *wings*.

"After we left Milford Haven, in the early part of the time (weather permitting and the tides not too strong), we used to try an' fish orf Bardsey Island. We used to work roughly about twenty-five miles south-west from Bardsey and we were mostly after conger, and a few rooker [Thornback Ray—*Raja clavata*] and a few cod. If the weather wuz too bad, we used to go orf Holyhead—and we used to work either Caernavon Bay or Cardigan Bay as well. We used to go into Cardigan Bay after the ol' *studded rooker*—the real ol' thornybacks! Yes, we used to go in as far as we could to shoot our lines, so we had to use the leadline an' test how

---

3 Swivel-hooks were also intended to prevent certain species from twisting up the lines once they had been caught. Conger eels particularly would rotate themselves and the swivel prevented this movement from fouling the gear. See, Davis, *Fishing Gear*, p. 137.

4 The development of steam line-haulers was a great step forward in fishing technology and relieved crew members of a great deal of hard work. It also made possible the use of longer lines (and, therefore, a greater number of hooks), thereby increasing the catching potential of the vessel.

much water we'd got.

"You always shot with the tide, and the early part o' the time we only shot twelve baskets o' lines. Only twelve. That wuz because you had to shoot, haul and do everything within the six hours of the tide. And when we shot our gear, we used to have a right-hand man and a left-hand man baiting.[5] But the mate used to sit on the *rail* and pay the lines over. By hand. Yes, everything was done by hand. When we started to shoot, we used to throw the *dan* over first and that would have three *buffs* on. And then, fastened to the buffs, wuz a 120 fathom o' *dan-tow*, and on top o' that wuz the *anchor*. Yes, and we threw that lot over. The dan-tow was ordinary rope. Yeah, no chain. All rope.

"When we started to *shoot*, we were head to tide. Then we brought the boat round and went with the tide. They used to call down to the engineers (and, as a matter of fact, I wuz down there!) what wuz happenin'. A man on the deck, he'd say, 'We're goin' to shoot.' So, therefore, we'd set the engines to what we thought wuz the speed they wanted. If we weren't goin' fast enough, they used to call down to the engine-room, 'One faster!' One rev faster, see. Well, that'd be two revs by the time we'd done. Ha, ha, ha! We always used to keep the *mizzen* [sail] up while we shot—that used to be up the whole time—an' that used to take us about three-quarters of an hour altogether, for about twelve baskets o' lines.[6] You didn't bait up before you shot. You baited as you went along—a left-hand man an' a right-hand man, like I said. And what you did wuz, when you finished one basket o' lines, wuz have one o' those men bait about eight or nine hooks on the next one and just stick them on the edge o' the basket, ready. The other man would sit there and hold the line tight, what'd been shot, so it didn't get tangled up on the bottom. Then, the two lines were tied together and those hooks, which were already baited, were thrown over right quick. An' then you'd go back to normal again.

"The baskets that the lines were in were about a yard across an' two foot six tall and they had a coil o' small rope tied all the way round on the top. And then, on top o' the rope, there used to be a piece o' *spunyarn* that wuz rolled round and round the rope from one end to the other. And the hooks were pulled down in between the rolls o' spunyarn right round the top o' the basket and you pulled 'em out as you baited. There wuz an art in it, and we were a long while before we learnt the art because everybody was strange to the job.

"You didn't have anchors on the lines. No, no. You had an anchor at one end, on the dan gear, and an anchor at the other end with a dan. You'd have *flags* on

---

5   This was because the hooks were set alternately on either side of the line.

6   The mizzen sail was set, to act as a steadying influence on the vessel as it moved down-tide. The engine also served this purpose and was able to supply instant power if, for any reason, it should have been needed.

yuh dans in daylight and a *battery light* in the hours o' darkness.[7] You'd shoot as soon as the tide turned from a *flood* to an *ebb*, and you knew when that tide had finished by the position of the buffs on your dan. You see, with the tide running that one way, your buffs would be the other [far] side o' the dan. But, as soon as the tide finished, you see, your buffs would come towards the boat. That was a signal. And, as soon as you got that signal, you used to go an' call the skipper out. He used to come on deck and away you'd go an' haul your lines.

"You had to haul as soon as the tide turned and you had to be very, very quick on your job, do otherwise the tide would ha' gradually moved and moved a little faster and pushed you past your lines. So you had to work as fast as possible. The *line-hauler* made the job easy, but it could still be tricky. If the wind wuz awkward and that wuz blowin' the hooks towards you, you had to sometimes stand back.[8] What the mate used to do [from his position near the line-hauler], as soon as he could see a fish comin' out o' the water, was lean over and get the snud and just pull the fish in. Pull it in and drop it in the *kid*. And the man who wuz on the winch [line-hauler], he'd still keep carryin' on as if nothin' had happened. And if the fish had swallered the bait and the hook wuz fairly well down, the mate used to put a *disgorger* down the fish's throat, give a half-turn and take it out. That's right, yeah.

"As you were coilin' your line back inta the basket, after the fish had been *backed orf*, I learnt that the best way wuz to start from the outside and work in, and then work out agin. And the art was to coil your line as small [tightly] as possible inta the centre and work out from there—otherwise you'd finish up with a big hole in the centre o' the basket and all your hooks would fall in an' get in a tangle. Now, after you'd finished coilin' that basket orf the winch, you had to take it aft and coil the line back into another basket an' put all the hooks round the edge, so that was ready for the next shoot. Everybody took his turn at that, just like on the *guttin'*.

"Like I said, the lines were made from manila and the fishin' was very hard on the hands because you all had to take a turn at pullin' up on the line when you were hauling. One man heaved up all the time to keep the line at the right tension for the winch and you knew you'd done it when you finished your spell. It was important to keep the boat as near your lines as possible, so you could control them as they came aboard. That was no good bein' too far away from 'em and, o' course, as the boat rolled you had to pull up hard to keep the line nice and tight. I remember once, the wind was blowin' very, very hard one day onto the ship, as we were hauling, and a chap named Sidney Fisk (he lived at Kessin'land) had a hook blow into his face. Right inta his mouth! We'd got a few baskets left to haul

7 A twelve-basket shoot gave a total line length of a little over two miles, which meant that the light on the far dan would usually have been visible from the boat.

8 This refers to hooks which did not have fish on them—especially those from which the bait had been taken or had fallen off. These would sometimes catch the wind and be blown inboard, causing a high risk of injury to anyone who got in the way.

at the time, so we put a dan down right quick and then went as fast as we could to Newlyn an' took him to the hospital. And they didn't want to cut the poor chap, not to disfigure him outside—so they cut him inside. Two years in succession he had that—in the face! But they were the only times we ever had anybody git hurt. We were fairly fortunate, really.

"Another thing, too. We never lost bait or had trouble like that. I don't think our lines would ever have been attacked by starfish or anything like that, because we never hauled at dead low water. The starfish lays on the bottom (he's what we call a *lazy fish*) and the tide would keep the bait up, so he wouldn't git up after it. The lines wouldn't shift far, though, because o' the anchors at each end. They were a good-sized anchor, too. There wuz praps a little movement in the middle, but not much. What used to happen, after we'd finished shootin', wuz that the skipper used to tell the person who had the watch the position o' the boat.[9] So whatever position he said, you knew that the boat would drift in the direction he'd told you. We used to let the boat drift a certain distance (not too far) and then steam back to the dan to start haulin'. If the weather wuz bad, you used to let the boat *dodge* up to wind'ard and keep a reasonable distance from the dan. But you only done that if the weather wuz exceptional.

"The depth o' water dint make any difference on linin', but when we were fishin' with all forty-five baskets o' line we'd shoot at the finish o' daylight and let the lines be there all night. And then, the next mornin', about half-past six, we used to call the cook out and have breakfast an' make a start. And that would take us till dinner-time before we'd finished haulin' the lines—and guttin' at the same time. Forty-five baskets o' lines and we were tired! Yeah, and we used to have a dan in the middle on that, as well as the ones on the end. When we were workin' Anglesey, we were puttin' out roughly about fifteen baskets. Yes, where there wuz a lot o' tide, or where the weather wuz unkind, you didn't overdo it. It was left entirely to the skipper.

"Now, if you got a lot o' fish, wherever you were, you'd go over that piece o' ground again. Which meant that you had to turn the boat round, right quick, and steam roughly about three-quarters of an hour back over the ground what you'd previously done. And then, when you turned back again, you'd still have the tide with yuh, so you could cover that same ground again to get yuh fish. In a twenty-four hour period, you usually used to get four shoots an' hauls. See, you worked each tide, and took your meals when you could. You never had a set meal-time, and you also slept when you could. Sometimes, you'd only get one hour's sleep in the six, and you never got more'n two. Another thing you'd do wuz spell each other round on the different jobs. You know, the *fireman* would help the *chief* and

---

9 Once the lines had been shot, the chief engineer and the stoker worked the engine-room watches between themselves. The deck and wheelhouse watches were arranged between the other crew members—with the exception of the skipper and the cook, who never took a watch.

someone would go in the wheelhouse and take over from the skipper.[10]

"We used to gut the fish up while the lines were bein' hauled. Six people gutted. See, we had ten in the crew—same as we did on a drifter [i.e. when fishing for herring]. Yes, yes, everything was just the same: *'awseman, waleman, three-quarter and half-quarter*. Yeah, just the same. Same names. Same everything. And, as I said, we used to spell each other round for meals, and the people who were not haulin' the lines at the time used to gut the fish as they came in. But we didn't hafta gut conger. No, we never gutted a conger. As soon as ever they fell in the *kid*, we used to put our two fingers inta the gills, lift them up an' drop 'em down the hold out o' the way.[11] Never saw 'em no more, till we wanted to pack 'em away. Leave them! They'd die. No, you dun't never want to touch them! No, no. Definitely not. O' course, we had to gut rays and cod, or any *long fish*—anything like that."

The usual procedure on the *Contrive* regarding shooting the lines was as follows: skipper (wheelhouse), chief engineer (engine-room), cook (galley), mate (shooting the lines), hawseman and waleman (baiting), and the other four crew members bringing baskets of lines to be shot and taking turns at baiting-up when able to do so. For hauling, the skipper remained in the wheelhouse, the chief engineer in the engine-room and the cook in the galley, but the rest of the crew took turns at manning the line-hauler, disengaging fish from the hooks, coiling the lines back into baskets and gutting the catch. The mate spent most of his time bringing the fish inboard, but he was relieved of this task periodically. Tom Outlaw's vessel would have operated a similar routine and his account of the Westward lining voyage can now be heard (tape-recording made, 4 October 1983). He was only fifteen years old when he first went to Milford Haven, nine years younger than George Kent, and the experience must have been a testing one for him, both physically and mentally—especially with his father being skipper and part-owner of the vessel in which he sailed. And, in connection with this fact, it is interesting to observe that, as with the *Contrive*, evidence is again to be had of how a resourceful skipper could earn sufficient money to purchase an interest in a fishing vessel—if not to own it outright, as some of the more successful operators did.

"I first went longlinin' in 1930. My father an' his partners had bought the ship the year before and their idea was to work it, if they possibly could, for twelve months o' the year. So that's the reason why the ship went longlinin'. She wuz the *Boy Scout* (LT 17), a small drifter about eighty-two foot long. I wuz on that

---

10 On the daily pattern of six-hour shoots and hauls, sleep was only taken when all the gear was overboard and everything on board was neat and tidy. The cook was mainly kept on galley duties and only assisted on deck (cutting up bait, usually) in fine weather.

11 Conger eels were too dangerous to handle, but once their bodies had lost contact with the deck they were manageable. The insertion of the index and middle fingers, on each hand, into the gills enabled them to be lifted and disposed of relatively easily.

Plate 5:   Boy Scout (LT 17)

The steam drifter "Boy Scout", outward bound, astern of another vessel. Built in Lowestoft, in 1913, four of her crew are present on deck: two of them, standing near the little boat and two more up for'ad near the steam capstan. The boat's rounded counter-stern (often referred to as a "tug-stern") enabled it to ride a following sea: as long as it wasn't too large a one!

voyage for five years. Yeah, I wuz there 1930, '31, '32, '33 an' '34. You went away in January, and you'd go inta Newlyn to coal an' pick up bait there if yuh could. Then, if you got some bait, you'd fish a trip from Newlyn to Milford and work from Milford for the rest o' the voyage. An' I can remember one year that we dint come hoom till early June. Yis, yis. Five months away wuz nothin'. And there wuz one or two occasions, when one or two o' the ships done very well, that they went back there for a summer voyage instead o' goin' down to the Shetlands, herrin' catchin'. I think that Colley Forster done that in the *Supernal* (LT 750) or the *Reclaim* (LT 227).

"We used to go away with the lines all in *hanks*, and the lines had to be made up as you were goin' round to Milford. We used to take away about 30,000 swivel-hooks and each line, each single line, would be made up o' seven hanks, or sometimes eight hanks, yuh see. Each hank wuz about forty fathoms long and made o' *manila* or *hemp*, which wuz very hard an' would be slightly less thicker than my little finger. And these hanks would be made up into one long line, which would be 280 to 300 fathom or more. And on that line you'd have about 100 hooks. The *snuds* would be about a fathom long an' they'd be two fathom or more apart. I think they were tarred manila and, o' course, they were a finer twine than the lines. Yeah, they were sim'lar to the twine used in trawls [trawl-nets]. The *shank* o' the hooks wuz about four inches long an' the *bowl* wuz about three-quarters of an inch. So they were fairly big hooks. Oh yes.

"The first year I went, I wuz just the *cook,* but the second year I wuz on deck—as *cast-orf.* And, o' course, to be quite frank, the cast-orf an' the *three-quarter share* do more or less the same as the others, but the senior men (like the *mate* and the *'awseman* and the *three-quarter and half-quarter man*[12]), they would be the men that shot the lines. I did git round to baitin' up the lines myself, and a-shootin' on 'em, but that wuz the last year I wuz round there. The other years, there wuz better men than me there to do the job, yuh see. They had more experience. They'd bin round there several years before I ever went.

"When you got round to Milford, you would take in bait. An' the bait in those days wuz squid, caught by the trawlers. They used to bring it in and sell it on Milford market, at about 12s 6d [62½p] a *kit.* We used to buy about twelve kits for a trip. An' if you couldn't git squid in those days, the agents ashore used to arrange for Norway herrin' to be brought to us.[13] On one or two occasions, when we were fishin' in the Irish sea, praps we couldn't get hold of enough bait for an entire trip, so my father would arrange for Norway herrin' to be taken to Fishguard. See, we'd be workin' somewhere in that area and then, on a certain day, we'd go inta Fishguard and pick the bait up. I only know of one ship that carried *bait-nets*: Crabby Hudson in the *A. Rose* (YH 69), he used to shoot a few nets. And, in actual fact, I have bin shipmates with one o' the men that wuz in his crew. Yes. And he said in actual fact that the *Scotch nets* (q.v.) and the lines together were a damn pest! He said he would ha' much rather had just the lines alone and bought the bait.[14]

"We used to have ice for the bait, o' course. And the squid (*fantails* we used to call 'em) wun't be too bad for the first two or three days. But, after that, they'd smell like blazes. Yeah, awful smell! That used to be somebody's job between shoots to cut them up for bait for the next shoot. You used to take hold o' the squid an' slip yuh finger down and pull his head out. Then you'd chop the tentacles off the top o' his head—but not too short. Conger used to like the heads. Yeah, if you caught conger, you'd always catch some on the head o' the squid. There wuz an ink sac behind the head, so you'd cut that orf an' push that to one side, then slip yuh knife down the inside o' the squid an' split it open. That would then open out to a piece o' flat, leathery-lookin' stuff about four inches by six or seven, an' you would cut that up into praps six pieces. Yeah, we always used squid, herrin' (Norwegian herrin' as a rule) and mackerel from Newlyn. The Norwegian herrin' used to cut up into about seven baits, an inch an' a half acrorss. See, they were

---

12 This last-named member of the crew was sometimes known as the *waleman.*

13 One of the Lowestoft fish-selling companies acted for the *Boy Scout,* handling all the onshore business in return for a commission payment.

14 Albert ("Crabby") Hudson was skipper-owner of the *A. Rose* and one of Great Yarmouth's best-known fishermen.

fairly big, Norwegian herrin' were.

"In the early part o' the season, which would be January and February, we'd be workin' in the southern part o' the Irish Sea, orf Lundy Island and the Smalls. Yeah, or we'd run across to the Irish side: Old Head o' Kinsale, Arklow, Coningbeg, in the region o' Dunmore and that area. And sometimes we'd get further north and work the Kish Bank and the Stacks, off Holyhead. And that area, if you were fishin' there at the tops o' the tides, the tides in the Stacks area particularly would be fairly fast. And if you didn't have enough *buffs* on your *dans*, the tide would pull your dans down. Oh yes, yes. See, you had a dan to start with, and on that dan were three herrin' buffs. And then there would be a *dan-tow* of about 120 fathoms o' manila (that'd be about an inch an' a half, two inch, diameter) and an anchor tied onto that. And then the first line would be *bent* onta that anchor. And then, as that anchor wuz dropped, they'd sing out 'Shoot-o!' and the men would then start to throw the line away.

"We used to bait the hooks as the lines were bein' shot. There'd be a *bait-box* on the after-end o' the drifter, on the starboard quarter, near the *lifeboat*, and two men would stand there—one fore side an' the other aft. The basket o' lines would be on a platform between the two men and another man would be sittin' on the rail, payin' the lines over. And that could be an extremely dangerous job. The hooks were all round the top edge o' the basket, and they had to be picked orf one at a time and the bait put on'em and then thrown over the side. And the men used to be very good at gittin' inta unison so they never made any mistakes.[15] If there was a mistake made, and a hook dropped down inta the centre o' the basket when you were shootin', there allus used to a couple o' sharp knives right handy, so that if anything went wrong they could just grab hold and cut. Yes, cut the *snud*, so the hook wouldn't foul the line. An' sometimes, if you were a bit unfortunate, and they made a mistake and a hook *hefted* up in the wrong place, they'd sing out, 'Stop her! Come astern!' And then hooks and lines would be flyin' in all directions, and someone would finish up with a hook in his hand or finger, or somethin' like that. I only see it happen once, but you did have to be extremely careful when you were shootin'.

"Once you'd shot the first dan and the first basket o' lines, the bottom end o' that line would be stickin' out o' the top o' the basket, see, so you could *bend* the next basket onto it, and so on, until you got to the end. When you got to the end, you would bend an *anchor* onta the last bit o' the line, then the *dan-tow*, and then the *dan*. That's right, so you had a dan at either end. And the lines were shot in more or less a straight line before the tide. After you'd finished shootin', you'd just drop

---

15 A platform ran from the rail of the vessel to the bait-box, along which the lines were drawn. One man stood fore-side of the bait-box and one aft. They baited the hooks and cast them over alternately by hand. Another man, sitting on the rail, paid out the line itself. It was customary to keep these three crew members in the same job. The first twenty fathoms of line, either side of a dan, had no hooks on them in order to prevent fouling.

away from yuh lines and let the drifter lay orf. And, o' course, there wuz always a man on watch to keep an eye on that last dan, so you didn't lose yuh lines. We used to shoot anything up to eighteen baskets o' lines and never had no anchor in the middle—just one at each end.

"One thing I didn't say wuz that when you'd just shot one basket over the side, and you'd got another basket riddy to go, the man who wuz shootin' the lines would hold the joint, where the two lines were made fast, across his waist. And as the ship wuz steamin' through the water, he'd tow that basket what'd bin shot out tight behind him, until that come reasonably tight to the anchor. Then he'd sing out, 'Stand by! Let go!' An', o' course, he'd let go o' the line an' away they'd go agin [shooting hooks and lines]. And he'd do that every basket until you got to the end. Now, if he didn't do that, when you went to haul sometimes (and, by the way, you always hauled yuh lines before the tide), you'd finish up with what wuz called *bunches o' grapes*. Instead o' the lines bein' out straight, they would congregate together and you'd have a bunch o' lines and hooks to untangle.

"The whole business o' shootin' and haulin' wuz carried out over six hours. Now, if you arrived on the area where you were goin' to shoot, and say you'd got about four hours o' tide to go—well, you'd shoot. Praps you'd take about three-quarters of an hour on that and the ol' man would say, 'All right. Turn in.'[16] And the *watch* would take over, and the men who went below would git about an hour and a half's sleep. As soon as ever the tide wuz *makin' round*, you'd call the lads out and haul the lines back to the other end. You used to start to pick up the lines at slack water and work back with the tide. Occasionally, you'd git a *heft* on the bottom—what we called a *fastener*—and that'd be quite a pantomime movin' the ship to break the fastener out. Sometimes (and I've seen this happen once or twice) the man on the winch would have a few fathoms o' line in and then, all of a sudden, the ship would pay orf and that line would whizz out. And, o' course, the hooks would whizz out with it and then you'd have hooks flyin' through the air agin! So you always had to be very careful.

"The first year we went, we had a Scotch *line-hauler* that fitted on the rail, on the *port side*. And it wuz very unusual—down this way, anyhow—to have the line-hauler on the port side.[17] But, apparently, it wuz the only one they could git at that time. It wuz up the fore end o' the kid and it wasn't as good as some o' the other winches that some o' the other ships had. We got one by Elliott and Garrood the next year. They had a very good line-hauler out, which wuz called a *lighthouse hauler*, for some reason or other. I think that wuz simply because the pedestal which the haulin' wheels fitted on stood about four foot high. See, this

---

16 The expression *old man*, in this case, has dual meaning. It refers both to a traditional nickname used for commanders of vessels and to Tom Outlaw's own father.

17 Starboard was the preferred side to work on East Anglian lining vessels, just as it was in steam trawling and drift-netting.

pedestal stood just inside the rail near the fore *thwartship-board* an' you could ship the line-haul wheels onto it. And when you were in harbour, the outboard wheel would stand out over the rail and, o' course, you had to unship that an' take it off the pedestal. They were very good winches, they were. There wuz a steam-pipe went direct to it, underneath the thing, and an exhaust pipe as well—just the same as in their *steam capstans*.

"Given that you didn't git too many complications, haulin' wuz about an hour, hour and a half's job. O' course, it all depended on how many lines you had out, see. What used to happen, if you had an extraordinary big fish come in, wuz that the man who wuz standin' at the rail, *backin' the fish orf,* used to sing out, 'Garf!' And you'd git the *hook* and use that. And sometimes, as a fish wuz comin' out o' the water, he'd drop orf. And, o' course, the man backin' orf would sing out, 'Garf!' agin—and someone would *garf* it. I never did see a *didall* used—though that woulda bin a good idea. I remember once, when I wuz along o' my father, seein' the only *hollabut* [halibut] we ever caught round there. That come up onta the top o' the water and the mate wuz at the rail and he sang out 'Larnch!' Because *'larnch'* to us wuz 'stop'. And he looked over the rail and he say, 'Well, I dun't know what the hell this is, but thass a damn big fish!' Well, o' course, when we looked over the side, this damn great big flatfish wuz layin' on top o' the water. This wuz west o' the Scillies. And, o' course, we got two or three garfs into it, and that still laid on top o' the water and hardly moved even when we got the garfs in. And, you can believe me, that took all hands exceptin' the skipper, the driver and the cook to git that fish up over the rail. I've never sin anything like it! I reckon that musta bin at least eight foot long from the mouth to the end o' the tail.

"If you worked fairly deep, you had to lengthen yuh *dan-tows*. And as long as you had yuh dan-tows deep enough, that din't matter how deep the lines were. We did work in shallow water as well. Yis, oh yis. Like when we worked Oxwich Bay, we'd be in close—right close to the shore.[18] As close as we dare get. And, on another occasion, I remember we were orf Aberystwyth, after rays again, and we were in pretty close there. The more baskets you worked on a tide, the less sleep you would git. More often than not that wuz a dozen baskets, but occasionally you'd have eighteen. The *driver* [chief engineer] dint take an active part in it, but the *stoker* did—yis. And, o' course, the skipper used to spend plenty o' time in the wheelhouse, though after you'd shot he'd be like the rest. He'd hand over to the watch and git his hid down. The *cook*, he wuz cook an' cook only. That wuz his job. He would just look after cookin' the meals. He wun't hev much to do on deck, though he'd sometimes come an' lend a hand guttin' if you were gittin' plenty o' fish.

"Once the line had bin hauled over the winch and the fish had bin taken off, you'd gotta take that basket o' lines you'd bin coilin' in (another man would take

---

18 Oxwich Bay is on the south side of the Gower Peninsula, not far from Swansea.

over from you) and go an' sit on the ship's *rail* and clean that basket o' lines riddy to shoot agin. And, o' course, the hooks would invariably be coiled round the line and you'd hefta unravel them and put them up on the edge o' the basket.[19] Oh, it was a *tired voyage*! You weren't gittin' enough sleep, see. And sometimes you'd be unfortunate enough to get a *fastener* and break yuh line, and then you'd hefta go to the other end and pick that dan up and haul the lines back aginst the tide. I've seen two men tryin' to haul the line, and that wuz with the help of a line-hauler!

"You always tried to keep your lines in good repair and do the maintenance while you were at sea.[20] The line wuz examined by the man who wuz cleanin' that line and gittin' it riddy for the next shoot. And, as he wuz goin' through the line, he would renew chafed snuds; and, if the line wuz badly chafed anywhere, he would cut that and knot it. And he would knot it with what wuz known as the *longlinerman's knot*. Some people call it a *fisherman's knot*.[21] And the harder you pull that, it gets tighter and tighter and will not pull apart. Yeah, the harder you pull it, the tighter it gets. And, before it parts, the line will part. In some ships, when they were goin' inta harbour, especially in warm weather, they'd lay a few o' these knots out o' the side o' the baskets. Then they'd splice them up while they were in the harbour. But the line had to be fairly dry before you could do that.

"Another thing about that voyage wuz, once you'd started it, your hands were sore up till the time you finished. Because you were always prickin' yuh fingers, yuh see. Specially when you come up aginst thornback rooker and that sort o' thing. Yeah, you were always prickin' yuhself wi' them. And when we were workin' orf the Melville Knoll, we struck a type o' fish there I've never seen anywhere else.[22] They were a big skate, but instead o' bein' bluish-grey one side an' brown the other, these were brown on one side an' white on the other. Damn gret things! About three of 'em would cover this room! But they wun't very saleable and, on top o' that, they had rows an' rows o' spikes down each side o' the nose, so you had to be terribly careful o' them.[23]

"The hooks were all *swivels* an' that wuz because the conger tends to twist like

---

19 Each basket of lines was joined to the next one by a sheet-bend knot, using the loop in the end of the line. When the join came inboard, it was untied by the man whose basket was being prepared for the next shoot. He would have already coiled the incoming line into the basket, dropping the hooks into the space in the middle. The latter would then have to be put around the edge of the basket, ready to use again—work that was done when the line and hooks were checked for damage.

20 This made good economic sense and was better than losing earning-time by staying in harbour and carrying out maintenance work on gear.

21 This knot was formed by tying two *overhand knots*, one in each end of the cut line, and sliding them together.

22 The Melville Knoll was a fishing ground, about eighty-five miles west-south-west of the Scilly Isles.

23 The fish referred to here was probably the Pale Ray (*Raja lintea*).

nobody's business. Sometimes they'd come up with a *muzzle*. They'd swivel round and git the snud wound round the jaws. They used to say that congers would bite through broom staffs and people's boots an' things like that—well, I never saw it happen. And providin' you could git yuh fingers inta the gill o' the conger, to lift him up and put him down the hold, you've got nothin' to worry about. They stayed alive a fairly long while, if they were in the kid or even down the hold, but as soon as you put 'em inta the *wings* and chucked ice on 'em they'd be dead within a very few minutes. See, you'd have yuh hatch covers orf when you were haulin' and the conger would go straight down inta the hold. I have seen one or two o' the men, as a conger come over the rail, use a special *backin'-orf* tactic. Yeah, I've seen the fish come over the rail and, as he's movin' through the air, he wuz backed off the hook and he'd go straight down the hold without ever touchin' the deck! You used to take a turn round your hand on the snud (see, you always wore woollen *hob mittens*) and then the line would go inta the bowl [curve] o' the hook, and you'd turn your hand upwards and the weight o' the fish would take him off the hook.[24]

"If the hook went right down, then you'd hafta git a *gobstick*—what we used to call a gobstick—and ram it down his throat an' twist it around. And if it dint come out then—well, you din't play around with it—you just cut the snud and let it go. Sometimes, you'd git a conger with a muzzle on and you couldn't git him off, so you'd simply lay his head (this is a cruel thing to say) up aginst a basket and hit with the gobstick until his jaws broke. And that wuz the only way you could git him off. The gobstick wuz the best part o' two foot long, with a notch in the end, and that had to be fairly thick—though it didn't matter if it wuz flat or round. Sometimes, you'd git a ray or a skate and, instead o' gittin' the hook in his mouth, that'd go through what we called the *mull*—the soft bit on the outside o' the mouth. You'd have a job backin' him off, then. Yeah, yeah. I've seen hooks (and, as I said, they were four inches long and three-quarters of an inch acrorss the bowl) bent, bent badly. You know, by the fish, while you were strugglin' to get the damn thing off."

The expositions given here, of longlining in western waters, are sufficiently clear as to leave the reader in no doubt regarding the nature of the work and the demands it made on those involved. Both men were obviously familiar with the technical details, but they were also able to convey those same details in a style of language that was straightforward in describing working practice and colourful when embellishment was needed. It is easy to be nostalgic about ways of life that are past and gone, but the lack of false sentiment in the preceding pages prevents such an attitude from developing in the reader. The work was there to be done and the account given of it, fifty years afterwards, conveys that sense of practicality. Lowestoft was once a town almost wholly devoted to maritime trades and allied industries and its population had little choice of employment outside

---

24 *Hob mittens* were knitted from wool that had been treated with oil.

them. The problem of adjustment since their collapse and near-disappearance, both in economic and psychological terms, is still apparent in the town.

Back in the 1930s, the terminal decline of Lowestoft as a major fishing port was sixty years away. George Kent and Tom Outlaw were young men following an age-old tradition of going to sea and their westward lining voyages formed part of a pattern of migratory labour that had been a feature for centuries of not only British fishing, but of much of Western Europe's also. During the later part of the nineteenth century and the earlier part of the twentieth, Lowestoft vessels began to establish regular visits to fishing grounds off Cornwall, Wales and Lancashire as part of their annual activities—leading eventually to long-term (if not permanent) settlement in ports such as Newlyn, Padstow, Milford Haven and Fleetwood. Neither of the respondents in this chapter made that kind of migration, but each of them was well aware of the necessity of working far from home if regular wages were to be earned. George Kent continues his account of longlining out of Milford Haven.

"It wasn't often that we had to stop fishin' when we were round there. You know, with the weather. We would get in somewhere. Under the *lee*, if we could. And we were very fortunate, as regards linin', because we had two Milfordmen friendly with us who had a lifetime's experience. One wuz skipper o' the *Surmount* (M 231) and one wuz skipper o' the *Marguerita* (M 11). We used to work wi' them, and they took to us, and they showed us every hole and corner that a Milfordman fisher would know. And then, when the bad weather wuz more or less finished, we used to go out about 120 mile from Milford Haven, right out inta the Atlantic. We'd be orf the south-east o' Ireland. Sometimes we'd run as far as he Fastnet [Fastnet Rock], an' that wuz 150 mile.[25] We used to go an' fish orf the Tuskar [Tuskar Rock] as well an' that wuz when we used to shoot our forty-five baskets o' lines.[26] What we used to do wuz shoot half of the lines first, to see what the ground wuz like, or what fish wuz there, before we started to shoot the full lot o' lines.

"We never went further north than Holyhead. That was our northern limit. And sometimes we'd be a lot closer to Milford. We used to have two trips off the Smalls [Light], which is about twenty miles from St. Ann's [St. Ann's Head]. Yeah, we used to have two trips there each year and we used to get nothin' only rooker—all lovely, white, blond rooker.[27] This would be April, roughly the latter part o' April, but the fish would only last two or three hauls. I don't know why, but you'd hev two or three hauls and then you would shoot your dozen or fourteen baskets o' lines and you wouldn't two kit o' fish. You were there, and you got the

---

25 The fishing grounds off the Fastnet Rock were about 180 miles from Milford Haven, on a west-by-south bearing.

26 The Tuskar Rock was about fifty miles north-west of Milford Haven, not far from the entrance to Wexford harbour.

27 The fish referred to here is the Blond Ray (*Raja brachyura*).

fish, and then they were gone. If we got any quantity o' fish close to Milford, we just used to slip back into port, sell them, get provisions and out we'd go again.

"Your time at sea was usually between seven an' eight days. Then back to Milford and sell yuh fish. When the fish wuz put away down the hold, in the *wings*, each wing had a different class o' fish. Conger wuz in one, and so forth and so forth. The most wings o' skate that we ever got in the *Contrive* was 864. The ol' blue skate—864 wings. Two wings each fish, so divide that number by two. We got them roughly about 110 miles west-south-west of St. Ann's. They just simply come up, and they were that big that we had to have a garft. See, the weight wuz too much for one man, so they were garfted from each side and pulled in that way.[28] And, as soon as they were in, every fish wuz winged [i.e. the wings were cut off].Yes, they were winged in less than two minutes after they'd come in. All we had to do with the rooker was gut them. Just turn round and take the gut out. We didn't wing any. No, no. Just take the gut out. We used to take the *rolls* [roes] out o' any cod we got and put them down below in a wing, separate. But the livers, they didn't pay to keep. We never got no money for them, so we used to leave them in front o' the wheelhouse for a period of time, then throw them over the side.

"We always got more fish in the hours o' darkness than what we did in daylight. Yes, yes, we'd get a lot more. I remember once, when we went and fished orf the Fastnet, the skipper come down the cabin with his chart and said, 'I think we'll go an' hev a go where the *Lusitania* was supposed to be lost.' And we got a tremendous lot o' conger there.[29] Whether we were right near the wreck, I wouldn't like to say. But some of our hooks, when they came aboard, had got bent. So I should say they were caught on wreckage or somethin' down there. We never came fast, though. We never came really fast anywhere that I can remember. The main trouble that we had on linin' wuz if we weren't haulin' fast enough. If you didn't play smart with yuh work, the tide would beat yuh and you'd be runnin' past yuh lines. You'd hev a lot o' trouble then!

"One o' the best places to work wuz down the Bristol Channel, orf Bardsey Island. You couldn't really beat that—after the conger and rooker. But when we were out westerly and gettin' the big skate and that sort o' fish, that wuz good as well. You could go out anywhere from Milford between west-half-south and west-by-south-half-south and get a *trip o' fish* any time.[30] But, of course, the trouble

---

28 Two men with gaffs (one on either side of the line-hauler) stood ready to bring the fish inboard, assisted at times by the mate, who pulled up on the snood to give extra leverage. The Common Skate (*Raja batis*) is the largest Atlantic ray, reaching a maximum length of 2.5 metres and weighing up to 100 kilos.

29 Good catches of fish are often to be had near wrecks, which create suitable habitat for many species. This has to be set against the risk of damage done to the gear, if any of the wreckage is fouled.

30 These compass directions refer to fishing grounds off the south-east coast of Ireland.

was that you could get the fish and it still meant a low price if two or three of you landed at the same time. Mind you, conger wuz usually worth a good bit o' money, because the French people had a quota for that. So many fish, so many conger, were allowed to be landed in France on their quota system; but as soon as they'd took their quantity, the fish then went down very cheap.[31] And most o' the conger then went to the mining districts in England for the *frying trade*. Except for the *whips*, as we called 'em—you know, the small conger. People would never buy them, on account o' all the sharp bones they had in 'em. Ling wuz never worth a lot, either, except at Newlyn—but we weren't allowed to gut them, because the buyers at Newlyn wanted to buy their fish and the roll [roe] in at the same time. Yeah, a ling wuz nothin' at Newlyn without the roll in!

"After the herring were finished in Norway (they were bein' landed in Hull and then transported to us at Milford, see), we used to go to Newlyn after mackerel, for bait. We used to take in about twenty-five hundred o' mackerel and then, when we come out o' Newlyn, we used to fish a trip back there. We'd go orf to the Scillies, round Tresco or somewhere, and we used to git turbot there *chance time*. That'd be round about the end o' April, beginnin' o' May. We only baited on Norwegian herrin', squid and mackerel. Nothin' else. Now, the *A. Rose* (YH 69)—Albert Hudson, from Yarmouth (Crabby, as we used to call him)—that used to carry *bait-nets*. He wuz very friendly with our skipper, very friendly indeed, and he used to go across to Ireland sometimes and shoot his nets and get his own bait. That'd be either herrin' or mackerel, so he wuz pretty fortunate at gettin' fresh bait.

"The squid what we had from Milford, we used to make about seven or eight baits out o' each one. Roughly about two inches square. We used to get seven baits out of a herrin' or mackerel, but we never used the head or tail. No. And the skipper said, 'If you starve a fish, that'll starve you!'[32] You used to pull your hook right into the bait and up the shank, so the point wuz just showing out o' the end. And with the squid, at night-time, when we used to get them out o' the hold for baitin' up (they were on ice, see), the eyes were a-shinin' just like stars—and so were other parts of 'em. Yeah, shinin' just like stars![33] I think the trawlers out o' Milford used to catch 'em orf the Irish coast and bring them in for bait. And, in that day, they were pretty cheap.

"We were workin' mainly grounds which weren't too rough, but in certain parts there wuz a tremendous lot o' *sea louse*. And when the sea louse are there, they'll eat the flesh off the fish. They'll eat the fish themselves even before they're on the hooks! This wuz orf the south-east coast o' Ireland, in the spring o' the year— about May. May time, yeah. You never saw a sea louse on a fish, but you knew

---

31 French buyers were able to purchase conger eels in Milford Haven through middle-men based in the port (usually local fish merchants).

32 In other words, the baits needed to be a good size in order to be effective.

33 This was due to phosphoresence.

they'd been there. We've had fish come up on our hooks which were nothin' but the frame o' the fish! They were nothin', only skin an' bone. And when that happened, we had to change our ground—you know, steam about nine or ten mile further orf. They were mostly conger and big ol' skate we saw like that. The fish were still alive, but the meat or flesh wuz all eaten orf.[34]

"Round the *West'ard*, we caught mainly conger, skate an' rooker. We never saw whitin' round there. Nor plaice, dabs, soles. No, no *prime fish* o' any sort, really—just a few turbots orf The Scillies, like I said. You might git a chance hake there as well, but they were few and far between. We never got pollack round there, neither, but one thing we did get occasionally wuz a *monkfish*.[35] And once he wuz in the kid, we let him die. Yeah, if you started to do anything with a monkfish—well, you know, they've got teeth as long as my finger an' they'd bite through your long rubber boots! We used to get some o' them off Anglesey and a few off the Scilly Isles as well. Dogfish wuz another thing we used to get. You know, the *spurs* [i.e. Spur-dogs]. Yes, you'd get them, but we never saw the spotted ones and we never saw a *nurse*.[36] You used to get plenty o' dogs orf Holyhead, just clear o' where the ferries were goin' across to Ireland, an' sometimes they would make money. It all depended on what the trawlers had got.

"If we had anything like a good trip, we'd have roughly about 150 kit o' fish. But, o' course, Milford kits were twelve stone [weight], not ten like the Low'stoft ones, and that wuz Milford kits that were landed. You took your turn to land, as you came down the haven. So, if you were the fourth one in, you were the fourth one to land. Everything wuz fair. We used to hev Arthur Mitchell sell for us. He wuz our *salesman* and our *coal agent* as well, and he used to order the ice from the ice comp'ny. He saw after the ship. Mitchell Brothers had trawlers down there too, yuh see, an' he looked after them as well. The skipper would git in touch with the man from the grocer's shop and he would come aboard and ask for the list. The cook ordered what he wanted; that wuz left to him. With bread, we used to take so many loaves each trip, and we used to take flour an' yeast as well and make our own bread till the trip wuz up. If we used too much o' the flour an' yeast an' what have yuh, we used to hefta come down to what we called *Cooper's old*

---

34 The sea louse referred to here is some kind of isopod (probably *Caligus curtus*)—a family which resembles woodlice. The poor physical condition of the fish referred to may not have been due to attack by isopods, but could have been the result of the deterioration that sets in after spawning—a terminal condition, in the case of conger eels.

35 This was (and still is) a commonly used nickname for the Angler (*Lophius piscatorius*)—a fish that increased in value during the 1960s and thereafter, because the tail section of its body makes a good scampi substitute.

36 The two species referred to here are the Lesser-spotted [*Scyliorhinus caniculus*] and the Larger-spotted [*Scyliorhinus stellaris*] Dogfish.

biscuits.[37] Yeah, we'd soak them and put some corned beef in them, and that wuz our meal till we got in the harbour. Ha, ha, ha!

"You hed good food on board, though, and o' course you caught fish! When you went to sea, you had roughly about seven *cookings* [joints] of meat. Praps four or five would be beef an' the rest would be a piece or two o' pork. They were four and a half pound cookings. Yes, four and a half pounds. An' then, for the rest, you could have fish, you see. When we were in harbour, we never had our own fish. Mitchell Brothers had trawlers there, landin', like I said, and we used to have a sole or two from them and what have yuh. And Arthur Mitchell, he used to come with us and have his breakfast. He never would go home [i.e. to his lodgings].

"When we went out o' Milford, if the weather wuz bad, we always used to bring up in Deal Roads.[38] Yeah, you'd be out o' the harbour an' inta Deal Roads. And then, as soon as the weather moderated, you were gone. Milford Haven is a tidal place, you see, so you always tried to git a start. We hed ten berths on board: seven in the *cabin* and three in the *foc'sle*. So there wuz enough room for everybody. We were paid the same as what we were paid if we were herrin' catchin'. Same *share*; same crew. All the ol' *half-quarters* and that. The early part o' the time [i.e. the first year or two], we made a livin', but the latter part o' the time we did not hardly, sometimes, pay our way. The price o' coal begun to come a little dearer and bait wuz £9 a box for Norwegian herrin' and about £1 a hundred for mackerel.[39] Squid wuz pretty cheap most o' the time, but that did get so your bait bill wuz sometimes more than yuh coal bill. When you finished the voyage round there, that'd be gettin' towards the end o' May. Yes, we'd be home about the end o' May, or the first week in June, an' then go straight down to Shetland after herrin'. One weekend at home. That wuz all!"

George Kent's remark, in the paragraph above, concerning the increasing difficulty of making the Milford Haven lining voyage a profitable venture is worthy of comment. There was always a fine line between a boat making money and failing to break even; and (as was pointed out earlier in his testimony) even good catches did not necessarily result in good prices at market. Fishing was a precarious way of making a living and, in the case of *share fishermen*, this financial risk was increased during periods of unemployment. Under the terms of employment law, they were classed as self-employed and were therefore not eligible for dole payments [unemployment money] when out of work, because

---

37 These were ship's (*hard tack*) biscuits. In Lowestoft, they were usually known as *Cooper's rusks* –a name with two possible derivations. The first is a comparison with the hardness of wood, a material that a cooper (barrel-maker) worked in. The second, more likely one is a reference to W.B. Cooper Ltd., a provisioning company in the town which made biscuits and supplied many of the fishing-craft.

38 This was a sheltered area just to the east of the small Dale Peninsula, which itself terminated in St. Ann's Head.

39 Norwegian herring came in boxes containing about twelve stones weight of fish.

66

they had not paid for such benefits. If unemployment reared its ugly head, they had to go on poor relief—whereby a bare subsistence (judged according to individual need) was provided by vouchers for food and other necessitites, which then had to be earned by physical labour of some kind.[40] Trawlermen were treated differently. They earned a weekly wage and paid unemployment contributions (known as the *Lloyd George stamp*, after the man who had introduced the scheme, in 1920) and were therefore entitled to dole payments. This basic (though not generous) security was important and was the reason why many Lowestoft men preferred to go trawling. For share fishermen, however, the main consideration was how to keep working all year round and avoid the laying-up of a vessel in between major drift-netting seasons. Going on longlining voyages was one way of doing this. Tom Outlaw resumes his narrative.

"There used to be several well-known Low'stoft ships round the *West'ard*. There wuz Benny Uttin' in the *Forerunner* (LT 1160), when I first went. He later had the *Silver Crest* (LT 46). There wuz Colley Forster, in the *Supernal* (LT 750) first, and then the *Reclaim* (LT 227)—the ship he wuz lorst in. There wuz Lonnie Harvey in the *Paisable* (LT 1149), and wherever Benny Uttin' wuz in the *Forerunner* or the *Silver Crest* you could bet that Lonnie Harvey an' the *Paisable* wun't be very far away! They were Kessin'land men. Yes, they were Kessin'land men.[41] And we had a mate with us the first year I wuz there by the name o' Frank Curtis. He wuz a Kessin'land man, and we also had three or four other Kessin'land men who were unfortunate enough to lose their lives later on in the loss o' the *Reclaim*, with Colley Forster. A chap by the name o' George Doddington wuz one an' Trouncer Catchpole wuz another. But that's another story.

"I was thinking this afternoon an' I can't remember whether there wuz many Yarmouth men there. Crabby Hudson wuz about the only one I could think of. Yeah, that wuz mainly Low'stoft men. I've mentioned some already, but there wuz also my father in the *Boy Scout* an' Frank Uttin' in the *Shipmates* (LT 1134). Then there wuz Jack Clarke in the *Contrive* (LT 1123), Wag Spillings in the *Infinitive* (LT 705) an' Teddy Beckham in the *Rajah o' Mandi* (LT 736). He wuz the one what used to use a sextant. That wuz when we were out on the Melville Knoll. You know, praps you'd bin out five or six days from Milford and the skipper would have a bit of a job makin' sure o' his position. Now, Teddy Beckham used a sextant and he wuz the only drifter skipper I ever saw do that. Once or twice, just after midday, we'd go up to him and ask his latitude. And he'd give us that and then the ol' man would check on his *dead-reckonin'* so he'd know more or

---

40 In the case of Lowestoft men, this *test work*, as it was known, often meant joining sea-defence gangs or performing tasks in the gardens of Oulton Workhouse.

41 Kessingland was a long-established fishing village, situated five miles south of Lowestoft, and many of its men worked on vessels belonging to its much larger neighbour. During the first half of the twentieth century particularly, a number of the more important boatowners and most successful skippers lived in Kessingland.

less where he was.[42]

"Another boat that wuz down there wuz the *Merit* (LT 231), an' then there wuz the *Confier* (LT 658) as well. I think a man by the name o' Charlie Reynolds wuz skipper o' her. And I remember there once, we were about ninety to ninety-five miles from the Scilly Isles and we got a bad weather report. Then them big *swells* started comin' in, so that we knew there wuz wind an' water comin'. Well, we got the lines aboard and we runned for the Scilly Isles.[43] And, o' course afore we got there, we hed a roarin' gale behind us. And I remember us runnin' inta the Scilly Isles, and the *Confier*, which wuz a ship about the same size as us, she *pooped one* and nearly filled herself up. And I wuz in the wheelhouse when this happened, and all you could see o' that ship when she pooped this sea wuz the wheelhouse, the casin' and the funnel! The hull o' the ship wuz completely covered wi' water. She shook herself clear, but that wuz a close thing. Oh, that wuz very bad weather, that day.

"I think that Benny Uttin' and Lonnie Harvey and their two ships had bin round there for quite a few years before I went. And, also, there wuz one or two Milford liner-men, such as the skipper o' the *Surmount* (M 231) and another man in a wooden standard drifter called the *Fleck* (LT 599). An' there wuz also a firm there by the name o' Peter Hancock, an' they hed a big trawler by the name o' *Sydnelsie* (FD 352) [formerly *Lysander* (H 800)] an' she wuz long-linin' as well. But, o' course, I can't go too far back—not beyond 1930. I think possibly durin' the twenties, up till about 1928, most o' the drifters wanted to do somethin' else other than herrin' catchin', so they were either *trawlin'* or *seine-nettin'*. My father wuz seine-nettin' up till 1928. When that finished, they had to find somethin' else, see. To be quite truthful, we never made a fortune at linin'. Yeah, there wuz men like Colley Forster, Benny Uttin' an' Lonnie Harvey who seemed to do better than what we did. But we earnt a little bit o' money—nothin' to shout about—and we kept out o' debt.

"One thing that did happen while I wuz round there, which hadn't happened previously, wuz that the mackerel boats fishin' out in the Atlantic, round about 100 miles from the Scilly Isles (I think it wuz about west-south-west o' the Scilly Isles) were workin' *handlines* and gittin' a lot o' conger.[44] See, the tail end o' the season, we used to go from Milford if we couldn't git squid an' steam to Newlyn and buy mackerel for bait. Then we'd fish orf The Scillies and that area. Well, we arrived there and this tale wuz goin' round that conger were pretty thick on this

---

42 *Dead reckoning* was a means of estimating a vessel's position from the distance recorded on the log and the course(s) steered by the compass, with allowances made for the direction of current etc. No astronomical calculations of any kind were made.

43 This was done in order to seek shelter closer to land, hopefully off a weather shore.

44 These were crew members of the Lowestoft drifters that had gone round to Newlyn for the late winter and spring mackerel voyage. The grounds being fished would have been somewhere in the Melville Knoll area.

shoal west-sou'-west o' The Scillies. About 100, 120 mile. And the *Abidin' Star* (LT 451), Dutch Turrell, she wuz linin' there that year, and another ship whose name I can't remember. And they went out there to try and find these fish, and o' course they did find 'em. Yeah, and as they were haulin', they were gittin' a fish on nearly every hook, so they were back inta Newlyn within three or four days with a big trip o' fish. And these fish were actually found by boats what were mackerel catchin'. A man by the name o' Dudley Durrant, in a drifter called the *Renovate* (LT 307), wuz one of 'em and there wuz another one besides him. They were mackerel fishin' and they used to work handlines as well, see.[45] The men themselves. Yeah, they used to work *rippers*. And, o' course, they were pullin' these fish out o' the water as hard as they could go! And that's how we come to be out there. Well, when we got onta them fish, we pulled 160 kit inta my father's ship in three days! So, then we decided to hit the road for Milford and land there.

"I would say that conger made the most money out o' what we caught. But the funny part about it wuz that if you caught a really large conger, they never made as much money as a good-sized medium conger. And, o' course, the *whips*—well, they only made peanuts, really. I have caught conger off the Melville Knoll that we used to hafta land one at a time. They were so big that you couldn't git 'em inta a quarter-cran basket.[46] No matter how you tried, they wouldn't go in! So we used to hook the *cran-hooks* inta the gills, one on either side, and land 'em like that. Yeah, we used to git 'em up onta the *capstan pulley*, on at a time, and run 'em ashore. They were tremendous big fish. All the fish wuz *kitted up* on the quay at Milford inta the ol' wooden kits. They never hed the tin *trunks* there then. Not in them days, no.

"We used to try to get in the harbour when other ships weren't there, but that wuz exceedingly difficult. I mean, sometimes you'd come up the *haven*, and the skipper knew what time the tide would be, but if you dint git in through the lock-gates you were stuck outside till the next tide. Yeah, and the deep-sea trawlers would be there, landin' hake, and the *scratchers* would be landin' megrims and whitins. You know, the small trawlers. And you mighta had a bit o' competition wi' them as far as rays were concerned, but not as regards much else. The fish wuz sold by auction at Milford, sim'lar to how it wuz at Low'stoft. There used to be quite a lot o' hake sold there and, for a few years while I wuz linin' round there, there wuz also Spanish hake fishermen landin' their catches. And there wuz quite a lot o' trouble over the Spaniards landin' hake at Milford Haven and affectin' the

---

45 It was customary for crew members on steam drifters (on both herring and mackerel voyages) to fish over the side with handlines while their vessels rode to the nets. This was done to catch various demersal species, which could then be sold in port as a means of creating a modest income.

46 A quarter-cran basket was the standard measure used for landing herrings. It held seven stones weight of fish.

Milford ships.[47] I can't remember any foreign *liners* bein' there, though. No.

"You were continuously in and out o' Milford, but sometimes you had a rest day in the harbour. See, you'd come in and land yuh fish, git yuh coal and ice, and then praps you'd hev that night in and go to sea the next day. Sometimes, you'd go out on a midnight tide, or an early mornin' tide, because Milford is a locked harbour. With *locks*, yuh see. So you went in when the locks were open and you come out when the locks were open.[48] Our *agent* round there, if I remember right, was Kerr—W. Kerr & Son. Yeah, they were widely associated with Low'stoft ships, in the past. They handled most of our business [specifically, the coal and the ice]. Not the provisions, though. That wuz done on the same lines as it was in the herrin' drifters, when you went away from hoom. Yeah, nine times out o' ten, the grocer boy and the butcher boy would come bowlin' over the bow o' the ship and tell the skipper, 'Well, I'll git you so much discount orf us', and that sort o' thing.

"We were paid similarly to herrin' catchin'. Yeah, yeah. We went away with that agreement. The cook wuz half-share or half and half-quarter. There wuz the three-quarter share and the cast-orf. Yeah, they used all the same names as they used on herrin' catchin'. You'd hev a three-quarter an' half-quarter for'ad and aft, and the 'awseman and the mate. Yeah, and the stoker, he'd either be three-quarter share or three-quarter an' half-quarter.[49] And I'm almost sure we used to get four pound and half-a-crown [£4 2s 6d, or £4.12½d] as the full share. Yes, four pound an' half-a-crown.[50] And we also used to get *stocker bait* when we first went round there. We used to sell certain fish, like dogfish and that sort o' thing—and the rows [roes] out o' the ling used to be sold and all. But, durin' the latter part o' the time, there wuz some dissatisfaction, because on some trips the men would not get enough stocker bait. And it finished up with a payment of ten shillins on the hundred. That wuz the *gross hundred*. So if you made £150 on a trip, you got fifteen shillins a man. Hobson's were our sellin' agent round there; my father worked through them. We also got paid the *allotment*, like we did on herrin' catchin'. So the cook would be about ten bob [10s, or 50p] or 12s 6d [62½p] a week, and the 'awseman would be £1 a week, and the skipper 26s 9d [£1.34] I think it wuz.[51]

"The trips were invariably, I spose, eight or nine days. Sometimes that might be ten. That all depended on how far you went, as far as findin' the fish was

---

47 Too many landings of any one species would have brought the selling-price down.

48 The rise and fall of the tide at Milford Haven is pronounced and the tidal currents strong. Sea locks were built to protect the harbour works and vessels moored up at the quay.

49 The chief engineer would have been a full share.

50 This meant that, for every £100 of net profit made at the end of the voyage, a crew member on the full share received £4 2s 6d [£4.12½p].

51 This weekly payment would have been collected by wives or other members of crewmen's families from Hobson's office on the Lowestoft fish market. It was deducted from the payout at the end of the voyage.

concerned. I mean, over on the Kish Bank[52], you'd probably be gettin' skate, whereas down in the southern Irish Sea you got conger. Like that trip I told yuh about, when we got that 150 or 160 kit and filled her up in about three days. Yeah, we were fishin' near where the *Lusitania* wuz sunk that time. If you really struck the fish, it wuz nothin' to git one on every hook. Oh yes, that wuz really excitin' then! But, o' course, it dint happen very orften. We never got many *blondie rays* in the Irish Sea, but there wuz a ray which you got, which hed a very sharp nose, like a blue skate, and a brown back and a white belly. This may not be the correct name, but we called 'em *sand rays* and we used to eat a lot o' them.[53] We used to git the little *jinny hannivers* as well. The nickname for them in those days wuz *butterfly ray*, 'cause they wun't very big and they've got that design on the back.[54] But they're very sweet to eat—very sweet.

"Towards the latter part o' the season, we used to go fishin' down towards the Scilly Isles and you would catch a lot o'rays down there. Yeah, you'd git the blondies and you'd also git blue skate. We never got many cod, but we did use to git quite a lot o' ling. And we got them in the Irish Sea and all. They're a long, thinnish fish and, o' course, when they're in season, they git a very big pair o' *britches* in 'em [a reference to the female's roes]. And, like I said, we used to save them up and land them for stocker bait in Milford. Same wi' dogfish. We used to land them for stocker bait as well. They were nearly always *spur-dogs*, though sometimes you'd git a few *nurse-hounds*. I don't remember that we ever saved the livers or anythin'. No. But I do remember occasions, when we were on skate and dogs and that sort o' thing, when we were guttin', that I've bin standin' in the kid up to me ankles in guts and livers. That all finished up over the side. Yeah, you'd have streams o' gulls behind yuh. O' course, you dint gut conger. No. they went straight down the hold and they were always landed ungutted. Occasionally, we got hake. But we very rarely landed them, because we only got one or two now and again. Nine times out o' ten they finished up in the oven and we hed them for tea.[55]

"Sometimes, when we were fishin' in the Irish Sea (especially in the early part o' the season), the gannets would be very hungry and they would foller you while you were shootin'. Yeah, and they would see the bait goin' down on the line and they used to dive and take the bait—and, o' course, they used to take the hook as well. And that wuz nothin' to see four or five dead gannets come up in the course of a haul. Oh yes, that often happened. And another thing: we used to have one

52 This fishing ground was about six miles east-south-east of Dublin Bay.

53 The species in question was the Shagreen Ray (*Raja fullonica*), which presumably had had its skin used at some time as a substitute for leather.

54 This particular species is the Cuckoo Ray (*Raja naevus*). It has a marking on each wing that is analagous with the roundels on the wings of Peacock butterflies.

55 Lowestoft fishermen usually cooked hake by baking them, often in meat gravy with slices of onion.

awful scavenger, which used to attack ling an' whitin' occasionally. It used to attack the fish after the fish had took the hook. And I can only call it a *sea lice*; I dun't know what the real name would be. An' these sea lice (it's hardy credible), they used to get into the fish and they'd eat the fish alive, inside. So, when the fish used to come up on the hook, there'd be his head, the backbone and the skin—and nothin' else! Yes, yes. They were just like—how can I describe it? You know them little woodworms what roll up into a ball? Yeah, they'd be like them, only about twice as long an' white, like a shrimp.[56] Yes, if you got in amongst them, you'd hev quite a few fish what'd bin eaten. And the funny part about it is that it wuz invariably long fish that they attacked, like ling and whitin'. I can't really tell yuh where we struck most of 'em, but there wuz particular places for 'em and that wuz in the Irish Sea.

"I remember an occasion when we weren't findin' too many fish in the Lundy [Island] area. We were playin' about, tryin' to find a bit o' fish, and the ol' man say, 'Well, I dun't know where the blazes to go!' And one o' the crew, a man by the name o' Billy Evans (longliner-men would remember him well), had bin round there at one time with a Milford man who wuz a *don skipper*—in a boat called the *Surmount* (M 231). And, o' course, he knew a lot o' nooks an' crannies where fish would be at certain times. And he said to the ol' man, 'Well, why not have a go in Oxwich Bay.' That wuz inside the Helwick Light Vessel. Well, we went in there an' shot as close to the beach as we could git. An' Billy Evans said, 'If they're here, you'll hev sore hands afore the trip is up.' Well, they were there all right! Armour-plated rooker, and we dint go too much on them. Yeah, and I spose we got about sixty kit o' them in a couple o' days. But they were wicked! And no matter how you tried to gut them without gittin' pricked by them thorns, you'd git pricked.

"It wuz funny how things used to work out. I remember us haulin' one day and gettin' a lot o' fish. Yeah, we were gettin' a fish on nearly every hook and the ol' man said, 'All right. Plonk a dan down." See, you did that to mark the place. Well, we dropped a dan, but after we'd hauled about two baskets [of lines] the fish disappeared. He couldn't understand this at first. Then, I suppose, as we were finishin' the haulin', he must have thought to himself, 'Them fish lay in a *gulley*.' So what he done then wuz say to the mate, 'How many dans ha' we got aboard? How many anchors, dan-tows and that sort o' thing?' And, o' course, the mate wondered what he wuz thinkin' about, so he say, 'I intend to shoot four sets o' lines, if we've got enough, over the gulley.' And that's what we done. So, instead o' shootin' one fleet o' lines, we shot four short fleets, and that meant a devil of a lot o' work gittin' dans ready, dan-tows, buffs and all that sort o' thing. And by the time we'd got them four short *fleets* over (there wuz about three or four baskets in each fleet), we hent got nothin' left. But that paid orf, yuh see. We got the fish.

---

56 This creature was obviously the same *isopod* as that described by George Kent on p. 64.

Yeah, we got a trip o' fish out o' that alone.[57] And, o' course that is the thing—to git the trip as quick as you can and get inta harbour.

"If you had to stay out, that's where the *ice* come in. And I can remember one unfortunate trip about ice. We went away wi' four o' the *wings* full up wi' ice, and we had a lot o' hot weather, and we didn't catch no fish durin' the early part o' the trip. And, o' course, the ice wuz slowly meltin', and then we struck fish. Well, by that time, a third o' the ice had melted. And the *mate* kept worryin' about the *ice* and the *ol' man* kept worryin' about gittin' a *trip o' fish*. And the mate kept sayin, 'Thass no good, Tom. We'll hefta git away to market, do we're goin' to finish up with a bad trip.' And the ol' man say, 'We must git one or two more. Let me worry about that.' And, o' course, the mate say, 'Well, thass all right for you to say that, but I'm the one who's gotta worry about it.'[58] Howsomever, the ol' man hung on until he'd got a satisfactory trip aboard. An' most o' the fish were rays. Rays and skate. And, o' course, the rays used to be landed as they are, with the gut out. But the skate, we used to take the wings orf them and chuck the middles over the side. Anyway, we come inta Milford harbour, and we rigged up tarpaulins over the hold 'cause that wuz a hot day. Yeah, and we hed hoses runnin', tryin' to keep the decks cool. We landed the fish the next day and they looked all right as they were goin' out. We couldn't see nothin' wrong with 'em. But within two hours o' them bein' on the quay, they all turned yeller! Yeah. And, instead o' makin' 150, 160 quid, we made less than thirty! And, o' course, in them days 150, 160 quid wuz a very good trip."

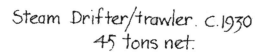

Steam Drifter/trawler. c. 1930
45 tons net.

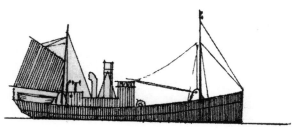

---

57 It is a well-known fact, among fishermen, that many species congregate in gulley-ways on the seabed.

58 The mate was the crew member responsible for the storage and good condition of the catch.

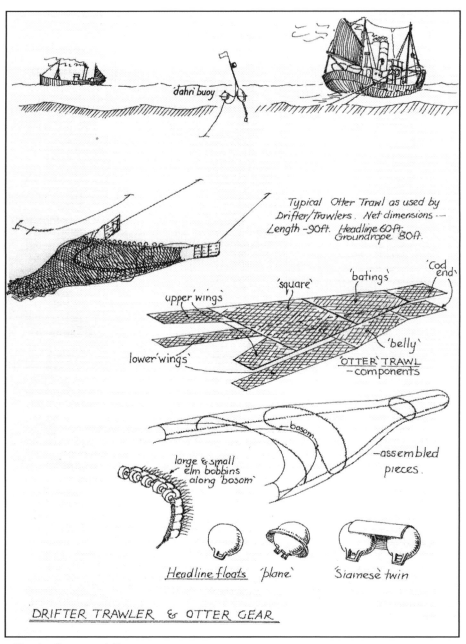

The following text labels appear within the illustration:

'dahn' buoy

Typical Otter Trawl as used by
Drifter/Trawlers. Net dimensions –
Length –90ft. Headline 60ft.
Groundrope 80ft.

upper 'wings'

'square'   'batings'   'Cod
                                  end'

lower 'wings'

'belly'

OTTER TRAWL
– components

bosom

–assembled
pieces.

large & small
elm bobbins
along 'bosom'

Headline floats   'plane'   'Siamese' twin

DRIFTER TRAWLER & OTTER GEAR

Fig. 4: Otter-trawl Gear

Line-drawings of a typical otter-trawl's structure and working practice. Both steam trawlers and drifter-trawlers used this type of gear and "Oscar" Pipe had developed his own version of it, as described in this chapter.

CHAPTER FOUR

Inside the Line

We'd been a week at sea, when we hit a Christmas tree,
And the wind blew off the skipper's wooden leg.
Lower the funnel, stop the ship, heave the anchor chain.
Throw the cargo overboard and haul it back again.
(Fisherman's nonsense rhyme)

The trawling activities of Lowestoft vessels and the men that crewed them were covered in detail in *The Trawlermen*. Among the many aspects of the work examined was the fishing which took place in the Atlantic Ocean, the St. George's Channel and the Irish Sea, together with the pattern of migratory labour that resulted from such voyages. In the case of some fishermen, seasonal migration became permanent settlement, especially in the Lancashire port of Fleetwood, where a body of expatriate Lowestoftians became a notable feature of the fishing community. Harry Colby (1902-95), whose distant-water experiences were recorded in the earlier book,[1] was one of the earliest East Anglian fishermen to make the move to Fleetwood, before eventually returning to his native Pakefield in 1955. However, his going there in the first place was not the result of summer fishing activity in Morecambe Bay; he left Lowestoft during the autumn herring season of 1924 in unusual circumstances. He was *stoker* on a steam drifter called the *Berry Head* (LT 966) and was assisting with the unloading of 200 *crans* of herring on the Lowestoft market, when the vessel's owner appeared, ordered the crew to return to sea and told them to *dump* the remaining fifty crans on their way out to the fishing grounds.[2] Harry Colby refused to be part of this, walked off the boat and went straight to The Royal National Mission to Deep Sea Fishermen's office, which was situated nearby.[3] There he saw an advertisement, which stated that three deckhands were needed for craft in Fleetwood, and within a few hours he was on a train and heading out of Lowestoft.

On his arrival in Fleetwood, he soon found a berth on one of the local mid-water vessels, but had to learn all the basic techniques required because he had had no previous contact with trawling. Ten years later, he was a very experienced fishermen and it was at this stage of his career that he became a crew member of a steam trawler called the *Blanche* (H 928), a vessel that had been built at

---

1 D. Butcher, *The Trawlermen* (Reading, 1980), Chapter Nine.

2 Dumping fish happened periodically during the 1920s and 30s and was usually the result of a surplus of herrings on the market, which caused the selling-price to fall.

3 It stood in Suffolk Road and later became the town's library. The building is still in existence and once formed part of R.J. Pryce's and (later) L.R. Godfrey's store and café.

the height of the trawling boom in 1907 and had once been part of the fleet belonging to Hellyer's Steam Fishing Co. Ltd. (many of them named after leading Shakespearean characters, male and female). The skipper of this boat was a Lowestoft man called William Pipe, universally known as "Oscar", and the rest of the crew (with one exception) consisted of Lowestoft men also—though the craft was operating permanently from Fleetwood at the time. Oscar Pipe had been a byword for singular behaviour in his home-port for many years and his move to Fleetwood, at some point during the early 1930s, saw him become something of a legend on the other side of the country.

Harry Colby served with Oscar Pipe for three years and what follows is an unbroken account of his experiences on the *Blanche* (tape-recording made, 14 May 1980). As will be seen, fishing may have been the boat's official function, but much else was going on as well. Indeed, a good deal of the material in this chapter would seem to be the stuff of fiction rather than that of the working world. Yet it all happened. The observations made give a wonderful picture of a very unorthodox skipper, who was a master of his craft (in all senses of the word) and who found the time and opportunity to engage in different kinds of commercial activity—not all of it strictly legal. The picture that emerges is of a man whose life needed a degree of risk to make it interesting and worthwhile and who enjoyed

Plate 6:   *Rosalind (LT 977)*

The steam trawler "Rosalind" (LT 977), sister-ship to the "Blanche" (H 928). Both craft had originally belonged to Hellyer's Steam Fishing Company Ltd., being built at Beverley in 1905 and 1907 respectively. A small "handkerchief" mizzen sail is a prominent feature of the vessel's rig: as is the ladder used for work on the funnel.

flouting authority—especially that which sought to impose coastal limits, within which it was illegal to fish. But the sense is also derived of someone who cared for the men who sailed with him and did his best to put money in their pockets, at a time when fishermen's earnings did not always reflect the amount of toil that the job entailed and were certainly not commensurate with the risks.

"I joined Oscar in 1935 and wuz with him up till the beginnin' o' 1938, when the boat wuz sold. The *Blanche*, yeah. And when I wuz in her, I looked in the almanac and found she wuz built in 1907.[4] She wuz registered in Hull, but the real owner wuz Countess Howe, of London. She wuz an old aft-side job, an old *fleeter*, and there were nine in the crew. Oscar Pipe wuz *skipper*, Tranny Swan wuz *mate* and I wuz *third hand*. Coolo wuz *chief* [engineer]—a bloke called Coleman, he got lost in the *Westholme* (LT 216) arter he'd come out o' us—and Tarzan wuz *second*. He wuz a Milford bloke, and I couldn't tell yuh his other name, but we allus used to call him Tarzan. Chuddy Hutson wuz *deckie*, and Ronnie Mullender wuz deckie, and Siddy Drake wuz *fireman*,[5] and Dick Cornish wuz *cook*. Now, he wuz my uncle, an' things were a bit sticky in Fleetwood then, and that wuz through bein' friendly with him that I joined the crew. He wuz a first-class cook, my uncle. Yeah, he used to work in a bake-office [bakery], and old Oscar liked his grub, so there wuz plenty o' good grub on the *Blanche*.

"She wun't too bad to live on, either. The skipper, the mate, the chief engineer and the second [engineer], they all slept down the *cabin*. The rest slept for'ad. She wuz all open for'ad—what they called an open-bowed ship—and yuh quarters were down below the deck.[6] Yeah, thass where you used to sleep, down there. She used to ship a lot o' water and she used to stink like hell too. Bloody ol' tarred nets! See, you were right alongside the room where you used to keep keep yuh *trawls* and tarred *bellies* and that. You used to go through a little door and they were all there—all yuh spare gear. You used to have yuh meals down aft. That used to be rough, livin' up front, when you were steamin' hid to wind, but you got used to it. Yeah, you used to shut the door up—the bottom door—and leave the other half open. You hed these half-doors, see. There wun't no toilet neither. You used a tub or went over the side o' the boat.

"O' course, all them ol' ships rolled. That woulda bin a sorry thing for yuh if they

---

4 The almanac referred to was *Olsen's Fisherman's Nautical Almanack*, an annual publication containing navigational data and other information relating to the British fishing industry.

5 In East Anglian parlance, *fireman* was a Great Yarmouth term for the second engineer on a steam drifter. In this case, it meant a dual-purpose crew member who had duties in both the engine-room and on deck.

6 In other words, the *Blanche* did not have a protective whale-deck, to provide cover for gutting and other tasks, as many of the later trawlers did.

dint roll![7] But she wun't too bad—though she did used to tairke plenty o' water, because she wuz so deep [close to the water] in the middle. You used to git some rum weather goin' acrorss that Morecambe Bay. Yes, that yuh did. But the ol' *Blanche* stood it all right. Well, we used to look after her. We never used to drive her too hard. You start drivin' 'em and you'll git inta trouble. She wuz a smart ol' ship. Yis, her wheelhouse wuz all boards [tongue-and-groove or lapped] an' they were spotless. That they were! Deck and all, just the same—'specially when you wuz comin' inta harbour. Yes, yes. I wish I hed a photo o' her with all them pigs' tails round the top o' the *wheelhouse*. Oscar allus used to git a bit o' pork with the tail on, cut the tail orf, varnish it an' then nail it round the wheelhouse. That wuz to show he wun't superstitious.[8] And round the bottom part o' the winders [windows] wuz pigs' feet, all varnished, and on top o' the wheelhouse, at the front, wuz a pig's hid! Oh, Oscar wun't superstitious. Nothin' worried him!

"He'd bin round on that west side a fair time, but I think he'd also bin out o'Yarmouth on the *Ralph Hall Caine* (YH 447) at one time. He hed the *Veracity* (LT 685) from new as well—the first *Veracity*.[9] I'm talkin' about the steam one, though I don't think he wuz ever much of a herrin' man. And o' course, he lived in Pakefield at one time, but I dint know him then. I knew about him, 'cause I lived there, and I knew his daughter, but that wuz all. When he wuz in the *Ralph Hall Caine*, there wun't many boats hed wireless in them days and they said he come inta Low'stoft one day wi' wireless aerials up. You know what they used to hev in the 1914 war—that bar with four wires comin' out of it. Well, he rigged one o' them up with old tarred twine, so people thought he'd fitted up a wireless![10] Yeah. Yeah, he wuz up to all them tricks.

"Cor, an' the number o' mates we had! Tranny Swan wuz about the only one who got on with him. Yeah, his word wuz law. If he said you were goin' to sea, you had to be there. He'd be there hisself and you'd gotta be there. But I'll tell yuh one thing about him. We wuz never out a penny. We allus had a shillin' [1s = 5p] in our pocket, and things were bad when I wuz in the *Blanche*—really bad. Yeah, we allus had money and that wuz more'n a lot of 'em did at Fleetwood—poor buggers! Thass when the hard times were. Yeah, there wuz allus plenty o' *stockie*

---

7 The implication of this remark is that, if the vessel hadn't rolled with the swell of the sea, it might have foundered in bad weather. This particular class of trawler was very low in the water amidships—a deliberate feature of the design, which was calculated to allow a heavy swell to wash across the vessel without putting it in jeopardy.

8 Many British fishermen were extremely superstitious where pigs were concerned, often to the point where the word "pig" itself was taboo on board ship. Some people attribute this to unease generated by the New Testament story of the Gadarene swine (Mark 5. 11-17 and Luke 8. 32-36), but there may also have been a more ancient connection with the Celtic goddess Ceridwen, one of whose many manifestations was that of a large black sow.

9 The second vessel to have this name was a diesel craft built in 1926, which features in Chapter 11.

10 This simulated four-strand aerial ran from the top of the wheelhouse to the foremast.

bait when you were along o' Oscar and he dint work yuh very hard either.

"There wuz one chap there, who wuz in the *Ethel Taylor* (FD 363)—. Now, I dun't know what really happened aboard her, but I think the crew had bin worked a long while and they were shiftin' grounds. And I spose, with one thing an' another, this chap fell asleep on the *bridge*. And, o' course, the *Winooka* (GY 465), a boat from Grimsby wuz laid there and she got hit and sunk. This wuz somewhere at *Kildas* [St. Kilda]. Yeah, an' two or three of 'em were lorst.[11] And, o' course, when they come in, this chap couldn't git a ship. He couldn't git a ship anywhere and he started to sell his hoom. And Oscar say, 'We'll want a deckie when we git in, wun't we?' He say, 'What about that boy who can't git a ship? You go and tell him that I want him.' So I went and fetched him down aboard the ship an' Oscar say, 'There you are. I'll put yuh on yuh feet, boy!' He did do an' all. We took him with us. He'd bin walkin' about weeks an' weeks over that Kildas job. Oh yes, he helped him.

"I allus found him all right and all, though I know he wuz a rum bugger. Yeah, but he wuz a marvellous fisherman. He often used to sit in the *galley* when we wuz fishin'. Yeah, and he allus used to watch what wuz goin' on—but not to watch you. Just to see things. He used to say to me, 'I want you to do so and so.' Then praps he'd say, 'Do you know what?' So I'd say,'Whass up?' He'd say, 'You aren't goin' where I told yuh to, yuh know.' I'd say, 'Well, I'm goin' where—. ' Then he'd say, 'No you aren't! I know by that *towin'-block* that she ent where she should be.' And you bet your life he'd be right![12] And another thing about him wuz that he never took chances. No, no, there wuz never a lot o' bad weather fishin' with Oscar.

"That wuz always *on-the-door gear* with him. He never used *bridles*. And we were *chain* right through. He used to make his own gear. Right? We never had no *foot-ropes* or anything. There used to be a chain go right the way through from door to door, with *dangles* on it, and with a *combination fishin' line* (made o' wire an' rope) fixed to that. Yeah, he made that idea hisself and that gear used to fish well. Coo to hell, yis! That wuz about sixty foot long on the *hidline* [headline] and about 100, 110, along the bottom. And there wun't many *floats* on the hidline either. You only used to hev one or two. Yis, he made that idea hisself and that wuz so he could tow through what they called *bladed weed*. That hed long stalks, and we used to hetta tow through all o' that when we were workin' close in.[13]

---

11 The Fleetwood Steam and Sailing Trawler Website (*The Bosun's Watch*) records the vessel as being lost on 15 March 1936, off St. Kilda, with three fatalities—all of them Fleetwood men.

12 Oscar Pipe was able to tell by the set of the towing-block and the tension of the warps whether the boat was fishing in the exact place he had wanted it to, or not.

13 The gear described in this paragraph was a variation of the basic otter trawl, designed to be effective in relatively shallow water, which had Oarweed (*Laminaria digitata*) and Sugar Kelp (*Laminaria saccharina*) growing on the bottom.

"We carried a trawl both sides, but we hardly ever worked the *port gear*. That wuz always *starboard gear* with Oscar. Yeah. And, the latter part o' the time, what we did wuz pull like these here stern trawlers do. We hed an *eye* spliced inta the *after-warp* and then, when we used to shoot the trawl and *block up* the warps, this eye would be out aft o' the *towin' block* . Well, we used to put the *messenger's hook* inta that. Now, that messenger would already ha' bin made fast round the after-deck bollard, on the port side, and bin passed under the stern to the starboard side. Then, as soon as yuh gear came tight onta that messenger, that wuz pulled round squareways. See what I mean? Yuh gear wuz more open, so you were gittin' more fish.[14] Cor, we used to work some tight *nips* sometimes! And he never used to block up for that. Right? The warps used to be left in the messenger, and you'd heave up on that till it wuz good and tight. Then he used to say, 'Right. We're now comin' round. Let go!' And we used to let go o' the messenger an' the warps used to spread orf the side o' the boat, and that used to pull yuh round quicker when you were workin' a tight nip near any rocks. And that wuz all measured orf and marked out on the warp and the messenger how far you had to let it run. Oh yeah, he wuz a clever bloke.

"That all depended on the fishin' how long yuh *towed*. Three hours, four hours. Yeah. And we used to be out about seven or eight days when we were out o' Fleetwood and worked Ireland. Praps nine or ten. He used to go after mixed fish, Oscar did. We used to git soles, cod, plaice, bass—all sorts. But he never really bothered with hake—though you mighta got the odd one now and agin. Oh, he knew what he wuz a doin' on! He hed a book with everything writ down, all the fishin' grounds and that, and I say to him one day, 'I'd like to hev that, if anything happen to you.' He say, 'Dibro,'—'cause thass what I wuz called round there— 'when I go, that go with me! Yeah,' he say, 'I'll tell yuh one thing, ol' boy. There's no one that'll use my bloody brains!'[15]

"Alec Keay used to sell for us in Fleetwood and we used to sort all the fish out on board, o' course. *Prime* wuz allus kept separate (you know, soles an' that); so wuz cod an' plaice. Yeah, an' you allus used to git a good *fry* when you come in along o' William! We used *crushed ice* on board and you used to hetta chop it up yuh bloody self when that got down the fish-room! See, when I wuz workin the White Sea [after the Second World War], when I used to go up there, that'd be *flake-ice*. Yeah, and when you went aboard, you could just go down the fish-room

---

14 Again, this method of working the gear was something devised by this particular skipper— so, instead of the trawl being towed off the starboard quarter, it was pulled along square to the stern of the vessel in a similar fashion to the gear worked by modern stern-trawlers.

15 Many skippers kept a record of catches made, the grounds fished, prevailing weather conditions and particular times of year for different species. They were usually referred to as *skippers' logs*.

an' shovel it up as you wanted. You dint hefta put a chopper into it![16]

"That wuz allus Ireland and Padstow what we fished. Ireland and Padstow, yeah. We did land in at Milford once, but there wuz a fishermen's strike on and we come out and brooke the rules. Yeah, we come out, back to sea, and wun't allowed to go there no more. They were strikin' over more money or somethin'. This'd be about 1935, '36. Padstow, though—William allus used to be there for the *hobby horse*.[17] Oh, that wuz a smashin' time! Yeah, we used to go round there as soon as that wuz time—Trevose [Trevose Head] an' Godrevy [Godrevy Point] and them plairces. And if the tides were right, we used to be in and out every day. We never even bothered to take ice on. Yeah, I've worked Pendeen [Pendeen Light] with him, and Godrevy with him, and Trevose with him, and never put a *needle* in a net! And other blokes ha' bin there and got *paralysed*—lorst gear and all sorts.[18] Yeah, thass a deadly ground, that is—Trevose. Yeah, there's rocks there. Hell, yeah! But we never got split, and we never had no *hides* on the cod end—just ol' bits o' net. *Bellies*, yeah. And a few *bobbins* on the *bosom*. Thass how he used to work it.

"I know one partic'lar day he say to me (o'course, we wuz just laid there; we allus shot in the dark), 'Who the hell is that come there, Dibro?' I say, 'That look like Johnsey's lot to me.' Johnsey. Johnsey Gamble, in the *Encore* (LT 929). Yeah, and he come alongside an' say, 'What're yuh gittin', William?' So he say, 'Oh, we're gittin' a good livin' here in the dark. You know, plaice an' soles an' turbot an' that.' So Johnsey say, 'All right. We'll hev a go with yuh tonight.' William say, 'Thass fair enough.' And when that come dark, o' course, we shot. But, before we did, he say to me, 'All right. Shorten them warps up.' See, we shortened the warps and heaved the gear up so that wuz just travellin' the bottom. O' course, when Johnsey come along the next mornin' at daylight, he hent got a stitch left! Yeah. Oscar knew where to work, yuh see. Johnsey wuz follerin' us round the *dan*, but we wuz goin' the opposite way to what we generally used to do!

"One year there, in the summertime, we went to Newhaven for an experiment and we shot orf the Needles two or three times. You used to git what they call *nurses*. They call 'em *huskies* round there.[19] Gret big things! Cor, they're huge what yuh git round there. Yeah, and when we landed at Newhaven, he say, 'Right. There's three kit o' them to go to Peacehaven. They were sold on the market, but the money went to Peacehaven to some orphanage place for musicians' children

---

16 Crushed ice was coarse in nature and the pieces would soon coalesce and stick together. Flaked ice was much finer in texture (being produced differently) and did not degenerate in the same way.

17 This is a reference to the famous Padstow May Day celebrations.

18 The Padstow fishing grounds were notoriously rough, owing to outcrops of slate on the seabed. This particular voyage (largely for soles) was well established among Lowestoft vessels. See Butcher, *Trawlermen*, Chapter Six.

19 The fish descibed here is the Great-spotted Dogfish or Nurse Hound (*Sycliorhinus stellaris*), which can attain lengths of up to a metre or more.

and that. Gracie Fields hed somethin' to do with it. Oh, William hed his good points. Like when one o' the Boston boats got lorst out o' Fleetwood.[20] We hed about ten or fifteen *kit* o' crabs this partic'lar trip. See? An' my uncle Dick used to hefta boil 'em. So William say, 'I tell yuh what we'll do. You can all hev one or two each to tairke hoom and we'll give the rest to the fund.' Well, that wuz fair enough. So, anyway, after we landed, he come down the cabin with the *stockie bait* (ol' Duke wuz mate then). And he say, 'All right. Here's yuh stockie bait together.' Then he say to Duke, 'You can't hev as much as the rest of 'em. That wun't be right.' So Duke say, 'What've I done wrong now?' William say, 'I see yuh, yuh know. I see yuh give some chap three or four crabs. I mean, that ent right! They were for that purpose, what I said [the disaster relief fund].' Yeah, an' he cut him orf his money. That he did.

"He wuz a marvellous man when that come to fishin', though. Yeah, we used to work the Kish [Kish Bank] and the Codlin' [Codling Bank] sometimes, but mainly we'd be further down, near the *Coningbeg* [*Coningbeg Lightship*] an' the Tuskar [Tuskar Rock] and all them grounds.[21] And when we worked the Barrels, just inside the *Barrels Lightship*, he used to hev a *dan* at one end with a red light on—which wuz for the rocks, the Barrels Rocks. And then, at the top end o' the Saltees [Saltees Islands], he used to hev a dan with a green light on. Yeah, and he wuz the only bloke who could work it. And I don't think I ever shot outside the limits with him, except when we wuz at Padstow. Yeah, that wuz allus *inside*—as soon as that come in dark. We used to go right inta Wexford nearly, and there wuz a huge buoy there, an' that used to mairke this hummin' noise in the still o' the night. If the weather got bad, we used to lay in. We laid in Dunmore that night when the *Shorebreeze* (LT 1149) wuz lorst at Milford.[22] Yeah, you could allus run in somewhere when that blew hard. Sometimes we used to run inta Rosslare, close in, and then drop the *hook*. They dint mind, as long as you wun't fishin'.

"Yeah, that wuz allus the Irish side with him and we usually used to lay all day. We used to git the gear riddy for when that come in dusk. We used to overhaul the trawl and one thing and another. And he used to watch the *Lucifer Lightship*, see [off Wexford Harbour]. He used to look after them chaps aboard the *Lucifer* like he looked after his own son. He used to give them everything they wanted, because he used to git all the information from them about when the *gunboat* used to leave Dun Laoghaire. See, that used to come that way, round the Tuskar. And I used to say to the ol' man, 'They're now pulled the the mizzen up. She's left.' An' when that gunboat went past, that'd look at us—but, o' course , we wun't fishin'.[23]

---

20 This is a reference to a vessel belonging to the Boston Deep Sea Fishing & Ice Co. Ltd.

21 In other words, Oscar Pipe usually worked grounds in the Wexford/Waterford area rather than in the Wicklow/Dublin vicinity.

22 This occurred on 5 January 1936. There were no survivors.

23 The gunboat referred to was an Irish fisheries patrol craft, whose task it was to enforce the three-mile limit within which it was illegal for foreign vessels to fish.

Oh yeah, the boys on the lightship used to hoist the mizzen to let us know.

"Mind yuh, he hed one or two bits o' luck while I wuz with him. We shot one night in Wexford, right over Wexford Bar, and he left it too late. And when the water [tide] fell, we were high and dry with our gear out! Yeah, we wuz on the bottom. And, do yuh know, that come in thick o' fog! Yeah, and we laid there till the water flowed agin and lifted us orf. Next trip he run her ashore on the Saltees! Same thing happened there. That come in thick, so no one dint know we were there, and we got her orf with a *kedge anchor*.[24] O' course, when she went on the slip at Fleetwood for a clean bottom, they found out what had happened. When they come an' surveyed her, one o' the blokes say to me, 'Whass this under your bottom?' See, that wuz where she'd bin ridin' the rocks. 'How long ha' you bin here?' So I say, 'Only about two or three trips. I dun't know nothin' about that.'

"The *harbour master* at Fleetwood say to us one day, 'I can never tell your ship.' Our ol' man say, 'Why?' He say, 'Because you've allus got a different funnel when yuh come in!' See, while we were out, we used to paint the funnel a different colour when we'd bin inside the limits, poachin'. Yeah, we allus used to paint the funnel different. He fired at us one day, the *bogeyman* did, just as we were a-haulin'. Yeah, and he shoved a bullet through the compass and one through the engine-room door! Coo to hell! That wuz a little ol' lifeboat thing and that hed a machine-gun aboard. How the hell we got away that day, I'll never know.

"Another thing Oscar used to do wuz bring vegetables acrorss from Ireland and sell 'em in Fleetwood to Pilkington the grocer. He'd buy 'em orf the Irish, see, and charge double the price when he got 'em over here. We used to hev all sorts aboard her—nanny goats, bloody chickens! Yeah, he wuz fetchin' 'em acrorss for somebody. One o' the goats died there once an' he dumped it orf the Stacks, on the Welsh side.[25] We used to tairke all sorts acrorss to Ireland as well—bloody canaries, french letters, guns and ammunition. Everything that wuz sellable! He used to run the guns to Rosslare. They used to come arter 'em in a boat, the Irishmen did. Yis, they used to think the world o' him in Ireland! Uncle Oscar, they used to call him. The little ol' kids thought the world of him as well. Coo to hell, yis! One time we were there, just afore Christmas, and I'll tell yuh what he did. We *hauled* Saturday tea-time and he say, 'Right! Thass yuh lot. You wun't *shoot* no more till after Sunday midnight.' Yeah, an' we steamed inside the *Lucifer*, orf Rosslare, and anchored. Out come all the people in motor boats, and little ol' kids, and the ol' parson [priest]—and we hed a service aboard the boat!

"Yeah, an' another Christmas he say to me—. See, they allus used to go hoom for Christmas [to Pakefield]. But I dint go, because I lived at Fleetwood, and I

---

24 A kedge anchor was dropped and the boat was pulled off against its resistance, using the engine.

25 The North Stack and the South Stack were two small promontories on the western extremity of Anglesey, near Holyhead.

allus used to look after the boat.[26] He used to hev a couple o' them covered-in railway trucks full o' stuff and he say to me, 'What do yuh want for a Christmas box?' I say, 'I'm all right.' He say, 'Now, look here. I'm goin' to tell a bloke to put a ton and a half o' coal in yer house.' So I got a ton and a half o' coal Christmas box! That wuz the Christmas he say to me, 'We're goin' to crawl in here tonight, close in. There's a motor boat comin' out and I want you and Ronnie [Mullender] to go ashore.' He say, 'I want you to go to Rosslare Station, where the mail boat is, and you'll see two blokes there. They'll know who you are.' So away we went. When we got there, one o' the blokes say, 'All right, let's git this load onta the lorry.' So I say, 'What the hell's there?' He say, 'There's parsnips and so forth. And in these boxes there's about a dozen turkeys.' See? So we got these aboard and then William say, 'I'll go an' see the ol' lightship.' O' course, she ent there now, the *Lucifer* ent. But thass where we used to git all the news from. If we used to see her with her mizzen up, we knew the gunboat hed left Rosslare or Dun Laoghaire, or wherever he wuz comin' from. Yeah, so we give the blokes on the lightship a turkey and then away we come hoom.

"Now, afore we got in, he say, 'I tell yuh what we'll do. We'll put all the stuff in that spare *pound* an' fill it up with ice. So thass what we done. And after we'd landed, there wuz an old Irish bloke who worked down there as a *watchman* an' he say to me, 'Do yuh know what? The customs had bin aboard here.' I say, 'Hev they?' He say, 'Yis. And they're bin swearin' about you. One of 'em went down the *fish-room* and nearly went up to his neck in water!' See, William hed half filled the hold up wi' water, so no one couldn't git down there. Anyhow, we pumped her out and then William say to me, 'How're we goin' to git these ashore?' I say, 'I dun't know.' So then he say, 'Will yuh be available early tomorrer mornin', about half-past two, you and Ronnie? I say. 'Yeah.' He say, 'All right. I think I've got it weighed up. I've got some old net here.' And thass what we done. We got 'em orf on a wheelbarrer, hid under this net!

"People used to hefta watch him when we wuz laid in. Yeah. What he used to do wuz cut the floats orf the hidlines if he found a trawl layin' around. And if there wuz any dan-gear layin' on the quay, he used to hev this little anchor on a long bit o' wire, an' he used to hook that onta the dan-gear, git inta the wheelhouse an' drag that along the quay to the boat! And he'd pinched the wire he wuz usin' an' all![27] Blast, yis! Oh, he wuz a rum bugger. Yit if we wuz in at the weekend, he'd allus go to church with his missus and daughter. Yeah, you'd see him, bowler hat on, and a walkin' stick or umbrella, an' one o' them *jillanut coats* as I call 'em. You know, with a split [vent] at the back. Yeah, there he'd be, with all o' that and

---

26 The crew of the *Blanche* (including the skipper) returned to Lowestoft for the festive season.

27 George Stock, another Lowestoft expatriate, who fished successfully out of Fleetwood for over thirty years, was skipper of a vessel called the *Amalia* (LT 241) during the 1930s. He often laughed about Oscar Pipe's social visits to his boat and what had gone missing afterwards.

a little ol' Pekinese dorg. Cor, you'd think butter wun't melt in his mouth!

"Now, you wanted to know about that time we got caught by the gunboat. Well, I'll tell yuh. He say to me, when we wuz gittin' riddy to come hoom, 'We're goin' inside the Barrels on the way back.' I say, 'All right. What for?' He say, 'I've got some spuds to pick up for ol' Pilkington the grocer, in Kemp Street.' Well, we kept layin' there and layin' there and, o' course, they never come orf [rowed out to the *Blanche*]. So he say, 'We mustn't lay here no longer, do we'll be on the bottom.' Then he say to me, 'All right. I'll go and hev my breakfast. You know which way to go. Take her right through Carnsore Point.' Thass inside the Tuskar.[28] So I say to him, 'What about these doors?' See, we hed our starboard doors out, 'cause we hed bin poachin' durin' the night.[29] Definitely. So he say, 'Well, git 'em in.' O' course, as soon as we started the winch to git 'em in, steam started to come out o' the little pipe at the top o' the funnel. Then I see the gunboat there. Well, as soon as he see that steam—blast, he come after us! I went down an' told Oscar. He say, 'All right. Keep you her a-goin'! I'll tell yuh when to stop. You don't want to worry about bloody gunboats.' So I kept a-goin', yuh see, and he opened up on us! Fired at us. I thought, 'This is plenty far enough.' So I stopped her. O' course, Oscar come up and played hell wi' me!

"Anyhow, away come the gunboat and two blokes with revolvers jumped aboard—you know, like cowboys. And one two-ringed bloke went to the bridge an' say to the ol' man, 'You've bin illegal fishin'.' So the ol' man say, 'We hent bin.' The bloke say, 'Well, I've now bin down yer hold and all the fish were alive.' Which they were, 'cause we hed bin poachin'.[30] So one thing led to another and Oscar say to me, 'Dibro.' I say, 'Whass up?' He say, 'Who's that bloke there?' I say, 'What bloke?' He say, 'That bloke there wi' two rings and a purple ring up.' I say, 'Hell if I know!' So, anyway, I say to one o' the Irish sailors on the gunboat, 'Who's that bloke there?' He say, 'Thass the chief engineer o' the gunboat.' So I say, 'What do he want aboard here?' He say, 'Well, he's now goin' to take you to Waterford. You've bin had up for illegal fishin'.' So I went and told ol' Oscar. Coo to hell, you oughta heard him! Anyway, the commander o' the gunboat wuz leaned on our winch and Oscar say, 'Do yuh hear, sir?' So the commander say, 'What can I do for you, skipper?' Oscar say, 'Well, I'm goin' to tell you one thing. Do you see that man stand there? Thass my chief engineer. He's bin along o' me for seven year, and if he can't tairke her inta Waterford without any o' yer bloody crew aboard! Do yuh see that rock there? Thass where she'll go!' And he meant

28 All three locations referred to here were close to Rosslare.

29 The otter doors of the trawl were not properly secured in the galluses.

30 The live fish in the hold's pounds were the ones caught during the night, which had been put down below, to be gutted later. The usual procedure on the *Blanche* was to trawl in the dark, leave the fish on deck, get back outside the limit-line at daybreak and start gutting. On this occasion, the fish had been put down below because of the consignment of potatoes which was to be taken on board.

it, too. He'd ha' run her on![31]

"Anyway, away we go to Waterford, behind the gunboat. And as soon as we got alongside the quay, all the people turned out. The gunboat boys thought that wuz marv'llous, 'cause they'd bin after him for years. He wuz one o' the biggest poachers there wuz and they could never catch him, till this partic'lar day. So we laid alongside the gunboat, and away go me and Tranny [Swan] and the ol' man, and they locked us up. In jail. In Waterford. So I say to Tranny, 'Blast, I tell yuh one thing, Tranny. Our ol' man wun't last the night out if he stop here!' See, that wuz like a concrete plairce. So Tranny say to the bloke [warden] what wuz in the prison, 'What about lettin' our ol' man go aboard? Me and Dibro will stop.' And this bloke went and see the officer in charge and he say, 'All right. You might as well all go.' So they took us aboard under armed guard and they hed an armed guard aboard all night.

"Next day, we hetta go and see the *sheriff*. He says, 'You're so-and-so skipper and you've bin illegal fishin'. We'll tairke some o' yuh fish and yuh gear.[32] But,' he says, 'Somethin' I can't understand about you. Why is the reason that your starboard gear wuz wet and your port gear wuz dry?' O' course, we hed two trawls, but we never used the port side. 'Well, sir,' Oscar say, 'thass easy answered. When you were a little ol' boy and hed the arse out o' yer trousers, yer mother put another pair on yuh. And thass how we do.' He say, 'If we git split, we change over.' And, o' course, we never did 'cause we never got split. So the sheriff say, 'All right. So-and-so and so-and-so.' Then Oscar say, 'I appeal!' I kidded him up to this, yuh see. 'I appeal!' he say. 'I appeal!' So, anyway, they let us orf, though we hetta appear agin at Waterford in six weeks.

"When we got aboard the boat, we were goin' away that night 'cause that wuz tea-time when we come out o' the court. So the gunboat captain, he say, 'I tell yuh what, skipper. We're goin' down to Dunmore. I tell yuh what we'll do. We'll escort yuh down there.' Oscar say, 'Look here, sir. Years ago, I couldn't write my own nairme. Now I've got a *skipper's ticket* and a *master's ticket*.' He say, 'I dun't want no one to show me out o' here. I can go out o' here by myself, blindfolded.' O' course, when we went out, he say, 'We'll be hoom in about forty-eight hours, I spect.'[33] Yeah, and we run straight down to Dunmore and shot that night. We put

---

31 The rock referred to was the South Rock, near the Tuskar.

32 Confiscation of catch and gear was standard punishment for illegal fishing, often followed by a heavy fine when the case came to court. The Fleetwood Steam and Sailing Trawler website records that on 30 September 1937, at a special court in Waterford, William Thomas Pipe was found guilty of fishing in territorial waters off the Saltees Islands and fined £50. Fish to the value of £160 was confiscated. This must have been the result of the preliminary hearing.

33 It would have taken less than half this time if the vessel had gone straight back to Fleetwood. Oscar Pipe was implying that some fishing was to be done, before returning to the home port.

100 kit o' plaice down below while the gunboat wuz still in Waterford! Thass how artful he wuz.

"He dint live far orf me, then, and Maudie, his daughter, come round to mine after we got in. She say, 'Do yuh know what, Harry?' I say, 'Whass that, Maudie?' She say, 'I want you to tairke my father's *skipper's ticket* and also the *ship's pairpers*. Will you look after 'em?' I say, 'O' course I'll look after 'em.' And thass what I done. Now, when the time come, away go me and Tranny and the ol' man. We left the *Blanche* in Fleetwood and went acrorss in the *Scotia*, one o' the crorss-channel boats from Holyhid to Dun Laoghaire. Yeah, and then we went the rest o' the way by train an' stopped at the *Grenville Hotel* in Waterford afore the case come orf. Then we went to this gret big court—a big, round circle, like a bull ring—and we set down at the bottom. There wuz Lord an' Countess Howe sittin' there (they were the boat's owners) and the ol' man, with his trilby on. Anyhow, the ol' man went up, then the mairte went up, and then I went up last. And the judge say to me, 'Can you place the models up where you were?' I say, 'Certainly I can.' And I placed the models up where we were, from the Tuskar and the gunboat.

"Then the ol' judge say—and I can picture him now, with his hair [wig] all hangin' down—'I don't see any point in proceedin' with this case.' So they say, 'What do yuh mean?' He say,' Well, who does the ship belong to? Where'd she come from?' And, o' course, the captain o' the gunboat, Captain Doone (I'd know him now if I saw him), he got his report out from when they first nipped us. He say, 'Well, this ship belong to Lord and Countess Howe, o' London.[34] 'Well,' say the judge, 'that ent no good to me. I want the proof. I want the ship's pairpers.' And, o' course, I hed 'em! Do yuh understand what I mean? And Oscar's skipper's ticket. If I'd ha' produced them, we'd ha' got jailed. But I never produced 'em. No one uttered a word and I dint neither! I kept them and we got away with it.

"Afterwards, we went back to the *Grenville Hotel*, where we'd bin stayin', and o' course we hed two or three drinks, you know. And as we set there hevin' these drinks, in come the chief o' police. You know, three pips up. And he say, 'Come on, skipper, and the two o' yer crew. Hop in the hurry-up wagon, 'cause if I leave you here you'll be dead in the mornin'. He say, 'I'm goin' to tairke you aboard the *Scotia*.' See, we went back on the sairme ship, the crorss-channel boat. He say, 'I'm goin' to put you aboard her and lock you up, the three of yuh, for your own sairfety. And I'll tell the captain when to let you out.' He say, 'When she git clear o' the Kish Lightship, he'll let yuh out.'[35] Cor, that wuz a rum carry-on, that wuz!

"The last trip we ever mairde in her [the *Blanche*], we lay waitin' to go to sea. O' course, I aren't goin' to swear. That wun't do for the mike [microphone], what he said! High water wuz at half-past four in the afternoon and we laid agin the

---

34 Francis Curzon, 5th Earl Howe, and his wife Mary. The earl was an ex-Royal Navy officer and a notable racing driver of the late 1920s and the 1930s.

35 In other words, when the vessel had left Dun Laoghaire and was safely out to sea.

lock-pits, waitin' to go out. William say to me, 'Is Chuddy [Hutson] aboard yit?' I say, 'No. He hent arrived yit.' And, o' course, time we wuz waitin', they shut the lock-gates up. Then along come Chuddy. Paralytic! So, anyhow, we lowered him aboard an' he went an' turned in. When we got out, he shoulda bin on my watch, but I took her on my own. That dint make no difference to me. So William say to me, 'We'll go up as far as the *Bar Lightship* [Mersey Bar], arter them small plaice.' I say, 'All right.' That wun't a very long steam—only orf Liverpool. So when we got up there, I called him out. I say, 'We're come far enough to shoot.' He say, 'Oh, I aren't goin' to shoot. Let her lay here till he roll out.' He say, 'And you tell him I want him when he do!'

"Well, o' course, Chuddy rolled out in the early hours o' the mornin' and we still laid there. Yeah, we'd got all the gear riddy to shoot, and I see Chuddy come along and I say, 'Chuddy, the ol' man wanta see you.' O' course, he went down the cabin and, cor, there wuz such a commotion! Effin' and blindin'! Coo, to hell! Anyhow, things went quiet. Up come Oscar. He say, 'We're just hed a little row over it.' He say, 'He don't see my point and I don't see his.' Then he say, 'All right. Pull her round. Ring her on full and tairke her back. Tairke her hoom. Thass the last. Thass the last for William!' And he never went no more! Yeah, he never went no more. He musta known she [the *Blanche*] wuz sold afore we went out. He musta done! See, 'cause when we got in, Jimmy Mair bought her.[36] Yeah, bought her for his boy—the one what got blew up the first year o' the war. The last plairce she come to wuz Low'stoft.[37] I wun't here then, but I understand the last man who had her out o' Low'stoft wuz Jack Reeder. Oscar went back to Low'stoft an' all. He died there. Yeah, and he went blind after they sold the *Blanche*. I think me and Chuddy Hutson are the only two left alive out o' her now."

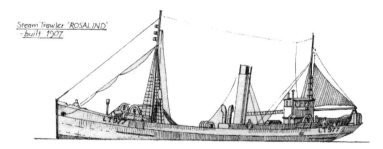

Steam Trawler 'ROSALIND' - built 1907

---

36 The vessel was sold in 1938 to J.W. Kates, c/o Mair & Co. of Fleetwood (managers of The Sun Steam Trawling Co. Ltd.). The Earl and Countess Howe had divorced in 1937 and this was what had probably triggered the sale.

37 The Fleetwood Steam and Sailing Trawler Website does not record this move. After the Second World War, the boat was sold to the Wendover Fishing Co. of Grimsby in December 1945 and re-registered as GY 133. It was broken up in 1952. As the fishing company named above was connected with Consolidated Fisheries Ltd., of Grimsby (which, in turn, ran a Lowestoft operation), it is possible that the vessel worked out of Lowestoft in the immediate post-war period.

CHAPTER FIVE

Along the Shore

Pray God lead us;
Pray God speed us.
From all evil defend us;
Fish for our pains send us.
Well to fish and well to haul,
And what he pleases to give us all.
A fine night to land our nets
And may we do well with what we gets.
Pray God keep us from sand and shoal
And grant that each may have fair dole.
Pray God hear our prayer.
(Traditional: *Mundesley Fishermen's Prayer*)

The town of Lowestoft and its neighbour, Great Yarmouth (together with Gorleston), were long-established centres of large-scale commercial fishing, which expanded particularly during the nineteenth century as the country's population grew and the national railway network developed. But the whole of the East Anglian coast had many other, smaller communities along its length which relied upon the sea's harvest to underpin their economies and provide a living for indigenous families. The types of fishing carried out were no different in basic working method from those practised by vessels from the two large ports, but everything was much smaller in scale and much more localised. Such activity was usually referred to as *longshore fishing*, the first element of the phrase being an abbreviation of "along the shore", which is itself an indication of the limited distance from land within which the boats operated. However, this way of working was as labour-intensive at every stage as its deep-sea counterpart and its employment capacity was considerable.

Nor was the operation confined solely to the smaller coastal communities (such as Southwold, where important recording-work carried out by Bob Jellicoe, contemporary with the writer's own, reveals similarity of practice). Both Lowestoft and Great Yarmouth had longshore fishermen engaged in this smaller-scale industry, working their craft either directly off the beach or from within the harbour. The catches tended largely to meet local needs and usually travelled no more than a few miles from where they were landed, but their quality was such that there was usually a demand for them—though this was not always reflected in the price paid to the fishermen. One of the most frustrating constraints imposed on longshore fishermen was the limited market available to them because of small-scale catches. And such buyers as there were to purchase these knew that they could often dictate the price paid. Even when an attempt was made to transport the fish, there was not necessarily public auction on a well patronised market— just an offer made, in the knowledge that there was no real competition for what was available. Whether on the fish market itself, or a local beach, a good price was usually dependent on there being a scarcity of a particular species at any one time—something which did not occur very often because of the sheer number of large vessels landing regularly around the clock.

Even so, a number of fishermen in Lowestoft managed to make a living from longshore activity—though it was sometimes combined with other work. George Stock (1903-85) was brought up in such a household and remembered his boyhood clearly. His grandfather had owned a small fleet of *smacks*, but the business had failed before he was born and his father was in reduced circumstances compared with what had once prevailed. However, by a combination of hard work and enterprise, he succeeded in remaining his own master and exercising choice over what he did. Young George (along with his brothers) was expected to make his contribution to the father's commercial activities and it prepared him for a life at sea once he had left school—though, initially, he was apprenticed to the trade of shipwright with Colby Brothers. During the 1930s, he joined the Lowestoft migration to Fleetwood, eventually settling there before the decade was out and becoming one of the most successful mid-water trawler skippers out of the Lancashire port. Retirement during the late 1960s brought him back to the Lowestoft area (to Pakefield, in fact), where the writer of this book was fortunate to make his acquaintance. He was always ready to share his extensive knowledge of fishing and was a first-class respondent. The material used here was recorded on 16 November 1976 and 25 January 1979.

"My father wuz a fisherman through an' through. Yeah, he'd bin goin' for years on his own, since he lorst his couple o' *smacks* and my gran'father's fleet went broke.[1] And, o' course, at the end o' the South Pier, he kept all his salvage gear. Underneath, at the end, where the light is, there wuz a big platform and he used to hev big *bass* ropes there, and big *manila* ropes, and about fifty *Dutchman's bowls*. I used to go down and paint them, in the spring o' the year, and I used to give him a hand to grease the big drums o' wire he had there.[2] There wuz all manner o' things! He lorst one or two little boats when he wuz tryin' to run a rope out to

---

1 Walter Stock Snr., the grandfather, had lost his money by investing in three early steam trawlers and forming the Lowestoft Steam Trawling Co. in 1887 (the vessels were sold the following year). The *Bonito* (LT 106), the *Dolphin* (LT 100) and the *Greencastle* (LT 101) were probably ahead of their time for the port, but they failed to make money and brought bankruptcy to their purchaser (see Butcher, *Trawlermen*, pp. 16 and 24). Walter Stock was born in 1839 at Ramsgate and had moved to Lowestoft at some point during the second half of the nineteenth century—part of a large-scale migration from Kentish ports which brought trawling to the Suffolk town.

2 The Dutchman's bowls referred to were large wooden casks used as floats in salvage work and the drums of wire were reels of steel cable.

Plate 7: Lowestoft Harbour Entrance (Edwardian postcard)

An Edwardian postcard showing the entrance to Lowestoft harbour. A "Belle" pleasure-steamer is heading in, with a local shrimper (lugsail set) accompanying her. Moored up to the southern pier-head is the local lifeboat, "Carolina Hamilton"—named after the wife of Lord Claud Hamilton, Chairman of the Great Eastern Railway Co. Ltd., which owned the whole of the harbour works including the Fish Market.

boats what went down in the harbour's mouth. Yeah, and in his box, he used to hev photos o' different ships sunk in the harbour mouth. One wuz the *Sparklin' Nellie* (LT 750); I allus remember him showin' me that.[3] There wuz three [marine] insurance companies in Low'stoft and my father wuz to do with all of 'em. He got a retainer for seein' after all that gear. He wuz in with the tug skippers as well. He used to put his gear aboard and go out wi' them if there wuz a salvage job. And the last time he went out on a tug wuz after the *Blencathra* (LT 1243), a smack, that went ashore the other side o' Yarmouth (California or somewhere) and they salvaged her.

"Now, as regards fishin', my father hed suffin all year round. Come fishin' time [i.e. the autumn herring season], he'd start *linin'* for cod. Now, my brother Spider, when he hed his boat, he used to go in for *sprats* an' *longshores* [longshore herring], but my father never hed no sprat nets or longshore nets. No, and when the herrin' and sprattin' season wuz on, he used to row round the market (I used to go with him) to different drifters after bait. *Mackerel* wuz a stronger bait, but sometimes we'd bait *herrin'* as well. And he used to send away to Fred Parkes at

---

3 The *Sparkling Nellie* was a smack which sank in the harbour mouth at Lowestoft, close to the north pier head, on 20 November 1902. Explosives were used to break her up and thus remove a major hazard to shipping.

Boston (him who wuz originator o' the Boston fishin' fleet[4]) for *whilks*. Sacks o' whilks and sacks o' *mussels*. An' they used to come inta the railway station an' we used to go an' git 'em on our big ol' barrer.

"He used to send away to Redditch for his hooks and us boys allus used to give him a hand puttin' 'em on. He used to hev the line run down the hall from the front door knob and acrorss inta the kitchen, and he used to space out the *snuds* with the hooks on. There'd be about two or three feet between the snuds, so they dint tangle. Then, once the hooks hed all bin tied on, he hed baskets with mackerel net corks tied round the top to stick 'em in. Then he used to take them baskets down to his shrimper, the *Ocean Queen* (LT 614), which wuz moored alongside the South Pier, and bait up aboard o' her. O' course, she'd be dismasted by then and the mast and sails would be in our shed at hoom.[5] He used to put the whilks and mussels in baskets, cover 'em over with sacks and bits o' net, and keep 'em alive by hanging 'em over the side o' the *Ocean Queen*. He used to bait up with a whilk, a mussel, a herrin' and a mackerel, in that order, and then away we'd go over agin. Mussels dint hang on as long as whilks, so you dint use many o' them in bad weather—but the cod seemed to go for 'em. I're bin down there with him (I wuz only young), blowin' my hands an' crackin' them whilks with a *rollick* [rowlock] up in the front o' the boat.

"I used to go out with him and all. He hed two boats what he used and he allus rowed. He never hed no motor. Yeah, he hed the *Myra* (LT 229) an' the *Anglia*, an' the *Anglia* wuz a big ol' boat.[6] How he rowed her, God knows! He used to put out about 1500 hooks. There'd be *dan* at each end with a flag on an' three or four metal cans, joined together for floats, every so orften between the dans so you hent got one great *swing*.[7] Then there'd be about twenty little anchors to keep the lines down on the bottom. When he shot the lines, he used to let 'em go hisself. He'd say, 'Stand clear!' And you used to hetta stand clear. I used to be up for'ad. 'Git out o' the way, boy,' he'd say. He'd go out twice a day, mornins an' afternoons, from the beginnin' o' October till after Christmas—right inta January. He used to hev his *garf* with him when he hauled. Cor, and I've sin him git hooked up once or twice! He just used to git his pliers, snip the hook an' suck. He never did worry about it an' he never got poisoned hands. Yeah, he allus hed his pliers handy to pull the hooks out! I wuz only young then, and I've come in with my feet up on the *thwarts*, as cold as yuh like.

---

4 Boston Deep Sea Fisheries Ltd.

5 The Stock family lived at No. 14, Stevens Street, Lowestoft.

6 Fishing vessels of three net tons or more were usually listed in official publications, such as local port directories. Smaller craft were not, and their registration numbers are therefore much harder to find. *Olsen's Fisherman's Nautical Almanack* listed vessels of fifteen net tons or more.

7 The improvised floats served to keep the longline from forming into a large curve.

Plate 8: Kirkley Cliff & Claremont Pier (Edwardian postcard)

An Edwardian postcard view of Kirkley Cliff, looking northwards. The Claremont Pier is prominent in the mid-foreground, while the Lowestoft harbour's South Pier is discernible on the skyline—the mass of its pavilion clearly seen.

"When he went linin', he used to tairke his bearin' from St John's Church and run away up as far as the Claremont [Claremont Pier].[8] But not anywhere close, so there wuz people fishin' orf the end. Or sometimes he'd put 'em a little further out, along the Barnard [Barnard Sand]—though he'd be out o' the way o' the traffic, when the boats could git through the Pakefield Gat. That silted up afterwards and, o' course, the boats couldn't use it then. I think one or two o' the smacks tried, and they bumped [the bottom], so they couldn't git through no more. Some years, my father did well on the cod. Mind yuh, we're goin' back a long while. Some years were good years and other years were lean. He sold his fish on the Market. I used to be round there with him. I'd be down in the boat, a-hookin' 'em on. See, he'd lower a *hook* [gaff] down and pull it up, 'cause you hed the *walins* there then, you know. There wuz a lower one (and if that wuz high tide, the water would be over that), and then there wuz the second one, and then there wuz the market.[9] He'd pull the fish up, sep'rate. I used to git hold o' these gret ol' cod and hook 'em in

8 St. John's Church was built in 1853, on a site not far to the south of the harbour bridge, to serve the new parish created by Samuel Morton Peto's building development on the old Lowestoft South Common. It was demolished in 1977-8 and its parish merged with that of St. Peter, Kirkley.

9 The quay on the main part of the Lowestoft Fish Market was stepped, with two lower stages below the floor of the Market itself. It had been built like this, to facilitate the landing of fish by hand at different tidal levels, at a time when vessels did not have steam capstans and winches to run catches ashore.

the gills. Then he'd pull 'em up. They were laid out on the floor o' the market and one o' the salesmen down there used to sell 'em.

"He wuz allus on his own, my father—except when he hed me or my brother Spider. He'd never employ anyone. He wuz a big chap and them boats musta took some rowin'. He used to take anglin' parties out. Yeah, he hed a lot o' high-class people aboard the *Anglia* for fishin' trips. She wuz twice the size of a normal rowin' boat and there wuz a space at the back in her where women could sit. If he just took two or three chaps out, he'd use his smaller boat, like the *Myra*, and the one he hed afore her, the *Emily*. He used to start tairkin' fishin' trips out about the end o' September till the real cod set in. And even then he'd try to do both jobs. Yeah, he'd run so many lines out and praps go over them afore he'd tairke the people out; then he'd bring the people in and go over his lines agin. There wuz one *toff* he used to tairke out regularly—Captain Ferguson Davison—and he used to give us boys many a half-crown [2s 6d = 12½p]. Well, a half-crown in them days wuz really somethin'! Yeah, he used to bring parties down for fishin', though I dun't know where he lived, and every Chris'mas he'd send a turkey and a big hamper o' everything.

"Durin' the summer, my father hed rowin' boats in the yacht basin and he'd let them out for people to row up the river—not to go out to sea! No, that wuz no good tryin' to go out o' the harbour. He'd tell the people where to go and what to do. The boats wun't for fishin', like on the *broad* [at Oulton]—just for rowin'. In the end, he come out o' that and sold the boats to the broad people and kept mainly to *linin'* and *shrimpin'*. I know durin' the winter time he used to tairke these boats up to Darby's yard—him what kept the *Commodore*—to be gone over.[10] I've bin up there with him, and he's bin rowin', and there's bin praps three o' these boats towed along behind.

"The *shrimpin'* used to start about the beginnin' o' May. My father hed the *Ocean Queen* for that. She wuz a *clinker-built* boat, with a fore-deck and a sail, and in them days there wuz quite a few of 'em. The Swans and all them on the North Beach had sim'lar ones. And theirs used to be anchored from the lifeboat quay right through to the Hamilton Dock. My father kept his inside the South Pier, though, near his other boats. When we were gittin' things riddy in the yard at hoom, say for the first o' May, there'd be the trawl there, and the sails, and the mast. Yeah, and us boys would scrape the mast and he'd varnish it. Then my mother used to hetta make the little red and white flag for his mast-hid. That wuz the Stocks' flag goin' back to their *fleetin' days*. Durin' the First War, he saved nine out o' nineteen crew on the *Astrologer*. He wuz fishin' well out, just in sight o' land, and he see this ship on fire—so he went in among the wreckage and got

---

10 The references here are to a boatyard and a public house on the water's edge at Oulton Broad, which were owned by the same family. *The Commodore* public house is still in operation.

nine o' the men. He got a big, gold, framed parchment for that.[11]

"The *trawl-beam* he used to work wuz about twelve feet long, with the *iron heads* on the end [trawl-heads], and his *ground-rope* used to hev just a little bit o' chain on. When the gear wuz stowed, the *after* trawl-head used to hang out over the stern, just like on a smack. Yeah, and he used to work that all on his own. He knew just how much *warp* to go out, and he'd haul the trawl on his own as well. Yeah, he could do that all right. He'd shove the boat up to the wind and—oh, he wuz very strong. People used to call him the *East Coast Giant*. Yeah, he wuz a big chap. He used to work the tides. Yeah, we used to go up [southwards] with the tide an' then come back with it.[12] He'd weigh up the tides, so praps you'd go out durin' the day and be back at the close [dusk]. Or praps you'd go out in the evenin' and come in about six or seven o' clock in the mornin'. Yeah, sometimes we'd go up orf *Sowle* [Southwold] and that way.

"You used to git the shrimps mainly on a sandy bottom. He wun't tow along above an hour, and that'd be mainly with the tide. Then he'd haul and shoot away agin. That wuz a life where you'd gotta know every item—weigh up the wind and the swell and everything. Otherwise, you'd be in trouble. That wuz very, very rare that he went down the North Roads. He did at odd times, but you got so many pink shrimps down there and Thain's wun't take pink shrimps very much.[13] You come on them where that sewer pipe run out there, at Corton. Well, the Yarmouth and the Gorleston men, they'd git the pink shrimps down there. And when you used to go on Yarmouth prom and that, you'd see all pink shrimps. We used to hetta pick them out, though!

"The Swans and all the *Beach gang*, they were nearly all *shrimpers*.[14] Yeah, they hed their own boats and some o' them used to work down the North Roads, 'cause sometimes they'd git a little bit more soles down to the nor'ad. A lot o' the time, my father would set out in the evenin' durin' the summertime. You know, about seven or half-past seven. He'd weigh up how the tides run. Sometimes that'd be about four o' clock in the afternoon, but he'd still go for the night—providin' that wuz fine and everything wuz all right. Oh yeah, he'd work through the night.

---

11 This rescue was reported in *The Lowestoft Journal* of 22 July 1916. Mr. Stock also received a £20 reward. The wreck of SS *Astrologer* itself occurred on 26 June 1916, when it struck a German mine five miles S.S.E. of Lowestoft. The captain and nine of the crew perished.

12 In the North Sea, the flood tide runs south and the ebb tide north.

13 Edward F. Thain Ltd. was a firm of fish merchants, which had a shop just to the north of the Lowestoft harbour bridge. The pink shrimps referred to were Aesop prawns (*Pandalus montagui*), which turn pink on being cooked. The common shrimp (*Crangon vulgaris*) turns brown.

14 The Swan family were well known longshore fishers and lifeboatmen, who lived on the so-called Lowestoft Beach Village, a community that had grown up north of the harbour on former manorial waste-land. The inhabitants themselves never used the term; they always referred to their home-area as *The Grit*.

"We used to hev a big barrer and we used to hetta take the shrimps down to Thain's. Father used to bring 'em hoom and we hed a gret big copper to boil 'em in. And you dint only git shrimps. There wuz a lot o' small things like *miller's thumbs* and you hetta pick all them out.[15] And little odd bits o' log and stuff like that, you know. They'd gotta be clean shrimps, so ol' Thain would take 'em. I know the chaps that used to work there would say, 'Ah, these are the best!' They used to shoot 'em straight out onta a big marble counter that went all round the shop and showed in the winder [window]. There wuz big square wooden things, wi' no bottom in 'em, standin' on this counter and the shrimps went in them. My father sold his shrimps by the *peck*.[16] He hed the pint-sized, round, wooden measures, you know. Then he hed the next size up [a quart] and the big *half-pecks*. He hed all the measures, yeah.

"He got *flatfish* an' all when he went shrimpin', but he always kept to his usual trawl. My mother used to make the nets. She'd be a-doin' and us boys would be a-fillin' the *needles*. As far back as I can remember, I can remember fillin' them needles! My father used to do his own mendin', though. Yeah, and one thing he dint like wuz easterly winds. I mean, that took him all his time to keep out [from land] and he'd hefta *tow* on the cant. Many a time he'd say, 'Well, thass no good goin' out today, boy. Bloody easterly wind!' And all the ol' boys used to be the same.[17] He'd keep on shrimps till about September time, praps a bit longer, and he never went only to git flatfish. If you're a shrimper, you're a shrimper, and whatever else come is extra. If he got a good lot o' plaice or soles, sometimes we used to take 'em round in baskets and sell 'em on the market. But a majority o'times Thain's used to take his fish. We used to git a bill when we took the shrimps and fish down; then he'd go down the end o' the week and git the *dibs* [money]. Yeah, an' give us a treat, praps.

"I spose there wuz a livin' in that sort o' thing, but all fishin' in them days wuz not a very profitable game. Not for the small man. Nor for some o' the big ones. I mean, look at the boatowners what *went through* [became bankrupt]! I can remember cleanin' the *slips* and that. We never used to take the small stuff to Thain's. We used to sell 'em from the house at thrippence a plateful—slips, little plaice, small dabs and that. Yeah, as far back as I can remember, I've bin cleanin' fish! You know, skinnin' dabs and that. My father used to git the odd turbot and brill as well, but not very orften. He got weevers and *gurnets* [gurnards] as well. You've gotta mind them! Orf Low'stoft here, you used to git them little tiny

---

15 The Miller's Thumb or Bullhead (*Cottus gobio*) is a freshwater fish. The species referred to here may have been the Armed Bullhead (*Agonus cataphractus*), which is to be found in shallow coastal waters.

16 A peck measured two Imperial gallons by volume.

17 Easterly winds were also unpopular with fishermen because the counter-current they created, beneath the surface of the sea, caused fish to move further out from land. They also caused flatfish to dig themselves into the seabed.

weevers and, cor, did they sting! So did the biguns and all. Yes, he'd git them, but he used to throw 'em over. Same wi' gurnets. He never used to save them. No. Or little *latchets*. Though we orften used to hev a nice big, stuffed, cooked latchet. Yeah, they're lovely and white.[18]

"The beginnin' o' September, my father used to dismantle the shrimper, the *Ocean Queen*. You know, take the trawl-beam, the trawl-net and everything out of her. Even the mast and that. Yeah, an' he allus used to clean the bottom on what we called the *Harbour Beach*. That wuz lookin' straight acrorss from the Herrin' Market. We tilted her well over on there and cleaned her down.[19] And my father knew ol' Billy Wooden, up Commercial Road, who used to make spars and that. He went to school with him; he wuz an ol' pal o' his. And Billy Wooden used to say, 'What wood do yuh want? What size?' Then we'd go up there wi' the ol' barrer and bring it down to our yard. I remember puttin' a couple o' new planks in the stern and a bit o' iron that went round where the *iron reel* for the *warp* wuz.[20] I even put half a keel in her once! See, my father said to me, 'Boy, you're not goin' to sea no more!' That wuz when I first left school and the Germans were blowin' up seven or eight smacks a day. The submarines used to come up alongside and put a bomb aboard.[21] He say, 'I've bound you to a shipwright, so you can mend my boat when that want anything.' Oh yeah, we all hetta do somethin.That we did!"

Ten years or so after George Stock had observed his father's longshoring activities and been part of them, Ernest ("Jimmy") Fisher (1912-89) was beginning to become acquainted with the same kind of fishing in neighbouring Pakefield—but not through a direct family link. He was one of a number of boys in the village who gravitated to the beach as a natural playground and became involved with the fishermen who had their storage sheds there and whose boats were pulled up above the tide-line. Even at that time, Pakefield had become part of the Lowestoft built-up area, following the town's rapid expansion after the development of the harbour and the arrival of the railway during the 1840s, but it still retained something of its old identity.[22] A little of this can even be detected today, particularly in the collection of boats and sheds which are still to be found

18 *Latchet* was a local name for the Tub Gurnard (*Aspitrigla cuculus*). These were regarded as something of a delicacy and were usually stuffed with minced beef and chopped onion and baked in the oven, in gravy.

19 The "Harbour Beach" was an area of shoreline within the outer wall of the herring basin, where many of the local longshore craft underwent maintenance. It was also a favourite playground for local boys.

20 There was a sheave in the stern of the vessel, which helped the warp to run freely.

21 For accounts of German U-boat activity off the local coastline during World War I, see Butcher, *Trawlermen*, Chapter Three; D. d'Enno, *Fishermen Against the Kaiser*, vol. 1, chapter 7; R. Malster, *North Sea War 1914-1919*, Chapter 4; and A.J. Curtis, *Lowestoft Fishermen's War 1914-1918*, passim.

22 In 1831 Lowestoft's population was 4,238. By 1921, it stood at 44,323.

Plate 9: Pakefield Beach (1930s postcard)

A 1930s postcard view of Pakefield beach, showing the local holiday industry in full swing with deck-chairs, tents, huts and bathing-machines. A longshore boat is beached just in front of the last-named, to remind us of the fishing carried out here, while the square tower of the parish church is visible above the line of the cliff.

on the beach below the parish church of All Saints and St. Margaret. However, no one is a full-time longshore fisherman at Pakefield these days and the craft are there to provide a hobby or leisure interest. Having said that, it may still be possible at certain times of year to buy fish on the beach and have it in the pan within an hour or two of it being landed.

Jimmy Fisher had his first contact with longshore fishing when it was still a means of livelihood for some of the local men, but it was already in the final phase of its existence. The growth of Lowestoft and its fishing industry during the Victorian period dominated all maritime activity locally and created a demand for labour whose effect was felt well beyond the boundaries of the town. One of the attractions of going on the *big boats*, as opposed to fishing off the beach, was the more regular nature of the work and its greater earning potential. Longshore fishing (largely through using small craft close in to land) was much more susceptible to the effects of bad weather and was usually not capable of creating a good level of income from its catches. Most of the younger local men preferred to work for wages or shares on the Lowestoft trawlers and drifters, leaving the longshore enterprise in the hands of older men, who had either done their time on the larger vessels and now preferred to work for themselves or who had always followed longshoring (often combined with other interests). Jimmy Fisher recalls his early experiences on Pakefield beach (tape-recording made, 20 February 1979).

"I've lived here in Pakefield Street for all but two years o' my life and that'd be about 1925 when I first started *longshorin'*. That wuz when Beach Street wuz still standin' and you had all the boats down below there.[23] This wuz long before the sea wall wuz built and you had all the ol' fellers with their boats, such as Bo Martin, Fred Thompson, Dinks Allen and Doddles Allen. He wuz the feller who used to go round the roads, when the *maroons* went orf, shoutin', 'Who roar! Ship ashore!' Then everyone used to turn out to help larnch the lifeboat.[24] Then there wuz Isaac Benns. He wuz one o' the mean fishermen, he wuz. You could go and lend him a hand to git his boat up the beach and cart his fish up, but you never got a fish out of him—so he never used to git much help.

"Now, in regards to us boys, you never got a ride in a boat unless you could row. If you could row, you were all right, because in them days, when you were fishin' for herrins and sprats, you would pull as far as Kessin'land if you'd got an ebb tide runnin'—which meant pullin' aginst the tide. And the boy would be on the for'ad oars and the man in charge o' the boat would be on the after oars, and the boy would hefta keep time with the man. Yeah, you'd pull up as far as Kessin'land and shoot yuh nets and then drift back to Pakefield on the tide, providin' there wuz enough tide runnin'. All us youngsters went, when we were about thirteen or fourteen year old.

"Thass like durin' the summer months. All these ol' *longshoremen* hed these here varnished boats and they used to git a licence from the council, which cost 'em half-a-crown [2s 6d = 12½p]. That wuz a blue badge with white letterin', and they used to put that on their arm and leave Pakefield Beach and go down to the South Beach [at Lowestoft] and run passengers orf at a shillin a head. You know, pleasure trips. Yeah, there used to be quite a fleet of 'em go down. Well, o' course, us boys used to lend 'em a hand to push orf and then we'd row the boats down to the South Beach time he sit aft and hed a ride. And then we used to run hoom. Well, later in the afternoon, about three or half-past, we used to go down and row the boats hoom and help pull 'em up the beach. Well, if you were pretty good at that, you'd git a chance to go orf fishin' with 'em—such as herrin' catchin' or after sprats. But that wuz very rare they let you pull about with *line fish*.[25]

"It wuz more or less a scratchin' along livin'. I mean, there wuz one or two of 'em made a livin' or entirely relied on longshorin'—but not many. There wuz times when they had a bad season, durin' the summer, and hetta go inta the drifters

---

23 Pakefield had two serious phases of sea erosion during the first half of the twentieth century, which carried away a lot of the cliff-top area. The first occurred between 1900 and 1907, the second during the early 1930s.

24 *Who roar* may have been a corruption of "hurrah", because a ship in trouble might well have resulted in a salvage payment to the first vessel to reach it. Pakefield men were known as *roaring boys* and the phrase cited here may have had something to do with the nickname.

25 The fishermen were unwilling to take boys out longlining because there was more chance of them getting injured—especially from hooks fouling their hands.

for the hoom fishin'. See? That would all depend on how the year's work had gone. Ol' Isaac Benns wuz about the only one who thrived on it, because he used to catch his fish, bring it ashore, smoke it, and then run down town with it in a basket on his head a-sellin' *bloaters* an' *kippers*. His smokehouse wuz right alongside *The Trowel an' Hammer* [public house]. Yeah. And that wuz where he used to cure his fish. Ol' Fred Thompson wuz another ol' longshoreman, but o' course he used to have his *bathin' machines* on the beach and work his boats at the same time. Same as Frank Lincoln. He used to have all the ol' *bell tents* along the beach and work his boats, and he sort o' made a livin' that way.

"I used to go orf with Cromwell Warford quite a lot. He lived in St. George's Road. He had a boat called the *Three Sons* (LT 1283) and durin' the hoom fishin', when the drifters used to lay in, he used to go down the Market as a *watchman*. I've been down there on a Saturday night and slept aboard the drifters with him. Yeah, I used to look forward to goin' down there. He got paid. Oh yeah. But I didn't. No, that wuz more or less just a pleasure trip for me. Well, with the aim o' gittin' a *sea biscuit*! You know, the big ol' hard sea biscuits. I didn't mind them.

"I started longshorin' on my own not long afore the war.[26] I had a boat called the *Cheerio Lads*. She wuz a seventeen-footer and we used to go *longlinin'* and shoot about 500 hooks then. We never used to go out far. There used to be a reef o' rocks called Hubbard's Rocks, just opposite Pakefield Church, and we used to shoot either just outside o' that or just inside. That wuz an old sea wall and sea defences which a man called Hubbard, who built half o' Pakefield, had built to protect his property and, o' course, it didn't come orf.[27] With longlinin' you allus started round about the end o' October, beginnin' o' November. That all depended on if the fish were in early. But generally, when the sprattin' season come inta bein', you could say there wuz cod there as well. You used to go right through to the end o' January, weather permittin', and you went after *cod* an' *whitin'*. And, o' course, prior to that, you had the herrin' in October.

"We used to bait up with herrin' or sprats, or we used to go over to Oulton Broad and dig up *clams*. You know where the Petrofina depot is and them ol' wrecks?— well, thass where we used to go and dig up clams. And you used to git bags of 'em! They used to be biguns, too.[28] I used to go down there two or three times a week. See, when you baited up wi' clams, the hard gristly part would hang on the hook a long while. Yeah, I used to use them; that wuz very rare I used *whelk*. I hev used *mussel*, but there wuz always difficulty keepin' them on the hooks. You'd hefta bind them with a bit o' cotton or wool to hold 'em on. Sometimes I used

---

26 Mr. Fisher stopped going to sea on the Lowestoft trawlers because the money earnt was not good at the time and because crews were often laid off at the end of unprofitable trips.

27 Hubbard's Rocks contained debris from the houses destroyed by sea erosion during the first decade of the twentieth century.

28 This bivalve was probably the Sand Gaper (*Mya arenaria*). The area where they were dug up was on the southern shore of the Lowestoft inner harbour—Lake Lothing.

mackerel, too—especially when the whitins were about.

"Now, the 500 hooks, if you can weigh it up (if your mathematics are good), were a fathom apart and the *snuds* used to be about two foot long. And, o' course, you put them on like you do a *norsel* on a herrin' net, so that they don't slip. We had *anchors* every so often and, when you put them on, you sort o' judged the distance. I mean, all the lines were in *shanks* about thirty fathom long, and them shanks were joined together, and I spose you'd put an *anchor* about every two shanks. We used to have the lines in tin baths. There wuz a few who had baskets, but the only thing with baskets is that if the hooks drop down they'd catch in the wicker work. But with tin baths, they couldn't hook into anything. The lines were *danned* at both ends. Definitely, yis. And if you had an extra long run o' lines, you used to have a *dan* in the middle—so that if you got *parted*, you wun't hafta go to the extreme other end before you could haul 'em. See, you could go to that halfway dan. Oh yeah.

"We used to go out late in the evenin' and then leave 'em till next mornin'. I mean, I've even bin out Chris'mas mornin' and hauled lines. The wife'll tell yuh that. Oh yeah. I mean, that wuz in the days when a shillin' wuz a shillin'. Like I said, we'd be outside or inside o' Hubbard's Rocks. See, the rocks were there and they enticed mussels an' winkles, small fry and all that, and the cod and whitin fed on it. Anywhere where there's rocks, you git cod. And you don't always need cold weather for cod either. I mean, in November, you don't git a real nip in the air. At the time I'm talkin' about, the rocks would be about seventy or eighty yards out. I've actually bin on 'em on at extra low water. There wuz a strong south-east gale there once, and a very big ebb, and Tom Colby and me walked out from the shore. And inside the rocks there wuz big *ross* banks. Ross. Thass a marine life like a little worm and it's encased in a sort of honeycomb sand.[29] Thass similar to coral. And that wuz a big attraction for cod as well. Yeah, and we had to step from bank to bank on that to get out onta the rocks.

"We never went out to the Barnard [Barnard Sand], not from Pakefield. Well, one or two mighta done, but not very many and not very orften. We used to git good catches on the lines. I mean, I've hed bathfuls o' cod in the kitchen here. There wuz only two of us to a boat. There'd be one on the oars and one shootin' the lines, or one on the oars and one a-haulin'. The man on the oars wuz the most important man. He's gotta back her up to the tide and you rely on him in case you happen to git a hook in yuh hand. He's gotta hold the boat steady then, until you can cut the snud and git yuhself free. Oh yeah. See, when you were *shootin'* the lines, you used to shoot 'em with yuh hands. Well, o' course, when you *coiled* the lines in the bath, you allus took that bit o' care in coilin' 'em in fairly steady, so that when you paid the lines out the hooks run nice and free. You just used to git hold of a few coils o' line and give it a flick and that'd fly out. You couldn't afford

---

29 The creature referred to is the polychaete worm *Sabellaria alveolata*.

to hev three men workin'. No, just the two. And you allus hed a *gaff* with yuh. Oh yis. If you got a decent fish comin' alongside, you'd gaff it and get it inboard. That wuz very rare you got anything apart from cod and whitin'—a dogfish or two praps [Spur dogfish], or a *chance* dab. But that wuz all.

"You could sell yuh fish in the village if you wanted, but mainly the outlet wuz the Fish Market [at Lowestoft]. Yeah. We used to put 'em in boxes and the local carter used to come and pick 'em up and take 'em down. He used to charge you so much a box. Yeah, and Mitchell Brothers were the ones who used to mostly sell the *longshore fish*. Yeah, they used to specialise in that. An' that wuz there for anyone who liked to buy it. You could git *cod* up to ten or twelve pound on the lines, but the average would be about three or four pound. You got an occasional *slink* as well, and sometimes you'd git a cod wi' just the head, the backbone and the tail—no flesh on it at all! Thass what the seals would do. There's bin a good cod on the line and a seal has come along. Well, he couldn't git it orf the line, but he'd take all the flesh orf just as if someone had took a knife an' filleted it. Durin' the war, Alan Page (one o' the ol' longshoremen) got permission to have an army feller go out with him and shoot seals. Yeah, he contacted the Army to git permission for somebody to shoot 'em, because they were robbin' the lines."

The autumn and early winter proved a busy time of year for the longshoreman because, as well as longlining for cod and whiting, there was a period of overlap during which herrings and sprats were caught. This necessitated using a completely different kind of gear, the drift-net—a series of which were joined together and floated up near the surface of the sea to catch the fish as they rose from the bottom. A crude analogy (but one which is broadly accurate) is to make comparison with a number of tennis court nets, joined end to end and allowed to stream out along the tide—though with a much smaller mesh-size.[30] This method of catching pelagic shoaling species goes back well into the medieval period, and may be even older, and wills and probate inventories relating to people who lived along the East Anglian coastal fringe (women as well as men) contain many interesting references to drift- nets and their use.

All fishing gear, regardless of its nature, is labour-intensive to set up and maintain—drift-nets particularly so. Herrings and sprats required two different sizes of mesh (the former being a good deal larger than the latter) and, once in use, constant *cleaning* was required in order to keep the nets effective and free from deterioration. The battle against wear and tear was unceasing and, if not undertaken, only led to costly and unnecessary replacement. Thus, the investment of time in maintenance was worth making. Longshoremen, in the nature of the work they did, tended to be individualistic—and this was often reflected in the way they rigged their gear. Local conditions, such as tidal features and the nature

---

30 For a detailed explanation of the drift net and its operation, see Davis, *Fishing Gear*, pp. 54-61, and Butcher, *Driftermen*, Chapter Two.

of the seabed, dictated the fishing operation itself, but each man tended to have his own idea of how his gear should be set up to give the best results. The basic principles were the same across a whole range of equipment, but fine details might vary considerably. Jimmy Fisher describes his drift-netting operations, beginning with fishing for herrings.

"A *longshore net*, on average, wuz about twenty-five to thirty yards long, and the ones we used to work orf this beach were made o' *white cotton*. We used to cure the nets in *linseed oil*. There used to be half raw an' half boiled, with a little *driers* [thinners] in it. I cured my last nets in 1957 and I've still got some down in the shed. A white net allus fished better inshore than a tanned one and I think that wuz because the tanned ones made a big brown shadow in the water. Once you'd soaked the *lints* in the linseed oil, you put 'em on a chute so the oil could drain away. And you had to keep turnin 'em over in the meantime so they didn't heat up—otherwise the cotton would just automatically disintegrate. Once the oil wuz drained out, you laid 'em out on the grass to dry, and you'd go and turn 'em over two or three times to make sure the oil took and they dried evenly. If you got a really good dry with the weather, they'd be ready in two or three days and you could set 'em up on the *frames*.[31]

"I used to buy the lints new from someone like Stuart's or Beetons. Some o' the blokes used to buy *Scotch nets* and cut 'em down. I've done that myself, because you git a Scotch net, which is about fifty-five yards long an' eighteen *score* deep—well, that's six longshore nets out o' that one net.[32] Longshore nets were mainly six score and you'd buy that size o' lint. Now, praps a Low'stoftman, who'd got a bigger boat, would work some six scores and some eight scores, because he wuz out in deeper water. But, mainly, us Pakefield men used to have *six scores*. There used to be flat corks on the *net-rope* and they used to be rounded and smoothed orf so the lint dint catch when you shot 'em.[33] I spose the corks were about a foot apart and the *norsels* used to be put on every four *mashes* [meshes]. Yeah, and there'd be three norsels between every cork. There wuz a *hoddy* on the net, and *hiddins* [headings], and the hoddy wuz just at the top o' the net—about eight rows deep o' heavier cotton. There wuz nothin' on the bottom, but sometimes we used

---

31 Once the nets had been oiled, they were not treated again. Proper drying was essential for effective preservation and, if carried out correctly, would give nets a working life of fifteen years or more. The frames referred to were the ropes and cords within which the meshes were set.

32 J. & W. Stuart Ltd. and Beetons Ltd. were two net manufacturers in Lowestoft. The depth of drift-nets was always reckoned in scores of meshes. Thus, with an average herring mesh being about an inch square, a net of eighteen score meshes was thirty feet deep.

33 The corks alone were sufficient to keep the nets floated up near the surface of the water and, as long as a boat remained attached to its nets, no other floats were used. But if a vessel left its nets to drift on their own for a while, or if under-running was practised, floats were fixed along the net-rope at periodic intervals so that the nets remained visible. These floats were often large tin cans, worked singly or tied together two or three at a time.

to have a little piece o' lead wrapped up in calico bound on here and there. Or praps a piece o' *reinin'*. That wuz an old piece o' net rolled up, which wuz laced along the bottom. But, quite orften with the white nets, you dint need nothin' on the bottom to make 'em hang prop'ly in the water. In our boats, these here seventeen-footers, we used to shoot about twelve or thirteen nets, 'cause in them days you could find yuhself wi' more herrins than you could handle. I can't tell yuh orf hand how many rows to the yard longshore nets were, but they were only just a shade smaller than the ordinary Scotch net.[34]

"Now, we allus reckoned on a full moon wi' herrin'. See, when the moon is bright, we reckoned that brought the herrins to the top.[35] But I hev caught herrins without a moon. Another good sign wuz *thick water*. Yeah. *Sheer water* wuz never no good anywhere, so you allus looked for thick water—what we used to call *puddly* water.[36] We used to like the weather fairly fine as well, but if you got a flat-a-calm you never got many fish. But when you were a-jumpin' and a-heavin' about a bit, then you'd catch plenty. And sometimes that could be thick wi' fog an' you'd git 'em. You'd shoot on the flood, of an evenin', and drive up [southwards]. And if you worked the tail end o' the flood, you'd drive up so far and then come back on the ebb. That all depends on how the fish swim. I mean, you could push orf the beach and shoot straight away if they were there; but if you dint see many a-swimmin', well, you'd hang on then. You could go up as far as Benacre Ness. Oh yeah. I mean, you could go round Benacre Ness, as long as you kept yuh nets inshore. O' course, with a wind orf the land, yuh nets would set orf. An' if they set orf too far you could run onta the East Barnard buoy, so you hetta be careful. You could drive well down the other way on the ebb and all. I mean, I've driv right down to the Claremont Pier, and past there.

"Anything bar an easterly wind wuz generally all right to fish in, though sometimes a northerly or north-westerly wasn't too good. See, you got that *logie swell* wi' them—that big ol' heavy swell in the water. Mainly, we kept inside, if we could. The only time we used to be a little orf from the beach wuz comin down on the ebb. Yeah, and if that wuz gittin' to the bottom o' the water [tide] abrist o' the church here, you'd expect to be further orf.[37] You'd come drivin' down over the flats and then, by the time you reached the village, you'd expect

---

34 The size of drift net meshes was reckoned in rows to the yard, which was the actual number of meshes per yard's length of net. Longshore herring nets were usually thirty-six or thirty-seven rows to the yard, which meant a mesh size of one inch.

35 East Anglian fishermen believed in the influence of the October and November full moons as a positive factor in autumn herring catches (with the October one being of more significance for longshoremen), either because of its brightness or because of the effect of lunar "pull" on the tides. For a discussion of the true, scientific significance of lunar periodicity, see W.C. Hodgson, *The Herring and Its Fishery* (London, 1957), pp. 103 and 160.

36 The *thick* or puddly water referred to was caused by air bubbles resulting from shoaling activity, together with the presence of herring oil and (perhaps) zooplankton.

37 Herrings shoaled further out from land on the ebb tide than they did on the flood.

to be out a bit. And if the herrin' hent swum, you'd want your nets to lay orf a bit at that partic'lar point. We allus used to reckon that the *October herrin'* were at their peak round about the seventh. Yeah, but they hev bin here durin' the last two weeks in September. The autumn season used to go right inta mid-November and then you'd come onta yuh sprats.

"As soon as you went orf an' shot yuh nets, you'd keep *under-runnin'* as they call it. You'd git hold o' the lint, and pull that till you got to the bottom, and pick out any fish what wuz in the net. A good man on the oars would keep you alongside the nets all the time. See, and as you under-run, you could see where the fish were swimmin'—whether they were inside, towards the beach, or whether they were further out on the flats. Well, when you found out where they were swimmin' most, you transferred nets from one end to the other. Yeah, and there's bin times when herrin' were so close in that you'd shoot yuh nets right at the back o' the breakers. And as soon as ever you shot, the nets would be goin' down with so many herrin' in! But that wuz always a bad sign, because there wuz this this ol' sayin' that they were kissin' the beach goodbye. Yeah, if you caught any quantity o' herrin' right in the breakers, the ol' boys used to say, 'Well, they're kissin' the beach to say goodbye!' And they used to thin out after that. Oh yeah.

"That wuz very rare you got *double-swum herrin'* on longshorin'. Very rare. No, that allus seemed as if they were one way or the other. The only time you used to git a double-swim wuz when yuh nets lay up and down o' the tide. That wuz when you were streamin' up and down wi' the tide and left yuh nets in the water and hent looked at 'em. See, herrins swim aginst the tide, so if you'd bin drivin' on the flood an' hent looked at yuh nets, and the tide changed to the ebb, then you'd hev 'em on both sides.[38] But not otherwise. No. Sometimes they'd be in the middle o' the net an' sometimes you'd git 'em right at the top. An' sometimes you'd git quite a *shimmer* in the bottom o' the net. That wuz just how they *lifted* [rose from the seabed]. Yeah, just how they lifted. I never parted with the weight o' fish, though. The only time I wuz parted wuz one night in a thick fog, when one o'the motor boats from the harbour went through the nets. But, fortunately, we were able to git hold on 'em and tie 'em back together agin.

"The autumn herrin' swum in heavier lumps than the spring an' summer ones. Oh yeah. I mean, in 1957, I had just over thirty *cran* in one boat in eight days, and I landed another two cran in Freddy Cable's boat 'cause his mate couldn't go off with him and my mate couldn't turn out.[39] Yeah, so I went off with him, and we got two cran o' herrin', and they were right inta the beach in the first half-dozen

---

38 Herrings actually swam in the opposite direction to the wind, taking advantage of the compensating mid-water current created by the wind's effect on the surface of the sea. This was why an easterly wind was bad for fishing, because it drew fish away from the land, further out to sea.

39 A cran is a measure of 37½ Imperial gallons. It was adopted as the official unit for the measurement of herrings in 1908 and weighed out at 28 stones of fish.

nets! Yeah, that wuz a good year and we averaged £6 a cran, which wuz a good price in that day. There wuz another good year after that one, but there hent bin another one since. What I actually done in 1957 wuz work Danny Allen's boat, the *Molly* (LT 27), 'cause I hed a smaller one, the *Young Harry* (LT 25). And by workin' a bigger boat, I could shoot more nets and catch more fish. Mind yuh, that first shoot, I had four cran o' herrin'! That wuz a very fine night, luckily, and we only had about eight inches *freeboard*. We come ashore, cleaned our nets on the *tarpaulin*, took all the loose herrin' out o' the boat and boxed 'em, left 'em all on the beach, pushed orf agin and got another two cran! We brought them ashore, done the same wi' them, went orf agin an' got another two cran! This wuz between half-past five at night and half-past six the next mornin'. And then we had to carry eight cran o' herrin' up the cliff—and that wuz eleven o'clock in the mornin' afore I got hoom!

"Another time I hed a large haul wuz in 1937. Yeah, we got about 4,000 herrin' that night [about four crans]. I wuz *bendin'* the nets inta the boat [i.e. joining the *head-ropes* together] and ol' Billy Thompson come along and he say, 'What're yuh doin' on, boy?' I say, 'Well, I'm just goin' to git a *fry*.' So I pushed orf and went orf on me own. That wuz Saturday afternoon. Anyway, I saw my cousin on the beach near the Rifle Range, so I pulled inshore.[40] He say, 'What're yuh schemin'?' and he asked me if he could come. And I wuz damn glad he did, because that happened to be a full moon that night and we were gittin' a steady swim all the time. And what we were doin' wuz haulin' half a fleet, cleanin' the herrin' out and then shootin' agin. Then we'd haul the other half and clean them and shoot away agin. And thass what we done, right through the night till half-past five the next mornin'. And when we come ashore on the Sunday mornin', I dun't know how the news had got round, but there wuz a heck of a scamper down onta the beach. We took the herrin' down to the market and sold 'em, but we hetta leave the boat down there because a *fresh o' wind* come up from the south-east and we couldn't row back.

"I never did go down the north end o' Low'stoft, fishin'—not even when I wuz shrimpin'. No. Yuh see, in them days, when you used to hetta pull a rowboat, that wuz a long way from Pakefield beach to the harbour. And then you hetta go down past all them groynes along by Links Road and then come back agin. See, and you couldn't nicely tide with yuh nets in a channel-way where there wuz shippin' because that wuz agin the law. That wuz all right if you could keep well inside, but once you got up towards Ness Point, well, you hed the Inner Shoal buoy and that sort o' thing, so you couldn't really work it.

"Very occasionally, you used to catch little *winter herrin'* in February, but you dun't see 'em now. They were small herrin' and they hed little *rows* in 'em. Yeah,

---

40 There had been an army firing-range on Pakefield cliff, to the south of the village, for many
   years.

they were smaller than the ordinary autumn herrin' and they were a little shoal or specie [*sic*] that used to come in about February and March—just afore the *spring herrin'* come in. See, after the *linin'* finished, the end o' January an' February wuz a sort o' *makin' up* time, when you prepared yuh boat for the spring o' the year, but if winter herrins were there you'd go after 'em. You got the spring herrin' from mid April through inta May. That all depended on how long they actually stopped. I mean, you got short seasons and you got long seasons. Now, the spring fishin'—that wuz good and that wuz bad. You could go orf one day an' git praps half-a-dozen boxes, and another day you'd be lucky if you got a box. And then, on the odd occasion, you could go orf an' praps git a dozen boxes. They were *spent herrin'*, but they allus made money.[41] Yeah, you got more for a spring herrin' than you did at autumn time. There wuz nothin' else about, yuh see. And I think another reason why they made a bit o' money is because people hed bin orf the herrin' for a while and, o' course, that ol' first taste allus eat good. Yeah, but the cream o' the herrin' were the *midsummer* ones. I never did see many o' them, but you sometimes got 'em in July time after a good shower o' rain. Yeah, after a thunderstorm and a good downpour, you stood a better chance o' gittin' them. They were a full herrin' and right fat. And when you cleaned 'em and *snotched* 'em, you only just wanted a tiny nobble o' fat in the pan. Then, when you fried 'em, by the time they finished cookin' they were nearly floatin'.

"When you landed herrins, whatever you couldn't git rid of round here you'd send to the market. Yuh see, in them days there used to be so many boats here that you had a hard job to sell all the fish locally. Oh yeah, and thass the reason why you had to send 'em to the market. See, in them days, as soon as ever people saw a boat come ashore, they used to bring their plates down an' git the herrins straight out o' the boat. They used to be seven for sixpence. Well, I remember one time when I had five or six hundred herrin' and I wanted to git shot of 'em, so I decided to sell 'em at ten for sixpence. I had a hard job to git rid of 'em! For the simple reason that people knew the price of 'em on the beach and thought that these wun't fresh herrin' what were bein' sold. If you got big hauls, the Market [Fish Market] wuz the main place and the herrins went up for sale there. Ol' man Mitchell [of Mitchell Brothers] wuz pretty good for longshoremen. I mean, if you come in, like on a Sunday mornin', with a big load o' fish, he'd git in touch with somebody. When I went down wi' them 4,000 herrin' in 1937, Mitchell found a buyer. Thass the photo you're seen, wi' me in the boat. Yeah, and we hetta tally all them out by hand. Four herrin', one *warp*; thirty-three warp, one *long hundred*.[42]

---

41 Spent herrings were ones that had spawned and had less flesh on them than their autumn counterparts.

42 Before the Cran Measure Act of 1908 was passed, herrings were often counted out by hand. The long hundred was an old measure, going well back into the medieval period. At one time it had been 120 herrings (thirty warps), but during the nineteenth century it had increased to 132—the extra twelve fish being known as *overtale* or *overtail*, the second syllable being an old variant of *tally*.

"Yeah, you allus counted herrins out at one time. That wuz durin' the war that faded out. Then you hed these here tin boxes or wooden trunks. They used to be eight to the cran. Then they brought in *tin boxes* what were six to the cran.[43] Then they settled on the cran basket, 'cause we hetta go an' buy *quarter-cran baskets* to measure the herrin' out with an' then shoot 'em inta the boxes. Like I say, ol' Mitchell handled most o' the longshore stuff. Yeah. And we used to hev an ol' carter here, Stew White, who used to cart most o' the fish down to the Market.

"We were robbed a lot o' the time, though, a-longshorin'. In 1937, I got half-a-crown [2s 6d = 12½p] a hundred that Sunday mornin' for them 4,000 herrin'! Half-a-crown a hundred! But there agin, see, as the markets fluctuated, sometimes if you got down there nice and early, you got a good price. That all depended on the quantity what was there, whether you got a good price or not. Most o' the longshore herrin' went to small people—like shops an' *hawkers*, who used to go out inta the country, and such like. But if any big buyers got them, they used to send 'em up to London or Birmingham. Yeah, they put 'em in boxes what they called *margarines*—little wooden boxes about that long and about that wide [using hands to indicate a size of about 22 inches by 14]—and iced 'em down. That wuz for the London trade and that sort o' thing over the country. Oh yeah. I mean, if there wuz no other herrin' in and they were good-quality longshores, they'd buy 'em. You sometimes got a buyer up here on the beach and he'd take 'em direct. Oh yeah. But that dint happen very orften. That all depended on how bad they wanted 'em. That wuz the thing, see. The only reason why a buyer would come up here after herrin' wuz because there wuz no prospect o' him gittin' 'em down on the market. Now, if he'd got a demand for 'em, he wuz goin' to git 'em wherever he could.

"You got a few *horse mackerel* in the nets sometimes. Scads. Oh yes, you got them in amongst the herrin'. This wuz autumn time. And you'd git loads o' whitins, too. Oh yes, they were there. They used to strike the net and then roll up in it. They just happened to be there in the bay time the herrin' were there. You'd be a-drivin' up, and they'd run foul o' the nets. Yeah, you could catch quite a load o' whitins. You got the odd dogfish as well, *chance-time*, and sometimes you'd find a cod rolled up in the net.[44] But only rare did you git a flatfish. I'll tell yuh what else yuh got occasionally as well—*pilchards*. Yeah, there wuz an occasional pilchard. Autumn time this wuz, agin. Yeah, they used to mash [mesh] with the herrin' sometimes and you hetta pick them out before you sent yuh herrin' down to the Market.

"There used to be *mackerel* caught orf here as well. Some o' the Low'stoft boats used to go out after 'em. This is pre-war days. There wuz a bit of a craze there at one time, when all the *motor boats* congregated and went out to the Crorssin'

43 The so-called tin boxes were actually made from aluminium.

44 Whitings, dogfish and cod all feed on herring (among other species).

[Cross Sand] an' got mackerel.[45] But I never did see any real mackerel fishin' orf here. That wuz very, very rare that you any in wi' the herrin'. You might git a chance *cock mackerel* (they're the little ones), but that wuz all. They tell me people used to git mackerel on *flies* [lures] out by the South-east Buoy in July time [the South-east Newcome], but I never did go out there myself. These were the *feathered flies*. Any ol' colour, that dun't make no odds, or you can put a bit o' *silver paper* on. One or two o' the boys here hed canoes an' they used to catch a mackerel or two orf here wi' *spinners*, but you hardly ever got 'em in the nets.

"Whatever you got, though, you allus hed continuous *mendin'* on longshorin'. Oh yeah! Oh, you very often got split *mashes*—'specially if you're got a mate who's not very careful when he's takin' 'em out o' the boat. If he can't git 'em out easy, he'll break a mash. And then, yuh see, you hed all yuh various little *hefts* in the boat—like on the *roves*, if one o' the *clinkers* is a bit rough, the net'll hang up. Or if the man on the oars is rowin' too hard, and you can't shoot 'em quick enough, they drag over the stern an' you're likely to tear 'em there. Yeah, you allus hefta hev a *needle*. Well, see, this is in the winter time when you do yuh repair work, but you'd allus do some as you went along. I mean, if you come ashore and were all squared up, you'd git a bit done then. And, o' course, in them days the main thing with the *oiled nets* wuz to dry 'em whenever you can. Lay 'em out on the beach, on the stones, see, and dry 'em and then put 'em on yuh *net-barrers* [barrows] and cover 'em up. Well, then, if you hed a bit o' time on yuh hands, you'd run through one or two o' yuh nets and see if there wuz any *sprunks* or *crowfoots*."[46]

While the autumn herring fishing was the longshoreman's main drift-net enterprise, the sprat season was also of some importance, and there was a short period of overlap during which both types of fishing might be carried out according to local conditions and opportunities. Sprat fishing was a long-established activity along the East Coast, with references to the boats and gear used frequently occurring in sixteenth and seventeenth century wills and probate inventories. The word commonly used for the fish in such documentation is *sparling* or *sperling*, which has led to a degree of confusion at times because the term was also applied to the Smelt (*Osmerus eperlanus*). However, it is clear from the many occurrences of the word in connection with nets, boats and curing practice that it is sprats largely being referred to and not smelts. Jimmy Fisher describes his own sprat fishing activities off Pakefield beach.

"After the herrin' we went onta *sprats*. Yeah, we'd usually start on them the first week in November. The nets were about eight foot deep. I couldn't tell yuh

---

45 The motor boats referred to would have been longshore craft with petrol engines installed—some of them probably small car engines converted to another use.

46 These were terms used for broken meshes. A spronk was one damaged strand; a crow's foot was two.

how many mashes; I never bothered to count.[47] They were nets we used to hetta buy; you couldn't do 'em yuhself. They used to average about thirty yards in length. And you could git *double nets* as well, so instead o' thirty yards you got a sixty-yard *lint* made up as one net. Bit we never used to work them. Yeah, they used to be ready-made, sprat nets did, an' they'd be from Stuart's or Beetons or Bridgeport [Bridport Gundry Ltd.]. They had *flat corks* on 'em as well. All the longshore boats used flat corks. There wuz no round corks, like they had on the drifters, because they'd hang up on the *gunwale* when you were shootin', see, and they'd take up so much room in the boat when you stowed the nets. The nets hed a *hoddy* and the *hiddins* [headings] and some of 'em worked little bits o' lead along the bottom to sink 'em quick in the water. They used to be all white cotton, the original ones, an' you oiled 'em like the herrin' nets. Then, later on, they got onta green ones, which used to be soaked in some sort o' *capon oil* [Cuprinol].

"You'd only work about twelve or thirteen nets orf here. Oh yeah, because if you got a real *shimmer* o' sprats you could sink the boat. I've sin a boat sink in the breakers with so many fish in. You'd hit the beach when you come in an' then the boat'd go over. You used to sort o' *under-run* wi' sprats, but all you done wuz pull the lint up just to hev a look to see how many wuz a-swimmin' and whether they were up, down or in the middle o' the net. And when sprats strike, I've actually sin the whole depth o' the net come to the surface—an' all you can see is little green noses stickin' up out o' the water. You'd go *break o'daylight* after sprats, if you could, or just before the break o' daylight—providin' the tide wuz right. Because you hed to rely on the tide, an' it all depended on what time o' day that come.

"You allus shoot on the ebb for sprats and you'd keep *inside*. Not right in to the beach, like you did for herrin', but fairly close in. Yeah, you'd shoot acrorss the *flats* an' in, so yuh *halfway bowl* [float] would be right on top o' the flats, and half the nets would be outside o' that and half would be inside. You always had *cans* with yuh, because you always put cans on sprat nets just as you do herrin' nets. Any *tin can* would do; a gallon can or anything like that. Yeah, you allus worked them. And if you dint hev 'em on yuh nets, you'd hev 'em in the boat, because if you struck an extra heavy *dollop* what you'd do is whip a can or two on where the net-ropes were beginnin' to dip, to help support 'em. And then, o' course, when you do strike like that, you start a-haulin' afore they go down. On average, we used to only put about four floats on: one at each end and a couple in between. We couldn't afford *buffs*. No, we used to git gallon cans an' paint 'em black. Yeah, you never saw anything fancy like buffs, not on longshoremen's boats.

"Some years, I're bin here after Chris'mas on sprats. But, there agin, sometimes you'd git a long season and sometimes you'd git a short season. After Chris'mas,

---

47 The usual dimensions of a longshore sprat net were as follows: thirty yards long off the loom (set in to twenty-one yards working length) by ten score meshes deep. The mesh-size was sixty-two *rows* to the yard, giving an individual measurement of about half-an-inch. See Davis, *Fishing Gear*, p. 57.

you wun't git any real quantity, not like you did in November. I mean, I hev caught sprats as late as March, but that only used to consist of about two or three boxes, and they'd be mostly *yowlers*—little herrin'. An' if you hed too many yowlers in, you wun't git a very good price for 'em. That wuz with Alan Page. I used to go orf wi' him sometimes. When you got a real *muddly* mornin' on an ebb tide—when that wuz sort o' close and muggy—that wuz good weather for a sprat. I mean, I can remember ol' Frank Lincoln; he used to go up on the cliff an' put his nose up to wind'ard and he'd tell yuh within a little what the weather wuz goin' to be like. When you were out in the boat, you hed the water to tell yuh—the ol' *thick water*—and you allus caught more sprats on a southerly wind, or a sou' westerly, than you did on any other.

"If you went outside o' the South-east Buoy, out that way, you got 'em on the flood.[48] But inside, orf here, you only got 'em on the ebb. Yeah, you could start at Southwold on the first o' the ebb, if you wanted, and come all the way down and finish up on low water here. Then, after the ebb, no sprats. If you wanted to git 'em, you'd hefta shoot outside o' the south-east buoy and take the first o' the flood up. That seem as if they went up on the flood to Southwold and then come down on the ebb. Thass how they swum. We used to go only as far as Kessin'land, at about half-tide, and then drive down. And if you dint *strike* inside, well, you used whip the nets in and try a little bit further out. But, o' course, we never used to go right out to the South-east buoy. We used to shoot betwixt an' between. See, you were on oars then; you hadn't got the fancy motor boats.

"As soon as you got a catch, you'd pull yuh nets inta the boat, then come in and shake 'em out on the beach—same as with the herrin' nets when you got a big catch.[49] When we were boys, we used to rely on that—you know, to go and pick 'em up orf the beach to git a fry. The ol' boys dint mind too much, but that all depended who they were. I mean, we knew the best blokes to work for, and you'd carry a few boxes up for 'em and git a fry that way. They used to *smoke* a lot o' sprats in them days. Oh yeah, there were a lot o' sprats smoked, and sprat fishin' used to be a big thing. The longshoremen used to rely on it.

"Sprats were sold by the *mand*. That wuz a basket and I should reckon that held about two stone. Thass a funny thing, but I only got rid of a mand basket not so long back. That wuz a round basket about that high [hands indicating a length of about twenty inches] and about that wide at the top [about eighteen inches], and then that tapered down. Yeah, that tapered down a little at the bottom and, o' course, that had the *seal* [the official mark] on for weights and measures same as a quarter-cran basket. Sprats used to vary in price accordin' to how the demand was. I mean, I've seen 'em sixpence [2½p] a mand in the old days, a long while

---

48 The buoy referred to here was the South-east Newcome buoy, which marked one extremity of the Newcome Sand.

49 A tarpaulin would usually be put down first, to prevent the fish from getting covered in sand.

before the war—and I think, just prior to the war, if you got five bob [5s = 25p], that wuz an exceptionally good price. There wun't many sprats about to git that— or not many on the market, anyway. Sometimes you got a *klondyker* who wanted to top his cargo up and, if he could git enough of 'em, he'd take a load o' sprats. You'd git a decent price then. But that did vary. Yeah, one year wuz allus different to another."

The klondyker referred to in the preceding paragraph was someone involved in the export of fresh herrings from Lowestoft to Germany, packed in large wooden cases, with a certain amount of ice and salt added as preservatives.[50] Most of the fish was shipped to Altona, on board German freighters, for different kinds of curing treatment when it was unloaded. Certain quantities of sprats were also purchased from time to time, to accompany the herrings. However, such occurrences were not common and the longshoreman could not rely on sporadic interest of this nature as a regular generator of income. He had to look largely to the established outlets for his catches: the local community in which he lived and certain merchants on the Lowestoft Market who specialised in buying longshore fish. And of no activity was this more true than of the spring and summer endeavour with *beam-trawls*, catching shrimps and flatfish.

"When we went beam *trawlin'*, we hed a *fish-trawl* and a *shrimp-trawl*. Now, a trawl is governed by the length of your *beam*. I mean, I used to work a fifteen foot beam and you hetta set your net up to suit that beam. See? The only difference in a fish-trawl and a shrimp-trawl is the size o' the mash.[51] They both used to hev *wings* in and I used to make my own trawls up. I *braided* 'em. I've got one out the back there now, which I braided up myself. I used to have a *flopper* in as well, and then o' course I worked the *pockets* in to trap the soles.[52] And I used to hev *chafing-pieces* on the bottom o' the *cod-end*. My *ground-rope* wuz made up from a small chain [i.e.one with small links], with *lint* wrapped round it, an' then I used to bind a length o' net-rope round that so I got a good thickness on the ground-rope. The idea o' the lint wuz that the sand got into it an' made additional weight. I used to put an extra bit o' chain on the ground-rope if I found it wuz a-jumpin' about as I towed, but sometimes that happened because you were pullin' too hard.

"With the big *beam-trawl*, I hed an inboard motor, which wuz a Stewart Turner. This wuz on a motor boat now, the *Joyce Ann* (LT 84), not a rowboat. I hed a six foot beam afore the war, but I never worked it much with a sail. No, 'cause we were out there one day and we were goin' so damned hard that we caught a

---

50 This trade first developed in the late 1880s and early 90s, at about the same time as the *Yukon* gold-rush—hence the name. It was revived after the First World War and continued throughout the 1920s and 30s, but it did not carry on for very many years after the end of the Second World War.

51 Shrimp trawls had smaller meshes than the beam trawls used to catch flatfish.

52 For a good explanation of the set-up and working of a beam-trawl, see Davis, *Fishing Gear*, pp. 88-95 and Butcher, *Trawlermen*, Chapter Two.

cod instead o' shrimps![53] That wuz squally, and we were goin' too hard, and we couldn't keep the trawl on the bottom. I didn't do much shrimpin' then, until 1957. Thass when I really got goin'. I mean, in the old days o' shrimpin', they used to work a small beam an' they hetta row the boat. Yeah, an' if there wun't much wind or tide, there used to be one man git out o' the boat with a long length o' rope, tied one end where the *fore-rollicks* [rowlocks] go in, pullin' the boat along the beach while the other one rowed! You don't hefta move very hard, just as long as you're movin' a bit. You allus tow with the tide. You never pull aginst it. Mind you, you can with a motor boat. Oh yeah. But you hefta turn yuh engine on a little harder. When you're trawlin' or shrimpin', as long as you're just beatin' the tide, thass all you want. You dun't hafta go skimmin' along, otherwise the ground-rope would be jumpin' orf the bottom.

"You'd start trawlin' in April. You could git small plaice orf here in April and May, and then from there onwards you'd come inside for shrimps. And then, o' course, when you're shrimpin', you git soles with 'em an' all. I know I'd got a shrimp-trawl on, but if there's any plaice or dabs or soles come in the way I got 'em in my trawl. When you're trawlin' out here, you like to see yuh *markins* [markings]. You can't just shoot out here and pull a trawl just anywhere. It's all right for these here big forty-footers. I mean, they're got a winch to haul with. But when that come to a longshore beam-trawl, you're gotta hev markins what you can see because you can't just pull where you like—not even out orf here. They're took the main one away now—St. John's Church—an' they're took the end orf the Claremont Pier. But there's a winder [window] up on the inside o' the pier, on the southernmost gable, and we used to line that up on the Birdseye [Factory] chimney. The only trouble wi' Birdseye is that it used to be black an' you could see it, but then they changed the bugger to silver![54]

"The way you towed all depended on where you were *towin'* and if you were towin' flood or ebb. If you're towin' ebb, well then, you motor to the south'ard and then git yuh bearins. Thass like St. John's Church—you'd git that halfway up the Claremont Pier. An' there used to be a winder on the end o' Pryce's Warehouse, which some people used. Then there wuz the houses on the Kessin'land Road: you'd either git the trorffin' [troughing, guttering] level with the top o' the cliff or you'd git the chimney stacks level wi the top o' the cliff. See, an' you mustn't tow in between.[55] How long you towed all depended on the distance you wanted to

---

53 Trawling successfully for shrimps necessitated covering the ground slowly, in order for the gear to work effectively.

54 There are mixed references regarding time-scale in the last three sentences of this paragraph. The hammerhead end of the Claremont Pier (built originally for the Belle Steamers to take on and discharge passengers) was removed at the beginning of World War Two, so as not to provide the Germans with an easy landing-stage should they have invaded! The Bird's Eye food-processing factory was not established in Lowestoft until after the war.

55 This was because the ground had obstructions and a trawl would either come fast or be damaged.

cover. I mean, I hev shot at Claremont Pier an' gone right up to Pontin's [Holiday Camp], and thass a good three-quarters of an hour towin', but not so long motorin' back.

"They were Dover soles you used to git. An' we hev hed a spare turbot or two. Oh yeah, but they were never very big—about a foot or fifteen inches wuz the usual size. No brills, though. No. You mainly got the *soles*, the *dabs* and the *plaice*. A chance *skate*, maybe, but they never used to be very big. These were the smooth-skinned ones, the skate. You never got a great lot o' flounders neither, but you'd git several *eels*. Oh yeah. Well, o' course, when you're towin' along the bottom, you get all sorts. I mean, we hev hed a *John o' Dora* [John Dory] inside here. Oh yeah. Mind yuh, that wuz small, but we've hed one. Now, *cucumber smelts*, we used to git no end o' them. An' them lesser weevers. You'd git loads o' them, a-shrimpin', and plenty o' crabs. We even used to git good lobsters, but my mother allus had them.

"Now, them rocks I mentioned earlier—them there Hubbard's Rocks—they're bin sunk a long time now.They don't hardly exist now, not above the sea bed. See, the beach has bin scoured out so much that the rocks eventually sunk, and now the beach has built up agin and the rocks are covered up altogether. But there used to be *crabs* and *lobsters* round them. We never set *pots* for 'em, though. See, the trouble wi' crab pots and that sort o' thing round here is that they git sanded up so much, for the simple reason that you're got so much shiftin' sand. The sea bed shift about so much, and if you worked a pot you can guarantee you were goin' to lose it some time or other. We hed trouble wi' weed sometimes as well. There's bin times when we hauled lines an' thass bin like a two and a half inch rope! But you take all that in yuh stride.

"There were little patches where we used to tow reg'lar for soles. Yeah, we used to start from just below here, with the Claremont Pier winder [window] lined up on St. John's Church [tower], and then tow until we got up abrist o' those wooden steps down the cliff near the caravan site at Arbor Lane. Then we'd set orf out a little from there and git the Birdsye chimney in the centre o' the pavilion on the South Pier an' work up from there. You hed to git that just right, because there's a wreck abrist o' Pontin's, and thass bin there a number o' years and there's bin a lot o' trawls lost on it. Yeah, I've even lost one meself! And once you git on it, you dun't git orf!

"I used to git some good ol' *gran'father soles*, what'd got beards on! Yeah, yeah. They used to be a couple o' foot long, some of 'em! Yeah, gret big ol'—well, we used to call 'em gran'father soles. We used to git hundreds o' *slips* as well. Oh, you allus got more slips than you did soles. And you could sell 'em, provided they were the nine inches [length]. Then, from slips you went down to *tongues*. Well, you wun't supposed to land tongues, so we used to smuggle them hoom and then hev a right good ol' fry-up.[56] I dun't think I ever caught a lemon sole, but I used to git plenty o' whitins in the shrimp trawl right throughout the season.[57] A lot of 'em were *slinky*, though, because there used to like a maggot or a worm in the gill. We used to look at 'em carefully if they were slinky, because I allus used to bring whitin' hoom for the dog. We used to git a few *pout whitin'* in the shrimp-trawl as well, but they were never no size.

"I hev sin the time, when I've bin towin' up orf Pontin's with a fish-trawl, that I've hed a bag o' dabs as much as I could pull in over the side! Mind you, they were big and small dabs together, and you had a lot of other rubbish in with 'em. You had to pick out what wuz accordin' to size. Seven inches used to be the measurement for dabs in them days and what wuz big enough to sell, well, you used to take 'em down the market. You never got many big plaice inside, though. They used to be just out, inside o' the Newcome [Newcome Sand] there, the fore part o' the year. I used to sell my shrimps on the market as well, but I also used to sell five or six *peck* round here. Oh yes, there's an art in boilin' a shrimp and I could easily git rid o' five or six peck around here—no bother at all. Most of 'em used to down to Cole, the fish merchant [J.T. Cole Ltd.], and he used to take the soles and all. I used to boil the shrimps aboard. I had a propane gas bottle an' a boiler, and the propane hed a special burner so that you got a fierce force of flame.

"There used to be quite a good sale for *smelts* in pre-war days. Mind yuh, this is goin' back to 1925, 1930. There used to be little heaps o' smelts on the market, which used to be sold. Oh, they're beau'iful, cucumber smelts! And you dun't taste a bit o' cucumber either. I mean, if you git a cucumber smelt in a boat, you soon know you're got it because that stink the boat out. Oh yes, as soon as you're got one in your net and bring it aboard, you can smell it. The boys used to go down to the harbour and the market and catch 'em on their bent pins, but orf here you'd git 'em in herrin' nets and shrimp trawls. If you wanted *mullet* [Grey Mullet] or *bass* orf here, you'd hefta shoot hook an' line—but people never used to fish for 'em, 'cause you could never git rid on 'em! No, there wuz no demand for mullet or bass. Thass only these last few years they seem to ha' caught on an' people ha' bin fishin' for 'em. They never used to sell in the old times."

Longlining, drift-netting and *beam-trawling*: the account of longshore activity is almost at an end. Only the *draw-net* and its use remain before the list is complete. And whereas all the other modes of fishing required only one or two people in the boat (usually the latter), draw-netting required the efforts of four men in order to be effective.[58] The net itself was a long *seine*, with corks spaced along the *head-*

---

56 Very small soles were below the regulation length for catching and sale, but they were also extremely tasty.

57 Shrimps constitute part of the diet of whitings.

58 For an explanation of the draw net and its various forms along the English and Welsh coasts, see Davis, *Fishing Gear*, pp. 65-6.

line and small lead weights set periodically on the *foot-rope*. Two men held one end of the net on shore, while two others went out in the boat, one of them rowing a semi-circular course and the other paying out the net. Once it had returned to the beach, the boat was grounded and the two crewmen took hold of the other end of the net, which was then pulled in towards the shore, trapping any fish that came within its compass. Jimmy Fisher ends his lengthy and detailed account of longshoring from Pakefield beach with a description of draw-netting.

"The *draw-nettin'* we did wuz mainly after trout. *Sea trout*.[59] There used to be four men on that, 'cause the net wuz 100 yards long. That'd be nine foot deep at both ends and twelve foot deep in the centre. And that used to made out o' mackerel net. Yeah, and then you hed a *net barrer* [barrow] (or just the top of it), which you stored the net on, and then that laid acrorss the stern o' the boat. You left two men ashore and they would hold the shore end an' keep the net inta the beach time time the other two shot the net and brought it back inta the beach. There'd be one man *a-rowin'* and one *shootin' the net*. Now, the two men on the beach, they'd be walkin' along as the tide carried the net up. You fished with the tide; you'd never pull aginst it. You just hed *lead pellets* along the bottom, every four or five foot, and *flat corks* along the top. There wuz a *net-rope* on the top and then you had *bridles* (that is, two ropes) on each end—one from the top o' the net and one from the bottom—and they were connected up to one main rope. The bridles were about thirty foot long.

"I spuz by the time you shot the net and by the time you got it in, you'd cover a distance of about 100 yards up or down the beach. That'd take about three-quarters of an hour altogether. Yeah, I mean, haulin' only took about twenty minutes. What used to take the longest wuz sortin' the net out after you'd got it ashore, then stowin' it onta the net barrer afore you shot away agin. This wuz a *night fishin'*—night fishin' in the summertime. That used to be from May right through till September for trout. You dint git many usually, but I hev hed as many as forty, big and small, in one night's fishin'. That wuz me, Danny Allen, Fred Cable and Umshie Thompson. We used to go reg'lar, Friday nights. That would all depend, but we're bin out all night sometimes. See, that would all depend how the fish were. And wi' trout, you had to have it fairly still. You used to git a sole or two sometimes, and I have adapted the net so that the *norsels* were right tight down to the *ground-rope* so that there wuz no space for fish to git between.

"I know one time there, one partic'lar night, they were gittin' a taste o' *soles* (I wasn't present at the time) and were shot right on the dead low water so that the net wuz out onta the flats. And in one drag they brought a *conger eel* up! That wuz about six foot long, but I wasn't present at the time so I never did see the fish. They buried it up on the cliff, in one o' the gardens. There hev bin odd times when

---

59 The sea trout and brown trout are one and the same (*Salmo trutta*), the former simply being one which spends part of its life in the sea.

we were draw-nettin' for trout that we hed so many *horse mackerel* in the net that we had to let the ground-rope go and spill 'em out because we couldn't git the net ashore. And then we had to stand on the beach an' pick 'em out because, as you know, a horse mackerel has got a spike for'ad and one aft.[60] Anyway, I picked out half-a-dozen o' the biggest an' brought 'em hoom, skinned 'em an' filleted 'em, rolled 'em in flour [prior to frying them] and they were beau'iful!

"In the old days, we used to go draw-nettin' in November for *codlin'*. Oh yis. Yis, you could git codlin'. But the only trouble today is that you can't use a draw-net on the beach now because there's so many fishin' leads [weights] bin lorst out there and you can't git clear of 'em.[61] Like I said, I have had as many as many as forty trout in a night. And I believe I've still got a bill upstairs for the last two trout I caught—though that wuz in a *drift-net*! That wuz pre-war days an' just after the war that I used to go for trout. You could git 'em up to a couple o' foot long or so. Oh yeah, five or six pound, seven pound—and that wuz a good un, if you got one that size. Yeah, you mainly got 'em a pound an' a half, two pound—that sort o' weight. They used to go down to the market. Oh yeah, the only time you hed a buyer up here wuz when they were out o' season. I shouldn't ought to ha' said that, should I!"

---

60 This is a reference to the spines on the front of the first and second dorsal fins, which can inflict a painful puncture on the hands and would have snagged up in the meshes of the net.

61 This was one of the results of the increasing popularity of rod-and-line fishing from the beach—especially during the autumn and winter months.

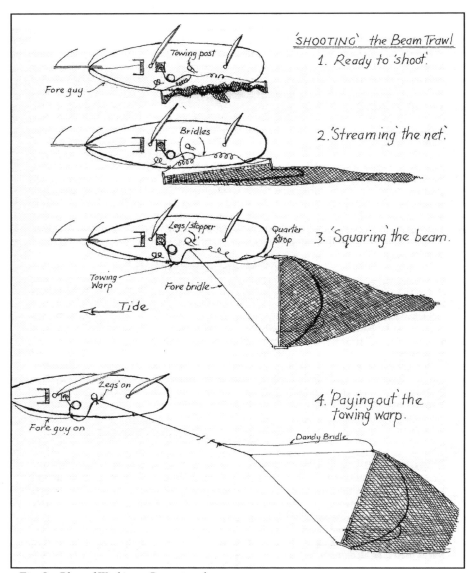

Fig. 5: Plan of Working a Beam-trawl

The drawing shows the basic method of working a beam-trawl from a smack. This method of fishing covered the ground slowly (c. two knots or so), which was far less injurious to the quality of catches than steam trawling. It dates back to the second half of the 14th century.

CHAPTER SIX

A Right Old Blow!

Oh, it's threescore and ten boys and men
Were lost from Grimsby town.
From Yarmouth down to Scarborough
Many hundreds more were drowned.
In herring boats and trawlers and fishing smacks as well,
They had to fight the bitter night and battle with the swell.
(W. Delf: *Threescore and Ten*)

Two vessels, above all others, serve to symbolise Lowestoft's fishing industry during the twentieth century—the *steam drifter* and the sailing trawler, or *smack*. Each type of craft developed its own mythology almost, coming to represent not only a particular way of making a living but also a distinctive way of life. The sailing smack did not continue its working life beyond the outbreak of the Second World War (though a number of motorised ones operated well into the 1950s), but the folklore surrounding it continued as part of Lowestoft's collective memory for decades after it had ceased to put to sea and has still not entirely disappeared from some people's consciousness. The purpose of this chapter is not to investigate in detail the method of trawling carried out by sailing smacks on the favoured North Sea fishing grounds, but to recount some personal experiences from a man who spent his later teenage years working on board such craft.[1]

Edward ("Ted") Quantrill (1911-88) was not a career fisherman, for want of a better term, but he went to sea during the later 1920s and never forgot his time on the sailing smacks. He was well known in Lowestoft, over many years, as an entertainer, largely due to his prowess on the chromatic accordion, which he played entirely by ear with great verve and heavy rhythmic swell. His repertoire of tunes was enormous and consisted largely of popular songs, music hall items and revivalist hymns (his wife belonged to the Salvation Army), many of which he sang in his characteristic high-tenor voice.[2] Another claim to fame locally for him was that he was one of the twenty-seven people arrested for his part in the so-called *Town Hall Raid* of 8 May 1933—a fracas that resulted from a protest march made by about 100 unemployed men, complaining about the withdrawal of

---

1 For an explanation of the working of a beam trawl, see Davis, *Fishing Gear*, pp. 88-95, and Butcher, *Trawlermen*, Chapter Two. The latter source also includes a number of details concerning life on board sailing smacks. Another very useful reference is W. Finch, *The Sea in My Blood* (Weybread, 1992).

2 Ted Quantrill may be heard on at least one compilation of Suffolk folk musicians: *Songs Sung in Suffolk, Vol. 5* (Veteran Tapes, VT 105, 1989).

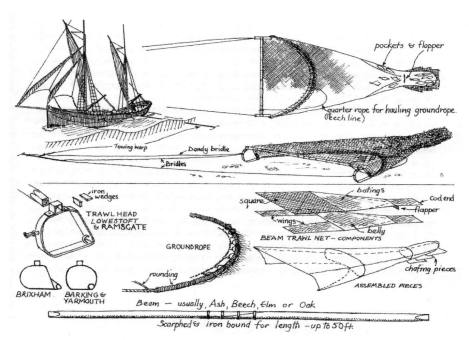

Fig. 6 : Beam-trawl details

Line-drawings showing the make-up and operation of a beam-trawl. In 1376, the earliest-recorded type (known as a "wondyrchoun") was blamed for the depletion of fish-stocks in the Thames Estuary. The length of the beam at that time was 8-10 feet long, compared with the 40-50 feet used on board the larger Lowestoft smacks.

the *coal relief voucher*.[3] Always a colourful character, Ted Quantrill had an ironic way of looking at what went on around him and a singular way of expressing himself (tape-recording made, 5 July 1983).

"My first job, leavin' school at fourteen, was for a deaf and dumb man by the name o' Mr. Pretty—21, Alexandra Road. He wuz a brother to George Pretty, the coal merchant, and he wuz an expert upholsterer. Yes, I wuz with him and I wuz gittin' 6s 6d a week [32½p], and he writ me a letter out to take hoom. Well, I wuz nosey, so I opened it and that said, 'Dear Mrs. Quantrill, your boy is a fine lad—honest, etc., etc. I would like him to come apprentice.' See, Mr. Herbert Cook, who belonged to the Elim [Pentecostal] Church wuz just out o' his time. Full tradesman. Yeah, and I read the letter an' took it hoom, and my mother said, 'They're goin' to cut yuh down to five shillins [5s = 25p], but that'll save the *indenture money*.' Which wuz £50 then![4] Silly fule, I dint take it! Not my fault, though—my mother's! She said, 'Ted, thass no good. Try and git somethin'

---

3 A full account of this incident may be found in Butcher, *Living from the Sea*, Chapter Six.

4 This refers to the premium payment, customarily made by the parents of any boy or girl about to embark upon an apprenticeship.

better.' So I ran away to sea. I'd bin with Mr. Pretty about a year, so I wuz about fifteen.

"The first *smack* I went in wuz the *Pilot Jack* (LT 1212). Belonged to Mr. Arthur Podd. LT 1212. New Scotland Yard's number, one-two, one-two.[5] Skipper's name, Bradley Soloman. Twenty-two stone and never saw down the *fish-room*. Couldn't git down! Ha, ha, ha, ha, ha. Truth! I used to hetta clean his fish afore I went hoom, him and the mate's, and they used to give me tuppence [2d, or 1p] each.[6] A penny each way the tram [i.e. to and from the fish market]—a penny there and a penny back—and don't be late in the mornin' 'cause we're sailin' on the tide. Right? I wuz *cook*, yeah. And you'd gotta be one, too! That wuz yuh job. After a bit, I come out o' the *Pilot Jack* and went cook in the *Ivan* (LT 1098). Mr. Podd agin, so I couldn't ha' bin too bad. Skipper's name. Leggy Foster—one o' the toughest smack skippers in this town. Do yuh know what I've sin him do? Honest! May I never move from this armchair! I've sin him take a whitin' (or any *long fish*), when we were *split*, an' hoist that up the *jib halyard*. Right? Then he'd shout, 'Come down, you ol' bastard, if you think you're more entitled to fish than we are! Come down!' And thass the truth. And Lou Cook, who wuz mate, he dint go much on that. He liked a drink and he wun't religious, but he dint do that sort o' thing. No, he wun't blarspheme like that.[7]

"I wuz in the *Ivan* about eighteen months, and then up we come to Mr. Podd's firm agin—a ship called the *Energic* (LT 1195). I wuz in her quite a time. Harry Blowers wuz the skipper and he wuz a tough bloke. Got a medal there once, for towin' a ship in. And I wuz cleanin' his fish one day, and the mate's, and he come to me and say, 'Teddy, hev yuh finished cleanin' mine and Wally's fish?' I say, 'Yis, skipper.' He say, 'Well, we want you down the cabin. We're got a discussion on.' He say, 'They're nearly all *dressed*. But I want you down before you git dressed.'[8] So I went down the cabin and there they all set. 'All right, skipper. Hev I got the sack?' (Just for a laugh, like!) He say, 'You hent got the sack, ol' son. Will you come in the *Dusky Queen* (LT 895)? Transfer.' She wuz a *tosher*. Carried four men in the winter and three in the summer, 'cause three men could do the work o' four in good weather. I say, 'Whass it all about then, skipper? Comin' out o' a big smack. I'm gittin' on lovely. Riddy to go *deckie*, and I're gotta come out.' He say, 'Well, you're goin' to better yuhself. We're hevin' a motor put in, and we want

---

5 Whitehall 1212 ("one-two, one-two") was the telephone number of the Metropolitan Police headquarters at one time. It was periodically heard on BBC radio programmes, when it was given as the contact number for any response made to emergency items in news bulletins.

6 This refers to the allowance of fish given to crew members.

7 It was not unknown for some fishing skippers to challenge the Almighty if things went wrong or catches were poor. Such behaviour tended to leave church-going members of the crew feeling uneasy.

8 The reference here is to the crew members having changed from their working clothes into conventional attire, prior to going home at the end of a trip.

you to come *cook an' deckie* at the same time. You'll do yuh cookin' and work on deck as well.' That wuz bloody hard work, I'll tell yuh! But I took it 'cause I got more money. Yeah, I got my cook's pay and half a deckie's wage on top.

"Now, the engine wuz put in at Richards.[9] She laid there approximately six weeks and then we went out on our trials. Now, the man what wuz hid o' the motor side o' Podd's ships wuz Mr. King, and he come out with us and we done all right. We wuz averagin' eight or nine knots. That wuz good, that wuz. Then he come out for a full trip, to see how the engine worked, and I hetta see after him. He pillowed up on deck under the bow, rather than come down below, and we rigged up a canvas shelter for him. Luckily, that wuz dead calm for the whole o' the eight days, and after he'd got over his little bit o' sickness I saw after him for his meals. We hed the full crew aboard, but he come out a-supervisin' the engine. He only come out that one trip and he wuz satisfied, and he give me £1 for my trouble.

"Now, a man by the name o' Fisher wuz *chief engineer* and I, bein' cook and deckie, hetta go and help him pump the *bottles* up.[10] And when he wun't down below, if anything happened, I used to hefta go and tell him and go back down with him and learn a bit. So if he couldn't be there, I knew what to do. After a time, we got a full cook and I went full deckie. But after about four trips the orffice found that din't pay, so they got rid o' the cook and I hetta go back to bein' deckie-cook agin. We tried a *beam-trawl* to start with, but then they put *otter-boards* in 'cause they found that the *otter-trawl* wuz best. That wuz a slickin' gret motor we hed; too big for her, really. That used to shake the guts out o' yuh! She wuz only a little ol' tosher, so they cut the engine down. I dun't know how they did it, but Mr. King come out with us agin. We used to go right down orf Cromer and that way, the sairme as the [sailing] smacks did. And when the fish finished down there (they're like us; they travel about), we used to go what they call *Up and Along*. That wuz south about. Yeah, we used to go up to the Galloper [Galloper Bank], the Hinder [North Hinder Bank], right up as far as the Thames Estuary.[11]

Now, can I say somethin' in regards to sail? O' course, I can! When you go deckie, you're responsible for a *watch* and you're gotta know a *lee tide* from a *weather* one. Common sense would tell yuh that anyway. A lee tide is runnin' with the wind; a *weather tide* is runnin' agin it. Now, when we wanted to *shoot* on a weather tide, we used to hetta take the *warp* and the other ropes round the stern—

---

9   Richards Ironworks Ltd., shipbuilders and marine engineers, Horn Hill. This famous company, located on the southern shore of Lowestoft's inner harbour, had been established in 1876 by Samuel Richards, a young Cornish shipwright from Penzance.

10 Bottles of compressed air, which were used to turn diesel engines over until they fired.

11 The Galloper and the Hinder were fishing grounds near sandbanks, about twenty-five miles and forty miles east of Clacton. Fishing on grounds off the Norfolk coast occupied the summer months; working off the Essex coast was done during the winter.

an' that wuz hard work![12] Big as your arm, the warp wuz! Oh yeah. Six strands o' wire and rope. We used to tow six hours and the ol' skipper allus used to be holdin' onta the warp, so he could feel how the trawl wuz a-goin'. Now, when you hauled, if you wuz cook, you hetta go down below and *coil* the warp. Oh, that wuz heavy work. Not bloody much that wun't! That wuz like manual work ashore, only longer hours. Oh, hellishly long once you started buggerin' about wi' *reefs* and things like that. See, that wuz the cook's job to *reeve the pennants* through the holes and make a figure-eight knot so that couldn't pull through. Yeah, as soon as that come on a breeze o'wind, you'd put a reef in. And if that come on more wind, you'd put two in. Now, if that really started to blow, you'd reef yuh *fores'l* as well as the *main*. And praps you'd put a smaller *jib* out. Say you'd got a *seven-clorth* one on, you'd hefta go and hunt for a *five-clorth*. I know! I're done it. But I dint mind. That wuz better'n standin' about in the three million dole queue at that time o' day, wun't it?

"Another thing you hetta do, when you wuz cook, wuz keep an eye on the *boiler* and see what steam she'd got by the gauge-glass. You hetta build that up so you'd got about 100, 120, pound [i.e. pounds per square inch pressure] for the next haul.[13] Or any emergencies. Then, as soon as the crew hed done haulin', they all wanted a drop o' tea. You made that in the ol' *shoe* [shoe-kettle]. Yeah, you allus hed yuh shoe in the boiler, ready to use. Sometimes, if that wuz cold, you'd mairke a hot pot o' cocoa. *Thames Mud* we used to call it! Ha, ha, ha, ha, ha! An' if that wuz right cold, ol' Harry Blowers in the *Energic* used to hev a drop o' hoom-made mustard in it. In the cocoa! Oh yis, there wuz mustard in there. He liked his mustard, he did. 'Are yuh mairkin' cocoa, boy?' (O' course, if you wuz cook on a smack an' you were sixty year old, you were still 'the boy'. That dint matter how old you were.) 'Yis, skipper.' 'Easy on the sugar, then. We might be out another couple o' days.' Yeah, if you run out o' anything, you were in trouble.

"If you felt like it, you could go up on deck and *gut*. That wun't forced work, like when you were deckie, but sometimes they wanted yuh to help. I used to try and git ahid o' my cookin' the day before, if I could. Beef puddins used to hefta be made second day out, anyway, when the meat wuz fresh. We used to make 'em in an enamel platter and tie 'em up in a clorth. We dint make bread on board, though, and if we run short we'd hev *sea biscuits*. The biguns. Yeah, with all the holes in. Give 'em about a minute's soakin' [in water] and then fry 'em or bake 'em in the oven. Most o' the grub wuz cooked in the *beef-kettle*. That wuz a big, cast-iron, oval-shaped pot, with handles each end—more like a gipsy's cauldron. Yeah, and we used to put everything in there, tied up in clorths—though at different times,

---

12 Lowestoft smacks customarily worked their trawls off the port side, so shooting on a weather tide meant moving the gear round to starboard after it had been released in order to avoid the maximum turbulence of wind and tide working against each other.

13 A smack's upright boiler provided the power for the steam capstan, which wound in the trawl's warp and performed other lifting operations on board.

o' course.

"We used to eat a lot o' *steamed dumplins*—unless we hed a stew on, when there used to be *light duff*. What you did wuz lay a puddin' clorth on the table (but make sure thass clean first, afore yuh git the sack!) and make up yuh dumplins for steamin'. You used to hetta put bakin' powder in and you only made the five. Only five. Oh yes! Yes, flour might be short. See, just one each. You'd sprinkle some water on yuh puddin' clorth, put yuh five dumplins on, tie yuh four corners up and then tie them ends to the handle o' beef-kettle's lid afore you put the lid back on. See, yuh dumplins must not touch the water, 'cause they'd go heavy. And the reason for cookin' 'em like that wuz that if you hed a long job up on deck, you could leave 'em two hours—as long as yuh water wuz boilin'. An' when you took 'em out, they'd bounce. Lovely!

"That wuz all fresh grub every trip, what you had of it. There wun't a lot, but what you had wuz fresh. I're heard some o' the boys say that some o' the boats hed an orange box for the groceries. Well, we hed a margarine box—and that wuz it![14] There'd be about three tins o' condensed milk, three or four pounds o' flour—and you hetta look in the flour locker first for that, 'cause if you dint want any you mustn't order any. Then there'd be tea an' sugar and that. The meat used to come down sep'rate; so did the vegetables. I said earlier about how we made the tea, in the shoe, but sometimes we used a kettle. Tea, milk an' sugar, all in together.[15] Just too bad if some of 'em dint like sugar! Oh yeah, we allus carried a kettle and put that on the stove. There used to be four iron bars round the top o' the stove and they'd stop the beef-kettle from rollin' about. Yeah, but the water'd come out when the boat rolled! One thing I never could mairke out wuz how a dish-clorth (you know, a wool one, like some o' the ol' chiefs used to wear round their necks for a sweat-rag) would stop things movin'. That dint matter how much wind you hed, if you put one o' them down on the floor and put yuh kettle on it, that'd never move. The bloody pan used to slide about, though—the pan for yuh fish.

"See, we hed trawl-fish every mornin' for breakfast. Every mornin'! You used to hetta git all the smallest ones you could find. You'd even open the bloody *pockets* o' the trawl to find 'em! When we sorted the fish out, we hed a thing called a *thole*. That wuz a bit o' pointed stick, which you stirred the fish about with so you dint git stung by a bloody weever. The deckie used to make 'em; the cook used to

---

14 A margarine box was a lot smaller than an orange box.

15 This particular brew was commented on by Ernest Holt, the eminent late nineteenth century marine biologist, in relation to vessels sailing out of Grimsby. He deemed it capable of giving a person "most of the sensations of sea-sickness without the trouble of going to sea". See E.W.L Holt, 'An Examination of the Present State of the Grimsby Trawl Fishery', in *Journal of the Marine Biological Association of the United Kingdom*, new series 3, (1895), pp. 337-448.

make 'em. Tholes.[16] Yeah, you used them instead o' yuh fingers, 'cause you never wore gloves. Oh, moost o' the small stuff went for grub in a smack, I can assure you o' that. Yeah, an' now and agin, if we hed a couple o' *rooker* [Thornback Ray] to spare, we used to clean 'em, skin 'em, put taters at the bottom o' the water and boil the rooker wi' the taters. The one thing you couldn't touch wuz *soles* an' *turbot*. The ol' man or the mate allus used to look after them.[17] The little ol' *jinny rooker* were stockie, if we got enough. We used to tie all the tails up an' tow 'em orf the stern o' the boat so they skinned easier. We used to tow an ol' *fiddle-fish* out astern as well.[18] Yeah, out on the lee side, if the wind wuz right.

"We used to git mainly the *rough stuff* for stockie, like gurnets and weevers. There wuz never enough o' one sort to do any good.[19] You know what I mean? We never called it *stockie*, neither. That wuz the real name, but we called it *dust*. Yeah. 'How much dust did yuh git, boy?' You know, when we met. 'How much dust did yuh git?' Sometimes we hetta go to the company orffice 'cause they wun't let the ol'man bring yuh the dust. No, some of 'em used to open the packets and tairke money out. There wuz one or two like that. O' course, you never earned £100 for a trip. Not in a smack. No, I can never remember it. £60 or £70 wuz a good earnin'.

"When I wuz in the *Energic*, we come in one Friday afternoon (I'll allus remember it) and landed on the Saturday and we made £75! Now, that night I went down the street along o' the young lady I wuz courtin'. She wuz a Salvationist and wore the uniform, and I backed a winner there. Married forty-nine years. And as we walked past the press office, that wuz on the fly-sheets outside: 'Smack beats all records—£75.' I wish I'd kept that 'Evenin' News'.[20] That'd bin worth a little money today, wun't it? £75. That wuz a trip, that wuz. Yeah, and we got half-a-crown [2s 6d, = 12½p] stockie as well. When I wuz single and got a shillin' [1s = 5p] stockie, I used to walk up Clapham Road to git hoom to Jacob's Street. But if I hed two bob [2s = 10p] or half-a-crown, I used to run hoom! Yeah, I used to run like hell up Clapham Road, holdin' that bloody half-crown! That wuz a lot o'

16 A thole (or thole-pin) was one of a pair of wooden pegs, which fitted into the top of a boat's gunwale and acted as a fulcrum point for an oar. The implement referred to here was obviously similar in size and shape. In fact, it is likely that thole-pins were used for the purpose described—hence the name.

17 Sole and turbot were the two most valuable trawlfish species and were therefore always treated with extra care.

18 Jinny Roker were small rays, especially the Starry Ray (*Raja radiata*). The fiddle-fish, or Angel ray (*Squatina squatina*), was a small shark whose shape roughly resembled that of a violin. It was believed to be a harbinger of good luck and, if caught, was traditionally towed off the stern of a smack.

19 In other words, there was never a sufficient quantity of any one species to make a respectable price on the market.

20 *The Eastern Evening News*, together with *The Eastern Daily Press* and *The Lowestoft Journal* were published at the Norfolk News Co. Ltd. office at 147, London Road North, Lowestoft.

money. I wuz only gittin' sixteen bob [16s = 80p] a week, yuh see.

"When I wuz in the *Flower o' Devon* (LT 302), along o' Teddy Pickess, we come in one day when all the trawlers come in white. Ice! Yeah, we come in and we couldn't git our sails down. All the *sheave blocks* up the top were all frooze up. Honest! May I never move from where I'm a-sittin'! She wuz a *tosher*. Belonged to Mr. Harry Painter. She hed four crew in the winter and three in the summer. And we never had a table in her. You used to hefta hev yuh grub on a rush mat on the cabin floor! Thass poor bloody seamanship really, ent it—the floor? And I say to Teddy Pickess one day, 'Why is it that I hefta lay on the *locker*?' That wuz the one down the cabin which hed all the bloody spare gear. 'What have I gotta sleep on that for?' O' course, you only hed one blanket, which you brought from hoom. 'Well,' he say, 'if you go in that bloody bunk,' he say, 'the bugs'll turn yuh out!'[21] An' thass the truth, yeah. A lot o' the ol' skippers used to sleep on top o' the grub locker, so if you were goin' to pinch somethin' they'd hev yuh.[22] And where you kept the flour used to be full o' bloody weevils! You wuz eatin' weevils all the time, wun't yuh? Yeah, they lived in the flour and you couldn't sift all them buggers out, could yuh?

"The worst thing that ever happened to me on board a smack wuz on the *Nelson* (LT 459). I'll allus remember it, 'cause when you're between life and death you never forget. Spot Howes wuz skipper and a man by the name o' Kemp, from Kirkley, wuz mate. I dint know his other name, and we used to hetta call him 'Mr. Mate' and all! Spot Howes's brother wuz third hand (I think his name wuz George), George Fisher wuz deckhand and I wuz cook. Now, this wuz in the autumn—about October time. 1928. And I can remember it as if it wuz today. We went out with a medium wind, about south by south-west. That wuz a Wednesday. Got out without a *tug*. Yeah, 'cause at times we hetta be towed out.[23] We wuz bound down, for Cromer. Yeah, the Cromer Knoll. And we'd got a few mile out—near the Cockle, I believe [Cockle Sand]—and a big ship wuz on our starboard side goin' south about, which wuz opposite to us.[24] We were goin' north about, see. That wuz one o' them big ol' Dutchmen, with all the little boys aboard what'd

---

21 Fishing craft, whether driven by sail or mechanical means, were notorious for harbouring bed bugs and were periodically fumigated by the local council—a process which only gave crew members a temporary respite.

22 Trawler skippers and mates, on both sailing vessels and steam-driven craft, were paid an agreed share of the net value of the catch after all expenses had been met. If the crew's food bill for the trip rose above a certain level, boatowners deducted the excess from the skipper's share. This was an incentive to keep food consumption (and therefore expenses) down.

23 Tugs were used to tow sailing vessels out of port when there was not enough wind for them to make way or when strong winds from the east were blowing directly into the harbour.

24 The Cockle Gat was two or three miles out from Yarmouth harbour entrance, near the Scroby Sands.

Plate 10: Nelson (LT 459)

The Lowestoft smack "Nelson" (LT 459), leaving port, fully gaff-rigged and with the foresail set. The wooden structure off her port bow was a lookout tower on the Fish Market, known as "The Mount".

hardly left school. We used to call 'em *workhouse ships*.[25] I dun't know why. They used to be out two or three months at a time, driftin' an' trawlin'. That all depended what season it wuz. They used to process the fish on board—ice 'em or whatever they did at that time o' day; *pickle* 'em. Yeah, he come up on our starboard side an' shouted to our skipper, who had the *tiller*. He shouted through a megaphone, 'Plenty o' wind down below!' [i.e. northwards] And the further out we got, the more that come on to blow.

"We got somewhere down north o' the North Float. Thass the *Haisborough* [a lightship].[26] Then she really come on to blow. We hed one haul that night. Yeah, we got far enough orf to hev one haul and we got about a basket an' a half o' fish altogether. We never got no more. And we dint tow the six hours [the length of a tide]; we hauled an' started *reefin'*. And, like I say, that wuz the Wednesday. Now, a normal trip wuz approximately eight days in a big smack and there wuz no such thing as callin' in, 'We're comin' in!' because we hed no wireless, no wheelhouse, no nothin'. The only things we relied on wuz a *leadline*, and the times o' yuh tides,

---

25 This is possibly a reference back to the 1870s and 80s, when the trawling fleets from Hull and Grimsby took on apprentices from English workhouses. It was at this time that the expression *sentenced to the Dogger* came into being, to describe the appalling conditions on board ship.

26 The *Haisborough Lightship* was about ten miles north by east from the coastal village of that name, which is actually spelt Happisburgh. In order to avoid confusion among mariners, charts have long used phonetic spelling to represent the word.

and a mariner's *compass*.

"Now then, the first night, we put put one *reef* in. Next night, we had two. And that wun't long afore we hed three! Fore an' aft! And that blew that hard we hetta have not only third reefs, but we hetta lower down as much sail as we could. You can't git any more'n three reefs down. That wuz the lot. And the *storm jib* wuz out after the five-clorth one, and you can't git no further'n that. Yeah, we got the storm jib out and made that nice an' tight. And that come on to blow so hard that we couldn't go about, and we couldn't *kneel* [heel over], an' we couldn't do nothin'. We definitely couldn't *shoot*. The trawl now lay dormant, if thass the word. All lashed up, o' course. An' I never took my *oily* orf, for what?—I'd say twelve days! And thass the only smack I ever went in where I see the mate and the skipper go down at the table and pray to the Lord. And if them men were alive now, or any of 'em—. Believe me, I know what I'm talkin' about. That wuz that bad.

"I remember, one night, standin' along o' the skipper, alongside the *tiller*, and I hed a *lashin'* round me what led down below—tied to the *sansom post*, which wuz in the cabin, aft-side. That wuz part o' the mizzen [mast]. I wuz lashed to that. And I'd sometimes hefta take the lashin' orf to do a job the best way I could. The skipper hed a *double-takle lashin'* on the tiller, and the words that man said to me—I'll never forget it. Somehow we were both down below together; I dun't know how it happened. But he say to me, 'Ted, look there. Look.' An' there wuz two of 'em on the tiller, with that lashin' holdin' it.[27] And he say to me, 'Ted, if we ever git out o' this, I shall never go smackin' no more!' And he didn't. He went driftin'. But I can't remember the name o' the first ship he went in.

"Oh, that wuz terrible! See, we couldn't *lay up*. The wind wuz about sou'west, so we couldn't pull her round to the south. We were goin' north! We couldn't really lay down to sleep neither. We more or less slept standin' up. You can do that when you're really tired out. We finished up right down past the Wash, down Grimsby way. We hed easy seventy mile to come back! Oh yeah, we hetta run. If we'd ha' went about, and went southerly, we wun't ha' bin here now. No, we'd ha' took *dollop after dollop* and the *scuppers* wun't ha' contended with it. We were all frightened. Dun't worry about that!

"I remember one night, standin' under the *dodger* alongside o'the ol' man, ol' Spot Howes. And the mate wuz along o' him at the double tiller. And a bloody gret boat come acrorss our stern—what we used to call *east-and-west boats*. They were like a bloody train, on a schedule. They'd go acrorss to Holland after the butter and bring it back, and they'd take somethin' out there—export, import. That come right acrorss our stern and you could nearly touch it! And that wuz [lit up] like a town. You'd think that wuz Low'stoft Central Station or suffin, wi'

---

27 A relieving tackle was used on a smack's tiller in heavy weather to assist with control of the steering.

trains comin' in.[28] And he sung out through an electric thing, he did: 'Everything all right aboard? Everything all right? Are you sure?' And I say to the skipper, 'Is that one o' the east-and-west boats?' He say, 'I believe it is, Ted. Yeah, boy. I believe it is one o' the east-and-west boats.' An' we watched him right out o' sight, like a train. And I thought to myself, 'I wish I wuz on him!'

"We got back inta Low'stoft two Wednesdays after we started out. Yeah, we went out on the Wednesday and we come in the Wednesday mornin', approximately. Now, how many days is that? Thass fourteen days. We were six days overdue. They all thought we were gone. When we got in, that wuz half-past three in the mornin' and ol' Long Taylor, Slater and Barnard's manager and *ship's husband*, say to me, 'Hello. How're yuh gittin on, Ted?' I say, 'I dun't really know. But dun't go down below,' I say, 'because I hent scrubbed out.' He say, 'Scrubbin' out is out o' the question. Dun't worry about scrubbin' out!' He say, 'We're goin' to take yuh in Bob Clow's for a hot meal.' That wuz a cafe near the market. But George Fisher and me dint go. We wanted to git hoom. Yeah.

"Now, when I got hoom, I'll allus remember my mother. She wuz sittin' up in bed with a shawl round her what I'd bought orf a Scottishman. A Scotch lady knitted it for her and I give a few shillins for it.[29] She wuz cryin' her eyes out. She hadn't bin to sleep for over a week, my mother—doin' the housework, the lot. The ol' man, my father, wuz down at the Market. You couldn't see Low'stoft Market for people! There wuz the old Trawl Dock full; they were all round the main Market and the Hamilton Dock; the North Extension wuz full o' people; and so were the South Pier and Yacht Basin. Oh, there wuz people everywhere yuh looked, all waitin'! We were one o' the last boats in. There wun't many out after us. I think the *Deodar* (LT 543) and the *Hepatica* (LT 1008) and the *Peaceful* (LT 99) come in after we did, and I think that wuz between the *Our Need* (LT 1270) and the *Star of Hope* (LT 225) for last boat. Cor, that wuz a rum trip. We hetta ration all the water and the food, to mairke sure we hed enought to last us out. Yeah, and we run out o' paraffin, so we hetta come in with candles in our *sidelights*! I shall never forgit that as long as I live."

---

28 Lowestoft had a North Station at one time, as well as the main one in the middle of town.

29 The Scottish and Shetland women who came to Lowestoft each autumn to gut and pack herrings were fine knitters, often "working from the belt" (as it was known) with great speed and precision.

STEAM DRIFTER/TRAWLER
'TOWING ALONG'

Fig. 7: Drifter-trawler Towing Along

This line-drawing shows a typical vessel of the time working her gear off the starboard side, with the warps nipped into the towing-block. Both galluses are clearly shown and the basket secured halfway up the foremast-stay indicates to other craft that the vessel is fishing.

CHAPTER SEVEN

The Sea's Grip

I will make you fishers of men,
Fishers of men, fishers of men.
I will make you fishers of men,
If you follow me.
(Harry D. Clarke — American revivalist chorus)

The town of Lowestoft was once as tightly bound to fishing and allied occupations as it was possible for a community of its size (a 40,000-45,000 population from c. 1920-60) to be, with a notable percentage of its adult males crewing drifters and trawlers, working on the fish market, or following trades that serviced and supported the industry. A sizeable number of the women carried out the essential task of repairing nets, either at the various fishing companies' *stores* or on a part-time basis at home, while the importance of the role (for many of them) of acting as surrogate family-head in the absence of a husband/father engaged in fishing voyages cannot be underestimated. In a wider context, the town's two or three main shipyards had their origins in producing fishing craft, much of the engineering (heavy and light) had a maritime element in its being, and even the three food-producing factories had started off with fish-processing (especially herrings) at least as important as the canning of fruit and vegetables. With the exception of a long-established company that built coach and bus bodies (which were fitted to the engine-and-chassis units driven up from Bristol) and a factory producing television sets (opened after the Second World War), Lowestoft was primarily geared to fishing and maritime activity. It was the life-blood of the town, without which much of the local retail trade would have ceased to function.

It was in this type of economy (so loosely and cursorily described in the interests of brevity), and the society it created, that the townspeople of Lowestoft lived for much of the twentieth century. William ("Billy") Thorpe (1908-94) was a man typical of his generation, both in terms of family background and working-life experience. He was a fisherman through and through, with a wide knowledge of different catching-methods and vessels, with Patrol Service experience during the Second World War as a skipper-lieutenant,[1] and with on-shore service as a *ship's husband* for one of the leading Lowestoft trawling conglomerates when he finally came ashore. His narrative is both fascinating and instructive (tape-recordings made, 9 March 1976 and 30 June 1980) and may serve to back up some of the other oral testimony presented in this book.

---

1   The rank usually given to masters in command of patrol vessels or minesweepers—most of which were converted steam drifters or trawlers.

"We left school at fourteen in them days an', o' course, you know, mum an' dad say, 'You're not goin' t' be like yuh father an' go t' sea.' Well, as things happened, there wuz no other work. I allus reckon about ninety per cent o' the boys who left school when I did (December, 1922) went fishin'. My mother hed died the year before an' Father say, 'You're not gorn t' sea!' What'd I do? Sold ice-cream for a little while, picked strawberries, picked peas—but then finished up down *the Market* [Lowestoft Fish Market], like you all did, an' went in an ol' *smack*. There wuz no other work; no other work t' do, only fishin'.

"Yeah, I first went t' sea in the *Lily o' Devon* (LT 96). She wuz a *tosher*; only carried a boy durin' the winter. In the summer, they'd hev just the three men. You all started orf as *cook*. You can picture a boy comin' out o' school at fourteen an' dun't know nothin' about cookin'. But you go aboard a boat an' you're cook! They give you a big bit o' meat an' tell yuh t' put it in the oven, an' you put so much water in an' cut an onion over the top, an you peel yuh potaters an' greens an' put them in. Then you hetta make yuh *light duff* [dumplings]. Now, there's an art in makin' light duff. You'd gotta roll it up an' finish it properly. If you dint do that, they'd come up as what we called *split-arses*. They were split because the water hed got in. Well, you can picture a young boy, straight out o' school! When you come t' think on it now, the cook wuz one o' the hardest workin' blokes. He hed t' coil the *rope* [trawl-warp] when you were haulin', as well as doin' his other jobs.

"My Uncle Harry was older than my father and he left a fishin' *smack* to go in one o' the *Mission boats*. Now, they all said he wuz a fool, because goin' in a Mission boat you din't catch no fish. You only got a weekly wage.[2] There wuz more money in fishin'. But he believed in it, and they all got on to him and said, 'You'll never stick it!' But he did stick it. Now, when I wuz young, he wuz in the *Thomas B. Miller* (LO 237),[3] and I wuz always goin' to sail with him—but I never did git round to it. I remember one day, comin' down Clapham Road, and I had my hand on the pub door. I wuz goin' in *The Clapham*. Thass it! And Uncle wuz passin'. 'Where are you goin' to, Billy?' I say, 'Oh, I've got a pal in here.' He say, 'You've got no pals in a pub!' He say, 'All your real pals are outside the pub.' Oh, he wuz a tough ol' boy!

"The Mission hed the *Thomas B. Miller* an' the *Ensign*,[4] an' they were all open

---

2   Vessels belonging to the Royal National Mission to Deep Sea Fishermen did not carry out full-time trawling. Their main purpose was to minister to the needs of crews working in the North Sea. Such fishing as was done was limited in nature, with the money earned from the sale of catches on the Lowestoft fish market going into RNMDSF funds.

3   The RNMDSF vessels, sail or steam, were all registered in the port of London, not in the different British fishing-ports from which they operated.

4   This vessel had been the *Ensign* (YH 701), one of Hewett's *Short Blue* fleet of smacks (built in 1877). She was later acquired by the RNMDSF and eventually became the *Thomas Gray* (LO 59).

boats [i.e. with no superstructure of any kind above decks]. An' my uncle hed the *after-boom* [on the mizzen sail] come down and take all his fingers orf on one hand, comin' in the pier heads. He still kept on the *tiller* till he got right moored up, with his fingers orf. See, the Mission smacks were based here in Low'stoft. Yis, the *Thomas B. Miller* (LO 237) an' them. Well, we hed some at Low'stoft an' the bigger boats were at Grimsby—the *Queen Alexandra* (LO 51) an' them.[5] Yeah, an' they were *hospital boats* [i.e. with medical facilities on board] an' they hed so many crew able to live aboard. The smacks here used to lay in the Trawl Dock along o' the rest o' the smacks. Yeah, the *Thomas B. Miller*, there's some good photos o' her. The last smack to be built wuz the *Sir Archibald* (I can't think o' the other name now)—yeah, the *Sir Archibald*. She wuz built at Fellows' yard in 1930.[6] An' she wuz the only smack which, instead o' hevin' a thick ol'eight-inch *rope*, hed a four-inch *combination rope* for her *warp*.[7]

"The Mission boats stayed out the ordinary time for a *trip*—seven days. Yeah, seven days. An' you always knew 'em 'cause their *sails* were white. When I wuz young, when I first went to sea in the *Lily o' Devon*, they'd always say, 'There's your Uncle Harry over there!' You know. An' you could hardly see it with your own eyes, but the sun had glinted on his white sails an' they knew it wuz him over there. Yeah. An, o' course, they sold socks, mittens, cheap tobaccer.[8] Yeah. An' on a fine Sunday afternoon you used t' git a crowd o' boats round, launch the *small boat* an' go aboard an' hev a little service. On the mission smack, yeah. The skipper would take the service. Yeah, yeah. An' he once said t' me, 'Do yuh wanta git inta these boats?' So I said, 'Uncle Harry, I could never be like you. I could never git up an' talk an' give a lecture like you do.' An' he said, 'Yes, you could. God would help yuh!'

"Now, I believe they made a recordin' o' his last speech. Ben Green [Superintendent of the RNMDSF in Lowestoft, at the time] wuz tryin' to git it. Thass a speech he made at the *Commodore Mission* in Oulton Broad [on Hall Road]. Yeah, the last speech he made afore he died. He wuz sayin' what a rough life they hed, an' the little money. Yit he brought up a big fam'ly. He wuz skipper all the time. Yeah. One skipper I sailed with, Big Noey Ayers, lived next door to my uncle, an' o' course he wuz allus pullin' my leg about him. He'd say, 'You say your uncle dun't swear?' He say, 'I heard him call one o' his boys suffin the

---

5 The reference here is to the RNMDSF steamers, the *Queen Alexandra* having been built in 1902, with a steel hull and a 65 HP engine.

6 This vessel was the *Sir William Archibald* (LO 401), built in 1927 at the yard belonging to Fellows & Co. Ltd. on Southtown Road, Great Yarmouth.

7 In other words, the vessel's trawl warp was four inches in diameter (using a combination of wire and natural fibre) instead of the usual eight.

8 These commodities were known as *fishermen's comforts* and had originally been sold by Mission smack crew members (during the 1880s) to men working in the trawling fleets on the Dogger Bank—a practice intended to counter the effect of the Dutch *grog ships*, which plied the fishermen with cheap gin and caused great misery thereby.

other day!' He say, 'He do swear!' So praps he did—but on the quiet. He used to say 'Beggar!' an' things like that, an' the fishermen used t' say, 'Well, as he might as well say the other! We know know what he mean when he say Fish it!—an' everything like that.'

"My uncle suddenly left [fishing] to go with The Mission, you know. They started up in 1881, the Mission boats, and they only carried an ordinary crew. Yes, there were five in a *smack*—while a *tosher* only used t' carry three in the summer and four in the winter. The Mission boats used t' keep with the Low'stoft ones nearly all the time. When the old [Hull and Grimsby] fleets used t' work the Dogger [Dogger Bank], the *Queen Alexandra* and the bigger steam boats used t' go see after them. But the ones out o' Low'stoft, like the *Thomas B. Miller* and the *Sir William Archibald* (that's the name, *Sir William Archibald*!) used t' see to the boats out o' here. To me, they done somethin' right, because when I was cook in the *Lily o' Devon* [early 1920s] an ol' Swedish boat come up an' we launched the boat [i.e. the smack's *little boat*, or lifeboat] an' the skipper an' that went aboard— an' the skipper come back drunk! See, we used t' give 'em some fish an' they used t' give out this ol' *grog*—an' a lot o' the blokes din't realise what that wuz goin' t' do to 'em! *Copers*, they used t' call 'em—them *grog ships*. Yeah, and the Mission boats done a good job aginst them. I think everybody realised that.[9]

"They would try to hail you if they could, when you were out there. You hed several skippers, who they knew, who would never fish on a Sunday, yuh see. An' the Mission skipper, he knew the chaps who would try to be near him on a Saturday night ready for Sunday mornin', to go aboard an' hev the service. Yeah. An' any bad accidents on the big boats out o' [Hull and Grimsby]—like in the *Gamecock Fleet*—the *Queen Alexandra* hed hospital beds aboard.[10] Part o' the *fish-hold* hed bin made inta a hospital room. Yeah, yeah. You always hed a little Bible aboard the Mission boats. Oh, yeah. And, in the latter years, the blokes would also walk round an' chuck a bundle o' books aboard for yuh, when you wuz *laid in*. Yeah, *Picture Post* an' things what we dun't see now (them glossy magazines), 'cause they were very nice to look through.

"I *signed the pledge* in Lerwick, in 1925. Yeah. Through the Mission. Yes. My father used t' drink, yuh see, an' I couldn't see no fun in it at all. I used to go in

---

9 The Royal National Mission to Deep Sea Fishermen had been founded by Ebenezer Mather of London, in 1881, to counter the malign influence of the alcohol sold by Dutch grog-ships (or *copers*) to the crews of sailing trawlers (or *smacks*) working the Dogger Bank. The word *coper* derived from the Dutch *kooper*, meaning "to buy or trade".

10 There were two steam trawlers named *Gamecock* once fishing out of Hull (H 205 and H 810). The former belonged to Pickering & Haldane's ST Co. Ltd., the latter to Kelsall Bros. & Beeching Ltd. The term *Gamecock Fleet* itself was applied to vessels belonging to Kelsall's.

[the pub] wi' the lads, but I couldn't see no fun in it, so I signed the pledge.[11] An' I wonder if I'm the only one what kept it up? I've never drunk in m' life—bar the odd sherry or port. Yeah. I remember one time, my brother wuz in hospital an' I'd made £60 for a twelve-week *voyage* [the local autumn herring season]. An' that wuz the time they were puttin' port in my lemonade! I looked at the clock an' that wuz five t' two. 'Five t' two!' I say. 'I've gotta be at the Hospital at two!' An' I asked someone the correct time because my hid wuz beginnin' t' go round round an' I realised then what the drink wuz doin' to me. Now, I hed sixty brand-new pound notes, an' I can remember takin' them t' my brother in hospital an' he say, 'Cor, let me hold them!' I think thass the most money I ever did take up on herrin' fishin', that sixty pound. That would be 1928. Things began t' drop after then—1929, an' the Thirties.

"The Mission smacks all flew the Mission flag. Thet wuz a *pennant*, really—with a long tail, yuh see. Blue, an' in white for the letters: "Mission to Fishermen". Oh, yis, they were well liked—the Mission boats. An' then, after the war [Second World War], we hed one o' the *landin' barges* [from D-Day] moored up in the Hamilton Dock. Yis, Percy Goldspink had her. Yeah, she wuz moored up there an' people could walk round to her for the evening service.[12] The Mission started here in 1881, with Mr. Mathier [Ebenezer J. Mather],[13] an' where it is now [in Waveney Road] used t' be called *the Fishermen's Shelter* when I wuz young. Yeah, The Fishermen's Shelter. There wuz a tea-room, an' you could go an' play billiards in there. That wuz run through The Mission, or *The Bethel*.[14] Yeah, an' you hed on the windows there, 'Fishermen's Shelter'. At one time, it used t' be up Commercial Road, where *The Petto* [Peto Coffee Bar] is now. Yeah thass where it used t' be. And, o' course, if you're goin' back before the war [Second World War], the old Mission buildin' used to be in Suffolk Road and wuz kept by a man named Harry Culley. Yeah, you allus hed one man there, full time."

The information revealed in the previous paragraph reveals a complex pattern

---

11 This was a formal promise, made under the auspices of the British Association for the Promotion of Temperance (founded 1835), not to drink alcoholic beverages. Nonconformist denominations and the Evangelical Movement in the Church of England were leading advocates during the 19th century of countering the harmful effects of excessive consumption of alcohol among the British working population. People undertaking to abstain signed a pledge-card.

12 The landing-craft was a floating base for the RNMDSF, with Percy Goldspink in charge of it. Woollen comforts could be purchased there, books borrowed, and religious services were held on board.

13 The first RNMDSF *smack* was based in Gorleston: the *Ensign* (referred to above in fn. 4, p. 132).

14 The Bethel was an independent Nonconformist chapel of no set denomination, located on Battery Green Road opposite the Lowestoft Fish Market. It now serves as the headquarters of the Lowestoft Players acting company, but was once a potent force in the religious and maritime life of the town.

Plate 11: *Sir William Archibald (LO 401)*

The RNMDSF smack "Sir William Archibald" (LO 401) towing her dinghy (al. little boat) and with foresail and five-cloth jib set. The mainmast's extension enabled a topsail to be used and the sails' appearance suggests that they may be the lighter ones adopted during the summer months. Both foresail and jib are white, as described by Billy Thorpe on p. 133.

of associations connected with maritime activity in Lowestoft during the second half of the nineteenth century and the first half of the twentieth. The RNMDSF headquarters was indeed in Suffolk Road at one time, in a building that later became the Borough Library and once formed part of R.J. Pryce's hardware shop (later, L.R. Godfrey's home-wares store). It moved after the Second World War into an office at 21 Waveney Road, facing the Trawl Dock. This had formerly been *The Fishermen's New Shelter*, successor to an earlier venue located on Commercial Road (*Kelly's 1937 Directory of Cambridgeshire, Norfolk & Suffolk* describes it as dining-rooms under the management of Horace Rivett). It is entirely possible that The Bethel had a role in its administration, because the *Port Missionary* (an employee of The British Sailors' Society) supervised activity at this chapel and was an important figure in ministering to the needs of local seafarers in the town. The RNMDSF had indeed begun its work of ministry to (initially) North Sea fishermen in 1881, concentrating on alleviating the appalling working-conditions on board the trawling-fleets working the Dogger Bank. Ebenezer Mather chose Gorleston as its first working-base, largely because Robert Hewett, owner of the mighty *Short Blue* fleet of smacks based there, was sympathetic to the Mission's work. With some necessary clarification having been made, it is now time for Billy Thorpe to resume his narrative.

"The Mission wasn't as big round the *West Side*—not in Fleetwood or the other places. But they did have missions ashore [i.e. offices] an' some of 'em were good. I mean, Padstow, he wuz very well liked—the bloke what kept the Mission there. See, you din't have no baths or washin' facilities aboard ship, but if you went in the Mission you knew you were clean when you come out 'cause you could have a proper wash or a bath. They had a certain number o' beds for yuh as well, if you were ill. They could see after yuh, yeah. An' there wuz a place where you could read as well, where you could pick old books up. Yeah, an' they'd allus come out on the quay an' give yuh a service [hold an act of worship]. Yeah, an' then afterwards the lads would sing when they all come out o' the pub! See, Padstow wuz the first *voyage* we used t' do after Christmas [when *trawling*]—a ten-week voyage, when you used t' go out for three nights an' never git no sleep for three nights an' three days! An' you'd be *a-guttin'* yuh fish up an' you din't know whether you were lookin' aft or for'ad!¹⁵

"Milford [Milford Haven] had a little Mission as well. O' course, I think that Milford had always bin a bit on the decline durin' my time. Yeah, all my lifetime Milford had bin goin' down. I don't know so much about Fleetwood, though we did catch fish orf there, which got in the *Fishin' News*. We caught soles what'd got whiskers on! They were that big! An' a photograph wuz in the *Fishin' News*, with a bloke holdin' one up in front o' him, an' that wuz as big as a *barmskin*! This wuz on the Morecambe Bay grounds. Durin' the summer, yes. Generally, after the Padstow voyage—say, from June. Yeah, June. Then you used t' come hoom an' do *the Fishin'* [the East Anglian autumn herring voyage]. In the end, that got so some o' the boats kept round at Fleetwood all the time an' you only came home for a week. Yeah, by the train. Then you had t' go back agin.

"When I wuz *drifter-trawlin'*, I wuz mostly in the *Ocean Sunlight* (YH 28).¹⁶ They were new ships; *Bloomfield's* boats, yeah. Big Noey [Noah] Ayers an' Kenny Thompson, two o' the *don skippers* out o' Low'stoft, took these boats. We used t' go over t' Yarmouth t' *make up*, but you could leave the ship in here [Lowestoft] otherwise. Bloomfield's hed two boats built every year an' they hed two well-known skippers, called Coddy Harris an' Arthur Muggins (or somethin') tairke 'em. Well, Noey Ayers an' Kenny Thompson then used t' tairke 'em orf them, yuh see. The *Darcy Cooper* (YH 370) an' the *Hilda Cooper* (YH 392) were built first [in 1928]. Then, the year afterwards, they hed the *Ocean Sunlight* an' the *Ocean Lifebuoy* (YH 29) built. An' then, the year after that, they hed the *Ocean Lux* (YH 84) an' the *Ocean Vim* (YH 88) built. Yeah, so they were a year old when we went

---

15 The Padstow trawling voyage started in either January or February, with soles as the main species caught (the venture having begun during the second half of the nineteenth century, with sailing vessels making the journey round to Cornwall). Even though the work was carried out relatively close to land, it was intense and tiring. See Butcher, *The Trawlermen* (Reading, 1980), Chapter Six,

16 Drifter-trawlers were dual-purpose vessels, which could catch pelagic species (herring and mackerel) with drift-nets, then convert to trawling for demersal (bottom-dwelling) fish. This enabled them to work all year round on different British fishing-grounds, thus maintaining earning-capacity and avoiding having to be laid up somewhere in harbour when not in use.

Plate 12: Ocean Sunlight (YH 28)

The Yarmouth drifter-trawler "Ocean Sunlight" (YH 28), on which Billy Thorpe worked during the 1930s. She and the "Ocean Lifebuoy (YH 29) were built in 1929 at Aberdeen, followed by the "Ocean Lux" (YH 84) and "Ocean Vim" (YH 88) in 1930. They were succeeded, during the 1950s, by six new "Ocean" diesel drifter-trawlers ("Crest", "Dawn", "Starlight", "Sunlight", "Surf" and "Trust"), all constructed in Lowestoft. They were sold to Small & Co. Ltd, of the Suffolk port in 1963 and re-registered there.

in 'em. An' they were lovely boats—jolly good boats, yeah.[17] They all ran on grease, an' every time you stopped the engine you were supposed t' tighten all yuh grease-caps up. Well, the skipper, Big Noey Ayers, he wun't hev none o' that. 'If you're a-gorn t' turn them, you'll hefta do it while we're *towin'!*' An' so they [the engineers] did—where Cods an' Muggins would let their blokes stop, say, for five minutes t' do what wuz needed. With us, though—oh no, the *trawl* hed gotta git over an' they used to hefta feel their way an' screw these caps down. No oil, yuh see [on the engine-bearings]. Whereas, on moost o' the ships, you used t' hefta oil when the engine wuz gorn round.

"There wuz no *bridle gear* on a drifter-trawler. They wun't powerful enough t' tow it. No. We used t' hev what we called *long legs*, about twenty foot long from the *doors*. An' we used t' work just one *titler*. That wuz the moost she would tow—where, nowadays, they work about seven titlers! You know how much fuel

---

17 The *Darcy Cooper* and *Hilda Cooper* were built in Selby, the four *Ocean* vessels in Aberdeen. All of them had steel hulls and triple-expansion steam-reciprocating engines, with those in the first two craft rated at 46 HP and the others at 39 HP. The *Ocean* boats were all named after washing-products made by Lever Bros. Ltd., as the Bloomfield company was part of that group.

they must be burnin' an' all; they're got a thousand horsepower! They just plough the sea up! An' thass why they're tryin' this new experiment. Instead o' hevin' *titlers*, they're tryin' to electrify the fish ahead. Sendin' a pulse, you know, t' stir 'em up. Yeah. But I dun't think they've hed any success yet. We used t' hev a sixty-five foot *headline*, an' that wuz a *standard trawl*. Yuh *square* wuz twenty-two foot long an' that'd gotta lay over where you were strirrin' the fish up. I've got all the dimensions in here [referring to his pocket-book]. We moostly used a *buff* on the headline. But, o' course, in deeper water a buff weren't no good after a while [because of water-penetration caused by the pressure], so we used t' hev the *bottles*. Green or red glass. They sell 'em now for souvenirs, t' hang up in rooms. But they used t' fill wi' water as well. You couln't see how it got in, but the pressure eventually got inta the bottles an' then they were chucked away. O' course, then the aluminium ones come in, an' now they're started on plarstic!

"*Soles* wuz the thing round on the West Side [of England] an' they used t' make sixpence [2½p] to a shillin' [5p] a pound.[18] That wuz yuh main trip. In here, as well [at Lowestoft].[19] An' when yuh think o' what we're eatin' now! When you think o' the *dorgfish* whass bein' brought inta Low'stoft now! We wun't ha' done. We used t' throw 'em over the side. I've heard people say, when they buy fresh fish in Low'stoft (they come from The Midlands), that they dun't like it. Thass too fresh for 'em; that ent a fishy enough smell! I remember takin' some children round the Market [on a conducted tour] an' they said, 'Well, down in Scarborough, they don't call 'em dogfish.' I say, 'No. In Scarborough, they call 'em *flake*.' Up in London, they're called *rock salmon*. Cor, the different names fish ha' got!

"The *silvery hake* is what made Fleetwood. Yuh see, Fleetwood an' Swansea, an' Cardiff, they'd all got boats goin' after hake [*Merluccius merluccius*]. They used t' go out on the continental shelf an' shoot (I think) a thousand fathom o' warp [in the area of The Porcupine Bank]. They used t' keep right on the edge o' the shelf, yuh see—the deep-water shelf. An' if you did fall orf that (you know, through neglect with yuh navigation), you soon realised it! Yuh *warps* were straight up an' down [instead of being out-length], an' you'd gotta git up onta the hill again. An' the water wuz so deep that, when I wuz fishin' out o' Cardiff, we'd have, say, forty *kit* o' good hake an' fifty kit o' broken hake. The pressure o' the water, you know, bringin' 'em up, used t' break the fish 'cause hake is very sorft. Oh yis, in bad weather, you'd hev more broken hake than yuh would whole hake.

"We mainly worked the *bays* [e.g. Cardigan Bay and Morecambe Bay] an' the Irish side. We did try the *grounds* where the Fleetwood boats used t' fish, but we never made a go of it [because of the depth of water]. No, we found our own

---

18 The wholesale price realised at auction on the fish market.

19 The Lowestoft steam trawlers and drifter-trawlers did not particularly specialise in catching soles, but the sailing trawlers (or smacks) did—landing high-quality fish because of their beam-trawls being a less injurious form of gear than otter-trawls.

grounds. There wuz a bit o' rivalry between us an' the Fleetwood people. I can remember one Easter Sunday, mendin' the net on board, an' the Fleetwood chaps were comin' orf their ship an' they all jeered us an' made a game of us. I think we left the deck. They wouln't work like a *Lowsterman* would. Whenever Lowstermen went t' Fleetwood, they would work any day. Whether that wuz Christmas Day, or what day it wuz, you worked just the same. But fishermen in Fleetwood wun't! As soon as they come in, they were like Low'stoft are now: they left the ship an' went hoom. But we used t' hefta live aboard the ship. Sleep aboard the ship. That wuz our hoom when we were away. Yeah. Fourteen t' sixteen weeks sometimes, you were away, so that wuz your hoom all the time. Yeah, you din't hev clean sheets every blinkin' *trip*, or anything like that. No, you used t' come down an' fill yuh bed up wi' straw! Yeah, but then we got so we hed the *flock mattresses* in the *Ocean* boats—or *kapok*. Yeah, yeah.

"Cardigan Bay an' Caernarvon Bay we used t' go to. An' then, across the other side [of the Irish Sea], we always used t' say when we towed towards the Kish [Kish Bank], 'Everything go swish, swish, swish!' Or suffin like that. Yuh see, The Kish an' the Codlin' [Codling Bank] lay t'gether. the Codlin' wuz very *rough* ground, but when you wanted some sleep they'd *tow* round the Kish, which wuz a *smooth* ground [hence use of the word "swish"]. Yeah, an' you're got all these different *lightships*. Yeah, the Barrels Light—we're steamed through there (I expect you're heard a lot o' people say that), between the mainland an' the lightship. Yeah, an' we used t' work the Chickens [Chicken Rock] as well. The Chickens. Yeah, that wuz moostly f' gittin' skate, orf the Chickens. Yeah, they were *blondes* [ref. the Blond Ray—*Raja brachyura*].[20]

"My biggest experience over there wuz when I wuz *mate* o' the *Neves* (LT 246). The skipper wuz ashore, an' I wuz *third hand*, so I went mate this trip [the regular mate taking over as skipper].[21] We were *poachin'* inside Irish waters, inside the Rathlin Island, up near Port Stewart. An' this gunboat come out, an' we see a man go aboard another boat (what wuz in the bay a-fishin' with us) with a revolver in his hand. An' he hed the skipper come out' o' the *wheelhouse*, yuh see. Yeah, we could see all this. An' we scrabbed the trawl aboard an' *steamed*! We even hed part o' the *ground-rope* hangin' out over the side. An' this gunboat come after us. He wuz a-firin' at us! One bullet went through the starboard *light-board*, one hit the *small-boat gripe*, an' as soon as I wuz a-gorn inta the wheelhouse one hit the *fiddley* top an' glanced orf. An' thass as near as I got to bein' shot! Now, when I got

---

20 After the references to the two Welsh bays, the fishing grounds mentioned were located in the Irish Sea. The Kish and Codling banks were to be found in Dublin Bay, the Barrels Lightship was on station off Rosslare, and Chicken Rock (with its lighthouse) lay about three miles south-west of the Calf of Man. The Kish Bank lightship was replaced by a lighthouse in 1965; an offshore windfarm is planned for the Codling Bank; and the Barrels Lightship was withdrawn in favour of a superbuoy in 2007.

21 The *Neves* belonged to a company called Seven Ltd. and its name was, in fact "Seven" in reversed letter-order.

inta the wheelhouse, the skipper (who wuz a queer character out o' Low'stoft—I shan't mention his name) say t' me, 'You'd better go aft, Billy, an' see if that engine-room door is shut.' He say, 'If a bullet go right down the engine-room an' hit somethin' vital—.' I say, 'Damn' the bloomin' door! I'm not gorn aft while this is gorn on!' See, we were tryin' t' git away. Anyway, they said this gunboat could do twelve mile an hour. Well, if he could go twelve, we went fifteen, 'cause we got away from him! She wuz a fast boat, the *Neves*. Yeah.

"See, we used t' fish just t' the nor'ad o' Lough Swilly. You could chuck a stone ashore! An' every time you hauled, there wuz all these lovely *blond rooker* [Blond Rays—*Raja brachyura*]. Beau'iful fish! See, that wuz Southern Ireland [the Irish Republic]. Yeah, Southern Ireland. Yeah, 'cause they wun't ha' fired at us if it had bin Northern Ireland.[22] Anyway, this all happened an' we got over it. The next trip, the reg'lar skipper come back. He wun't believe all this! He say, 'Dun't be silly! They dussn't fire at a bloomin' British ship!' He say, 'They dussn't do that!' So he went back t' the same place an' we nearly got caught agin. The bullets were hittin' the side o' the boat. Yeah. They were what were called *dum-dum* bullets, because they flattened when they hit. They wun't suffin sharp—t' go through, like [i.e. to penetrate]. They sort o' flattened an' they were from *rifles*. Rifles, yeah. Anyway, that other boat I mentioned [in the previous paragraph], what wuz fishin' with us, the Fleetwood ship, wuz called the *Pelican* (FD 7). An' they took her skipper ashore. She wuz renamed the *Cevic* (FD 7) afterwards.

"Now, after we'd got over this, we went an' fished a little further over, up orf Portrush. Yuh see, Portrush belonged to us. Yeah, that wuz it—that wuz Northern Ireland, yuh see. An' the man in charge, like the *fishery inspector* there, said, 'Oh, the *limit* here is a mile and a half.' So we used t' fish a mile an' a half from the land. Then, one dark night, away come a searchlight on us. Someone had called a British gunship orf to us an' caught us fishin'! An' the skipper wuz taken ashore, an' we lorst the catch [by confiscation], an' I think he wuz fined about £20. Yeah. But that chap told us we could fish there![23] There's a joke about Portrush, as well. Yuh see, they wun't really rigged up for fishin'. We hetta go so far after ice that—. Anyway, they were tryin' t' make Portrush a place to land fish, so we laid all the fish out on the quay an' the railway lines were like there [indicating close proximity with his hands]. An' when the train come in, the engine chopped all the

---

22 There is a certain degree of vagueness as to the position of the *Neves* in the preceding paragraph. The vessel was fishing off the northern extremity of Ireland, inside the official limit-line—probably in both Lough Swilly and Lough Foyle. Rathlin Island and Port Stewart are mentioned, just to give a generalised idea of the vessel's location. A reference to Buncrana would have been more accurate.

23 There had obviously been a misunderstanding of some sort regarding the distance from land within which vessels were not allowed to fish. It is possible that some local byelaw had been infringed.

tails o' the skate orf! Yeah."[24]

Billy Thorpe continued his trawling career during the 1930s, up till about the outbreak of the Second World War. His theatre of operations switched from the Irish Sea eventually and he found himself working in waters off Devon and Cornwall. This was familiar territory for many Lowestoft fishermen, because of *voyages* which had begun from about the 1860s onwards: notably, drift-netting for mackerel out of Newlyn-Penzance in the early months of the year and trawling for soles out of Padstow at about the same time. It was not a Lowestoft company (or even a Great Yarmouth one) with which he found employment, however, but one based in Plymouth. During 1936, Kelsall Bros. & Beeching Ltd. of Hull went into voluntary liquidation and what remained of its Gamecock Fleet of steam trawlers was sold to Heward Trawlers Ltd. of Fleetwood.[25] The following year, there was further selling-on of the vessels to other fishing companies, including the Plymouth Mutual Steam Fishing Co. Ltd. It was this last-named enterprise that Billy Thorpe found himself working for.

"I went t' Plymouth in 1937 as *mate* of a boat called the *Grosbeak* (H 108). Yeah, one o' the Gamecock Fleet. See, the Gamecock Fleet gave up in 1936 an' sold all the boats. Plymouth took four, Brixham took half-a-dozen. They were sold all round the coast, yeah. An', course, fishermen hev allus hed a name f' drinkin'—but I never drink, yuh see, an' the chaps in Plymouth couln't believe that. 'You come from Low'stoft an' dun't drink!' See, that wuz the idea they hed: every Lowsterman drunk! Well, anyway, I wanted t' have my wife come down, yuh see (I wuz married by then), so I'd gotta git her some lodgins. An' one or two' the places they showed me! Well, I wun't ha' took my wife there! Any rate, I found a nice place, nice rooms, an' told the lady who I was—an' when I looked in the rooms, they were lovely. You know, everything wuz clean an' the furniture all good. Now, the wife came down durin' the next *trip* an' I met her orf the [railway] station an' took her t' these rooms. Everything in the rooms hed bin altered! There wuz an ol' chair here, an' ol' thing there, an' when this woman looked at my wife, she said, 'Well, this ent your wife, is it?' She said, 'I thought about seein' her wear clogs an' a shawl over her hid!' I said, 'You're well away! You're years behind! The Scotch people still do that, but we dun't in Low'stoft. We dress prop'ly.' Anyway, we got round it, an' we got so friendly in the end that, when we left (eight months I had my wife at Plymouth), the women cried when they left one another!

---

24 In 1932, there was an attempt to open Portrush as a fishing-port, which didn't succeed. Railway lines ran along the quay, with insufficient space to lay catches out properly for sale.

25 The Gamecock Fleet had achieved fame in 1904, when its vessels were attacked in what became known as *The Dogger Bank Incident*. On 21 October, warships from the Russian Imperial Fleet attacked the trawlers as they worked, mistaking them (it was said) for Japanese craft in the opening phase of the Russo-Japanese War. One trawler was sunk, two men killed and thirty others injured. This huge error in Russian navigation almost involved the country in another conflict: this time with Great Britain!

"Thass like when I first started courtin' my wife. She wuz only about fifteen an' workin' f' Woodcock, the station-master, in Denmark Road. An' I went an' called for her one night an' her boss come t' the door, yuh see. He say, 'She's courtin' a fisherman. You aren't a fisherman!' See, I allus wore a collar an' tie. I dun't know why; that wuz just a habit I got into. I never did wear a *wrapper* round the neck an' I still like t' have a collar an' tie on now—even on a hot day. I used t' wear the *high-heeled boots* when I wuz younger, though. I can allus remember my sister (I'd bin at sea about a full year) sayin', 'You're not goin' t' hev fishermen's boots!' But they used t' be smart. Lovely boots! An the *duffel trousers* were good an' all. They wun't the proper *bell-bottoms* like they hev now (they call 'em *flared* now, dun't they?), but they were opened out a bit at the bottom. About twenty-two inches, I think they used t' be.

"When I wuz down at Plymouth, we used t' work orf The Eddystone [Eddystone Lighthouse] in bad weather, durin' the winter time. We were workin' orf the Eddystone late one night, when a Low'stoft boat passed us outside, an' through the glasses [binoculars] I could see that wuz a *Star* boat. An' that wuz the *Beacon Star* (LT 770). Now, that night, she got lorst an' never got t' Newlyn. She got lorst that night, an' I writ t' the Low'stoft *owners* an' told them the last time I had seen her. Yeah, she wuz *punchin'* her way outside, makin' hard work of it.[26]

"Another place we fished wuz orf the Scilly Isles. We never went round t' Padstow, though. No, we never worried about *soles*. You got a few soles—a stone or two a *haul*—which mount up, yuh know, if you hev about sixty or seventy hauls. An' you used t' git that number o' hauls a *trip*, where nowadays they only git about half that number. You used t' git *skate*, though, an' all the fish wuz sold on the quay. Yeah, you'd come back inta Plymouth, down the Barbican, an' land your fish. That wuz all laid out, yeah. An' you could be standin' there, watchin' your fish, an' they'd pull it out between yuh legs! Some of 'em would, some o' the men. Yeah, pinch it as it laid there! Yeah. See, the *mates* used t' hefta watch that fish.[27] An' I can remember comin' in one night, an' I just managed t' git hoom, an' I spuz I'd got about two hours before I'd got t' git down t' the Barbican. Well,

---

26 The Eddystone Light was eight miles south of Rame Head, off the Devon-Cornish coast. The *Beacon Star* had left Lowestoft on 17 February 1937 in company with the *Constant Star* (LT 1158) and the *One Accord* (LT 324). The vessels were not making for Newlyn to go mackerel-catching, but were headed for Padstow to trawl for soles. The two *Star* boats belonged to the Star Drift Fishing Co. Ltd. (an enterprise belonging to the Catchpole family of Kessingland) and the *One Accord* to George Catchpole and associates. The *Beacon Star* was last spoken to on 18 February, off the Eddystone, and reported missing the following day. Her Lowestoft port registration was terminated on 16 March 1937 and early in April her little boat was found off Cherbourg. There were no survivors of this total loss and the little boat had probably come adrift from its station on board rather than being launched by the crew. Details of this incident can be found on the Fleetwood Sail and Steam Trawler website.

27 The mate on board a trawler was the crew member responsible for sound and effective storage of the catch on board and for its handling and well-being after landing.

I went fast asleep. An' I had a bloke who used t' come an' knock me up with a big stick. You know, knock on the winder [bedroom window], yuh see. An' when eventually I did wake up, he said, 'I've wooke the whole street up t' git you out!' An' I wuz half-an-hour late gittin' down the harbour, an' a lot o' our fish'd gone. I'm almost sure it had. Yeah. But he said he'd knocked so loud with his stick. I used t' give him about five bob [5s = 25p] a trip, t' make sure he'd git me up. We hed no *watchman* when we were there. No, no.

"We used t' call at Dartmouth, yuh know. Dartmouth wuz a lovely place t' go in. I dun't know if you've ever been? Thass lovely, Dartmouth! If you ever do git down that way, you wanta go in Dartmouth. You go in, yuh know, an' you can't see nothin' when you first go in. Then you turn t' port an' you see all the houses on the high cliffs, all like little doll's houses. We used t' *coal* there. Yeah, we allus coaled when we called there. You used t' git a few soles, blond rooker, all sorts. Yeah, dabs an' plaice—a mixture o' everything. Every *garnet* [gurnard] you caught you sold t' the Frenchmen, if you were at sea. They used t' come an' git 'em. An' my money wuz £2 10s 0d, which is £2.50, an' we used t' earn that amount again sellin' the garnets t' the French sailin' boats what used t' come there. That wuz f' *bait*. Yeah, they had them little sailin' boats f' *linin'* mostly. There used t' be hundreds o' them lorst every winter, yuh know—them little ow sailin' Frenchmen, out o' there.

"Yeah, you made a *livin'* out of it, round there. That wuz only about the second time I got an income tax form in, 'cause I'd averaged over £5 a week. An' I got an income tax form in, yeah. I think what I paid in I got back eventually, 'cause that used t' be weighed up every year, din't it? In April time, I think. There wun't no *pay-as-you-earn* then, wuz there? We used t' make about a six or seven day trip. Yeah, an' the man who kept the cafe there [on The Barbican], Nicholls, wuz a well-known character. Everybody knew him, who'd bin there on the *Plymouth voyage*.[28] He'd bin skipper o' one o' the boats [steam trawlers] when they first had 'em there. Yeah, but they never had a really good market, yuh see. Never had a good market [i.e. a purpose-built fish market]. No, they hed the women buy 'em an' be a-sellin' 'em in the streets. The fish wuz all sold whole at Plymouth an' that got transported, as far as I can remember, by rail. That wuz all f' the local area, though—yeah, Plymouth, Devonport an' all them places.

"We worked what we called a *standard trawl*, which wuz a sixty-five foot long *head-line* an' *on-the-doors* gear. Yeah. Yeah, the boat wun't powerful enough f' *bridles*. See, an' we were workin' in twenty to thirty *fathom* [depth of water] moostly. Yeah, so we hever had a lot o' *warp* out. You know, you only hed about 200 fathom on each *drum*. Yeah. I remember one *haul* there, early on, we never caught a thing! The trawl came up blank. Seemed as if that hadn't been on the

---

28 A small number of Lowestoft and Great Yarmouth steam drifters used to fish for herring out of Plymouth during January and February.

bottom—an' that got me worried, bein' *mate*.[29] An' we tried t' weigh up what had happened, an' what had happened wuz that it wuz the first time the skipper had bin in this big ship [the *Grosbeak*]. An' he wuz twenty foot above the bottom, yuh see, an' we were fishin' orf a bit o' *ground* where you hed the Bishop's Light [the Bishop Rock Lighthouse] on the dip.[30] You were steamin' till you got the light just dippin'. You could just see it on the horizon, yuh see. Well, wi' him [the skipper] bein' up a little bit more, he should ha' bin not so far orf. He hadn't got that weighed up, so we din't have the trawl prop'ly fishin' this bit o' ground—which is where there wuz fish. Yeah.

"Another time round there, we were makin' in for Round Island, which is in the Scillies, an' that come down *thick* [fog].[31] That wuz a *red light*, the Round Island light, an' we thought we saw it. But we wun't quite sure, so we hed t' stop an' put her up, head t' tide, an' *dodge*. Now, all that night, whichever way we turned, there wuz rocks t' starboard an' rocks t' port.Wherever we turned, there wuz rocks! All the night, till that come in daylight! An' we were blowin' our *whistle*, hopin' someone would help us, 'cause we couln't see a thing. An' when me an' the skipper got the *chart* out—where we thought we were, we were right round the other side' o' The Scillies! Yeah, Tresco, or somewhere like that! Marv'llous, yeah. We allus tried t' weigh up wi' the the other skipper an' mates when we come in orf a trip [i.e. discuss aspects of the trip], but we couln't weigh up this time. No. But, anyway, we kept clear. Yeah, an' whichever way you turned that night, there wuz rocks on every side.

"Another place we worked wuz the Brixham grounds. Bin worked in *smacks* f' years. We worked all them grounds, 'cause there wun't many Brixham smacks in 1937.[32] No. I've got what number they were down to in '37 in this book [his pocket-book]. The ol' skipper I wuz with wuz a well-known character. He hed a big ol' pug nose. Joe Frude. Funny name an' a funny bloke when I first see him, but me an' him clicked it orf just like that! He wuz Plymouth through an' through; a proper Plymouth man. Yeah, proper broad speakin'. Yeah. An' when I wuz down there on hol'day in 1951, I run into him. 'You come up t' tea wi' the lads! You come up t' tea. Who've yuh got wi' yuh?' I say, 'I've got me daughter an' me wife.' He say, 'Well, you bring 'em round t' tea!' So I took 'em round [to the fishing vessel] an' he couln't do enough for us. An' when we were down there, on the Barbican, they all said (you know, you could remember 'em), 'Billy's here!

---

29 The mate being the crew-member generally in charge of the fishing operation's technicalities, while the skipper took care of the trip's overall strategy and navigation.

30 The lighthouse is located twenty-eight miles from the Cornish coast, in the westernmost part of the Scilly Isles.

31 Round Island is the most northerly point of the Scillies. The lighthouse there was built in 1887 and automated a hundred years later. The signal now is one white flash every ten seconds; it had formerly been one red flash every thirty seconds.

32 About thirty vessels, compared with sixty at Lowestoft.

Wuz here in 1937.' See, quite a few o' the chaps what I'd sailed with in them days were still on the Barbican. Yeah.

"The Barbican crowd were a proper close-knit fam'ly. Like *the Beach*, here [the so-called Lowestoft *Beach Village*]. Yeah, we hed one Low'stoft chap who came down there an' messed about with another seaman's wife, orf The Barbican. Now, that wuz a crime t' do anything like that. If he'd ha' gone up the town, all right! But he din't. Well, when they found out he'd done that, they threw him in the dock. Then he hed t' run all the way to the [railway] station, an' he just managed t' git onta the station an' went on his way hoom. 'Cause they were a close-knit crowd. They were. An' a decent crowd. Yeah, he wuz chased all the way t' the station, this chap. An' I dun't know whether you know where Plymouth Station is? That ent very far from the dock, is it! Not much that ent! Thass a good way, yuh know. That it is!"

The preceding paragraphs give the reader a sense of the camaraderie engendered by fishing, whereby the work undertaken drew men together regardless of their respective ports of origin. Billy Thorpe never forgot his year sailing out of Plymouth, nor the feeling of community found there down on the Barbican. His wide experience of fishing (which included herring-catching as well as trawling) made him a valuable man to have on board and, when he felt that it was time to come ashore, his experience and skills made him ideally suited to take on the role of *ship's husband* for one of the Lowestoft fishing companies. As he makes clear, the job was not without its difficulties, because the port was undergoing profound changes during the 1960s and 70s—the prelude, really, to its eventual decline and demise thirty years later. This was not apparent at the time, but hindsight (and the overview it brings) clearly suggests that the industry was heading for collapse.

"Now, you can't git too personal on this, yuh see, but my idea is that people come inta fishin' an' they dun't know nothin' about it. Which you hefta do t' make a successful comp'ny. See, you never hev the one owners now [individual vessel-owners] 'cause they couln't afford t' run a boat. You hefta hev comp'nies, an' all they think about is makin' money. There's no feelin' in the industry now. You know, you used t' belong. That wuz your ship an' you belonged to it, an' chaps used t' sail years t'gether. You dun't do that now. No, you dun't. No. there's no feelin' from the office. Nearly every trip there's a change, see.

"Yeah, only a few *skippers* can keep a good crew. An' I always say, skippers are ten a penny, but *cooks* are the main thing aboard the ships right now [1980]. A good cook—you can build a crew round him. I found that in my experience, in 1960 onwards, when I wuz a *ship's husband*. If you had a good cook, men would say, 'Oh yes. I'll go wi' him.' An' some skippers you just couln't *ship up*. See, you do git good food aboard a boat, but if you hent got no one t' cook it—well, thass only wasted bloomin' food. An' if the skipper's a bit lapsadaisy an' dun't git on wi' the chaps, an' if everything is layin' about, or if the *galley* is dirty when the cook turn out in the mornin'—well, yeah, you can see what I mean.

"Now, at one time, you hed all Low'stoft men on the boats. Then all the Low'stoft boys thought about wuz gittin' out of it. So then you hed t' go outside t' git crew from other ports: the chuck-outs out o' Grimsby or the chuck-outs out o' Hull. They all came t' Low'stoft. An', o' course, that got me down, bein' ship's husband.[33] When I wuz sixty-three, I suddenly chucked my hand in—just like that! That got me down, yeah. A boat is allus called a *she*, ent it? So thass your ship an' thass your wife. You're the ship's husband, so you're gotta see that everything is provided f' that ship. Whatever is missin' when she's out, thass your fault. If she's short o' *ice*, *water* [drinking water], or if the cook can't find his sugar or his bread or his tea, or suffin like that, the ship's husband is responsible.

"Like, one day, the *Jamaica* (LT 185) come back [having just gone out on a trip].[34] One o' the *deckies* wuz *queer*. He wanted a doctor. And the doctor went down inta the *cabin* an' say. 'I can't find him.' See, the chap wuz in his bunk; he wun't move. So I go down an' I said, 'Come on, Dick, or Tom,' (whatever his name wuz) 'you're in the harbour now. Come on, ow lad, let's git on the deck.' An' up he come. Well, we passed the doctor, an' the doctor say, 'How did you do that?' I say, 'Well, I know the chap.' I say, 'He wanta lay in t'night. He dun't wanta be at sea.' Yeah, he din't wanta go t' sea, an' that skipper always had t' be careful whoever he took afterwards 'cause you can't bring a big ship back. You lose money. Nowadays, you lose £300 or £400 for a day, dun't yuh? In them days that wuz, say, £100 or £200 a day the time that they lorst. Yeah.

"Yeah, you tried t' make sure a boat wuz prop'ly *crewed up* an' the biggest trouble I did hev wuz with our *don skipper* that year [1967]. He wuz top boat that year an' we hed the bus [minibus] ready. She laid at Grimsby, this boat did, the *St. Davids* (LT 494), an' we had the bus outside with all the crew on—barrin' one.[35] He never turned up. Now, I hed one *deckie* spare, an' I knew he wun't no good. Really, I shoun't oughta ha' put him there. But, at any rate, t' git her [the vessel] away, I put him aboard the bus an' away it went. Now, the boat brooke the record that *trip*. £5,000! The first time someone [from Lowestoft] had made £5,000. But the skipper came up t' me an' blamed me. He said, 'Look, we've brooke the record, but that chap you put aboard din't help at all!' But the boat did git away, an' that come in at the right time f' the right market. Yeah, we sent Billy Hitter an' his crew away t' Holland or somewhere for a trip, an' he brooke the record. We gave him a holiday f' that. But the boat wun't ha' got away if I hent put that

---

33 Billy Thorpe worked for an associated group of trawling companies owned by Gordon Claridge. He was one of a team of ship's husbands and was responsible for a certain number of vessels.

34 A vessel owned by the Dagon Fishing Co. Ltd. (built in 1947, with a 700 hp engine).

35 The *St. Davids* belonged to Claridge Trawlers Ltd. (built in 1947, with a 950 hp engine). She had landed her catch at Grimsby and stayed there for refuelling, provisioning etc., while the crew returned to Lowestoft (probably by rail).

man on board.

"O' course, you made sure you got the *provisions* for a boat. You'd have the *cook* come ashore an' say what he wanted. We hed one cook I used t' call 'Deadly', 'cause t' me he wuz so useless. You know, he wuz the first t' be called out an' allus the last one aboard the ship. An' he never could find all his stuff. He'd allus say, 'Billy, I can't find the sugar. I can't find the tea.' An' in the end, if I couln't find it, I'd go after a double dose an' put it aboard. Anything t' git her [the vessel] out. See, the cook used t' put his order in, but you hed a sort o' a *standard order* 'cause the cook hed only so much t' spend.[36] He couln't go above that limit. A good cook might be able to, though. Yeah, the *owner* [of the vessel] would call you up an' say, 'You've spent £2 too much this trip on food." An' when you told him that wuz a good cook, he dint mind then.

"Another thing you hetta do wuz make sure the boat's *gear* hed all the spare parts. They'd put a list in, when they come in, o' what they wanted. An' if their *net* wuz torn at all, you made sure men went aboard t' mend it, so she wuz all ready f' sea agin. Oh yeah. An' you used t' see to the *ice* as well. Yeah, the ice. When the *St. Martin* (LT 376) an' the *St. Lucia* (LT 362) came t' Low'stoft, they were the biggest boats out o' the port.[37] We thought they were too big f' the port, an' they used t' take in twenty-five ton o' ice. We thought that wuz a helluva lot, but now you've got boats what take fifty ton! The *lumpers* swear when they git the fish out 'cause there's more ice than fish—an' the fish is all spoilt. But you still can't teach these chaps. See, there's more weight on the fish. The ice is more weight on 'em. An' the people who git the fish out o' the boat, they stand at the back o' the *pound* an' kick it out—an' that damages it, too.[38]

"You made sure a boat wuz *fuelled* an' all. Yeah, an' *watered* [i.e. supplied with drinking water]. Yeah, there hev bin boats go out wi' no water, through some mistake, an' they hed t' call in Esbjerg, in Denmark, t' fill up. An' then you'd git a bollickin' up in the office! Sometimes the blokes would set fire t' the *galley* or the *dryin'-room*, where the *oilskins* were. We've even hed 'em chuck the fryin' pan overboard, or the big kettle [used for cooking meat and vegetables]. Things like that, yeah. Knives an' forks as well, just so they can git back inta port. Or they'd fall in the dock afore they went out an' say they'd swallered some water an' had gotta hev a day in! Thass bin like that since about 1960, I think. Thass the type o' man you've got. That never happened in the old days, 'cause you allus had enough good men t' pick from. No one would think o' doin' them sort o' things.

---

36 There was a budget for provisioning a vessel per trip and the food taken on board kept largely to basic foodstuffs: meat, vegetables, flour, tea, sugar, tinned stuff, etc.

37 The *St. Martin* belonged to the Colne Fishing Co. Ltd. and the *St. Lucia* to the Dagon Fishing Co. Ltd. Both vessels were built in 1961, with 845 hp engines.

38 Catches of fish were generally handled far less carefully in the post-war period than they had been in the 1920s and 30s. Using too much ice down in the fish-hold led to consolidation in the lower levels of the storage-pounds and the fish was difficult to remove.

That wuz your ship an' you took a bit o' pride in it.

"But thass nothin' like that now. No. I always remember sailin' the *Una* (LT 198) one Sat'day mornin' [i.e. getting the vessel to sail]. Yeah, the *Una*.[39] 'Cor, she's away! Lovely job! Now we can git away hoom. But afore we could git away, the *skipper* called up on the wireless, 'We're a *deckie* missin'!' Well, when she sailed, she hed a full crew. See? O' course, there wuz this business o' huntin' all round t' find where he'd fell over the side, but in the end we found him in his lodgins! He'd jumped orf the *Una* onta another ship afore she got out o' the Trawl Dock! Yeah, jumped orf his ship an' laid down on the deck of another one. Yeah—but that put a scare up o' everybody. The skipper thought he'd lorst him. Yeah.

"A skipper would hafta be pretty tough t' bring a boat back. You know, he'd hafta stand suffin [censure from his employers for breaking the trip]. Yeah, I think the first night out, the skipper an' the mate used t' take the *watches* 'cause you couln't rely on anyone else. No. That wuz a pity, really, 'cause some o' these chaps (what we call *winos*) were good workin' chaps once they were orf the drink. An' they were sometimes glad t' git t' sea away from all this lot. An' they'd be decent blokes when they come in. Then back they'd go on the ol' booze agin! Mind you, some o' the winos we've got here now, they've never been proper fishermen! When I look round, I only know about three who've bin on a trip or two! An' they wun't much good, anyway."

Billy Thorpe's concluding remarks may seem to have had something of a "not-like-it-used-to-be-in-my-young-days" quality about them, but they were founded in reality. The decade following the Second World War saw the decline and collapse of the North Sea herring fishery, which had been a staple industry locally for more than eight hundred years. This left Lowestoft with a severely compromised fishing capability, in that a substantial proportion of its fleet (totalling 151 port registrations in all, in 1966) had lost a major component of its annual working-cycle and the ability to earn money during the autumn months. The diesel-powered *drifter-trawlers* (either conversions from pre-war steam vessels or newer, purpose-built ones constructed during the 1950s) became increasingly incapable of pulling the heavier trawls needed to fish effectively in the North Sea and of sailing the longer distances required to reach profitable grounds. Put simply, overall increase in the weight and efficiency of the gear and in engine-size made these vessels obsolete. The total fishing-effort directed at the southern North Sea, from the European nations bordering it, reduced stocks and increasingly required greater lengths of travel (even as far as the waters of southern Norway) to find fish in sufficient quantities to make trips profitable.

---

39 This vessel belonged to Drifter Trawlers Ltd. It was built in 1950 for both herring-catching and trawling and had a 360 hp engine. The only firm in the Claridge conglomeration of fishing companies not to have been mentioned in recent footnotes is the Huxley Fishing Company Ltd.

With the herring industry gone, Lowestoft lost a number of its fishing craft and crews. Older hands retired from sea and found other, less physically and socially demanding work (ten-day trawling trips increasingly becoming the norm) and younger men found the traditional maritime way of life less attractive—in spite of the money which could still be earned. During the 1960 and 70s, the town was able to offer lots of alternative work to that found on fishing vessels: in shipbuilding, in light and heavy engineering, in television manufacture, in the construction of bus bodies, and in the food-processing industry. This caused a shortage of local labour on board the remaining trawlers, with the consequent crewing difficulties alluded to by Billy Thorpe in relation to his work as a *ship's husband*. An inward migration of men from the Humber ports (and from other places) was found necessary to maintain crew numbers—though the people who moved to Lowestoft were usually not of the highest calibre and had probably been made redundant in their own home-ports by a decrease in fishing-effort there. Given that they were mainly middle-aged and without close family nearby, there was an inevitability about alcohol becoming one of the main focuses in life—and their presence in town during the 1970s was certainly a noticeable feature.

Had Billy Thorpe been recorded a decade later, in 1990, the drastic shake-up in the British economy generally which had occurred during "the Thatcher years" would have produced a different picture again from that presented in this chapter. Trawling itself was now in trouble and a number of Lowestoft's traditional industries had either terminated or were heading for shut-down.

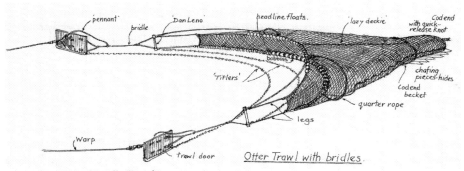

Fig. 8: *Plan of Bridle Trawl-gear*

A line-drawing which shows the bridle type of trawl-gear, referred to in both this chapter and previous ones. It gave the vessel using it a greater sweep of the seabed and therefore the opportunity to catch more fish, but it also required more power to pull it effectively than many of the drifter-trawlers (and even some of the trawlers themselves) had available.

CHAPTER EIGHT

Ministry Research

I'll sing you a song o' the fish o' the sea.
Way down Rio.
I'll sing you a song o' the fish o' the sea.
And we're bound for the Rio Grande.
(Traditional capstan and windlass song)

Systematic scientific research into the conduct of British fisheries was a development of the second half of the nineteenth century, when concern for the levels of stocks (and the livelihoods these supported) began to be expressed at national level. There were a number of reasons for the growing pressure on certain species, which included expanding urban populations which needed to be fed, a steadily increasing number of vessels at sea and developments in gear that led to greater catching-power. The establishment of a research laboratory facility at Lowestoft during the early 1900s was part of the programme inaugurated by The Board of Trade's Fisheries Department (and by its successor, The Board of Agriculture and Fisheries) to promote academic study of the marine environment.[1]

The first building occupied at Lowestoft (in 1902) was one of the houses in Waveney Road (opposite the Trawl Dock), followed by larger premises in the Marina (1905). In 1910, the Lowestoft laboratory was closed and the work moved to London—but ten years later the scientists returned and took up occupation in a pair of large, semi-detached, seafront houses on the Southern Esplanade, which had been built following the town's resort development of the 1840s and 50s. This link with the holiday trade was repeated later when the facility moved into the old *Grand Hotel* on Kirkley Cliff (1955), which had undergone conversion to its new function. Expansion of both personnel and buildings during the 1960s and 70s turned the *Fish Labs*, as they were known locally, into the largest marine study centre in Europe. Since then, as the result of privatisation of this branch of government scientific activity, the number of people employed is a good deal lower, though the laboratories still perform vital work in the field of fisheries and marine research.[2]

It is interesting to reflect that much of the work carried out at Lowestoft over the years, which was calculated to assist the fishing industry to conduct its affairs

---

1 For an illuminating article on the history and development of fisheries research, see J. Ramster, 'Government, Science and the Fisheries', in D. Starkey et al., *England's Sea Fisheries* (London, 2000), pp. 174-187.

2 The institution now carries the acronym *CEFAS* (Centre for Environment, Fisheries and Aquaculture Science).

more effectively and with an eye to the future, usually met with opposition from those it was trying to help. There were various reasons for this, but the main bone of contention was the need for *conservation* of fish stocks. The industry usually regarded this as nothing more than a restriction on its right to earn a living and customarily argued that there was plenty of fish to be caught—even when there was ample evidence to the contrary. The most recent example of this nationally may be seen in the controversy regarding stocks of cod in the North Sea, in which arguments in favour of reduced quotas and even a ban on fishing for the species meet with opposition from those who own and operate the boats. The main difference between agriculture and fishing as suppliers of food is that the former harvests what it has sown, whereas the latter merely takes what is present in a particular location—sometimes, without much (if any) thought for the process of replacement. The British fishing industry often failed to acknowledge that at least some of its problems, at any given time, emanated from the way it conducted its operations and it had traditionally sought to place the blame elsewhere.

Another factor in the lack of rapport between fishermen and scientists was the belief held by many of the former that research into fish behaviour and the marine environment had little use or relevance to the job they did. This was partly the result (or certainly had been in the past) of two completely different spheres of activity having so little in common with each other in terms of the basic pattern of work involved: life on board a drifter or trawler being so different from working in a laboratory environment. And even when scientists went to sea on research vessels, their experiments tended to be regarded with a mild scepticism at best and, at worst, condemned as a waste of time and money. The gap between mere utility and scientific investigation was further widened at one time by the sense that the latter sphere was the province of "educated people", who were not really a part of the everyday, working world. And there is no doubt that some of the scientists did tend to patronise the fishermen with whom they came into contact.

The value of this chapter is that it reflects something of the separation which still exists between the fishing community and the scientific establishment, as well as providing some interesting information concerning fisheries research during the 1940s, 50s and 60s. Herbert Doy (1900-87) was a fisherman from the time he left school up to about halfway through the Second World War. He had considerable experience of both drift-netting and trawling, but decided at the end of hostilities to continue his career at sea on board a Ministry of Fisheries research vessel. His knowledge of fishing in a wide variety of British waters must have made him a very useful employee and it also enabled him to view at least some of the activities he was involved in with an informed eye (tape-recording made, 23 September 1980).

"I come out o' the services after the war and went on *the Labour*, which you do. I never hed nothin' orf it, 'cause they said to me, 'We're got a job for you straight away. Go bosun o' the *Leeds* (LT 131). Bring her hoom to Low'stoft.' She wuz at Grimsby, but I refused it and went a-trawlin' for a little while along o' ol' Fred Nunn in the *Mill o' Buckie* (R 129). She wuz a *drifter-trawler*; she belonged to Ramsgate. Anyway, we kept a-comin' in and layin' for in eight or nine days, waitin' for people. We couldn't git the crews, so I packed me hand in and got a job as a *deckie* wi' *the Ministry*. Thass when we went away after the *Sir Lancelot* (LT 263). She laid in at Low'stoft at first and I signed up (we all did) on her mess deck on the tenth o' December, 1946. Yes, then they took her down to Leith to be converted. Ol' Oscar Pipes [ref. Chapter 4] wuz supposed to tairke her down, but I can't remember now whether he did or not. That wuz snowin' like hell when we got to Leith to bring her back and they brought us blankets up from Low'stoft in a lorry. We were there ten days altogether, in Leith, livin' in the *Mission* [The Royal National Mission to Deep Sea Fishermen]. Then we brought her back hoom.

Plate 13: *Sir Lancelot (LT 263)*

The research vessel Sir Lancelot (LT 263), seen heading into Lowestoft harbour. Built at Aberdeen in 1941, to Admiralty specifications, she had performed wartime minesweeping duties before taking up a more peaceful function after hostilities had ceased.

"She wuz a minesweeper durin' the war and they converted her to oil from bein' a coal-burner.[3] Yeah, she hed an oil burnin' steam engine put in her. We brought her back to Low'stoft on New Year's Eve, 1947, and the boiler give out as we come in. That packed up just outside the piers and the Yacht Basin wuz as far as we could git. The poor ol' *firemen* [engineers] were standin' up to their necks in water! The *tubes* blew out, yuh see. They fitted her out here. Took six foot orf the funnel, fifteen foot orf the foremast, nine foot orf the mizzen and done away wi'

---

3 The *Sir Lancelot* had been built in 1941, at Aberdeen, to Admiralty specifications. She was a conventional trawler of the time, but was used for minesweeping while hostilities lasted—as was much of the British trawling fleet, which had been requisitioned at the outbreak of war.

the two *lifeboats*. She hed one each side, but they done away wi' them and put one in the middle. Then we come down to the Trawl Dock and they hetta try her. Stability test. We all hetta git ashore. She passed out all right, though. Yeah, in the Trawl Dock.[4]

"Oh, she wuz a terrible thing when we first fetched her hoom from Leith. She bloomin' near turned over. Too much *top-weight*. And she wuz a *dirty thing* after she'd bin fitted out. The scientists' place down below wuz all right. They hed a lovely place down underneath the wheelhouse. Our place wuz aft. Our mess deck wuz right aft and I're sin that full o' water! Yeah, we shipped a sea once and filled that full o'water. Poor ol' Vic Dearlin' and me hung on the galley door, legs a-floatin'! That filled the whole mess deck up. Poor ol' Barney Smith wuz skipper of her then. Oh, she wuz a dirty thing! We went for a *trip* round the Muckle Flugga there once, round to Shetland. We were goin' down there fishin' and she bloody near turned over! So we hed to turn back and *run* her. We hed a Scotch scientist aboard and we shoulda landed him at Aberdeen. But instead o' that, we hetta run right to bloody Shields [North Shields] afore we could land him. Yes, she nearly went over. The water come aboard and she laid over, so we hetta turn her round and run afore the wind.

"There wuz only four *deckies* in her, then the *mate*, *skipper* and *captain*.[5] Yeah, and you'd gotta hev a *ticket* afore you could go mate o' her. The deckies did the watches; two on each one. Then there wuz the *chief engineer*, the *second engineer* and two *firemen*. You hed a firemen on each watch: one on the chief's watch and one on the second's watch.[6] O' course, they're got more of a crew now. Yeah, they're got six deckies now and they work three watches. We only used to work watch-on, watch-off, when I wuz in the job. We used to sometimes carry three or four scientists. That all depended on what sort o' job you were on. I mean, we hev bin out with only two. When we first went in her, we could only stop out eight or nine days, but that wuz because the chief only wanted to be out that long. The second engineer found out that she could stop out at sea longer. He say, 'She'll go ten or a dozen days!' So we started to do ten-day trips then. And the chief got the sack!

"We went every bloomin' where in her. All round the Irish Sea, up round Dublin and the ol' Hid [Head] o' Kinsale. We even went to Malta. Yes! Gibraltar. We took *frogmen* out there. You know that frogman what got lorst? He wuz one of

---

4 The stability test consisted of putting pig-iron all along one side of the vessel, to see how far it heeled over.

5 The captain was in overall charge of navigation; the skipper's main task was to direct the fishing operations.

6 The deckhands took the wheelhouse and deck watches with either the skipper or the mate; the engineering staff saw to the engine-room ones. The length of a watch at sea was usually four hours.

'em.[7] They were goin' down with the trawls, these frogmen. Yeah, as long as we were trawlin' close to the Rock, they were goin' down and takin' fillum. Yeah, you could see the bottom there. And one o' the frogmen went down inside the trawl and come out o' the *cod-end*. Yeah, and he took his shoes orf and tied 'em on the cod. So when I went to undo the cod-end, that wuz undone alriddy! Yeah, he undone that and tied his shoes on it. That could ha' bin dangerous, doin' that. He might ha' got hung up. O' course, yuh gear is right wide open when you're a-towin'.[8]

"We used to go trawlin' out here in the North Sea as well—down orf the Dorgger [Dogger Bank] and them places. We even went acrorss to Esbjerg in her. One time, we went and fitted out at Hamburg for suckin' up herrin'.[9] Yeah, we laid there ten days. I're got a photograph o' when we were out there, in Germany. Thass what they give me for bein' the longest servant in the *Sir Lancelot*. I wuz fourteen years in her altogether; then we went arter the *Clione* (LT 421) and I wuz four years in her.[10] She wuz a marv'llous ship! Yeah, she wuz a king to that other one! Yeah, you thought you were in heaven, a-sailin' in her. She wuz a lovely sea boat. That she wuz.

"The *Sir Lancelot* wuz powerful. She'd pull the gear all right. Yeah, she could pull the gear on top o' the water if you wanted. But she wuz just very dirty in bad weather. Yeah, you'd hetta *dodge* her up inta the wind then. We hetta hev all new *scuppers* put in her. She hed so much water aboard of her sometimes, the scuppers wun't big enough to let it out! So they hetta put some more in. Yeah, an' they wun't big enough to let the water out! She used to *lay over* so much, see. Take a sea aboard and she'd hold the water. She couldn't git rid of it. That frightened half them scientists up there [i.e. at the Fisheries Laboratories]. Especially when we first brought her hoom.

"We worked just the ordinary [i.e. *otter*] trawls on them boats. When I first went in the *Sir Lancelot*, they'd be seventy-odd feet on the *hidline* [headline] an' about 100 or more on the *ground-rope*. That all depended on the water how long yuh *towed* [i.e. on the depth of water and tidal conditions]. And if you were workin' up this way, you wun't hev above seventy-five fathom o' warp out. But if you were workin' deeper water, you'd hev 120 or somethin' like that. Sometimes even 150. That all depended on where you were workin'. You generally hev three

---

7 Commander Lionel ("Buster") Crabbe, who disappeared at Portsmouth in 1956, during the state visit of Nikolai Bulganin and Nikita Kruschev to this country. He may have been involved in espionage activity directed at the Soviet Union's naval vessels.

8 The film taken of trawls being towed off Gibraltar is still in existence.

9 This refers to suction or vacuum fishing, which drew herrings from the seabed. Both the Germans and the Danes used this method extensively during the 1950s and 60s, with much of the catch being processed into fish-meal. Such practice aroused critical comment among British drift-net fishermen.

10 The *Clione* was a new, purpose-built, research vessel, which was launched in 1961.

times the warp you're got water.[11] Yeah, three times. And you only hed about hour *tows* usually. Sometimes only half an hour. That wuz to keep the fish alive and stop 'em chafin'. If you tow too long, yuh fish are all chafed and they're no good for *markin'* [tagging]. Yeah, sometimes you only tew half an hour. Oh, I've bin knockin' about [killing time] longer aboard o' her than I did in a trawler![12] Only the watch used to haul. Yeah. Then, if that got a bit rough like, you'd *lay* for about two hours an' git some sleep.

"They marked plaice and all sorts. Well, they used to mark everything: cod, haddicks, plaice, soles, herrin'.[13] Yes, they tagged herrin'. Up here [indicating with his finger], on the top o' the neck. They were silver pins what went through inta the fish. I're got one somewhere what I had from when I wuz up on the *store*. The fishermen used to git five bob [25p] when they found a marked fish. Yeah, but the Lab people would wanta know where that wuz picked up. When I wuz on the store, they sent me a bit o' fish up from the *Clione* and this plaice hed a tag on. I remember once, when we were down orf *Kildas* [St. Kilda] markin' hake, and we lorst four trawls! That wuz the worst bloody turn-out we ever had. You could see the ground—rocks, stuck up like steeples! No one would ever tow there. But the bloke in charge kept a-sayin', 'Well, we're gotta experiment.' We hetta go inta Stornoway and git fixed up wi' new trawls, ready to start afresh. And we hed the four split trawls laid about. We were full o' gear! Tons of it! Expensive, too. I wouldn't like to tell yuh what I know—the money thrown away.

"O' course, there wuz a *laboratory* aboard. And *tanks*. We used to work the tanks all along the ship's side. Yeah, they were to keep the fish alive in, and there were taps runnin' all the time wi' sea water. When we first started markin' fish, ol' Wimpenny [R.S. Wimpenny] wuz in charge, and you hed a chute wi' water runnin' down it inta the sea so the fish din't hit too hard when they put 'em back. But, the latter part o' the time, they just threw 'em over. Some of 'em used to do such daft things and all. I used to keep quiet. The only time I spook out wuz about a *flow-meter*, when one of 'em shoved it on arse-uppards.[14] I say, "Thass upside-down." This wuz on the *Sir Lancelot*. Anyway, they made it right, but never say nothin' to me. But when I went on the wheel, Joe Sutton, the captain, say to me, 'I can see you goin' on a bloody leave there directly!' Yeah, because I spook about the flow-meter. 'Know nothin',' he say. 'When that come to them, if you know they're doin' wrong, let 'em do it.' So I used to do everything they said. Yeah, I

---

11 In other words, the length of warp used was generally about three times as long as the depth of water.

12 This means that the work was not as unrelenting and demanding as it was on a commercial trawler.

13 Tagging fish was carried out in order to ascertain the movement of species, in terms of seasonality, distances covered and the time taken. Electronic tags were introduced for some species later on [late 1960s].

14 A flow-meter was an instrument which was used to measure the speed of tidal currents.

kept quiet after that, all the years I wuz there. I could speak a lot if I liked.

"We used to sell some o' the catches on Low'stoft Market. Yeah, but that got stopped. There wuz a little bit o' fiddlin' goin' on. I dussn't say too much. Yeah, we were doin' the work [i.e. the crew] and they were gittin' the money. We got just a wage on board. £5 16s 0d [£5.80] a week, thass what we got. And you'd gotta pay for yuh food out o' that. Yes, yes. Yeah, thass right. We hetta pay for our own food. O' course, we allus got a bit o' fish at the end of a trip. I used to look after all that—ice it, share it out. I wuz a *deckie*, thass all. We din't carry a *bosun*. A bosun is like a mate on them sort o' ships and you'd gotta hev a skipper's ticket to go bosun o' her.

"There wuz no big hauls in her.[15] No, no. I remember we went herrin' catchin' in her once. *Herrin' trawls*. We went up orf Boulogne. Yeah, along o' the Frenchmen. Workin' along o' them. And we couldn't git the fish they were gittin'. They were fillin' theirselves up and we were gittin' nothin'! And we went inta Boulogne and laughed about it. We never hed enough bloomin' *warp*! We were givin' it the sairme as what we did when we were a-trawlin', but we hetta give it two or three times as much agin. We only just *tittled* the bottom, but that [i.e. the net] hetta lay right along the bottom. So when we come out agin, we give her another double that warp and we got sixty cran o' herrin'! We brought 'em inta Low'stoft. The trawl hed *kites* on. Yeah, kites an' *bottles* [on the headline], and *chain* on yuh *ground-ropes*. Just a little bit o' chain, thass all. That wun't heavy.[16] I couldn't see the good o' that sort o' fishin' myself, though. There wun't nothin' in it, wuz there? They shoulda gone somewhere else to see if there wuz herrin' there. Thass experiment, ent it? Not go where the herrin' alriddy are.

"That *vacuum fishin'* I told you about—oh dear, that wuz a pest. When we come out o' Germany, we went on the Norway Deeps and that way after herrin'. Yeah, we went a-suckin' on 'em up. We never got one! A German scientist come out with us. He hed all the lights. He hed all the lights fixed up on the deck, shinin' on the water, and he hed a thing lowered down inta the water [the suction tube]. That wuz separate. The whole thing wuz a washout. Another few thousand pounds went! We used to go midwater fishin' arter herrin' as well, with a *midwater trawl*. That'd be about halfway down, about half the depth o' water. That wuz all floated up wi' bottles—about sixty of 'em, I believe, on the hidline. We went down to the nor'ad there, down below the Long Shoal and them plairces, and we used to git some fish in that.[17] When I come ashore and worked on the store, I rigged one up for 'em.

---

15 This was mainly because the length of tows was simply not long enough to catch a lot of fish. Another contributory factor was the nature of the fishing, which was carried out for scientific experiment, not commercial gain.

16 For an explanation and diagram of the herring trawl, see Davis, *Fishing Gear*, pp. 108-110.

17 The fishing grounds referred to here are off the Norfolk coast, about twenty-five to thirty miles north-east by east of Cromer.

"The *Clione* used to go to just the same plairces as the *Sir Lancelot*, only she wuz a lot better ship. Yes, she wuz a lovely job, she wuz. You could do anything with her. She'd turn round in her own length, she would. One or two chaps in the orffice up there used to come out on her for pleasure when they were on their holidays. I're sin fish a-goin' inta the trawls on her. Sat down below an' watched 'em go in. Cor blimey, yes, you could see all of 'em down there. They used to call us down sometimes. Doctor Cushin' [D.H. Cushing] used to. 'Come down here an' hev a look,' he'd say. That wuz pretty good, that wuz. You could see 'em go in. You could see yuh trawl open and everything. They hed cameras hangin' on the warps and that shew up inta the lab. Yeah, on the screen there. Oh, some o' the scientists were all right; one or two would even help yuh *haul*. But others were a little more uppish and used to like lookin' over the *top rail*.[18]

"We worked gear only one side in the *Clione*, but both sides in the *Sir Lancelot*. Port side in the *Clione*. She wuz covered in the other side. Covered in. Thass right. And that din't matter her bein' covered in neither, because you can't work down the Shoals, down the Leman an' Ower and them places, with a starboard trawl anyway.[19] Yeah, the tide run that hard and that'll strike yuh over the top o' the banks. When you were towin' yuh port gear down there, that'd be right clean orf the side o' the boat. That wun't towin' behind yuh! Yeah, you'd be workin' inside the bank, inside the Leman, in about nine fathom o' water, and yuh gear used to be right orf the side. And you used to hetta hold the boat orf. Yeah, keep her hid about, oh, very near west, to keep orf the bank. See, the tide wanted to drive yuh over the top o' the bank. And if you hed starboard gear down, over you'd go!

"That wuz about the easiest job I ever hed in my life. Yeah, that wuz better'n haul-trawlin'. That wuz a lot easier. Cor, yes! That wuz *play* to what it wuz a-trawlin'. When I wuz trawlin' afore the war, we only used to git one night in. Thass all. Land yuh own fish, go arter yuh own ice, take her up alongside the coalin' quay and git coaled, and be down at eight o' clock in the mornin'. Then away yuh go agin! I hev bin to sea every day for sixteen weeks. This wuz here in Low'stoft, in the *Ocean's Shield* (LT 386), along o' ol' Sam Read.[20] I wuz along o' him in the *Cyclamen* (LT 1136) for nine years, then he bought the *Ocean's Shield*. And our first voyage, afore we settled, wuz sixteen weeks. And we'd bin at sea every day! I din't know, not afore ol' Jack Robinson, the *driver* [engineer], explained it to me. He say, 'Herbie, do yuh know? We're bin to sea every day for sixteen weeks.' I say, 'How the hell is that?' He say, 'Well, we come in this mornin' and landed, din't we? And we're bin doin' that and then we're bin goin'

---

18 In other words, view what was going on from the bridge and not get physically involved.

19 The Leman and Ower banks were favourite summer grounds with Lowestoft trawlermen. They are now largely inaccessible for large-scale trawling activity because of the presence of gas rigs in that particular sector of the North Sea.

20 This vessel had been built in 1896 for line-fishing but had later been converted to other work. She was originally called the *Craigievar* and was first registered in Aberdeen (A 782).

away to sea agin the next day. So we're bin at sea the day we come in, hent we?' And I told ol' Sam Read about it (I wuz *third hand* with him). I say, 'Do yuh know what, skipper? We're bin to sea every day for sixteen weeks.' He say, 'How the hell is that?' Hell if he din't shout! He say, 'You're hed a bloody night in, hent yuh?' I say, 'Yis, but we come in that mornin' and landed, so we were at sea that day, wun't we?' See, we used to come in about six o' clock in the mornin'. Yeah. This wuz summertime. We should ha' gone round to Fleetwood, but we stayed out here and worked the Long Shoal and the Leman and the Ower. We were gittin' good trips, so we kept a-goin' all summer.

"On the Ministry boats, we'd sometimes git three or four days in. But that all depended, that did. That wun't a reg'lar thing, not yuh time in. And when you were laid in, you did jobs aboard—yes, chip [rust, off metal], paint. I're bin up the *Clione's* mast, a-paintin'. I wuz up there once an' Joe Sutton told me to come out on it. He say, 'Let them young-uns go up!' Yeah, I wuz sixty odd then. Oh yeah, you hetta do everything yuhself. All the paintin'. Wheelhouse, funnel. I're bin paintin' the funnel at sea! Yeah, a-paintin' on her up. If they hent got much for yuh to do, you'd be a-paintin' while you were at sea. When we were in, we used to lay up-through-bridge.[21] Yeah just afore yuh git to where they are now, agin Mitchell's salt store.

"I come orf the *Clione* in the end and went ashore, because o' my missus allus bein' ill. Yeah, ol' Jack Wright hed died and they asked me would I take his job on, on the store.[22] Yeah, so I took the job on. I used to mairke up all the little trawls— *shrimp trawls* and *prawn trawls* and *sprat trawls*. *Push nets* as well. They're a net wi' two legs on. They're five and a half foot acrorss the *belly*, and then they part and they're got legs (six foot legs), like yuh trousers. Yeah, just the sairme as a pair o' trousers, and they used to hev them on a frame an' push 'em along for shrimps, just in front of 'em. They used to push it along the beach. Yeah, shovin' it along kept the legs out an' whoever wuz pushin' it wuz betwin the legs. That wuz on a wooden frame. I're got one up the allotment what they give me.

"Oh, I made up everything there. They used to send the papers down and I'd gotta work orf this plan. You give them one to do, though, and they couldn't do it! They'd got the plan, but they couldn't do it. Ha, ha, ha, yeah. You used all different-sized twine. Oh yis, yis. All different sizes. Yeah, and that wuz all *sisal* when I first went there [in 1965]. Then the *nylon* crept in and the *terylene*. That all come in then. Well, they hetta go and dump all the bloody sisal *cod-ends* and *trawls*! Dumped 'em somewhere in a pit. That wuz just arter I finished and come out on it. They went and dumped 'em because they'd got all this light stuff. The

---

21 *Up-through-bridge* was the description commonly used at one time to describe anywhere in Lowestoft's inner harbour, to the west of the road bridge.

22 The net store belonging to the Ministry of Agriculture and Fisheries (as it was then called) was situated on Commercial Road, just to the north of Lowestoft's inner harbour.

nylon and that. So they chucked all the sisal away. Cor, there wuz a helluva waste. I dun't dare begin to tell yuh.

"I once done a net up the labs there at Pakefield—a big net.[23] I couldn't do it at the store. That wuz a really big net, and that went up an' down the floor there [in the former ballroom] nine times, this net did. That wuz a *purse seine*. Yeah, we din't make it; we fixed it. You know, rigged it up for workin'. That wuz for the *Clione*. Yeah, that wuz a bloody job, that wuz! Thass when my boy come up and see me, 'cause he wuz foreman at Cosalt.[24] See, he used to do all the work afore I went on the store. Cosalt hed all them jobs. When I went there, I used to do 'em. They never sent nothin' out then. See, ol' Jack Wright, he might mairke a little shrimp net or suffin like that, but all the big trawls used to go to Cosalt. But when I went there, I used to do 'em. Yeah, done it all. Never sent nothin' out. And thass what I told 'em what come down from London [ministry officials]. The *Ernest Holt* (GY 591) hed three or four trawls condemned, and they sent 'em down here, and I mairde a trawl up for 'em out o' what wuz condemned. I went out on the Denes and done it.[25] Yeah, I cut all the parts out o' the condemned nets and made up a new one. Ol' Tinks Muttitt wuz with me. You oughta seen the visitors tairkin' our photo doin' that.

"Them boats used to hev all different kinds o' gear. Yeah, they used to hev all different turnouts for the different grounds. Praps they'd hev *rubber ground-ropes*, and then they'd hev the *wolded* ones. They used to work *titlers* and all. Sometimes as many as three! Yeah, I used to hetta rig three titlers on them little shrimp trawls and the small fish-trawls. They were only eight foot, ten foot and twelve foot beams. Yeah, they used to work one titler right acrorss from toe to toe, and another one shackled on so that hung about six inches from that other one, and then the last one would hang about six inches at the back o' that. We only used to work two on the big trawls. In the *Clione*, that wuz. She'd work a *long titler* and a *bosom titler*. I hev worked *on-the-door gear*, but the [otter] doors drive up all the shit inta yuh trawl. But if you hev wire *legs* on, the doors are further away from

---

23 As was mentioned in the introduction to this chapter, the Ministry laboratories were based at the former *Grand Hotel*, on Kirkley Cliff (they still are). Because the establishment's address was Pakefield Road, it was usually referred to as *Pakefield*, though it was actually situated in the old parish of Kirkley, which had long been absorbed into what became known as South Lowestoft following the town's expansion during the second half of the nineteenth century.

24 Cosalt was a marine supply company, which serviced the fishing industry and which had originated on Humberside as the Great Grimsby Coal, Salt and Tanning Company. It is still in operation in the town as Cosalt International Ltd., on the School Road Industrial Estate.

25 The North Denes, at Lowestoft—an open area of scrub grassland close to the beach, which had once been an area of manorial waste used largely for rough grazing and as an open-air wharf, prior to the development of the harbour.

the trawl and the less muck you git.[26]

"Another thing I hetta do wuz shove *pockets* in the nets. Oh yes, shove pockets in them. You used to run 'em from yuh *flopper*—run 'em up to a point. I're done all o' that. Oh yes. I're done *bunts, wings, squares, bellies.* Mended *cod-ends.* Rigged 'em up. Shoved half a cod-end in when one is chafed. I're put *blinders* in, to stop the fish from comin' up the net. You used to hev right a small mesh inside yuh trawl. Yeah, a small mesh the length o' yuh cod-end, inside. That wuz a bloody job, that wuz! That wuz to catch small fish, yeah. They used to lose so many small fish through the bigger meshes, yuh see, so they'd shove blinders in. We used to call 'em *covers* [in the Ministry]. O' course, I hev worked blinders on the *drifter-trawlers.* Yeah. You wun't allowed to, but you done it to git the *slips* [small soles]. Then you'd tairke the blinder out when you were in the harbour. Yeah, that wuz so when they used to come round an' check the gear, that wuz all clear.[27]

"I never touched *drift-nets* when I wuz on the store. No, I never hed nothin' to do wi' them. They used to hev 'em on the little ol' *Onaway* (LT 358), but I never touched 'em. I used to do trawls for the *Corella* (LT 767). Oh yeah. I're bin aboard her to do trawls, but I never worked aboard her [i.e. as a crew member]. No one ever interfered with yuh down on the store. No, they just used to bring the plans up and I used to carry on wi' the job. Yeah, I din't mind it at all. Sometimes you got it a bit hard, but sometimes you'd have it easy. I remember once there, one o' the blokes from Burnham [Burnham-on-Crouch] went out in the *Platessa* (LT 205) and they hed a prawn trawl which they couldn't mend aboard the ship, and that surprised me.[28] Skippers an' mates on board, and they sent it up the store to me! Anyway, this bloke come rushin' up and say, 'Herbert, can you git that done?' See, he wanted to git away in the afternoon. I say, 'I'll try.' And I got it done, riddy to go to sea at four o' clock in the afternoon. He say, 'I wish we could git you down to Burnham!' He say to me, 'I wish we could git you down there.' I say, 'Well, you git me and my missus down there, and git us a house,' I say, 'and I'll come down.'

"I wuz the oldest bloke in The Ministry at one time. I was, yeah. That wuz when I wuz at sea, latter part o' the time, and when I wuz on the store. I never wished

---

26 Otter-doors on a trawl act as paravanes and help to keep the mouth of the net open, but they also serve to stir up debris from the seabed and direct it into the net. If wire strops (legs) are used as spacers to separate the doors from the net, much of this debris escapes through the gaps created on either side of the gear.

27 Blinders were (and still are) illegal because they were a means of catching fish smaller than the permitted minimum size for the various species. Ministry officials used to carry out periodic random checks on vessels in port to check whether or not the regulation-sized meshes were being used.

28 There was a small marine research laboratory at Burnham-on-Crouch, Essex. It is now closed.

myself back a-trawlin', though. No, never! I used to git a lot o' leg-pullin' [from other fishermen] when I wuz on the Ministry boats. Oh yes. But I could put up wi' that. I used to say, 'You dun't git sore hands here!' Ha, ha, ha, ha. Yeah. And you wun't doin' half the work. You done some *guttin' up*, but not much. Cor, crikey, no! Nothin' near what you done a-trawlin'. Nothin' near the *mendin'*, neither. No. You ent after *a livin'* when you're in The Ministry. You'd say, 'Well, all right, we wun't shift over. We'll *lay* and mend that. But anybody aboard a trawler, he'd shift and shoot his other trawl, wun't he?[29]

"I lorst money by not keepin' trawlin'. O' course, I did! I coulda earnt tons o' money, the trips they were makin'. And they all kept a-laughin' at me about that. 'Look at the money you're a-losin'!' they kept a-sayin'. I say, 'Yis. But I got caught arter the 1914 War. A few years arter that, everything went down.' I say, 'I aren't goin' to git caught this time.' And thass how I come to join the Ministry. Yeah, I thought, 'If I hang in here, I'll git a pension when I finish. When I finish trawlin', I'll git nothin'. I see Joe Sutton not long afore he died.[30] He come up the pub here [the *Prince Albert,* in Park Road], a couple o' year ago. He say, 'You hed the laugh arter all, dint yuh?' See, thass what I hed in mind—the security. A lot of 'em on the trawlers earnt big money, but what did they do with it? They only juiced it away, din't they? Yeah, earnt a ton o' money and juiced it away and got nothin'! I know my wages wun't that good, but I finished up all right, din't I? Got a pension and a lump-sum o' money. I got two lots, I did. When I come ashore, I got a lump-sum and a pension. Then I got tempory civil servant—four years in the store—and I got another lump-sum an' another £1 a week extra pension."

---

29 If a trawl net got damaged on rough ground, the skipper would usually move his vessel to another area and use the port side gear. The starboard side net would then have to await repair for a convenient time between hauls. If the damage was extensive, the net was put ashore when the catch was landed and replacement gear taken on board.

30 The man who had been captain on the *Sir Lancelot* and the *Clione.*

'Shooting'
–the nets.

Mast & Gear
and Wheelhouse
omitted

Hauling

Fig. 9: Shooting and Hauling Drift-nets

Line-drawings which show drift-nets being shot and hauled. The former operation was relatively quick in favourable conditions (about half an hour or so), but the latter could be many hours at a time in the event of big catches of herring or the weather turning for the worse.

CHAPTER NINE

The Other Side of the Tracks

Railroad Bill, Railroad Bill,
A little way up on Railroad Hill.
Ride, ride, ride.
Kill me a chicken; send me the wing.
You think I work; I don't do a thing!
Ride, ride, ride.
(Traditional American folksong: *Railroad Bill*)

The development of the railway network nationally during the early Victorian period was of crucial importance in assisting the growth of the British fishing industry, and of nowhere was this truer than Lowestoft. Samuel Morton Peto, the builder-contractor, discovered the potential of the Suffolk town during the 1840s and, within a decade, had changed its character for ever. He bought the bankrupt harbour company in 1844 and proceeded to develop a larger and more effective facility; he purchased the old South Common land and laid out a model *seaside resort* of the time; and he established a railway link with Norwich, which opened in 1847. It is said that, at an initial meeting with the civic fathers in Lowestoft Town Hall (or, rather, its predecessor, the Town Chamber), Peto claimed that the fish landed by local vessels could be delivered alive in Birmingham and Manchester. This colourful image was of lesser significance where herrings were concerned, because much of the catch was cured for export abroad, but it was important for sales of demersal species.

Much of the *white fish* landed in Lowestoft at that time was caught on longlines and handlines by small craft working directly off the beach and was sold locally. The provision of rail links (a line to Ipswich, and from thence to London, followed that to Norwich) made it possible for large-scale catches to be moved to the industrial centres, and it is no accident that the development of trawling in Lowestoft mainly occurred during the third quarter of the nineteenth century. It was greatly assisted by the arrival of fishermen from Kentish ports, who were looking for new grounds to exploit—and then discovered them between the coasts of East Anglia and Holland. They had tried initially to get a share of the Dogger Bank activity, begun in the 1830s by men from Brixham, but had found the Hull-Grimsby fishing a closed shop effectively and therefore had to try elsewhere. Their arrival (and that of their families) in Lowestoft was one of a number of important factors in the town's expansion throughout the whole of the Victorian period. Let census figures alone tell the tale: in 1831, the town's population was 4,238; in 1901, it was 23,385.

Plate 14: Lucas Bros. Railway Station at Lowestoft

An engraving of Lowestoft Railway Station, dating from 1855 and showing the Italianate style of architecture so beloved of its creator, Samuel Morton Peto. The lines linking the town with Norwich (1847) and Ipswich (1859), together with Peto's harbour and fish market improvements, were foundation blocks of Lowestoft's growth and prosperity thereafter. The scene shown here has a restrained elegance about it, showing visitors for the Southern Esplanade resort arriving, modified to a small degree by the loaded handcart in the foreground.

By the first decade of the twentieth century, the role of the railway in assisting and servicing the Lowestoft fishing industry was well established. A line ran directly from the Central Station into the Fish Market and the passage of goods trains to and from the quayside became a daily feature of the town's commerce. William Thurling (1908-97) was a railwayman for forty-three years, but he had also been a fisherman in the earlier part of his working life and had had experience of drift-netting, trawling and seining. His recollections are therefore doubly valuable, serving as corroborative material for much that has already been covered in this book and providing an interesting account of day-to-day activity in a service-industry vital to the country's economic success. As with so many other boys of his generation, Bill Thurling's first contact with fishing began before he had left school, when he went to sea with a relative to get a taste of life on board and ascertain whether or not he liked it (tape-recording made, 7 April 1982).

"I wuz twelve years old, when my Uncle Micky (Micky Mewse) say to me, 'Would yuh like to come out for a *trip*?' This wuz on the *Iceberg* (LT 662). I wuz on my summer holidays from school, so this'd be the end o' August, beginnin' o' September [1920]. I say, 'Yis.' And away I go, you know. And we hent got far out to sea afore she started rollin' and jumpin', and I started feelin' a bit queer. My uncle say to me, 'You'd better go down in the bunk.' So I went down up for'ad, in the *foc'sle*, and I wuz in that bunk four days! And on the third day, my uncle brought me a *hunch* o' bread and jam down, and a mug o' tea. Do yuh think I could drink that? No! Or eat the other stuff. Anyhow, after the fourth day, that sorta calmed down a bit and I got up on deck and helped when they hauled the trawl. We were fishin' orf the Leman [Leman Bank]. And I also helped the cook to peel the spuds, 'cause I wuz only *pleasure-trippin'* and you hetta do suffin for yuh keep.

"Yeah, I sort o' mucked about and helped and then that started blowin' up a lot more wind. Well, that got nearly gale force, so we hetta clear orf the bank 'cause you git so much swell. And the ol' skipper say, 'I think we'll run in.' See, the bloomin' *mizzen* [sail] blowed out and we runned inta Yarmouth Roads. That wuz on a Sunday, and the trip wuz nearly up, so we runned inta Yarmouth Roads and laid there. And I could see the trams runnin' along the front [promenade]! Then the ol' skipper (Skipper Goldspink) say, 'What about hevin' Sunday tea at hoom?' And the crew agreed, so away we go. We upped anchor and drawed up to Low'stoft, yuh see, and went in so we had our tea at hoom. And the skipper say to me, 'You dun't wanta come no more, do yuh, boy?' I say, 'Yis, I wun't mind comin' another trip.' And I went the next trip with him. O' course, I'd got rid o' the sea-sickness then. They runned about a week, them little ol' *drifter-trawlers*, 'cause they couldn't carry enough coal to last much longer.[1] Anyhow, I enjoyed that trip, and I wuz never sick from that day to when I went in the war.

"Wel, o' course I hetta go back to school after them two trips. But durin' that time, my uncle, Billy Jenner, used to git me to go for trips with him on the *Hoom Fishin'*. He wuz a boatowner. He had about three boats: the *Our Allies* (LT 492), the *Nevertheless* (LT 1148) and the *Outline* (LT 1211). So he say to me, 'Are yuh comin' for a trip with us tonight?' I say, 'Yis, I'll come out wi' yuh.' So I used to go for a weekend trip with him, yuh see. Yeah, I used to go out with him and thass how I got used to goin' to sea. And, o' course, when I wuz about durin' the week, I used to work in his big garden up Kirkley Park Road.[2] Thass where he used to live.

"Now, when I come fourteen, my mother wuz glad to git me out o' the cupboard. She hed ten of us at hoom—ten! So ol' Billy Jenner say to me, 'Do yuh wanta come down to Shetlands with us?' I say, 'yis.' So on my fourteenth birthday [22

1 Drifter-trawlers used much more coal when trawling than they did when engaged upon herring- catching, because towing the gear (rather than riding to a fleet of nets) consumed greater quantities of fuel.

2 A number of local boatowners lived in this particular road in South Lowestoft and there are some fine residences in the Arts and Crafts style still to be seen.

May 1922], we were sailin' out past Low'stoft. We were goin' to Shetlands. Yeah, we were sailin' out down there. And the first land we come to, arter we sailed past Cromer, wuz Scarborough. Scarborough Castle, I could see that. And we steamed all the way down the coast till we left Scotland. Then we went acrorss to Shetlands. O' course, that took a while.[3] I dun't know whether that wuz two days altogether. I believe it wuz. You left Low'stoft and you were steamin' all night till the next night. That mighta bin longer. Then you'd *shoot* orf Lerwick when yuh got there.

"I enjoyed that trip down there. I used to help 'em push the ol' *trolleys* up the *stages*. You know, they used to run the herrins up on trolleys. You'd put about a cran on a trolley and run it on rails up to the stage where the girls were all guttin'. We were there all the while till September, then we come hoom. See, you hetta come hoom to change nets and then you'd go down as far as Grimsby and start agin.[4] I din't git nothin' for that voyage 'cause I wuz on a *pleasure trip*, but they'd learnt me a lot o' things—how to cook and that. An', o' course, when I come back to Low'stoft after that Scotch voyage, my uncle got me a berth as *cook* along o' Starcher Catchpole and young Noey [Noah] Ayers in the *East Briton* (LT 447). And I done the Hoom Fishin' in her and paid orf at £47 a share.[5]

"After I'd done *the Fishin'* in her, they say to me, 'Do yuh want to come round to Plymouth with us?' I say, 'No, I dun't think I wanta go to Plymouth.' So I went trawlin' in my uncle's boat, the *Outline* (LT 1211). He wanted a cook, out o' Low'stoft, so I went in her. She wuz a bran' new ship [built in 1920] and I went out in her, but I only done two trips. I soon hed enough o' that! Too long out at a time. Too long out. A week at a time. I din't go a lot on that. Anyhow, I come out o' her and went round the Market to look for a *berth*, like you always do—to see what little smoke wuz comin' out o' the chimneys [funnels] when the drivers used to start orf early in the year.[6] You'd look round the Hamilton Dock, and you'd see a little smoke comin' out o' the chimney, and you used to go aboard then and ask the ol' driver who wuz goin' skipper of her. And he used to tell yuh and then you used to say, 'I'll try an' find out where he live.' Thass how you could git a berth,

---

3 The distance from Lowestoft to the Shetland Isles was over 500 miles.

4 A preliminary week or two working off Grimsby signalled the start of the Home Fishing. The nets were changed after the Shetland venture because a slightly larger mesh-size was required for the East Anglian autumn herring.

5 Mr. Thurling, as cook, would have been on a half-share of the profits of the voyage, so his pay-off would have been £23 10s 0d [£23.50]. The voyage would have been about ten weeks' duration, which means that his average weekly pay was over £2 (he had not been drawing weekly allotment payments, which were then deducted when the final settling was made)—a good rate for a boy of fourteen years old.

6 This refers to vessels which had been laid up for a period of time, but whose owners had decided to get them ready for fishing once more. The engineer went aboard ahead of anyone else, to perform any maintenance work required on the machinery and ensure that the boiler was sound.

yuh see. And that wuz how I went on the *Livonia* (LT 545), an *Elliott pot*—a little upright boiler.[7] And the cookin' stove wuz all down below in the cabin, so you used to hetta cook down in the cabin in her.

"We din't earn no money in her. We went down to Shields. North Shields. That wuz summer and that wuz lovely down there—just like a holiday. Just like a holiday, 'cause you only steamed a little way out. You din't go out far. Ol' Albert Burrows wuz skipper, and I'll never forgit when you got all yuh food riddy (you know, when you laid all yuh food out)—you laid it on the floor, in the platters. And if you din't put yuh foot aginst the platter, the food would go over the side o' that when the boat rolled. I done the Hoom Fishin' in her as well. And once we runned inta Low'stoft in a gairle o' wind, and as we come through the Newcome [Newcome Sand] the sea wuz comin' up our stern and regularly pushin' us along. And when we got inta Low'stoft, the ol' *Sirius* (LT 317) wuz laid aginst where the South Pier readin' rooms used to be. She'd run ashore.[8]

"Like I say, we din't earn no money in the *Livonia*—though I did go in her agin as *cast-orf* the next spring and summer [1924].[9] In the autumn, I went cook in a *smack*, the *Early Blossom* (LT 16) and done two trips in her.[10] She belonged to Arthur Gouldby and the skipper wuz a religious sort o' man. He wuz a nice chap, he wuz. His nairme wuz Prior. I went cook in her. You hetta stand with yuh backside nearly in the furnace o' the little boiler what used to work the *capstan*! I used to stand down there, a-fryin' fish, and I used to hev the ol' *shoe* [shoe kettle] in the fire and all. That wuz a metal thing shaped just like shoe, and that hed a handle on the end, and you used to put that in the furnace fire and that used to boil the water to mairke a cup o' tea with, or pots o' tea.

"I liked the smack. We raced the fleet in once. That wuz the *Hoom Fishin'*—early Hoom Fishin'. We were comin' in an ol' Prior say, 'Look at all them Scotties goin' in!' They were runnin' in, see, wi' herrin'. And do yuh know what?—we beat one or two o' them goin' in! The boat laid right over, and the water wuz tricklin' through the *scuppers*, and she wuz really gittin' along. Yeah, I done two trips in her, but I did like to hear suffin goin' round behind me. A *propeller*, yuh see. Yeah, we laid there once four days in her, for wind! A gale o' wind. We couldn't put no gear down. We hed just a little *handkerchief* [storm-jib] out at the front an' *three reefs* down, and we just laid there. I used to poke my hid up out o' the little

---

7 The reference here to an *Elliott pot* is to a two-cylinder compound marine engine of about fifteen horsepower, made by Elliott & Garrood Ltd. of Beccles.

8 This vessel was an early steam drifter, built in Great Yarmouth in 1901 and originally registered in Banff as BF 657.

9 Mr. Thurling later explained (in a follow-up session to the tape-recording) that, at this stage of his fishing career, he was often "walking about" and doing odd jobs in between the voyages undertaken.

10 This vessel is not to be confused with an earlier sailing trawler of the same name, registered as LT 6.

ol' *hoodway* (you know, the entrance to the cabin) and hev a look every now and then. And thass how you hetta lay, like that. You couldn't do nothin'. Then that eventually calmed down. Yeah, that fined right away so there wun't hardly enough wind to tow yuh gear! Anyhow, I din't git much out o' that, so I finished. I believe I got twenty-five bob a week in her. Yeah, 'cause he allus paid a little more than what anybody else did—Arthur Gouldby.[11] He allus paid a little more money.

"When I come out o' her, I went in the *Lisburn* (LT 1262). I wuz on the Hoom Fishin' in her along o' poor ol' George Myall, a religious skipper, who used to read a bit out o' the Bible nearly every mornin'. George Myall. He got lorst in the *Shorebreeze* (LT 1149) round the West'ard, when she runned ashore on the rocks at Milford Haven. Yeah, he got lorst, poor ol' George did. Anyhow, I done one Hoom Fishin' in her, then I went *seine-nettin'* in the *Scadaun* (LT 1183) along o' my uncle Freddy Mewse. Another "Paddy" Mewse![12] He wuz skipper.

"We went down to the Dogger Bank after haddicks. All haddicks! Loads o' haddicks! Filled the decks up wi' haddicks in them days! I done a good few trips in her, but my uncle got took orf her 'cause he wun't earnin' enough money. Yeah, he din't earn enough money, so he got fired from the *Scadaun*. That wuz springtime we went [1925], 'cause I done another Hoom Fishin' after that. Yeah, I went in the *Constant Friend* (LT 1172), yuh see. What they used to do at seine-nettin' wuz to hev one end o' the rope hitched to the barrel on the winch and then steam away. I wuz on deck there. I wun't cook. And the ropes hed a winch what *coiled* 'em up inta little bunches. You used to lay them all carefully so they used to run out at nearly full speed. And they'd run the net out and go round more or less in a circle.[13] Yeah, go round in a circle and let the net go halfway round. Then, when you'd done steamin', you'd pull the two ropes in and pull the net towards yuh. And all the fish used to go in the end o' the net, like.

"Blimey, you'd work all day and night, if you hed the light! Though sometimes we used to lay a while arter that got dark. You'd go to sleep, if yuh could, arter you'd done guttin' all the fish up. But a lot o' the time, afore you'd gutted one lot, yuh net wuz in agin with another load! See what I mean? That only took about an hour and a half to shoot an' haul, so you din't git a lot o' time for yuhself. Anyhow, Uncle Freddy got the sack, so out o' that boat I come an' I went inta the *Touchwood* (LT 1150). Poor ol' George Myall agin. She wuz a little iron boat, a drifter. Yeah, I went seinin' in her. I went as cook. Din't earn no money, though.

"After that, I went along o' Pod Catchpole in the *Constant Friend*. He wuz

---

11 Arthur Gouldby was one of the largest independent boatowners in Lowestoft—especially of steam drifters. He lived in Kessingland.

12 Mr Thurling's relatives, the Mewses, had the family nickname of "Paddy".

13 The course taken was a triangular one, as fully explained in Chapter One.

Plate 15: Constant Friend (LT 1172)

The steam drifter "Constant Friend" (LT 1172)—built locally in 1912 –seen coming into Lowestoft, after a fishing trip. Three members of her crew are standing up for 'ad, while three others are aft—one of them stooping to a task near some stacked quarter-cran baskets. Drift-nets and buffs are visible, heaped neatly amidships, and the foremast's boom will soon be in use for landing the catch.

skipper-owner and he wuz a lucky chap as well.[14] I made a lovely model o' her an' thass down in the Maritime Museum [on Whapload Road, Lowestoft]. Thass in there now and you'll also see the number plate and the name-plate what they took orf the original boat afore they broke her up. I wuz in her two voyages that year, Shetlands and the Hoom Fishin'. I can remember poor ol' Pod a-fallin' over the side o' the boat, when we were moorin' up there aginst the quay, at Shetlands. An' he wun't in there long enough to git wet through, if you can believe it! They yanked him out right quick and he laughed when he come up over the side. We were in the harbour at Lerwick, yuh see, when he fell over. He slipped. Yeah, and he wuz laughin' when he come up over the side. I hetta laugh! And he say, 'That wuz a near un, wun't it?' Yeah, I enjoyed that voyage 'cause he wuz a good ol' skipper, he wuz. If he sent yuh ashore arter any baccy or fags, he never used to take no change back orf yuh. No, he used to let yuh keep the change. He wuz a nice ol' boy, he wuz.

"We earnt £96 a share on the Hoom Fishin' that year, and I wuz *cook*. An' I wuz gittin' a good cook then, so he give me the sairme share as what a *cast-orf* got—

---

14 The term *lucky* in connection with fishing skippers refers to their performance at sea and their earning abilities. Luck may have had something to do with their success, but there was a good deal of expertise required also.

half an' half-quarter.[15] Yeah, he din't want me to leave; he din't want me to finish as cook. And he allus used to stop aboard and have his dinner. But when he got the other cook, when I come out of her, he used to go hoom to dinner! We got the most herrin' I've ever seen on that voyage. We were workin' orf the Outer Dowsin'.[16] We shot our nets about late afternoon; there were plenty o' drifters about with nets out. About eight o' clock, a drifter come up to us an' the skipper shouted out, 'Pod, your *buffs* are dippin'!' So we hetta go to work and haul. A quarter-past eight we started and we din't git them all aboard till three o' clock in the afternoon, next day. 290 *cran*! We filled the ol' boat up. Four men orf the *Lord Howe* (LT 1257) come aboard to help us haul. They were so heavy in the nets, they were just fallin' out. The *net-ropes* bust 'cause there wuz so many of 'em, so we hed a *quarter-fleet* o' spoilt nets. Yeah, and by the time we'd pulled 'em all up agin and cleaned 'em, that wuz eight o' clock at night! Then we steamed orf to Ymuiden [Ijmuiden] with 'em and got there in the early hours o' the mornin'.[17] The Dutch sent men aboard to git the herrin' out, so that saved us. When we made up at the end o' the voyage, we'd earnt £3,900 and paid orf at £96 a share. I wuz a rich man that Chris'mas! I even bought myself a new bike from Curry's. £4 19s 6d that corst [£4.98].

"I went seine-nettin' with Pod Catchpole arter that Hoom Fishin' [in the spring of 1926], then I come out o' the boat and went on the railway. That wuz just afore I wuz eighteen. Yeah. I thought I'd git a job where I wuz more certain of a reg'lar wage. There wuz about three or four of us went up to Norwich to pass a doctor [i.e. to have a medical] and this bloke from the railway say to me, 'You're goin' to be a *greaser*.' I say, 'Yeah, all right.' He say, 'You know what to do, dun't yuh?' Well, I thought he meant I'd be cleanin' engines, 'cause you could git to be a driver from that. 'No,' he say. 'You're goin' to oil carriages up.' So I wuz stationed at Low'stoft, oilin' carriages up.

"You used to hafta go round all the trucks on the goods trains (see, there wuz four goods trains a day). Some o' the trucks hed *axle-boxes*, where you used to put fat in. *Animal fat*, yeah. You used to fill the box right full and when the truck runned hot, that'd melt some o' the fat. That wuz like a lubrication, yuh see. That wuz yeller [yellow] fat and you used to hev a gret ol' tin with it in. Yeah, I used to plonk that in. Sometimes, when I went round, I'd just touch the top o' the box and that fat would fall down to the bottom. That'd be nearly all melted away, yuh see. Yeah, I used to do all that. I used to hetta take an oil-can with me and all. There wuz some oil and some fat. Goods wagons, coal wagons and all like that, what

---

15 Mr. Thurling's pay-off at the end of the voyage would have been £60.

16 The Outer Dowsing was a fishing ground off the coast of Lincolnshire, about forty miles east of Donna Nook. Activity here suggests that the haul was made in the early autumn, before the herring shoals had moved further to the south on their way to spawning grounds in the Straits of Dover.

17 Lowestoft drifters used to land herrings at Ijmuiden fairly regularly, because a better price was often to be had there.

carry weight, yuh see.

"I used to hetta go up the sidins [sidings], night-time, and oil all the fish trucks up. I used to hetta git under all them ol' *runs* [wooden stagings]—you know, near the iron bridge [a footway across the tracks, downline, to the west of the station]. There wuz all little places where you used to walk along, where they used to put the fish on. Like *landings* [landing stages]. I used to hetta git underneath them and oil all them trucks up. And all ol' fish slime would be runnin' through, you know. Yeah, and I used to hetta go to the Fish Market and all and oil trucks up there. There used to be one fish-train leave for the North on the M&GN, at dinnertime.[18] And then you hed the 3.10 in the afternoon leave Low'stoft for London. That used to git up in London about eight o' clock time.

"Another thing I hetta do wuz put brake-blocks onta carriages. We used to go in Sunday mornin' to do that. I wuz set strad-legged over the rail there once and ol' Fred Reeve say to me, 'You dun't mind if I go now? I wanta catch my train to Norwich.' I say, 'Yis, you can go.' He say, 'Can I leave yuh to do that job? Put them other four up?' I say, 'Yis, I'll put 'em up.' So I sat with my legs straddled over the line in the middle o' this train. That wuz a York train, in the carriage sidins aganst Low'stoft Central Station. Yeah, I sat there, a-puttin' these brake-blocks up and, I go to charley, if there wun't a bloomin' shuntin' engine come on the other end! O' course, I hed a *warnin' flag* out, but he din't see it. Lucky for me, he pulled the carriages away from me. If he'd gone the other way, I'd ha' bin under 'em! They were all coupled up, but when he hit 'em they moved away from me, instead o' movin' towards me. That wuz the nearest escape I had, that wuz, I can tell yuh!

"Anyhow, I done that till I wuz twenty. Then they say to me, 'You're now comin' inta man's pay.' I wuz gittin' thirty-five shillins a week [£1.75], doin' that job, so they say, 'Now you're comin' inta man's pay, you'll hatta go to Norwich.' Man's pay wuz about £2 or forty-five shillins [£2.25] altogether and there wun't no man's job for me at Low'stoft, so I hatta go to Norwich.[19] I wuz with a *liftin' gang*—the heavy gang—on the *crane* and *traverser-winch*. There wuz six of us on the winch, three each side, and that used to travel along the rails and we used to lift engines right orf the wheels wi' that. Lift the whole body o' the engines right orf the wheels. Then they used to push the wheels away, if they wanted anything done to 'em. Or that'd drop the engines onta the wheels. See, whichever it was. O' course, that wuz an old way o' doin' it and, after I'd bin there a while, they had a *drop-pit* put in. So they used to run an engine over this drop-pit and the fitters used to unshackle everything from underneath. Then the set o' wheels what they

---

18 The Midland & Great Northern Railway (known locally as "The Muddle and Go Nowhere") and the Great Eastern Railway companies had a link-line built, joining Lowestoft to Great Yarmouth—and from thence to the Midlands. It opened in 1903, under the name of the Norfolk & Suffolk Joint Railway.

19 Mr. Thurling used to travel by rail each day.

wanted to work on (like puttin' new bearins in) would drop down and the engine could be pushed orf out o' the way on its other wheels.

"I wuz at Norwich about a year, then they sent me back to Low'stoft agin, as a *coal-man*. I used to hetta coal the engines up and do *fire-lightin'*—git steam up in 'em. Yeah, the drivers used to come on an hour afore time and they used to expect you to have twenty-five pound o' steam, yuh see, or fifty pound o' steam. Anyhow, we used to git steam in 'em, and if you smoked the front up inside the cab they used to swear at yuh. O' course, when you start them orf, there ent no draught and the smoke'd come out o' the front o' the *fire-box*. Many ol' drivers used to git onta me. 'Look at my front! I cleaned that the other day!' See, they used to keep the same engines. Yeah, and they used to think somethin' o' their ol' engines, them ol' drivers did, and they used to go round and polish all the brass up. And the *axle-boxes*, they were all brass, yuh know, and they used to polish them all up.

"That used to tairke about three hours to git steam. From cold. Yeah, that used to tairke three hours. And, o' course, you'd be coalin' up yuh *tender* as well. Do yuh know what?—I sometimes used to shift twenty-five ton o' coal on a shift. Onta the tenders, yeah. All hand-shovel. When the other man went orf, he used to leave a truck broke into so you could go straight to work. He used to throw the truck door down onta a little stool thing, so that wuz level, and you used to shovel the coal orf the truck door onta the tender. Well, then, you'd empty that one, you'd empty another one, and you'd start on another one for the next man. Do yuh know, I're bin inta an eighteen ton truck and emptied it! Emptied it on a shift! Fifteen engines we used to hetta do, and we hetta book 'em all. There wuz only one of yuh on a shift. Sometimes, the *fireman* [of the particular locomotive] used to come and lend yuh a hand if you were stowed up or if there were two or three engines waitin' for coal. I mean, some o' them big engines took five or six ton at a time. There were three shifts, all round the clock. There wuz six till two, two till ten, and nights [10 p.m. to 6 a.m.]. Night time, you used to go on at ten o' clock and you'd hatta coal the last three or four engines—like a Beccles last one, a Norwich last one. Yeah, the last one would come up the shed about half-past twelve, somethin' like that. They'd be *tank engines*, mind yuh. They'd tairke about thirty hundredweights, they would. And while you were coalin' them, you hatta keep lightin' the engines up in the shed what hent got fires in.

"O' course, some o' the drivers used to clean the fires. They all hatta be cleaned up when they come up the shed and some of 'em would leave a little bit o' fire in the corner so you din't hatta light 'em. I done that job for about four or five year, till they put an *electric coalin' plant* up. Then they stood us all orf. Yeah, they put an electric coalin' plant up and that used to tairke thirty hundredweight up at a time in the *bucket*.[20] That hatta be filled up out o' the coal truck, but instead o' chuckin' it up with a shovel you'd just push it inta the bucket, and that used to

---

20 There were eight buckets on the machine.

tairke it up and shoot it onta the tender. There wuz three of us stood orf. They hed us in the orffice one *Fishin' Time* [the Home Fishing] and say, 'We're gotta git rid of yuh.' See, there wuz only one man needed to work the new plant, so they got rid of three of us.

"I din't know what to do. I biked to Cantley to see if I could git a job there.[21] Yeah, I went there. Nothin' doin'. Then away round the Market I go. Mother couldn't keep me. See, there wuz nine of 'em at hoom besides me. This wuz 1930. An' I went round the Market and I see some smoke comin' out o' one o' the chimneys and I went aboard an' see the driver. She wuz a wooden boat, a drifter. I say, 'Who's goin' skipper o' this ol' boat?' He say, 'Young Turrell, the owner's son.' I say, 'Oh.' He say, 'If you come down one day durin' the week, you might see him. He might be down here.' So I went down and I copped him aboard one day, and I asked him if he wanted a crew. He say, 'Yis. Can you go as *cast-orf*?' I say, 'Yis.' So I went as cast-orf in her, the *Foresight* (LT 763). That wuz his first voyage as skipper in her. He wuz only a youngster, and I give him a model. I mairde a model o' the *Foresight* in a glass case and I give him that and, o' course, he took it.

"Down to The Shetlands we go. And, as I told yuh, that take yuh about two days to git down there. Well, we worked in and out o' there and we din't earn no money. And the skipper started bein' a little bit funny wi' me. He say, 'You can pack your bags when you git hoom! When you git to Low'stoft.' I say, 'All right, then.' He din't really mean it, but he kept tellin' me and I'd hed enough of it. And the mate say to me, 'Do yuh know what, ol' Bill? If he tell yuh that agin, thass what you wanta do.' I say, 'I will!' Arter we'd finished at Shetland, we worked out o' Grimsby a little while afore we come to Low'stoft. He say, 'Pack yuh bag when yuh git hoom.' So when we come inta Low'stoft one day about five o' clock (this wuz Hoom Fishin'), with about forty or fifty cran o' herrin', I went down the *foc'sle*. That wuz just gittin' dark and that wuz my job to git the *derrick* riddy to land the herrin', but I went down the foc'sle and started packin' my bag.[22] And he come to the foc'sle. I shall never forgit it; I can picture him now. Yeah, he looked down the foc'sle and he see me packin' my bag. He say to the mate, 'I din't think he wuz goin' to do that!' So the mate say to him, 'Well, you're told the chap time arter time he can pack his bag. He's now a-doin' it. Look!' I walked ashore then an' took my bag acrorss to my father in his little hut. He used to sweep the back o' the Market up (see, he worked on the railway, and so did my gran'father).[23] He

---

21 A sugarbeet-processing factory, on the Lowestoft-Norwich railway line. A bicycle journey there and back would have totalled about forty miles.

22 The derrick referred to was the boom of the foremast, which was used in conjunction with the pulley-wheel on the side of the steam capstan to lift the baskets of herring from the hold and run them ashore.

23 All the Lowestoft harbour installations were owned by the Great Eastern Railway Company (G.E.R) and by its successor, the London and North Eastern Railway Co. Ltd (L.N.E.R).

say, 'Whass the matter?' I say, 'I ent a-goin' wi' him no more!' I say, 'He told me to pack my bag, and I're packed it!'

"Next mornin', I wuz sailin' out o' the harbour in the *Elie Ness* (LT 1259)! Next mornin'! Yeah, sairme mornin' that I got the berth. I went out along o' ol' Harry Thompson and we were in front o' the *Foresight*, so I held up a rope to him [i.e. to the skipper] to give him a tow 'cause the *Elie Ness* wuz a faster boat. Yeah, I went the rest o' the voyage in her and I only took up £2 that Fishin'. I went as *cast-orf* an' all I took wuz £2. Yeah, and I took my gear acrorss to my father's hut agin, at the back o' the Market. Like I say, he used to sweep that all up, all the horses' mess and that, 'cause there wuz a lot o' horses about then. And he say to me, he say, 'You'll go agin, wun't yuh!' I say, 'No that I aren't! I aren't a-goin' fishin' no more!' And, o' course, I went hoom and then went down to the Market agin, you know to square up like. Ol' Harry, the skipper, say to me, 'What about comin' trawlin' along o' us, Pod?' O' course, thass what some of 'em called me. He say, 'You can be *trimmer*, can't yuh?' I say, 'Yis. I'll hev a go at it.' I knew that wuz a hard job, trimmer, but I say, 'Yeah, I dun't mind.'

"So I went trimmer on her out o' Low'stoft for a few trips. We were fishin' orf the Knoll [Smith's Knoll] and all out that way. That wuz bloomin' hard work, but I got used to it 'cause I wuz used to shiftin' coal on the railway. But that wuz a lot different on a boat, specially when you got a lot o' bad weather in the winter time. I're bin down in that *coal bunker* in only my dungarees and a vest, a-shovellin' for three hours at a time! You hetta shovel the coal from under the front o' the wheelhouse about twice to where the driver hetta git it out o' the bunker in the engine-room.[24] Then, if that wuz bad weather, she wuz nearly sunk amidships half the time. Them ol' *standard boats* were slushy things![25] They were so deep in the water.

"Anyhow, you used to hetta tap on the side o' the engine-room when you'd shifted enough coal, so the driver could hear yuh. You used to go down through a *bunker lid* when you started and a chap used to fasten that down. Well, when you wanted to git out, you hetta pile the coal up so you could git on top o' that to git out agin. Well, if that wuz bad weather, she'd ship a whole load over the side. And if the bunker lid wuz orf, that'd nearly drown yuh! Anyway, the driver used to say, 'Say when you wanta come out, Pod. Just knock on the wall.' [In other words, the bulkhead between the engine-room and the coal bunker.] So I'd do that and then ol' Arthur used to tell one o' the crew. Well, that bloke'd hev an *oily frock* and a *sou'wester* on, and he'd say, 'I can't undo it yit, Pod. There's a bigun comin'.' That'd go right over the *rail*, yuh see. You'd got yuh gear down. Yeah, you'd be

---

24 In other words, the coal bunker was located below decks, beneath the wheelhouse.

25 Standard boats were fishing vessels built to Admiralty specifications during and after the First World War, with the object of their being used for patrolling and minesweeping duties during times of hostility.

towin' along. So then he'd say, 'Come on! Right quick!' You'd hear him undo the bunker lid and, do yuh know, I'd lay a bet that afore I got up there I'd got a wet *shat* [shirt]! See, that'd come over the rail and some would go down the bunker. Then they used to screw the lid on agin, once I wuz out.

"I only hed a *duck-lamp* to work by. Thass all. Yeah, and that wuz hot down there on the engine-room side and cold everywhere else—all water drippin' down the sides and that. And the trouble wuz that you only had about eighteen inches [width] o' concrete on the bottom to work on, and then that bulged out at the sides where the *ribs* were. Yeah, that wuz very narrow inside, so if you hed lump coal you hatta pick the lumps up. You couldn't shovel it. And if you got lump and dust, oh, that wuz a terrible job! I're nearly cried down that coal bunker, thass straight! Twenty-eight bob a week [£1.40], thass all I got.[26] The trouble wi' the lumps wuz you couldn't break 'em up. You never hed no hammer, so you hetta keep chuckin' 'em onta each other. Then you'd heap the coal up where the *driver* could git it out. You done that from about the third day out. See, when the driver couldn't reach the coal, you hatta go and *trim* it over to where he hatta git it out, and you'd do that on both sides o' the boat.

"We done about two or three trips out o' Low'stoft, then he say to me, 'Do you wanta go round the *West'ard*?' I say, 'Yis.' Newlyn wuz the first place we called in. that wuz full o' Frenchmen—trawlers. We laid there a little while beside some Low'stoft boats, then we went out and fished orf Pendeen [Pendeen Point]. We went inta Padstow after that.[27] Yeah, we were arter soles round there, but we couldn't git on too well 'cause our *bobbins* were too small. Noey Ayers come up in the *Ascona* (LT 108)—Big Noey—an' he say, 'How're yuh gittin' on, Harry?' So our skipper say, 'I can't git along. Keep gittin' *hefts*!' We were all one night and all the next day there once, mendin' nets![28] I used about three or four balls o' twine fillin' *needles* up for the blokes to mend with. Yeah, and we were all dead tired, so the skipper say, 'We'll hetta lay for a couple o' hours, so you can git a sleep.' See, we hed bin gittin' soles, along o' all the mendin', so you know how hard we were workin' on the decks.

"There wuz one time there, when we were orf Pendeen, and I wuz never so frightened afore in all my life! There wuz a south-westerly gale blew up and you could see these big waves a-breakin'. Yeah, every now and agin, you'd see 'em curlin' up and then breakin' inta the *white horses*. I thought, 'Cor, if one o' them

---

26 All crew members below skipper and mate on trawling voyages were paid a weekly wage, with a small percentage of the profits (if there were any) on top. Skippers and mates were paid on a share basis.

27 The vessel was continuing to trawl, with soles being the main quarry. Pendeen Point is on the south-west coast of Cornwall, not far from St. Just.

28 Some of the Cornish sole-fishing grounds were notoriously rough, with outcrops of slate on the seabed. Large bobbins helped the trawl net to cover the ground more effectively and with less wear and tear on the meshes.

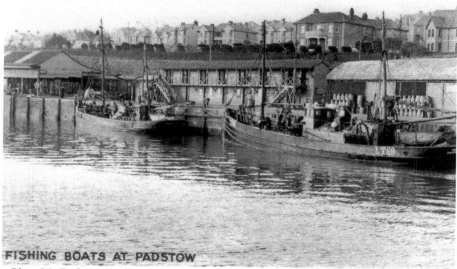

Plate 16: Padstow Harbour

This view shows the small Lowestoft drifter-trawler "Togo" (LT 69) moored up. Built in Great Yarmouth in 1905 and registered as YH 477, she was sold the following year and became LT 609. In 1920, she returned to Yarmouth as YH 248—before coming back to Lowestoft again in 1934. The following year, she was converted from steam to diesel propulsion and re-numbered LT 69, continuing to fish right up until the early 1960s, before being scrapped in 1964. The lack of craft here, at Padstow, suggests that the photograph was taken after the Second World War—by which time, most Lowestoft vessels were no longer undertaking the springtime voyage round to Cornwall to catch soles. It is even possible that the vessel was being operated out of Fleetwood by its owners, the Jubilee Fishing Co. Ltd., and trying its luck in Cornish waters.

was to hit us, that'd swamp us!' We were runnin' afore the wind, tryin' to git up as near to Padstow as we could, and the swell wuz comin' up the stern, yuh see. Comin' up the stern. Well, in the end, we did catch one. I wuz down the *foc'sle*. I wuz trimmer, yuh see, and my *berth* wuz down the foc'sle. And I din't know anything had happened, not till I felt the ol' boat shudder. And, do yuh know, when I put my hid up out o' the *foc'sle*, that wuz just as though she wuz sunk at the *stern*! The water laid halfway up her aginst the wheelhouse. This big sea hed just rolled over her—broke and rolled right over her stern. A good job they had the cabin doors shut and that! Yeah. Anyhow, he hetta wait for his chance to bring her round hid to wind. Yeah, and when he brought her round, we hetta pull the trawl inboard agin 'cause that wuz all washed over the side. Once he'd brought her round, he say, 'Now we'll hetta *dodge* it out.' And ol' Sonny Read in the *Inspiration* (LT 1211) come alongside o' us (that wuz the *Outline*, renamed) and he say, 'Blast, Harry, I thought you were gone!' And, do yuh know, all you could see at times as he wuz goin' down inta a holler [hollow] wuz the tops o' his masts!

"Sometimes, when you went inta Padstow, you hent even cleared yuh decks. There wuz soles on the decks still alive! Still alive. Oh, you used to git about two ton o' soles at a time. Two ton! O' course, we went to Fleetwood an' all on that voyage. Yeah, I wuz away all summer [1931]. Then I come hoom and got married. I done some more trawlin' out o' Low'stoft, and then I got wrong along o' the young *mairte* [mate]. He wuz about as old as I wuz. Yeah, the *driver* say to me one day, 'Pod, will yuh pull half-a-dozen buckets o'ashes up? I wanta relieve the *stoker*.' So I say, 'Yis.' And I went and pulled these bloomin' ashes up.[29] An', o' course, this young mairte come onta me. Coo, he wuz suffin raw! He say, 'You should be down the *ice-locker*, breakin' the ice up to help us ice the fish away.' We only hed about three baskets! I say, 'Well, the driver wanted me to help him, to relieve his man.' With no more to do, he shoved me over the *thortcher-boards* [thwartship-boards] onta my back. Yeah, and we hed a bit of a up an' down, and he tried to yank me over the side! Yis, he did. If I'd ha' reported him to Customs, he'd ha' got the sack. Anyhow, the ol' skipper say to me, 'We'll hev a change when we git in, Pod.' Well, I din't mairke no more bones about it. I come ashore when we got in, and that wuz the finish o' my fishin' career, that wuz.

"I wuz *walkin' about*, three months. And that wuz the worst three months o' the year for walkin' about.[30] I wuz livin' along o' my mother-in-law. And I wuz walkin' through the station one day and a chap (one o' the *shed masters*) come and saw me. He say, 'I're bin lookin' for you. Are you Thurlin'?' I say, 'Yis.' He say, 'Will you take a job at Norwich?' See, I'd bin on the railway, and they told us when they stood us orf that we'd git a job if they wanted us back. I say, 'Yis.' So I went as a *bar-boy*. I used to hetta do twenty-five engines a night, inside the *fire-boxes*, cleanin' the *furnace bars*. That wuz on the London engines. See, all the bars inside, you could lift them up. And sometimes they used to git burnt through, so you hatta change 'em. An you used to hatta clean the brick arch down [at the back of the furnace]. I spuz that wuz about as high as yuh chest, and on top o' that wuz all like gold dust what wuz burnt on the arch. You used to hatta git a long rake and push that through the back so that'd all run down inta the ash-pan.

"Then there wuz all the *tubes*, where the heat used to go through, and you used to hatta scrape all the *crow's nests* orf them. That wuz the clinker what used to lay on the tubes inside the fire-boxes. Yeah, I used to hatta clean all them over. I hed a scrapin' thing what I used to knock the clinker orf with. Them engines used to hev fifty pound o' steam when I hetta git inside the fire-boxes! There wuz no fire in there, but they'd still got fifty or sixty pound o' steam. What you used to do to cool 'em wuz pull the *blower* out. That used to blow all cold air up through the bars—

---

29 Waste from the furnace was usually put into buckets and drawn up one or other of the engine-room's ventilator shafts, before being thrown overboard.

30 Most vessels were fully crewed during the Home Fishing period and would only require a replacement in the event of accident, illness or unforseen circumstances.

draw the draught up and blow it out o' the chimney.[31] If you got a rough do inside, you'd be wet through wi' sweat after just one engine! I only wore dungarees, or a boiler suit. Yeah, and I hed an ol' sack to slip through the fire-box hole on. You hatta go in feet-first. Yeah, you couldn't go in hands-first 'cause you'd burn yuh hands on the bars. An' when you got inside, you could stand up straight. Yeah, they were six foot long, some o' the fire-boxes on them big engines. They were like a little room and you could stand yuh full height in 'em.

"You'd hev the ol' boiler inspector come round. And there used to be another boiler bloke on night-time with yuh. He used to say to me, 'Any *fusal plugs* leakin', Bill?' I'd say, 'No, she's all right inside.' So he din't hatta go in, yuh see. But if I did git one leakin', I'd git it down my neck. The engines hed got two fusable plugs inside the fire-box. They were *lead plugs* an' if the boiler run short o' water, this lead melted and dropped out and let the water out. That wuz to put the fire out. That wuz a safety device to stop the boiler from bein' burnt if they run short o' water. Yeah, all the water used to pour out o' these lead plugs. They were about half an inch acrorss. They're what they call *safety-plugs*, and if they started leakin' you knew as soon as you dropped inta the fire-box. Yeah, as soon as you got in and turned round, you'd git a drip down yuh neck. An' you'd look up, an' there'd be a fusal-plug leakin'. Just drippin'. Then the boiler bloke would hetta replace it.

"I done that job till a driver frightened me. He say to me, 'Do yuh know, ol' pal, if I wuz you I'd try an' git orf that job.' See, they used to put the engine-cleaners on it, but they took 'em orf 'cause that wuz ruinin' their eyesight an' their health. I stuck it five year and then he put the breeze up o' me. He say, 'Do yuh know what? If you dun't git orf that job, it'll tairke you orf.' So I went an' see the ol' man, the *superintendent*. His nairme wuz Fish. I say, 'Is there any hope o' gittin' back to Low'stoft, sir?' I say, 'Because if I don't go orf this job, that'll tairke me orf.' He say, 'All right. We'll see.' And he started talkin' about fishin'. See, he knew I'd bin to sea, so he stood talkin' about fishin'. He wuz a gruffy ol' boy; big ol' boy. And about a fortnight after that, he sent for me. He say, 'Well, Thurlin', he say, 'I're got a job for yuh at Low'stoft.' I say, 'Hev yuh?' He say, '*Shed labourer*. You can start next week.' So I went back on the shed [engine shed] an' I wuz there till I got called up for the Navy in 1940.

"Thass how I lorst my eye [the right eye]. I wuz on a big merchant ship called the *Castilian* an' we were bringin' aeroplanes and ammunition back from Canada. Yeah, Montreal. We laid in there a week. My eye got hurt when we were firin' a twelve-pounder gun. That wuz an old gun what'd come from the First World War and that wuz faulty. They took it orf when we got to Hull. I got a *back-blast*. The explosion come out o' the back and blew us all over. Yeah, out o' the breach. We

---

31 In other words, this device was normally used to provide a current of air to make the fire burn fiercely.

were practisin', gittin' riddy for when we'd gotta go across to England.[32] Anyhow, I reported it when we got in and, o' course, they sent me to see a specialist at Hull. He say, 'You're got an injured eye. You're got somethin' what'll hatta be seen to.' Anyway, I wuz then shipped up for a Russian convoy. Talk about bein' lucky! Three parts of it got sunk goin' there, in 1941. Yeah, we were shipped a 15,000 ton boat, me and my mairte, and they pulled me out o' the line. O' course, I knew I wuz goin' blind. I went to the specialist agin and he say, 'We'll hetta send you to Chatham.' And thass where they took my eye out, Chatham. I went to Grimsby first and had a night there, then I went down along o' all the wounded sailors an' soldiers to Chatham.

"They demobbed me the next year. I wuz at Epsom—Horton Hospital—and they demobbed me in the February, 1942. I come back on the railway then. Yeah, they took me back agin, and thass how I come to do forty-three year on the railway. Yeah, they give me a job, 'cause I'd hed my glass eye put in, yuh see. I hed several years doin' errands. You know, cartin' *side-rods* [connecting-rods] an' *springs* an' things between here and Norwich. I travelled backwards an' forwards on that. On a train.[33] On a train, every day. After that, I done odd jobs, like, in the shed and I used to clean the orffices out down Commercial Road. And do yuh know?—I finished up here on Corton Station, relievin' the ticket collector in the summertime! I actually come to the house here in 1938, when I finished the bar job in Norwich,[34] but I finished up on the station. Yeah, we used to hev a rush here in the summer, when all the holiday trains come."

Attending to the needs of holidaymakers, as they arrived in Corton for a summer break at one of the village's four holiday camps during the late 1960s, was a long way (in every sense of the term) from Bill Thurling's early years at sea and from his sweated labour on railway coal trucks and in locomotives' fire-boxes. His experiences speak eloquently of a world that is past and gone, serving to demonstrate unequivocally how the hard physical work of that era usually brought little reward for those involved. The shorter of his two careers was the great employment staple of Lowestoft for centuries and his long involvement with the railway saw him connected with a service industry which had done much to increase the importance of fishing in the town. The harbour works and rail facilities were all under the overall control of the railway company and it required a not inconsiderable bureaucracy to make sure that the whole operation ran smoothly.

One necessary part of the administration (though one which was not always popular with fishermen and market workers alike) was the Railway Police, whose

---

32 Mr. Thurling was part of a naval team, put aboard the merchant vessel to operate the gun.

33 Mr. Thurling travelled in the guard's van on passenger trains.

34 Mr. Thurling and his wife lived for many years in one of the station cottages at Corton—a village to the north of Lowestoft, which has long been the writer's place of residence.

task it was to maintain conventional law and order on company property and enforce any bye-laws appertaining to the same. Constant scrutiny was required to keep all kinds of petty theft in bounds and to make sure that more serious crime did not become common. Jack Turrell (1912-85) had been in the Merchant Navy during the late 1920s and early 30s and had then joined Trinity House as a lightshipman. He left this service at the end of the Second World War and became a member of the Railway Police at Lowestoft. His remarks concerning his work are illuminating and give a fascinating (though limited) insight into a less well documented aspect of the fishing industry and its freight-provider (tape-recording made, 1 December 1981).

"I'd made a vow to myself that, as soon as the war wuz over, I'd git ashore if I could. See, all lightships were withdrawn durin' the war, because they were just sittin' targets and the Germans shot them up. They kept one or two unmanned lights out there, but they weren't much of a success.[35] I come orf the *Haisborough* and went onta the *tenders*. Then, when they started on the Normandy landins [D-Day, 6 June 1944], they laid two lightships to mark the *swept channel* [i.e. cleared of mines] for them to go acrorss. Well, after they'd got the *bridgehead* established, the next lightship they laid wuz the *Silver Pits*, which wuz right in the middle of the North Sea [on the Dogger Bank]. Right smack in the middle. Now, that wuz all one big minefield out there, but they cut a way through to git the traffic across to build up the invasion fleet. I mean, a lot o' yuh supplies were comin' out o' the Humber and the Tyne. And instead o' goin' all the way down and goin' across from Dover, they could cut down through the Silver Pits. So they laid this lightship there an' called her *the Silver*. Just "the Silver". And Muggins was one of 'em who wuz elected to go! And there we were—stuck right out in the middle o' the North Sea. We hent got a peashooter aboard! And I weren't a brave man durin' the war. Believe me, when I wuz out there (I don't mind admittin' it), I wuz one o' the scared ones!

"Anyway, after the war, one o' the pilots here in Low'stoft (ol' Theo Page) offered me a job on the pilot boat.[36] They wanted a man to run the pilot boat out o' port. See, there's only one man and the pilot on the launch. When you're got a vessel comin' inta harbour here, they have to pick a pilot up. Well, the pilot launch takes the pilot out and drops him aboard. Then, alternatively, when a ship leaves, the pilot takes it out and the launch goes out and brings him back. So I would be the launch man. But at the same time as I come ashore, I also applied for the East Suffolk Police and the Railway Police and one or two other forces. Just as well, because the ol' pilot (he lived next door) came to me an' said, 'I'm sorry. The job's fell through.' And I said, 'Well, fair enough, if that's the case.' And, as luck would

---

35 These were small vessels, with a sealed top deck and with a controlled gas-burning light on a stem amidships.

36 The launch which carried the harbour pilots out to ships waiting to come into Lowestoft and brought them back in from vessels which had left port.

have it, the ol' Railway Police sergeant came up to have a look at me to see if I wuz a suitable candidate an' say would I please report to them an' submit to a little examination—a medical and an educational examination. And I did, an' passed, and I wuz put on a year's probation.

"A comical little story attached to that. We had a chief o' police, a Colonel McJasper, an' he used to be a colonel in the Guards. And when I finished my year's probation, I had to go up to Peterborough to pass out. Well, o' course, all the lads told me that, when you go in front o' the chief constable, you have to throw him up a good salute because he's a guardsman, you see. So, o' course, I went in an' threw him up a really smart salute. He wuz in right a long room, you know, and I walked up to his desk and saluted, and he says, 'All right, sit down. Take yuh hat orf.' Then he asked me several little questions—whether I liked the job and all that—and that wuz it. So away I go. I turned round and walked, and he let me git right down to the door. Then he shouted after me, 'Turrell! Come back here!' Then he said, 'What do you do when you leave a senior officer?' I hent got a clue what he wuz talkin' about and, o' course, I wuz dressed smart and I'd got me medal ribbons up, yuh see. So he said, 'You've got some medal ribbons up. What force were you in?' So I said, 'I wasn't in any force, sir. I wuz in Trinity House an' the Merchant—' He said, 'Oh, that explains everything! They had no discipline there.'

"That wuz the old L.N.E.R. I wuz workin' for, but the Railway Police were—well, if they weren't the first force, they were more or less level with the original old *Peelers*.[37] And they originated because we imported a tremendous lot of *navvies* and that from Ireland to build the railways. And as the railways progressed along, they had these sort o' labourin' encampments where these navvies used to live. And they were really only hutments, and as soon as the navvies got paid they were sort o' wreckin' the towns that they were near and all that. So they created a police force to see after these navvies. It was a crude police force to what you've got today, but that actually was the origin o' the Railway Police. And once the railway lines had been built, they maintained the police to see after them. Then, o' course, as the railways acquired docks, the Railway Police automatically policed the docks. They policed Low'stoft Docks; they policed Hull Docks, Immingham Docks, Cardiff Docks, Swansea Docks, you see. Grangemouth. Yeah, they were all policed by the various Railway Police forces. One first that we had, in the L.N.E.R., wuz that the police at Hull were the first force to have *dogs*. Tracker dogs and guard dogs and patrol dogs. And, initially, all the other forces used to hafta apply to Hull Docks to git their dogs, because they were trained there.

"When I first joined, there wuz six men and a sergeant to look after Low'stoft, but we came under an *inspector* at Norwich. And also at Norwich wuz the superintendent's main office. And the superintendent's office covered the whole

---

37 The L.N.E.R. was the London and North Eastern Railway Co. Ltd.

East Anglian area: King's Lynn, Ipswich, and all round. Now, our divisional inspector saw after Norwich, Low'stoft, Yarmouth; he wuz at Thorpe Station. Now, we did work in with the local police, but technically speakin' they had got no jurisdiction over the railway or the docks. As far as they were concerned, it was private property and like an ordinary household. They would only police there on request. You see, if an ordinary householder says to the police, 'I've got some trouble in my house. Will you come in and deal with it?'—well, they'll then go in. Otherwise, they've got to have a warrant, haven't they? The same thing was technically applicable to the railway and the docks. They were our jurisdiction.

"The whole job wuz a general police duty. The main railway crimes, as far as we were concerned—the tuppenny-ha'penny things similar to ridin' [bicycles] without lights and parkin' offences and that sort o' thing—you got that on the railway with *trespassin'*. Now, trespassin' on the railway doesn't sound much, but people takin' short cuts across lines are liable to get killed. And if somebody got killed on the line, you had to establish that the fencing wuz in good condition and (if you'd had trouble on there) that you had prosecuted a certain number of people, just to prove that you were tryin' to deter them from crossin'. Otherwise, they'd turn round and say [i.e. any lawyers involved in a case] that there wuz a darn great gap in the fence, which wuz an open invitation to cross the line. An' then you'd git sued for damages.

"We policed right down as far as Darsham, and Ipswich policed up to Darsham. So if there wuz any trouble, or anything on the line, between here and Darsham, that wuz our concern. I mean, just to quote one instance: one day, we had some kids at Beccles put some *sleepers* on the line. There wuz some sleepers just outside o' Beccles, ready to be laid, and some youngsters went and laid 'em across the line—and a train sort o' ploughed into 'em! Luckily, nobody was hurt and there wasn't a tremendous lot o' damage, but that could've been a really serious accident. We'd go on regular tours out on the train. Yeah, until we got a car. I mean, the latter part o' the time, we were supplied with a car to go out in. We'd use that sometimes to go down to Bentwaters in. See, when they put the new crossin' gates in at Darsham [an automatic barrier on the A12 road], American service men were always drivin' through 'em.[38] Well, we'd git in the car and go down to Bentwaters and contact the American base police there. 'Your car, number so-and-so, drove through our gates at Darsham. We'd like a word with the driver.' And they'd produce him, and we'd prosecute him for the offence.

"Now, apart from things like that, you'd have the various *dock bye-laws* and *railway bye-laws* passed by Parliament. For instance, there's a flashin' light on the pier heads, which says that no ship shall enter while that light is flashin'. It means there's a ship goin' out. And we'd prosecute ships for unauthorised leavin' o' the

---

38 Bentwaters is a former American airbase, near Woodbridge. It was the practice of some
    personnel, who were stationed there, to jump the red warning lights on the Darsham crossing
    and try to get through the barriers before they closed.

harbour. And another thing: you were only allowed to moor under the instructions of the *berthing master*. And the berthing master could come up to you and say, 'You will move.' And if you din't move, you'd be subject to prosecution.

"When I first joined, we still had Sparrow's Nest and St. Luke's Hospital under the Navy.[39] And we had all the naval personnel here. But although they were here, on Saturday nights they'd all shove off to Norwich and go on the beer. You know, have a rare ol' night out. The last train [from Norwich] used to come in about half-past twelve and then we'd hafta go and clear it. And there'd be all these drunken sailors there. Well, if that wuz too much, we used to phone The Nest up and ask for the patrol van to come down. And they'd come down, and you know these big ol' *parcel barrows* they had?—we'd run one o' them up along the train and hump these drunken sailors (you know, who were really out of it) on to the barrow. Yeah, just pile 'em up on the barrow, wheel 'em down the platform and sling 'em in the patrol van. And they would go in *naval cells* when they got back and be on a charge the next mornin'.

"We had one of our older men patrollin' one night in the goods yard and he come across a couple o' sailors breakin' into a truck. And, o' course he disturbed 'em and managed to catch one. Now, this wuz a bitter cold winter's night, and it wuz freezin' hard, but instead o' walkin' this sailor down the footpath round near the station he tried to take him across the lines—and he slipped. See, he'd got hold o' this sailor with one hand and had his truncheon in the other, and he slipped. And, o' course, he let the sailor go and lost his truncheon. So the sailor picked his truncheon up and really set about him—and he just managed to crawl onta the end o' the platform just as the *shunter*, the last man on the station, wuz then goin' down the platform to pack up for the night. And he [i.e. the shunter] just picked him up. Otherwise, he would have died of exposure. There's no doubt about it.

"Now, the next day, o' course, there wuz a hue and cry, and poor ol' Walter wuz in a bad state. But, after a couple o' days, he wuz well enough, so the Railway police and the East Suffolk Police mustered every sailor up at the Sparrow's Nest and had a parade [identity parade]. But Walter couldn't pick him out. They mustered 'em all up in St. Luke's. Couldn't pick him out. They mustered all the sailors that were in digs and got them in. And they'd got some more out in the country [i.e. billeted in quarters out of town], and they mustered them. But poor ol' Walter couldn't recognise him. And that wuz about four or five years later, in a pub up in Scotland, there wuz a copper sittin' and havin' a quiet drink. And, at the table next

---

39 During World War II, Lowestoft was the HQ of the Royal Naval Patrol Service, with administration facilities in the Sparrow's Nest gardens at the north end of town and a hospital for injured personnel in the old *Empire Hotel* on Kirkley Cliff (renamed *St. Luke's*). This vital part of the war effort is recognised in the presence of the national memorial to men killed in the service, which stands in Belle Vue Park (close to Sparrow's Nest), and in that of the Patrol Service Museum in the grounds of Sparrow's Nest itself. The whole of the Patrol Service base in Lowestoft was named HMS Europa.

to him, there wuz a bloke boastin' that when he wuz at Low'stoft, in the Navy, he wuz raidin' a railway truck and he din't half slaughter a copper! He knocked this copper about! But he wuz never caught! And, o' course, this copper who wuz sittin' there said, 'Come here! I want you!' and he brought him in. Yeah, and he wuz brought back to Low'stoft and he wuz done. He got time. And do yuh know why he wuz never found in Low'stoft? Well, he wuz a *stoker* and he wuz attached to St. Luke's, and he wuz under punishment in the cells there. And he wuz bribin' the bloke who wuz supposed to be seein' after him! Yeah, he slipped him a quid or so to let him out at night, when he wuz supposed to be in cells. Well, if you were musterin' people, and a bloke wuz in cells, you wouldn't muster him, would you?

"There used to be a lot o'stealin' from railway vans. Oh yis. Yuh see, there always is, and you'll never stop it. The thing that people don't realise is the degree of proof that a court requires. I remember bein' seconded to Norwich for six months as a *plain-clothes officer* and, while I wuz there, we had a whisper that some people were goin' to raid the Victoria *bonded warehouse* (a lot o' police work depends on information received). That wuz the big warehouse at Victoria Station, Norwich [on the corner of St. Stephen's Street and Queen's Road]. The station is gone now, but they had a big whisky and spirits bonded warehouse there.[40] And our inspector called a couple o' men up from Low'stoft; we had about four of us from Norwich; and there wuz a couple more from Ipswich and a couple from King's Lynn; and we ringed the station at night, as soon as it got dark. And we had *walkie-talkies* and were in contact with each other, all round this warehouse from dark till daylight. We were layin' out under the trucks; we couldn't git in anywhere else. And we had our flasks o' tea and sandwiches, and we stuck this for a fortnight—every night. We knew the three blokes; we knew their names; we knew everything. An' after a fortnight, the inspector said, 'What do yuh think?' We said, 'Call it off. Let's have a break.' You know, we'd had enough. Three days after that, the job wuz done!

"Now, Macarthy's [a fruit and vegetable wholsesaler] had a depot on that station for fruit and stuff. These blokes pinched a Macarthy's van; they loaded it fully up with whisky, gin and what have yuh; they drove it south about from Norwich and transferred the stuff to another van; and away it went up to *The Smoke* [London]! We had that van tested by forensic for fingerprints and anything like that. Nothin'! Gloves—fair enough. We picked these three blokes up. Now, o' course, it's obvious—they'd got together. 'If we git picked up, this is our story. We were all round your house, playin' cards.' But, o' course, what they don't realise is that we pick the three of 'em up separately, and we take 'em to Norwich police station and put 'em into separate interview rooms. 'Right. Where were you last night? We'll start at six o' clock and I want a detailed account. I want to know everything— what you had for tea, what time you started it, what you did when you finished, what time you went out, where you went, what time you got there, who you met, and all the rest of it.' Now, o' course, they start tellin' us their concocted stories.

40 The former coalyard is occupied by a Sainsbury's supermarket.

But they haven't gone into anywhere near enough detail. So when you get their three stories and compare 'em, you never see such a pack o'lies in all yuh life! But that don't prove that they stole the drink, so you're gotta let 'em go.

"With the policin' work we did in Low'stoft, we probably spent seventy-five per cent of the time over on the Market [i.e. the Fish Market]. They were a lot o' rogues there! Oh yis, especially night-times. And sometimes you'd get information. I mean, we got a nice little prosecution there once. We got a tip one night to watch the east end o' the Waveney Dock, where that arm runs out.[41] When you had a lot o' ships in, they'd be right up there, and some o' the *lumpers* would park their cars up that road there and then they'd be offloadin' fish inta the cars to take it orf up to Norwich Market! Anyway, we set our stall out one night and caught them. Yeah, lumpers. Oh yeah.

"When I first started there, we used to second people from Yarmouth and Norwich, and even as far away as Liverpool Street, and they used to come down durin' the *herrin' season*.There wuz so much traffic (lorries and that), we had to have point-duty on the Market to control incomin' an' outgoin' traffic. Otherwise, that just used to git snarled up. Yeah, so we had traffic duty there, as well as patrollin' the Market. That wuz the peak time, when they were doin' what they called *klondykin'*. They'd have ships layin' *through-bridge* and sometimes they'd even have a ship lay in the west end o' the ol' Trawl Dock, loadin' up herrins to take away. Yes, they were still klondykin' when I joined the Railway Police. Yeah, over to Germany. Then some o' the firms, like Phillips, used to do these rolled an' *pickled herrins* [roll mops], an' they'd send 'em over to America.[42] They loved 'em over there.

"They used to load fish trains at the back o' the Market and they also had big fish sidings up parallel to Commercial Road. There used to be three or four trains a day go from there. They had a proper staffed office up there to deal with it all—a goods office. Yeah. Oh, that wuz a tremendous thing! I can remember a comical little incident to do with up there and all. I wuz on duty there one day and I see one o' the porters comin' back with what they called a *margarine*. They were these little two-stone boxes o' fish, you know. He wuz comin' back orf the fish-sidins [sidings] wi' this. This wuz trawl fish, yuh see, and that wuz summertime as well—right hot. And, o' course, I stopped him and wanted to know what he'd got, and he say, 'You'll never believe it!' Well, what had happened wuz that they'd sent some fish away about a fortnight previous and this one hadn't bin offloaded. That'd bin left in the truck for a fortnight. And this porter had got a whole boxful

41 Waveney Dock had been originally built in the 1880s as the herring and mackerel market, but became increasingly used for trawlfish as well after the Second World War. The extension referred to here had been constructed at some point during the early twentieth century, as the fishing industry expanded, and was sometimes referred to as the New Quay.

42 F.H. Phillips & Co. (Lowestoft) Ltd. was a North Shields firm originally, which had a long-standing connection with the herring trade in East Anglia.

o' maggots! Beautiful big maggots. Yeah, and he took 'em round to Sammy Hook's [a nearby fishing tackle shop] and flogged 'em for bait. So, technically speakin', he wuz pinchin' maggots orf the railway. But that wuz one you turned a blind eye to. Good luck to him!

"A lot o' *salt* and *coal* used to come in on the railway. Now, when I first joined, we were losin' coal from the South Yard. Thass all gone now. That wuz near Mill Road, under the bridge there.[43] And I went round there one night and wuz standin' underneath the bridge. There used to be fencin' go along the side o' the yard, railings about six foot high wi' spikes, an' about forty yards from the bridge wuz a stile which you could cross over to git inta the Cleveland Road and Grosvenor Road area. Well, that wuz a beautiful moonlight night and I wuz standin' underneath the bridge (this wuz about half-past twelve/one o' clock in the mornin'), when all of a sudden there's this bloke walkin' along towards the stile with a hundredweight o' coal on his back! And, o' course, I realised that I'd got to get down to the stile to catch him. So there's this chap on one side o' the fence wi' this hundredweight o' coal [in a sack] on his back an' me on the other side, tryin' to tiptoe along the grass verge to git to the stile and catch him. Well, we were about halfway there, when I spose he heard somethin' or some sixth sense told him he wuz bein' followed, so bang go the coal [i.e. the sack was dropped] and he's gone!

"Anyway, I told the sergeant about this when I come off at night. 'Call yuhself a copper!' he said. 'You ent worth tuppence-ha'penny!' He said, 'I had exactly the same thing happen to me, boy. Do yuh know what I done?' So I said, 'No, sergeant.' He said, 'I put my hat down on the ground, then I took my big coat orf and crumpled it all up an' put it on my back an' went walkin' along like this. And,' he said, 'there wuz me on this side o' the fence with a hundredweight o' coal on my back, and there wuz a bloke the other side with a hundredweight o' coal on his back. Then I dropped my coat when we got to the stile and I caught my man!'

"There wuz a lot o' pinchin' orf the boats as well. That still goes on. Really, I could tell yuh quite a lot about that. Now, orf the record, they considered at one time that they hadn't got enough police and they employed some *security blokes* down there. They hadn't bin there a couple o' months before we knocked them orf for pinchin' ships' stores! Oh, it wuz a real problem, the stealin'. There wuz one old boy down there and he wuz a real rogue. A real thief, there's no doubt about it, but a likeable old boy. And he always used to address me as 'Master'. You know, 'Mornin', master' an' that sort o' thing. So I said to him one day (he wuz just about to retire), I said, 'Would you like to make some money?' He said, 'Yes, master.' I said, 'It's dead easy.' He said, 'What've I got to do, master?' I said, 'Just put it around that you're goin' to write a book about all what you know that

---

43 This part of the railway facilties was about a quarter of a mile from the central station, to the south of the inner harbour, off Belvedere Road.

goes on down on this Market. You'll be surprised how many people will offer you a fiver [£5] to keep their name out of it!'

"O' course, the *merchants* were just as bad. They condoned a lot of what went on. Yuh see, it's the old story. It's no good pinchin' anything unless you can dispose of it. Now, if you steal some fish, where's yuh best—? I'm not talkin' about takin' hoom a little fry. I'm talkin' about a quantity o' fish. If you steal a quantity o' fish, where are yuh goin' to git rid of it? Well, there's yuh answer. Oh, I could tell yuh all sorts o' little dodges that they used to get up to. I mean, when the merchants bought fish, they had little paper *tallies* and they'd put these on the *kits*.[44] Now, you git a big firm that buys in bulk. They don't buy just an odd kit; they buy twelve kits. Now, I wuz on the Market one day and I saw this firm's *buyer* take one of his tallies and give it to another chap, yuh see. So when that chap bought ten kits o' fish, or whatever, he tallied up nine for his firm an' the tenth one went to somebody else. Well now, when it comes to provin' somethin' like that, you try and do it! I went round to one o' the merchants and I said, 'This is what I've seen. Now, what about it?' His reply wuz, 'Well, you know, we often borrow ten stone o' plaice orf him, so the next day we give him ten stone back.'[45] So you couldn't git round it. And you couldn't proceed unless you got their co-operation. That wuz no good tryin' if they weren't goin' to back you up.

"Oh yes, you didn't get the moral support, you see. I could tell you a lot o' cases (if I had a mind to) where we'd git things like that and just didn't git the support. But, takin' the rough with the smooth, we really had a happy time of it. Yeah, except when you stood there all on yuh own and there wuz four big fishermen, drunk, and all of 'em without ships. They hadn't got lodgins or anywhere to go, and they wun't entitled to sleep aboard ships, and you were the one who wuz there and who had to get 'em orf the dock.

"Apart from the actual policin' o' the docks, I also did a fair bit of office work. You know, typin' up things and preparin' cases for court. Sometimes we were successful and sometimes we weren't. And, anyway, like I said, a lot o' things didn't even get as far as court because it wuz so hard to get the proof to make a charge stick. The merchants didn't give us much help, even when they were gittin' diddled. I mean, I told one about one o' his blokes pinchin' fish. 'I know,' he say to me. 'But what can I do? He knows as much about this business as I do, and if I give him the sack he'll only go and work for one o' my competitors and tell him all my customers and prices.' Mind you, there was a comical side to a lot o' the pinchin'. Yeah, you used to git the lumpers and the fishermen stuffin' soles down their rubber boots an' then tryin' to walk orf the Market with 'em! Oh, you always

---

44 The tallies were slips of paper with the different merchants' surnames printed on them in bold capital letters. These were placed on top of the kits of fish to indicate who had purchased them.

45 A kit of fish weighed ten stones—and plaice was the species which Lowestoft market was noted for.

got a laugh or two!

"O' course, a lot o' the time we wore *plain clothes* down on the docks. Yeah, you weren't so conspicuous then. We used to wear 'em round town as well, otherwise you'd get people comin' up to yuh an' askin' the time or where such-and-such a place was! Yeah, they'd get yuh confused with the ordinary police! I retired from the force in 1971, which wun't all that long after they put the *checkpoint* on the entrance to the Market. That wuz done to control the comins and goins of people, that was, and also because a lot o' the merchants complained about too many visitors and passers-by gettin' in the way down on the dock.[46] It wuz a pity in some ways to keep people off, but that did help to stop some o' the problems caused by visitors bein' a nuisance.

"Mind yuh, as regards o' the pinchin' what went on, most o' that wuz done by the blokes that worked down there. Then you used to git some o' the fishermen knockin' orf beddin' and cookin' utensils in order to set up house in various flats round the town . And then, o' course, latterly there wuz a fair bit o' stealin' drugs from the medical kits on board the trawlers an' *standby boats*.[47] The one thing you din't git a lot of wuz *smugglin'*. You got a certain amount o' booze bein' brought in on the fishin' boats from across the other side (you know, Holland an' France), but nothin' big. The favourite place to hide a few bottles wuz in a drifter's *mizzen sail*, when that wuz furled up in harbour. No one bothered to poke about in there because that wuz so filthy wi' soot and that from the funnel."

---

46 By the time that the security gate was placed at the entrance to the Fish Market, all harbour facilities had ceased to come under the jurisdiction of the railway company and had for some time been in the control of Associated British Ports. Some hilarity was expressed in local quarters when, among the reasons given by the port authority for preventing free access, was the number of complaints received from members of the public regarding the strong language used by fishermen and market workers.

47 Standby boats are vessels that anchor off North Sea oil and gas rigs and remain there, on station, for a month at a time, in case of emergency. A number of them are (or were) converted trawlers

Plate 17: Corton Lightship

A painting of the Corton Lightship, produced by a crew member (believed to be William Sharman) for the people of the village, during the 1930s, in recognition of the support given by them to the men serving on board—especially at Christmas, when a seasonal hamper was delivered. In this view, a Trinity House tender is seen approaching the lightship itself.

CHAPTER TEN

Going To Let This Little Light Shine

Will your anchor hold in the storms of life
When the winds unfold their wings of strife?
When the strong tides lift and the cables strain,
Will your anchor drift or firm remain?
(Priscilla Jane Owens: *Will Your Anchor Hold?*)

The role played by Trinity House, for nearly five centuries, in fostering safety at sea around the shores of Britain would require a substantial volume all of its own to explore thoroughly. This chapter will present just one aspect of the organisation's contribution to the well-being of mariners: the provision of lightships to mark the presence of coastal sandbanks. It was an important service—one that was instrumental in preventing countless vessels from foundering on a considerable number of treacherous shoals—but it has tended to be overshadowed by the attention given to lighthouses. These seem to have created greater interest in the public mind, probably because of their artistic appeal and architectural quality, but it is at least arguable whether they have been responsible for saving more lives than their floating counterparts. Tom Outlaw, whose longlining experiences were recounted in Chapter Three, was a lightshipman for thirty-seven years, and is therefore able to speak authoritatively about this important aspect of Trinity House's work (tape-recording made, 10 November 1983).

"I joined Trinity House in February, 1938. And the reason I decided to go in wuz that fishin' was gettin' bad. Even two or three o' the big companies had failed. Westmacott's out o' Yarmouth had [Westmacott Ltd.], and one or two more. They were towin' drifters away to Holland to be brooke up, and they were a-breakin' 'em up locally. When I wuz *mate* in the *Dorienta* (LT 185), I saw a drifter, fully rigged, ready to go to sea, at Wick. Yeah, in 1936, I stood and saw that ship sold for £5.[1] £5! As she stood. She never had her gear in her, but she had coal and steam and everything else. And the man who bought her, he simply hopped aboard with a couple o' other men (one went down the engine-room an' the other one let go o' the ropes) and they steamed her away to the breaker's yard. And, actually, the ship I wuz in at that time, the *Dorienta*, wuz bought for £75 at Hartlepool by Barney Smith o' Kessin'land and his partner, Jack Hayward. Smith & Hayward. And although we had a good year's work in her that year, and a fairly good year the next year, other ships an' other comp'nies were goin' to the wall. My father

---

1 The boat in question was the *Bon Avenir* (WK 254).

wuz skipper of his own ship (he'd had her several years), but I grossed three times over him in 1936.[2] I had a good year's work; he had a bad year's work. Herrin' catchin'. All herrin' catchin'. In the end, I decided that it would be best to get out o' herrin' catchin' and inta a secure job. And thass the reason I went inta Trinity House. And, o' course, I did on one or two occasions (durin' the war and after the war) think seriously o' comin' out, but my heart failed me. I never done it. I decided to keep in.

"When I first went in, you had to ha' done four full years at sea. That wuz no good sayin' to Trinity House, 'I're bin to sea for four years', and praps you'd only bin to sea actually for thirty-six months. You had to have forty-eight months on *discharges*. So, for instance, if you done nine months on a drifter—on that discharge, when you left the ship (let's say in 1936), that nine months to you would represent a year's work. But to Trinity House that wuz only nine months. So you had to have forty-eight months at sea altogether, and you also had to be a British subject. They would accept nobody else at that time, only a British subject. I remember Captain Moss sayin', when he wuz goin' through my discharges and he see my *mate's ticket*, 'Well, this'll help you get inta Trinity House. But I can assure you, Mr. Outlaw, once you are in, in a lightship, that mate's ticket will cut no ice whatever.' Yeah, the lightship skippers all worked their way up from seamen to skipper. Everybody started orf as *ordinary seamen*.

"I wuz in Trinity House thirty-seven years exactly. To the day! I went in on the fourteenth o' February, 1938, and I retired on the same day: the fourteenth o' February, 1975. I done about seventeen years as *seaman*, on what they call mannin' the boat; I wuz three or four years in the *tenders* durin' the war; and I wuz seventeen years *skipper* of several different lightships—includin' the *Smith's Knoll*, the *Dudgeon*, the *Haisborough* an' the *Inner Dowsing*. When I first went in, we used to go away for two months at a time—calendar months. So if you went away on the twelfth o' January, you'd come home on the twelfth o' March. Then you'd do a month ashore, workin' at the *depot* in Great Yarmouth every workin' day. Sometimes, if you were unlucky, you'd catch a *watch* at the weekends—or perhaps a *sea trip*. Perhaps there'd be a sea trip crop up, where they'd require one or two lightsmen to go on the local steam tender for jobs on *buoys* at sea.

"The first lightship I wuz in wuz the *St. Nicholas*, which wuz only about one mile and one cable [200 yards] from the beach at Yarmouth. And you can imagine what two months at sea on board o' that ship wuz like, lookin' at the beach all the time! I wuz in that ship until Christmas 1939 and then I transferred to the *Cross Sand*, outside a bit. She wuz about eight or nine miles east o' Yarmouth. Now, there wuz usually seven men on board a lightship, but the *St. Nicholas* only had five. She wuz what we called *a short-handed ship*. She never had no engine in her. All she had wuz a *mast*, with a *lantern*, and a *winch* to shorten up the *cable*

---

2   The vessel referred to was the *Boy Scout* (LT 17), which featured in Chapter Three.

[anchor cable] when required. Yeah, there were no engines in her. She wuz more or less a glorified hulk. Oh yes, yes. She wuz a wooden ship, and when I wuz in her she wuz over a hundred years old [close to the St. Nicholas Gat channel into Yarmouth Harbour]. I spose you could call her one o' the old wooden walls. And the size o' some o' the beams inside her, down the *foc'sle*! I measured one that went straight across the bow an' that wuz eighteen inches square! They were rare timbers; there's no doubt about it. When they built them ships, they were really built to stand bad weather. And that's the thing about a lightship: when you're out there, you face everything that The Lord send. You can't run away from it. You're simply gotta stick it out.

"When you went aboard, as I said, you went aboard for two months. And you arranged for all yuh own grub. You fed yuhself. Yes, an' they still do that today. So, o' course, you used to hafta take away grub to last yuh that time. You'd take four or five joints o' meat in a small cask about the size of a bucket, an' praps you'd have one fresh joint and the rest would be salt. So, a high percentage o' the time, you'd be livin' orf salt beef, corned beef and stuff like that. You were paid a monthly rate o' pay and you had to feed yuhself out o' that and maintain your wife and children, if you were married. I got £11.50 a month—or £11 10s 0d a month—when I first went in. And those in the steamboat, the *tender*, used to get about half-a-crown a week [12½p] more'n we did.

"At that time, we used to get tuppence [2d = 1p, approximately] an hour *fog-signal money*. So if the foghorn wuz goin' for an hour, we got tuppence. If that wuz goin' for twenty-four hours, we got twenty-four tuppences [4s = 20p], and so on. I spose that wuz *noise money*, really—inconvenience money. The *St. Nicholas* only had *a reed horn*. That wuz pedalled like a sewin' machine. You had a tank standin' about six foot high, with a diameter of about two an' a half to three feet, and you'd pump that up by *treadle* to a pressure of about five pounds to the square inch. Yeah, you had yuh treadle and two pumps (one either side) and that would pump the compressed air in. An' then yuh reed horn wuz above yuh hid, an' there wuz a little handle hangin' down, and when the clock went orf for you to sound the signal you just pushed the lever over and watched the air blast back to four pound. So you got rid of a pound o' compressed air to blast that note. Or two notes. Whichever the case might be. Then you hetta turn round and pump it up agin. I're done that for four hours at a time [the length of a watch]. Oh yes.

"The conditions on board were very spartan, when I first joined. Prior to the war, Trinity House hadn't got many ships that had livin' accommodation aft. Yeah, for instance, the *St. Nicholas* had nearly half her length as *foc'sle*. It wuz anything up to forty foot long, with four or five hammocks swingin' in it. There wuz a cookin' stove in the middle, a deal table and two deal forms. And in the *wings*, along the side o' the ship, there wuz three or four lockers each side, called *sea lockers*. You kept all yuh own grub and all yuh own gear in them, and that wuz it. That wuz bumpy in the foc'sle, too. Oh definitely, yes! But, o' course, fortunately for me, in the *St. Nicholas* (my first experience in a lightship), anchored in there underneath the *Scroby* [Scroby Sand], you din't know much about real bad weather—unless you got a northerly or southerly gale. If the gale wuz easterly or westerly, that wun't affect you all that much.[3]

"As I said, most o' the lightships up till about 1936 were all *foc'sle accommodation* for the crew. Then, in 1936, Trinity House decided to build three or four bigger ships with accommodation *aft*. They were for the London District. That wuz the *Eighty-five*, the *Eighty-six* an' the *Eighty-seven*.[4] Then, a little later, come the *Ninety*, the *Ninety-one* an' the *Ninety-two*. They all had accommodation aft and small *wheelhouses* on the deck, and they were mostly for London District as well. And then they built three more—yeah, the *Ninety-three*, the *Ninety-four* an' the *Ninety-five*. They were even bigger. They were 137 foot long and had a damn gret big *wheelhouse* on. Yes, they were *all-steel* and had *diesel engines*.

"When I first went in the ships that had engines, they had Ruston Hornsby semi-diesels. *Hot-bulb engines*. Yeah, you had to heat this bulb thing with a *blowlamp* before you could start the engine. I've seen some pantomimes wi' them, believe me! And, o' course, it was a godsend when Trinity House decided to put real diesel engines in the ships—which they did do in the later class after 1937.[5] They even had steam engines in some o' the old *Sixty Class* that were brought out in the 1890s, when they were buildin' them at Blackwall.[6] Yeah, they had low-pressure *steam engines*, fired by *coke*, but I don't know much about that because I never had anything to do with 'em. All I can do is say what wuz handed down to me by word o' mouth. I have bin in one or two ships where the *bunker plates* were still actually in the deck, where they used to put the coke through, but o' course they hadn't got steam engines in 'em any longer.

"On the *St. Nicholas*, you had that great long foc'sle, then the next compartment wuz the *chain room*. And the *mainmast* come down through that chain room. And then, aft side o' that, wuz the *skipper's cabin* and the ship's *magazine*. The chain room wuz where the main chains were kept—the *main ridin' cable* [i.e. by which the vessel was moored] and the *bower cable* either side. That is to say, the spare cables, yuh see. You had yuh main ridin' cable attached to a three-ton *anchor* (though one or two o' the later ships I wuz in had five-ton anchors), and then you had two other anchors on either side, port and starboard, called *bower anchors*. And, o' course, they were already rigged, ready to drop, if they were needed.

---

3   The land served to shelter the light-vessel from westerly gales and the sandbank from easterly ones, but it was less well protected from the effect of northerly and southerly winds.

4   These numbers were the ones given by Trinity House to the respective vessels.

5   The "real diesel engines" referred to were ones where the ignition process did not rely on the preliminary heating of an exterior bulb on the casing of the engine, but was mainly achieved by internal compression of the fuel.

6   Prior to World War Two, Blackwall (on the River Thames) had been Trinity House's main shore depot—a position assumed by Harwich during the post-war period.

"The magazine wuz where the *gunpowder* wuz kept. In those days, we used to have *signal guns*. Yes, we had old cannons and we used to use 'em to make a noise. That wuz all they were for, to make a noise—to attract attention. We used to put a *charge* o' gunpowder in, about the size of a coconut. That wuz in a *silk bag*. An' then you had a cannon ball made out o' *rope* what you used to stuff down, to help make a bigger bang.[7] After you'd put the charge in, you used to prick that through the *touch-hole* with a thing like a skewer, and you had a *friction-tube* thing with a *lanyard* on when you wanted to fire the gun. Yeah, you pulled on the lanyard and that struck a match in this tube and fired the gun. We used to use them for callin' out the lifeboat [at Gorleston or Caister]. Oh yes, thass what they were for. Yes, yes, they were sound signals, in conjunction with the *rockets*, yuh see. When I wuz in the *St. Nicholas*, we had two signals, because we were coverin' two sands and keepin' our eyes open for trouble on both of 'em—the Corton Sand and the Scroby Sand. And if you had a ship in danger on the Corton Sand, it wuz one gun an' one white rocket. And if a ship wuz in danger on the Scroby, that wuz two guns and two red rockets. That wuz how those ashore knew that there wuz trouble.

"Like I said, I wuz in the *St. Nicholas* till Christmas 1939, then I transferred to the *Cross Sand*. They were both oil lightships (*oil-bangers*, as we used to call 'em) and I din't go inta an *all-electric* lightship till after the war.[8] And about the same time as I changed to the *Cross Sand*, Trinity House altered the *relief system* so that the men done a month at sea and then got a fortnight ashore. And while they were ashore, that fortnight wuz all their own. But, I might add, that any time we lost in bad weather reliefs, we never got it back. So if you wuz three or four days late comin' ashore, because o' bad weather, you lost them three or four days. In all instances. You never got 'em back. No, you never got 'em back.

"When I went in the *Cross Sand*, the war wuz then beginnin' to hot up a bit. The renowned *Phoney War* had bin goin' on for a time and then things began to hot up on the European mainland. And I think on one or two occasions we had German submarines, or other ships, droppin' mines in our area out here, because there was at least two cargo ships mined not very far from the *Cross Sand*, where we were. And, also, one minesweeper was blown up. On one or two occasions, German planes flew round us and even waved to us. Yeah, they didn't attack the *Cross Sand* until—oh, I spose that would be round about Dunkirk time [June 1940]. I wuz ashore at the time, so I didn't experience that. But, in January o' that year, 1940, the Trinity House ship *Reculver* wuz bombed while he wuz steamin' between the *Newarp* light-vessel and the *Cockle*.[9] And I actually saw that lot happen, an' there were about thirty odd casualties aboard o' her an' one officer

---

7   This was to act as a *wadding* to keep the charge tightly in place.

8   The oil lightships referred to had their lamps fuelled by paraffin and required a great deal of attention in order to function effectively.

9   Both these lightships were located off the coast of Norfolk.

killed. And the same month, the *Dudgeon* wuz bombed on two occasions, and the crew went away in the lifeboat.[10] And the weather wuz so bad that when they tried to get back to the ship, they couldn't—and they finished up on Mablethorpe beach, all drowned except one.

"As the war progressed, one or two o' the ships got bombed and no one knew anything about it until the *relief ship* got there. I think the *Outer Dowsing* wuz bombed twice in two or three days and no one knew for the simple reason that, at the beginnin' o' the war, only two ships on the Yarmouth District were equipped with radio telephone.[11] One of 'em wuz the *Cross Sand* an' the other one wuz the *Lynn Well*. Why the *Lynn Well* had one, I don't know. I mean, she wuz stuck up there near Hunstanton. After the war had been goin' on for some time, an' they were changin' ships over an' re-arrangin' ships wherever The Admiralty wanted 'em, they put *RT* [radio transmission] into all of 'em. The *Outer Dowsing* was taken off station and she wasn't replaced—not durin' the war. In actual fact, I was on board the steam vessel when we towed her off station. Shortly afterwards (that wuz while Dunkirk wuz on), I wuz on the *Cross Sand* when the steam tender come to tow us in. We were towed right inta Yarmouth harbour and after, I spose, about a month most o' the Yarmouth District lightsmen were sent off to the London area.

"Trinity House and The Admiralty had decided they were goin' to lay a line o' lightships betwin the *Nore* and the *Sunk*. These lightships were about three and a half to four miles apart. Yes, thass right—right from the *Sunk*, orf Harwich, right up to the *Nore*.[12] I wuz in a light-vessel called the *Knob*, which wuz on the inner end o' the Barrow Deep.[13] The *Knob*, yeah. K-N-O-B. Number ninety-three. And she wuz bombed twice while I wuz in her, but both times I happened to be ashore. The Germans missed, and thass a good job they did. But, in the case o' the *East Oaze*, I'm afraid they didn't miss.[14] They hit her and sunk her, and all hands were lost. They were all Yarmouth crew in her, except the *mechanic*.

"As far as this area out here wuz concerned, they had already withdrawn the *St. Nicholas* and the *Cockle* and the *Cross Sand* about the time o' Dunkirk. They withdrew the *Smith's Knoll* at the beginnin' o' the war, then put her out again. They put her out again after Dunkirk and established a channel behind the Haisborough Sands, as far as I can remember, so that the convoys picked up the *Smith's Knoll*

---

10 The *Dudgeon* light-vessel was stationed off the coast of Lincolnshire.

11 The *Outer Dowsing* was another of the light-vessels stationed off the Lincolnshire coast.

12 The Nore is a sandbank in the Thames Estuary.

13 The Barrow Deep was near the Barrow Sandbank, off the coast of Esssex, opposite Foulness Island.

14 This light-vessel was on station off the Essex coast, to the east of Southend and Shoeburyness.

Fig. 10: Smith's Knoll Lightship

A line-drawing of the vessel which once marked the position of the Northern Hemisphere's premier herring-ground. "The Knoll" (as it was usually referred to) was said to have resembled "a city at sea" on autumn nights when the Home Fishing was in full swing—such was the large number of boats showing their lights as they fished for the "silver darlings".

and went down outside [to the east]. I think the *Haisborough* wuz still there.[15] But they removed the *Outer Dowsing*, and they also removed the *Humber* as well, and the *Dudgeon* wuz brought in severely damaged by bombin' after the crew had bin lost. I think, when we went down to London, there wuz only two ships left on the Yarmouth District—the *Smith's Knoll* and the *Lynn Well*.

"I wuz up in the London area until the December o' 1940. The lightships were beginnin' to get plastered by the Germans and, as I said, the *East Oaze* was destroyed altogether. The one orf Dover wuz sunk (I think four or five men were killed on board her) and there wuz two or three in the line I wuz talkin' about, from the *Nore* to the *Sunk*, that were damaged. And, o' course, we never had any arms on board. No arms at all. I suppose at that time Trinity House wuz of the opinion that we were non-combatant and were doin' a service to all the ships. All ships, yuh see, no matter what nationality they were. And so they never armed the light-vessels. It wuz only towards the end o' 1940, after these boats had bin sunk with all hands, that the Navy ships come down the River Thames and put a machine gun aboard one or two o' the ships. But I wasn't aboard the *Knob* at the time and I never did go back on board her. I went ashore that *relief* and, while I was ashore, they decided that they were goin' to bring the Yarmouth men hoom. An' that wuz the end o' my little part in the lightships durin' the war.

"I come hoom from London the tail end o' 1940 and I wuz standin' about on the Yarmouth Depot, doin' nothin' in particular. And just about the time my wife wuz due to have my eldest daughter, they decided they wanted two seamen for the *Alert*, a tender on the London District. Well, to be quite truthful, I tried to git

---

15 The Norfolk coastal settlement after which the sandbank and lightship were named is spelled *Happisburgh*. The sandbank itself is usually rendered as *Haisborough* on charts and the light-vessel itself at one time had *Haisbro* painted on the side. This variance in spelling has been previously commented on.

out o' joinin' that ship. They picked on me an' a Yarmouth chap by the name o' Morris to go and join this ship. And I tried to get out of it, but they wouldn't wear it, and I had to go with this chap Morris. We went down to *Hellfire Corner*—the Dover area. Yeah, The Straits. I joined this ship with this chap Morris at Southend. She wuz layin' orf Southend Pier, a-waitin' for us. We went aboard an' went and done some work in The Channel [English Channel], and that wuz where I wuz first dive-bombed.

"These were yeller-nosed Messerschmitts. They were equipped with one bomb only.[16] Thass a good job they were, really! And, o' course, they had these horrible cannon shells and all. We'd just done a wreck inside the Goodwins [Goodwin Sands]—somewhere in the Downs.[17] The name o' the wreck wuz the *Flamborough*. We'd just done it, so our boat wuz free. Normally, you were anchored while the work wuz goin' on, but we were free, so a little bit o' manoeuvrin' could be done. Now, there were German planes goin' up the other side, orf the Fench coast. That wuz a clear blue sky, so o' course we were watchin' them. What we didn't notice wuz that three of 'em took a wide circle an' come round behind us. Then they started to roar as they were comin' down. The ship what wuz escortin' us wuz a Naval *sloop*. The name escapes me now, but there wuz also a *minesweepin' trawler* with us by the name o' *Wardour* (GY 523). Now, we tried to screw our twelve-pounder round to get into contact an' have a go at these Germans, but we weren't fast enough. They were comin' down too quick and our gun wuz pointin' in the wrong direction to start with. And this *Wardour*, he got a shot away as these three Messerschmitts were comin' down one behind the other. And, fortunately for us, that shell burst right in front o' the first Messerschmitt and made him jink a little bit. He jinked and the two followin' him, they jinked also. So, instead o' the bombs comin' down our funnel, or inta the ship—as I thought they were goin' to—they all come down along the starboard side. And when they blew up, there wuz a helluva lot o' water come aboard an' two or three of us were smothered in soot. And, fortunately, not a man jack aboard the ship wuz injured. There wuz bits o' shrapnel flyin' about in all directions, but we got away with it. We were dead lucky.

"I wuz down there about three weeks. Then they brought us back. In actual fact, the ship I wuz in (the *Alert*), she came up to Yarmouth. And when I arrived at Yarmouth, they said, 'All right, Outlaw, you can come ashore now.' And I went hoom and saw the new baby. And while I wuz at hoom, I thought to myself, 'Well, there wun't be many lightsmen required now, because most o' the lightships on the East Coast are in harbour.' I thought to myself, 'I'm goin' to be a shiftin' spanner. I'm goin' to be shifted round all over the place.' So I decided I wun't goin' to have none o' that—so I volunteered to go inta the steamboats, the *tenders*, right away

---

16 The aircraft referred to were Bf 109s, carrying a single 250 kilo bomb.

17 The work carried out on this occasion was marking the wreck with buoys, to prevent other craft from running onto it. The area referred to was off the coast of North Kent.

an' stay there for the duration o' the war. An' thass what I done. I served the rest o' the war out in the *Satellite* an' the *Beacon*. They were sister-ships. The first eighteen months I wuz in the *Satellite* and the rest o' the war, right up till the day the war finished with Japan [14 August 1945], I wuz in the *Beacon*.

"We were on the East Coast all the while. The main work o' the tenders in wartime wuz to lay the *channel buoys* and keep them serviced, and also lay the *wreck buoys*. There wuz quite a lot o' wreck buoys needed and, while I wuz in the tenders, our work wuz never finished. Never. You used to come inta harbour and you were told to *grub up* (because we were still grubbin' ourselves then, durin' the war), then Trinity House at Yarmouth would get in touch with the senior Naval officer at Yarmouth and they'd work out a programme for the next trip. We'd go up river and coal at the Town Hall; our coal wuz always there, waitin' for us, in five or six railway trucks. Yes, they were always there, waitin' for us. And then, as soon as ever we were grubbed up and coaled, they would then decide what we were goin' to do for the next trip. And, as I said, we were never finished.

"The tender wuz 161 foot long. She wuz *twin-screw*, but she wasn't all that fast. She had two *triple-expansion engines* in her, and she wuz *coal-fired* o' course, and at the beginnin' o' her life I think she wuz *forced draught* down the engine-room. But I think she wuz so expensive to run that they done away with the forced draught and used natural draught. And if she done nine miles an hour, she was certainly going. Invariably, it was eight and no better. The funny part about them ships, although they weren't all that big, wuz that they had the power and could pull a lightship very near as big as themselves at about six to seven knots. Oh, they definitely had the pullin' power. Thirty-six men crewed 'em moost o' the time. Yes, it wuz a fairly big crew, and o' course we had extra hands for *lookouts* against German aircraft. And then, o' course, you had *gun crew*. We had a *twelve-pounder* aboard her, two *Hotchkiss* and four *Strip Lewis*.[18] Strip Lewis—they had a round magazine an' were an air-cooled gun. You carried 'em round like a Tommy-gun. The Hotchkisses were fixed. We had one on top o' the *bridge* and one on top o' the *engine-room skylight*. They were a pest! Nobody liked them. Actually, I'm pretty sure they were a gun used in the Cavalry durin' the First World War, and they were a horrible gun![19] The twelve-pounder wuz on the after-deck. And thass another thing to mention: in the early part o' the last war, all merchant ships were defensively armed. Yes, all guns were aft-side o' the bridge, the idea bein' that if a merchant ship wuz armed fore-side she then became a warship. But they did actually arm merchant ships with guns up for'ad towards the end o' the war.

"We had what were known as *D.A.M.S. gunners* aboard—Defensively Armed

---

18 The Hotchkiss and Lewis guns were types of machine-gun, named after their creators: an armaments factory, near Paris, started by an American, Benjamin B. Hotchkiss, in 1867, and Colonel Isaac Lewis (1911), a USA army officer.

19 The main problems were difficulty of handling and lack of reliability.

Merchant Ships. They were sent out by the Admiralty and the Royal Marines, so some were Royal Marines and some were Navy men. Now, we had three aboard our ship, so the rest o' the twelve-pounder's crew had to be members of our own crew, yuh see. So the *gunlayer*, who wuz in charge o' the gun, he trained about a dozen o' the crew to handle the twelve-pounder when that wuz needed. So when the alarm bells went, the first six onta that gun took it over. That din't matter who they were. We were attacked out here two or three times. We were first attacked in the *Satellite* in May 1941. That wuz a pretty bad year on the East Coast for air attacks, 1941. Yeah, that wuz a Heinkel what attacked us—a Heinkel.[20] And, funnily enough, we'd bin away in the *long boat* to do a job on a buoy, because the *motor boat* had bin troublesome and the engineer wuz doin' somethin' to the engine.[21] So we took the long boat away and done this job on the buoy.

"Fortunately for us, we'd just got back before the attack began. We'd picked the longboat up and *griped* her up and got down below for a cup o' tea. Then, all of a sudden, we heard the alarm bells go, and the next thing we heard guns—rattle-rap-rap! And, o' course, it was the Heinkel goin' over us. He wuz machine-gunnin' as he went over. And, o' course, we were all scrabbin' to git out o' the [living] *quarters* onta the deck. He ran over us four times after that and dropped two bombs each time. But he never hit us—though he wuz givin' us a good pastin' with his machine-guns. Fortunately, our skipper knew what he was doin', and he wuz swingin' the ship about, so that every time the Heinkel came for us it had to go over the ship broadside on. See, their idea wuz to try and run the length o' the ship if they could. Thass right. And that wuz the reason that The Admiralty decided to take a mast out o' all ships that'd got two masts, yuh see. The idea was that German aircraft could *line up* two masts from the air, so most o' the ships that had two masts had the *mizzen* taken out.

"The buoys that we were lookin' after had *ladders* put on 'em. We started to do that in late 1941. Yeah, we had ladders on 'em an' we also had *first-aid boxes*—very well-made boxes, teak boxes, and in them wuz first-aid equipment. I think, if I remember right, I only heard of one case of a man gettin' on a buoy, and that wuz in the Channel [English Channel]. We had these ladders hangin' over the buoy, right down inta the water. They were a *wire ladder*, with wooden rungs forced through the wire. And all a man had to do, if he could get there, wuz to simply climb up the ladder and then he could open up the first-aid chest. The chests weren't locked; they just had two handles on an' were easy to get into.[22]

"We didn't hev too much trouble wi' *mines*, because we were always escorted

---

20 Specifically, the He 111.

21 The *long boat* referred to was a craft carried on board (as was the motor boat, or launch), which was powered by oars and could, if need arose, serve as a lifeboat for the crew.

22 The ladders and first-aid facilities on buoys were placed there to assist any aircrew who might have been forced down into the water.

by trawlers. Yes, we always had an escort trawler with us and, whenever we went inta areas that were considered possibly dangerous, we were *swept in* by two or four (and, in some cases, eight) sweepers. They did the job, then come out again. Occasionally, when we went to pick up a buoy, you'd pick it up and then you'd find part of a *sweep-wire* underneath. Or praps a *kite*.[23] Oh yeah, you'd get that sort o' thing underneath. O' course, occasionally, a minesweeper would run up alongside a buoy—or his sweep would run up alongside a buoy. Then the sweep would run up the moorin' chain. And underneath the buoy wuz a bridle in triangular form attached to the chain, and the sweep would run up that as well, up the side o' the buoy, over the top, and cut the light clean off. So the *gas buoy* would then be just a buoy, like a can floatin' on top o' the water. The superstructure on a buoy wuz largely made o' wood, with three big bands o' steel, and the *lantern* wuz on top. And, o' course, that minesweepin' wire wuz a *serrated wire* and that'd go through the lantern like a breadknife through butter. Oh, that happened to us many, many a time. Yeah.

"As I said, we were never finished. Never finished. No. And we had the area from Orford Ness right up to the Farne Isands to look after! So we were always chasin' about. There wuz just the Yarmouth boat on that area. Yes, yes, just that one boat on the Yarmouth District. Occasionally, if we got bogged down with work, they'd send a boat up from Harwich to give us a hand. But all the buoys on that district, theoretically, were looked after by the Yarmouth steamboat. Oh yis, that wuz a hell of an area! At one time, durin' the war, we had (if my memory serves me right) 185 buoys on the district. There wuz all the *channel buoys* and the *normal gas buoys*, and then the *wreck buoys*.[24]

"We also laid automatic or semi-automatic lightships, wherever The Admiralty wanted 'em. We had two o' them on the Yarmouth District, but the *E-boats* used to play up merry hell wi' them.[25] They'd go aboard an' smash 'em up when they saw fit. We had one o' the old lightships turned inta a fully-automatic lightship for the Newarp Sand and the Germans went aboard o' her and smashed up the light equipment and foghorn, then stood orf and peppered her with cannon-shells. So when we went along side o' her a few days later, she wuz full o' holes as big as coconuts! And we spent the best part o' that day bungin' them holes up wi' *wooden plugs*. See, we allus used to carry bags o' plugs around for cannon-shell holes. Yes, they were varyin' sizes, yuh see. Small ones an' big ones, yuh see, and you'd just thump 'em inta the holes. But, unfortunately, that didn't save that ship, because when we steamed in that area two or three days later she was gone, completely—sunk!

---

23 This was a paravane, part of a minesweeper's equipment which helped to keep the sweeping-wire up to the required depth beneath the surface of the water.

24 Wreck buoys were painted green, with WRECK clearly visible in white.

25 The two vessels referred to were the *Cross Sand* and the *Newarp*.

"Another time, we went up alongside one o' the automatic lightships, and I jumped over the *rail* to make the motor boat's *bow-rope* fast and I saw some *fins* stickin' out o' the side o' the *deckhouse*. I looked at these fins and I thought to myself, 'Thass a bomb!' Well, I looked over the side and I said to the mate, 'Mr. Fisher, there's a bomb aboard here.' And he din't feel inclined to believe me, so he put his hid over the rail and, o' course, when he see the fins (I pointed them out to him), he said, 'Right. Come aboard.' Then we went back to the steamboat and told the captain and took him back to hev a look. And, o' course, he confirmed it wuz a bomb, sent a message in to the Senior Naval Officer, Yarmouth, and the naval squad came out and defused it. It wuz a thousand-pounder![26] Now, the automatic lightships had a deckhouse, with all the *acetylene gas* bottles inside, to supply gas to the *light* and to the *fog-bell*. This bomb went through the deckhouse, pushed five or six o' these gas bottles out o' the way and smashed through the main deck inta the lower hold.

"At the end o' the war, we took the *Beacon* up to London for a re-fit [to the Blackwall Depot]. Then I come back to Yarmouth, because I'd got some leave due to me. When I went back to the store, the man in charge said, 'All right, you can rejoin the *Beacon*. I said, 'No. I wanta go back in the lightships.' And, o' course, we had a bit of an argy-bargy in the office, and he said, 'All right, Mr. Outlaw, if you wanta return to the lights, proceed to Plymouth breakwater lighthouse!' And I done a month there! Ha, ha, ha, ha. Then, after I'd done that spell there, I come back to Yarmouth District and went back inta the lightships here.

"There wuz always a fair amount to do on board, because you did all the maintenance to do with the *general appearance* o' the ship, as well as maintenance on the *engines*. You know, in the way o' *filters* and *sumpin'* and that sort o' thing.[27] But to take the engines apart and *decarbonise* and all that sort o' thing, that wuz done by Trinity house mechanics. They were sent out every so often to do it. All the *paintin'* on board the ship wuz done by the crew, all the *chippin'* and *scrapin'*, and we painted from *truck to keel* every year. Oh yeah, every year, without fail! Sometimes twice a year! On the outside. Oh, you were never done on the bigger ships. No, no, you were never done. I mean, there wuz plenty o' days when the weather wun't let yuh git to it, yuh see. You just couldn't git to yuh work, because the weather wun't allow it, so you caught up when yuh could.

"In Trinity House, you were there to help the mariner—whatever he wanted. And you did your best to satisfy his wants, no matter what it is. I mean, I remember a strange ship comin' up alongside us, when I wuz in the *Haisborough*, and she wuz an admiralty ship bein' delivered by a civilian crew. And the skipper, he come alongside of us and he asked me to send a message to the Senior Flag

---

26 In this case (and given that it was German), a 500 kilogram bomb.

27 In other words, routine maintenance on the engines, such as cleaning or renewing filters and changing the lubricating oil.

Officer, Scotland, to tell him where he was and give him his approximate *E.T.A.* [estimated time of arrival] at Rosyth. He wasn't able to do it hisself; thass why he come up alongside. He'd got trouble aboard with his *RT* [radio transmitter], yuh see, so he come up alongside and give me the signal, and I simply sent it through.

"At one time, the *Haisborough* had bin a *Lloyd's Station*, but that wuz afore my time in her. Trinity House had one or two lightships around the coast that were Lloyd's Stations.[28] They were equipped with a *land telephone* and the wire used to go down the *cable* [mooring cable]. Yeah, the telephone cable went down the cable an' then went ashore somewhere to a *shore station*. That wuz to get in direct contact with those ashore. See, they were *Lloyd's signal stations*. A ship would come up close past the lightship and he'd have his signal flags flyin', yuh see. The men aboard the lightship would git the *code book* out, read the signal, check the code and just simply send the message ashore: 'Such and such a ship just passed the *Haisborough*, bound north.' Or 'bound south', yuh see. Well, that signal would be sent to the owners, or whoever wuz interested ashore. Yeah, they had two or three stations like that. Thass right. But that wuz all finished when I went inta the service.

"We used to send most o' our signals out here through the Cromer Coastguard, but I think I can only remember one occasion when I sent a message from a fishin' boat. It wuz somethin' to do with a fishin' vessel belongin' to Boston [the Boston Deep Sea Fishing Co. Ltd.], if I remember right. I can't remember the details about it now, but I asked Cromer to notify the superintendent that such and such a ship had passed the *Haisborough*, proceedin' south. On another occasion, I set down the cabin one night and I happened to be listenin' on the *distress band*, and I heard a ship callin', givin' out a *mayday*. It was a very slight signal. And I got in touch with him, and the people at Humber Radio an' Cromer Coastguard could hear me talkin', but they couldn't hear him. And I got the partic'lars from him. He wuz on the south end o' the Scroby Sands. He told me he thought he wuz on the Scroby, but he din't know for sure exac'ly where he was. The weather wuz thick. And while I wuz talkin' to him, yuh see, Humber Radio and Cromer Coastguard also formed the opinion, by what I wuz sayin' to this Scotch drifter, about where he was. And, o' course, in the meantime, the bells were ringin' ashore and out go the lifeboat. I never did meet with the man, but thass the only occasion I ever done anything like that over the RT.[29]

"In the old *St. Nicholas*, you were always seein' fishin' boats. So you did on the *Corton* an' the *Cross Sand* and the *Smith's Knoll*. Well, and the *Haisborough* as well. Oh yes, you allus had plenty o' fishin' boats around yuh. When I wuz in the

---

28 Lloyd's of London, the insurance agency.

29 Radio transmitters were fitted to all Trinity House light-vessels in the post-war period. The lifeboat referred to in the previous sentence was almost certainly either the Gorleston one or that from Caister (perhaps both).

Haisborough, we orften used to have a bag o' fish put aboard. Now, to be quite frank, the Senior Officer o' Trinity House used to frown on that sort o' thing. Oh yes, he used to frown on that, because if a ship come alongside and damaged the lightship, he wuz liable, yuh see. He'd got to pay.[30] And, to be quite frank, they shouldn't really have come anywhere near yuh.

"When I wuz on the *Smith's Knoll*, there wuz many a drifter had his nets cut clean through by the *cable* durin' the Hoom Fishin' time.[31] Oh yes, that happened dozens o' times! Dozens an' dozens o' times! And there were other things as well. I remember the first night I went aboard her as *skipper*, and I'd only bin turned in about an hour (this wuz just after midnight) when the *alarm bells* rang. I flew out o' the bunk an' went straight upstairs, towin' me *lifejacket* behind me ('cause you never know what's goin' to happen) and when I got on deck this French trawler had just cleared the bow! He wuz *towin'*. Yeah, towin'. And how the hell his trawl cleared our cable, I do not know. But we then hatta turn round and heave it in to make sure it wuz O.K. O' course, boats are warned. They never used to get any warnin' from us, but they are warned by Trinity House and articles in nautical almanacs and things like that to give light-vessels a wide berth.

"The cable wuz known as *Tayco cable*, an' in most lightships it wuz made o' inch an' five-eighths steel [width]. It wuz a damn great chain cable. Chain, yeah. An inch an' five eighths. I spose a link would be six inches long or so. If I remember right, there wuz eleven links to the fathom. The cables were made up ashore, an' they were made up in fifteen-fathom lengths. Then the lengths were joined together by *shackles*, which had red-hot pins put in 'em and the ends hammered down so everything wuz clinched solid. And every so often you had a *swivel-link*. See, you had yuh anchor, then forty-five fathom o' chain, and then (in the length from forty-five to sixty) you'd have a swivel. Then you'd go up to about ninety fathom, or praps even 120, before there wuz another swivel.[32]

"You had about 210 fathom o' cable on board altogether and the most I ever had out on a lightship [on station] wuz in the *Inner Dowsing*. We had 171 out there one night, when we had a northerly *buster*, and it wuz a very uncomfortable

---

30 In other words, Trinity House would have to bear the cost of any repairs.

31 A steam-drifter's fleet of nets was about one and a half miles in length, so it was almost inevitable that regular fouling of the gear on the light-vessel's mooring cable occurred. Smith's Knoll was the premier autumn herring ground and large numbers of vessels worked it every night.

32 The swivel prevented the cable from twisting, thereby avoiding extra strain on the links of the chain.

night.[33] And I can also remember bein' towed on the *Morecambe Bay* (the Number Nine) down to the Tyne in extremely severe weather. We'd bin inta the River Humber and out again, and we got towed right down to Shields [South Shields].[34] We wanted to go in there, and the captain o' the steamboat that wuz a-towin' us probably hoped that we might git a tug to tow us in. Howsomever, they refused to come out, so we hetta then turn round and run for shelter 'cause we'd now got to about *force ten* [storm or whole gale, on the Beaufort Scale] And we turned and started to run southerly again. He called us up on the air and told us he wuz goin' to run for Flamborough Hid.[35] Well, that wuz a helluva run! And while we were runnin' southerly, well, we were doin' everything bar roll over! She wuz *sheerin' about* from one side to the other and the water wuz pourin' over the rails. And I said to the lads on board the ship, 'I don't think she'll stand much more o' this. She'll *part*.' And one o' the lads say, 'Well, that'll be a damn good job! We can drop anchor then and *ride* more peacefully.'

"And it wuz in Robin Hood's Bay where we finally parted from the vessel.[36] And the captain o' the steamboat sung out over the RT, 'You're adrift, Mr. Outlaw. Drop yuh anchor.' I said, 'Yis, I know all about it. How much water ha' we got here?' And he said, 'Oh yes. Hang on a minute.' And he checked the chart. 'Yeah,' he say, 'You're got about twenty fathom under yuh. So watch how you drop that anchor.' See, you're got a five-ton anchor hangin' there and if you open the *brakes* on the *winch*, and dun't watch what you're doin', that'll run away with yuh and yuh *brake- blocks* will burn out before you can stop the cable runnin'. So, o' course, I eased the brakes open and the anchor started to go. The cable went up over the winch down inta the chain locker—a gret big room under the winch. An, that night, when we stopped her, we had 176 fathoms out. Yeah, that wuz a north-westerly that night, when we dropped—about a *force ten*.

"I saw a lot o' changes in my time wi' Trinity House, in general workin' conditions and in general comfort on board the ships. That class I mentioned earlier, when they changed over from foc'sle livin' to aft livin', the *Eighty-five*, the *Eighty-six* and the *Eighty-seven*, were definitely better livin' conditions than what we'd bin used to. And then the *Nineties*, they come along. Well, after the

---

33 The normal mooring length in reasonable weather conditions was 90 to 110 fathoms. Some of the Trinity House Elder Brethren thought this was excessive and might lead to the cable fouling its anchor (something which was feared by all light-vessel masters). If this happened, a tender usually had to go out with lifting gear. There was a maxim in the service that the length of mooring cable should be six to eight times the depth of water (it was usually reckoned at about three for other craft), but the Yarrnouth Superintendent would make no specific recommendation—he left the decision to be made by individual masters.

34 Every three years, a light-vessel was sent into port for a complete overhaul and refit. The contract for the work was put out to tender and the cheapest quote usually accepted. On this occasion, the *Morecambe Bay* was on her way to a shipyard on the Tyne.

35 A promontory just to the north of Bridlington.

36 Robin Hood's Bay is about five miles to the south-east of Whitby.

war, they brought in ships of all one class, 137 foot long overall and I spose about twenty-five to thirty foot *beam*. They were, without doubt, fine sea-ships, and all their accommodation wuz aft and they all had central heatin' in too. So, in my opinion, at that time, I considered that Trinity House couldn't do much more for the man on board the ship as far as comfort was concerned. Oh yeah, I saw a lot o' changes durin' my time."

Thirty-seven years' service, spent mainly on lightships, is an authoritative statement all of its own, requiring little endorsement. However, Tom Outlaw's experiences with Trinity House can now be usefully supplemented by those of a man with far fewer years at sea, but whose time on board made a lasting impression on him. In the previous chapter, Jack Turrell recalled his work as a railway and docks policeman at Lowestoft from the end of World War Two until 1975, briefly mentioning (by way of preamble) his career on Trinity House lightships and tenders. That phase of his working life can now be described in greater detail. It makes an interesting and complementary addition to what has already been recounted (tape-recording made, 1 December 1981).

"I left school at fourteen [1927] and went to the Prince o' Wales Trainin' School, in London, E. 14. It wuz run by the British Sailors Society, and I spose there wuz about sixty boys there, bein' trained for the Merchant Service. And, believe me, that wuz rough! You were trained by the old-time Naval *chief petty officers*, and they were hard! You were up at six o' clock in the mornin'and you scrubbed the school right through before you had yuh breakfast. That wuz that type o' thing. And you fell in at nine o' clock on the *signal deck* for orders an' all the rest of it. And, all of a sudden, they'd say, 'Port watch number one, over the top!' They had a big ol' sailin' ship's mast on the signal deck, an' you all had to scramble over that, and these chief petty officers they stood on the opposite side waitin' for yuh to come down—and the last ones got the *rope's end*! So you can imagine! And when you come to the *cross-trees*, you'd be standin' on the bloke below you. Yeah, you'd be standin' on his hands and kickin' him in the face, to make sure that you got over that top and down! And in the classrooms, if you weren't payin' attention—you know, they had little blocks, *demonstration blocks*, an' they just used to pick one o' them up an' smack it at yuh, just like that![37] Oh, that wuz a shockin' place!

"I wuz there about six months. And if you made a little bit o' trouble at night in the dormitories, yuh know, when the lights were out, they'd come after yuh and they'd turn the whole school out. And then you'd hefta run round the signal deck— rain or whatever it wuz like!—in bare feet, on this tarmac sort o' surface. You know, you'd be goin' round an' round, with yuh *beds* [i.e. mattress and blanket roll] and all that on yuh back! Well, I mean, if they tried to do things like

---

37 The blocks referred to were small blocks and sheaves, which were used to teach the trainees how to make different kinds of tackle to move weights of varying degree.

that today, they just wun't git away with it.

"Any rate, I left there and went to sea, fully intendin' to sit for me *certificates* an' all that.[38] This wuz in 1928 and I joined my first ship in Newcastle, a ship called the *Wendover*. It wuz the November o' 1928, and we sailed for Algiers, and that wuz one o' the worst gales that had ever blown for years and years. And we were a bran' new ship and we caught this in the Bay o' Biscay. The *awnin' spars* were carried away, the *fore-peak* wuz all flooded, and we very nearly lorst the ship. Yeah, we were three days overdue a-gittin' inta Algiers. She wuz a *general cargo* boat, round about nine or ten thousand tons, and she belonged to Watt & Watts [Watts, Watts & Co.]. They had quite a lot o' ships an' they were all named after places near London. There wuz *Watford*, *Wanstead* and *Wendover*—they were all sister ships—an' then there wuz *Twyford*, *Denham*, *Laleham*, *Cookham* and *Egham*.

"After a time, things got really bad and I got caught up with the unemployment situation. In the 1930s it wuz really bad. I came ashore and tried hard to get a job. Tried and done all sort o' stupid things. You know, anything to git a job. I even managed to git one or two sea trips in, but that wun't really very satisfactory, so I went and joined the lightships as a last desperate measure. I joined them in London and I went to a ship called the *Brake*, which wuz on the inside o' the Goodwins, orf Deal [Goodwin Sands]. Yeah, a funny little ol' wooden lightship. Well, o' course, they were then. A lot o' 'em were wood. An' they just had this mast, with the lantern built round it, and *oil-lamps* swingin' on *gimbals*. Yeah. And you had a *clock*, a big clock down below, which had to be wound up by hand every twenty minutes and which worked the light round.[39] And every time the clock run down, the bell clicked and away you had to go and wind it up again. Every twenty minutes, so that just kept goin' round. And you had to keep makin' sure, especially in gales o' wind, when the lamps were rockin' and rollin', that everything wuz all right. The lamps used to start smokin' and then up you'd hefta go and trim the *wicks*. Oh yes, oh yes!

"You hed six men and a skipper on board and you were out there for two months. Two months. Two months at a time and a month ashore, to start with. Yeah. When I realised there wuz a depot at Yarmouth, I applied to be transferred—and I got transferred to Yarmouth and I worked from there. When you were ashore, you had to work in the yard, cleanin' the buoys, scrapin' the chains [to get rid of rust] and general sort o' work like that. And, o' course, in those days, you couldn't afford cars, so you had to bike backwards an' forwards between Low'stoft and Yarmouth. I wuz on the *Haisborough* most o' the time when I wuz at Yarmouth an' she wuz an old wooden ship. I remember one night on her when all of us aboard thought

---

38 Certificates of maritime competence, finishing with that which enabled the holder to become master of a vessel. These qualifications were usually referred to as *tickets*.

39 In other words, a clockwork device which rotated the inner light mechanism.

we were never goin' to survive. I've never known a ship to be chucked about so much in all my life! Unless you've actually been to sea, you can't realise what it is. That wuz a strong north-westerly wind. Now, when the tide wuz on the *flood*, that run southerly with the wind, so you were hanging head-on to it—and that wun't too bad. But when the *ebb* tide come, you're got the tide goin' a different way to the wind. In other words, the tide now swings you broadside on to the waves. Cor, I shall never forget that night! I've never seen so much water shipped. And none of us in the crew really thought we were goin' to get through it.

"I wuz in the *Haisborough* when war started. Durin' the first twelve months, that wuz really a *phoney war*. Nothin' happened. And, o' course, we were just goin' out there, without even a peashooter aboard, and all we could see wuz *destroyers* and *sweepers* [minesweepers] playin' about. Well, then, o' course, the war started in earnest and the Germans started shootin' up the lightships an' goodness knows what, and gradually they were withdrawn. Well, when they were withdrawn, Trinity House sort o' reorganised us and I served a bit o' time on the *Patricia* and the *Alert*. They were *tenders* that did the buoyage work. Yuh see, the minesweepers were now sweepin' the *Channel* [the North Sea "swept channel", located east of the Haisboro Light] and we were buoyin' the Channel orf and doin' other sort o' work. We were still based at Yarmouth, but then we'd praps get a call that some buoys had been shot out by the Germans up in Grimsby. And we used to go up to Grimsby an' then go out on a *tug*. We'd hev a new lamp crated up and we'd go out on a tug, or praps on a *motor launch*, and put that new lamp on the buoy.

"We did some mad things, really. I spose, when you look back, you'd laugh now. I mean, we had to report to Southend once for orders an' pick up a naval escort. Well, when we got there, our naval escort wuz a little ol' Low'stoft drifter! She could do seven knots and we could do seven an' a half, and she'd got a little three-pound peashooter on her fore-deck and we'd got a few ordinary machine-guns. And we'd gotta go all round Dover, where the *E-boats* operated, and we'd got to go to all the buoys round there and put a special box on 'em, with seasick pills in and a syringe to inject cocaine. Yuh see, that wuz for the aircraft that come down. Yeah, we used to hefta attach a ladder to the buoy and strap that round, and we went all round *E-boat Alley* and underneath the guns at Dover doin' that.[40] And all we hed wuz a little ol' Low'stoft drifter as an escort! That wuz lucky we never fell in with any Germans.

"When I wuz on the *Haisborough* lightship, before the war, that wuz still two months on and one month off. *Oil lamps* then, too, o' course. I couldn't really give you a date for when the vessels went *electric*, but I spose that musta bin after the war. The *Haisborough* wuz a wooden ship, though she did have some metal superstructure, and she still had the big old-fashioned *foc'sle* with the cookin'

---

40 E-boats were high-speed, wooden hull, German attack vessels, capable of 40-50 knots and armed primarily with torpedoes. Protective armament (which could also be used offensively) consisted of machine-guns and cannons.

range in, up one end, and a big table down the middle an' lockers down each side. We all cooked for ourselves—took it in turns. You see, everybody sort o' mucked in. Oh yeah, you took yuh turn. And you slung yuh *hammocks* up and slept in them. Yeah, you just knotted them up and tied 'em to *eyebolts* in the timbers [i.e. the ribs of the vessel].

"You had three periods o' duty; you had two aboard and one ashore. And, o' course, that all depended on the weather whether you got ashore. I mean, if that wuz blowin' a gale, they couldn't get you off. You were sunk. You were stuck aboard. It was pretty boring while you were out there. But, o' course, I always did a lot o' reading and I wuz always a keen card player. We used to play a lot o' cards. We used to hev good card schools. Yeah, we used to sit an' play hours o' *solo* [solo whist]. And I wuz always a chess man. I always carted chess about with me and, wherever I went, I always taught somebody to play. And, o' course, a lot o' the chaps used to do model-makin'. You know, ships in bottles and that sort o' thing. I can show yuh how to put a ship in a bottle, if you wanta know how to do that! And we used to do mat-*makin'* as well—quite a lot o' that [rag or wool rugs].

"You did yuh *normal sea-watches* while you were out there: four hours on and four hours off. Yeah, four hours on an' four hours off. There was the two *dog watches*, o' course [4 p.m. to 6 p.m. and 6 p.m. to 8 p.m.], and we always used the mornin' watch [8 a.m. till noon] for maintenance. Yeah, you always worked on maintenance for the whole time in the mornin'. And then, after twelve o' clock (or after dinner, rather), you just kept watch—unless there wuz a little bit o' tiddly paintin' you wanted to do, or anything else. But that wuz never sort o' enforced. And, o' course, if you got a really nice fine summer's day, you used to lower the *little boat* and go scrub round the outside o' the ship (all the seaweed an' that, you know) and generally tidy her up. And, in the spring, you'd paint the whole ship up, right from top to bottom, and really get her posh and clean. And then the Elder Brethren would come, you know.[41] They'd come round and inspect yuh and have a word with yuh and all the rest of it. 'Any complaints? Blah, blah, blah.' And all that sort o' thing. Yeah.

"There wuz no engineer on board. You were all self-taught. I mean, you'd got no means of propulsion. All you'd got wuz an *air-compressor engine*. There wuz two big diesel compressors that compressed the air that worked the *foghorn*, yuh see. And if that come in foggy, you started this compressor up and that built the air-pressure up and you then worked yuh foghorn. You were towed out there by a *tender* after you'd bin in port and then you just hung to yuh *anchor chain*. O' course, if you were *master*, you hed to know a little bit about navigation. I wuz quids in on that, 'cause I'd studied navigation [as part of Merchant Navy schooling]. Yeah, the master hed to be able to take *cross-bearins*, 'cause if you got

---

41 The Elder Brethren were the most senior officials of Trinity House.

a gale o' wind you needed to know whether you were draggin' the anchor or not.[42]

"You hauled yuh anchor cable in, or paid it out, accordin' to the weather. In fine weather, you rode a short cable, but as the weather deteriorated you paid the cable out. And, o' course, every chain hangs in a *bight*, don't it, and that give yuh that bit o' play, see. That wuz just a big, heavy, iron anchor on the end of it. That'd be about three or four ton, I spose. Just the two *flukes*. Yeah, you'd be surprised how they dig in. You see, the harder you set back on an anchor and the more you pull, the harder that bite inta the ground. That wuz the only moorin' we had, though we did have a secondary anchor if we needed it. But you can't ride on two anchors because, as you go round, they'd foul. But if you lost yuh main anchor, you could drop a secondary one—though I never did hear of a chain breakin'.

"The biggest thing we had to contend with on the *Haisborough* wuz when you had a strong flood tide runnin' and a lot o' the ships passin' didn't realise that the tide wuz settin' 'em inta the lightship, if they got too close. Some of 'em used to try and turn, and then they'd be comin' at yuh broadside on! See, you had a six-knot current there, and I remember seein' one ship turn round completely when the tide got hold of it. Yeah, and if you'd bin standin' on our bow, you could ha' stepped off our bow onta his stern! As close as that! And I've known other ones only just *sheer* past, and you could ha' stepped aboard them as well!

"We used to see quite a lot o' the fishin' boats. Oh yes, oh yes. They used to stop sometimes, close to us, an' give us a basket o' fish. Yeah, the trawlers did. One or two of 'em especially, you know. We used to see the ol' sailin' smacks as well—and the Mission to Seaman smack, that used to stop.[43] Yeah, that'd always stop, and they'd lower the little boat and away they'd come and bring yuh a *fry*. Or they'd see if you wanted any woollens or anything like that, you know.[44] Yeah, they'd always give a look like that. Mind yuh, you'd have a little sort o' prayer meetin' and sing a hymn with 'em! We used to see all the drifters steamin' past out there as well. They used to be out to the east mostly. They were well outside us, but you could see plenty o' lights and that at night. Yeah, yeah. O' course, we were in radio contact with Cromer. The coastguards, you see. We reported in to them every day. We had communication with them, and we used to do the *weather report* and the *tide report* and send that in. Yeah, we used to give them a

---

42 If a light-vessel dragged its anchor to any degree, and finished up off station, it had to be towed back to the correct position by a tender.

43 This was the vessel belonging to The Royal National Mission to Deep Sea Fishermen, which was stationed at Lowestoft and which, as part of its Christian witness, minstered to the physical and spiritual needs of North Sea fishermen. The Mission to Seamen was a completely different, shore-based organisation, which attended to the welfare of sailors in merchant service from all over the world.

44 All the RNMDSF smacks carried a beam trawl, which the crew operated as part of routine trip procedure. Among the items distributed to any vessels visited were mittens, scarves and balaclavas.

barometric readin' and the state o' the weather as we saw it, and the state o' the tide and an *estimate o' the waves*—the strength o' the waves—and all that sort o' thing.

"Cor, they were strong, well-built ships! There's no messin' about. They were really good. Yeah, they were very warm and comfortable, them old wooden ships. They used to take 'em in for refits from time to time, but I couldn't tell yuh the exact period now [three years]. They had a fixed period at sea, then the *Alert* or the *Reculver* or the *Patricia* would tow a replacement out and pick you up and take you in. Yeah, an' you were liable to do this sort of relief business while that wuz your turn ashore![45] The ships used to be brought inta dry-dock at Yarmouth and be all cleaned up and hev a thorough overhaul, then be taken out on station again.

"You always had to take yuh own food aboard on the lightships. They reckoned that wuz allowed for in yuh wages, yuh see. But, I mean, o' course, that wun't much. We were only paid about £12 a month. Thass all. Yeah. But then you got one or two *allowances*, yuh see. Once the foghorn started goin', you got an extra tuppence [2d = 1p, approximately] an hour *noise-money*, yuh see. Yeah. And then we used to git another allowance, because we used to do this *tidal surveyin'* that I mentioned and reportin' on the weather. We used to get a few extra coppers [pennies] for that sort o' thing and that used to be shared out among us. Yeah, we had a *tide-meter* there and we used to hefta drop it over the side and record the tide every so many hours. That used to give us the direction and speed o' the tide, yuh see, and we used to make a note o' that and then we used to report it in on the radio.

"I always found Trinity House all right to work for. Yeah, they were quite reasonable. You got yuh *leave*, o' course, and that wuz taken out o' your *shore-time* (when you were ashore) so you din't hefta cycle to Yarmouth durin' that time. We had quite a decent depot there, at Yarmouth, and they didn't really push us a lot. As long as you got the required work done, nobody really slammed yuh. All the people there were Trinity House. And the head ones had worked up. Yeah, they'd started orf as *deck-apprentices* on the tenders and relief ships, worked themselves up to *skipper* and then gone *shore superintendent*. If you worked up high enough, you'd finish up at Blackwall, which wuz the main depot. And then the actual headquarters wuz at Tower Bridge—Trinity House, where the Elder Brethren actually met. Yeah, that wuz the top level o' Trinity House. I dun't know whether there wuz ex-naval men in it as such, but we certainly had ex-Navy men in the lightships and that sort o' thing. Yeah, we had an ex-naval signaller on the *Haisborough*, and he could read *morse* [Morse Code]. That used to be interestin'. There'd be a ship out there, blinkin', and he'd just automatically decipher it and be talkin' to me just like I'm talkin' now. I wouldn't say that bein' on lightships wuz the best life. But the trouble was that, with the unemployment situation, you just grabbed at anything as a job—and I managed to get in there."

---

45 In other words, some of the lightsmen might find themselves as relieving crew on a substitute light-vessel during the refit period of the ship taken off station.

Plate 18: Veracity (LT 311) pre-conversion

The diesel drifter "Veracity" (LT 311) seen heading out to the fishing-grounds during her herring-catching days. A moderate to heavy swell is visible and three crew-members are engaged upon some task next to the little boat—one of them much more plainly visible than the other two.

Plate 19: Veracity (LT 311) post-conversion

The "Veracity, after conversion, seen heading out of Lowestoft—with seven of the crew visible (one on top of the wheelhouse). Whether this is a trial or the start of her voyage to Cocos Island is not possible to say. Of the four people standing in line, the second from the left is a woman and almost certainly Mrs. Arthur, wife of the expedition's leader. The cabin built in front of the wheelhouse, referred to by Henry Leighton, can be clearly seen.

CHAPTER ELEVEN
The *Veracity* Affair

Were you ever down the Congo river?
Blow, boys, blow.
Where the fever makes the white man shiver.
Blow, my bully-boys, blow.
(Traditional American capstan song: *Blow, Boys, Blow*)

Lowestoft drifters were built to catch herrings, but one of them went hunting for much more valuable and elusive prey. The *Veracity* (LT 311) was the first purpose-built motor-drifter in England, constructed by Richards Ironworks Ltd. in 1926 and powered by a 200 h.p. Deutz diesel engine. Though having a conventional wooden hull, this vessel was revolutionary in her use of diesel power as opposed to coal-fired steam propulsion. As it turned out, she was twenty years ahead of her time, because it was only after World War Two that the Lowestoft fishing fleet adopted diesel power on a large scale. In his excellent monograph on the family firm, Lewis Richards (son of the founder, Samuel Richards) wrote of *Veracity's* significance, emphasising her superior speed to that of steam vessels and her economy in use of fuel and identifying innate conservatism on the part of local boatowners as the main reason why the diesel engine did not replace steam triple-expansion.[1] He saw the new means of propulsion as a way of enabling the local fishing industry to cope with a period of great difficulty, through its ability to reduce running costs, but the breakthrough never occurred and, within a decade of being built, the *Veracity* was withdrawn from herring-catching and laid up on the southern shore of Lowestoft's inner harbour.

The vessel's second career then began. She was selected by a consortium involved in the recovery of hidden treasure to go to Cocos Island (a remote Pacific Ocean location, about 340 miles south-west of the Central American republic of Costa Rica) and serve as the expedition's floating headquarters and supply vessel. She was converted for such work in the yard which had built her, the main task being to sheathe her hull in *Muntz metal* against the ravages of tropical marine worms (Lewis Richards refers to this in his book).[2] After completion of the refit, she set sail for the Pacific, with a Lowestoft man among her crew. Henry Leighton (1910-?) had encountered one of the expedition leaders completely by chance,

---

1 L.E. Richards, *Eighty Years of Shipbuilding* (Lowestoft, 1956), pp. 23-4. A weekly fuel cost of £5 12s 6d is cited for the vessel, which was far less than a steam drifter's coal bill. An earlier *Veracity* (LT 685) had been built at Richards in 1910 and was sunk by German destroyers (along with six other, similar vessels) in February 1918, while on patrol duties in the English Channel.

2 *Muntz metal* is an alloy of copper and zinc, named after its inventor, G.F. Muntz.

in a Lowestoft hotel, and had agreed to join the *Veracity* as cook and catering manager, using skills which he had already acquired. The voyage was to be one which he never forgot, with its overtones of piracy, buried gold and desperate deeds upon the high seas. It was the stuff of fiction, but every bit of it was real (tape-recording made, 15 February 1982).

"It all started one evening in January 1935, when I walked into the *Harbour Hotel* to have a drink. Now, in January, there's usually not many strangers about, but it happened that there was one this particular evening, and I got into conversation with him. And, during the conversation, he mentioned that he wuz in Low'stoft to buy a ship to take a crew and a party to Cocos Island in search of treasure. And I happened to make a remark that anybody might: 'Well, I wish I was goin' with you.' He said, 'Well, you can. There's one more wanted, and if you'd like to think it over and let me know in the morning—come and see me and we'll have a talk about it.' This was Captain Arthur. Now, the ship actually belonged to his wife. She'd bought it. It was laid up after fishing. And, anyway, the next day, I went along and I agreed that I would go. I wondered at the time whether I'd made a big mistake or not, having never been to sea in my life. But I'd made a decision and I was going to stick by it. We tied everything up and I signed the contract and went and had a look at *Veracity*. It was laying in Richards' yard and I was quite impressed by the alterations they'd done to it. They'd made a very comfortable yacht out of her and they'd encased her hull in *Muntz metal* because of the *tereda worm*.[3] And this all had to be looked at again in Balboa before we actually went on to the Pacific island—Cocos.

"The expedition organisers had actually written round to various ports, enquiring about vessels which might happen to be laid up or for sale, and there were quite a number apparently at Lowestoft—and they thought that their best bet was to come where there were most vessels available. And, going round the mudflats [in the inner harbour], they came across *Veracity*. Among others. But *Veracity* was the one that took the eye. This was up in the inner harbour. That's right, yes. And she was brought round to Richards' shipyard and they had a *ship's architect* come along and see what could be done. I presume it was Richards' ship's architect. And various suggestions were made, and these were agreed to and eventually carried out, with great success. There wuz a *direction-finder* installed and various other things to make her safe. The *fish-hold* wuz actually the *saloon*, where we had all the meals, but the crew's quarters weren't altered. The *bunks* where the fishermen used to sleep, they were still there, and I myself slept in one of 'em. There wuz two people slept in the *foc'sle* and a new *cabin* had to be put on deck in front o' the *wheelhouse*. This wuz a two-berth cabin, which was to be used by the *navigator* and the *commander*. In bad weather, of course, those two never left the *bridge*. They were there all the while and made a very good job of it, too.

---

3   *Teredo navalis*: a species of saltwater clam which burrows into timber.

"Another thing they did wuz raise the *foremast* and give her these two *cross-trees* for sailing with when we got into the north-east *trades* [trade-winds]. That was to save the engine and to increase power as well, when needed. We had every intention of doing quite a bit of sailing, to save fuel, and we found actually that when we did use the sail it was capable of six to eight knots in a reasonable breeze. Yes, we had a *square-rigged sail* and the *mizzen*. And we had an old seaman with us, a Commander Worsley, who went to the South Pole with Shackleton, and he knew all about the sailing side o' things. He was in charge of that. There wuz only four of us crew in Low'stoft and then we picked up the others in Dover, with the exception of another *cook*, a *cabin boy* and a *wireless operator*. The last three of

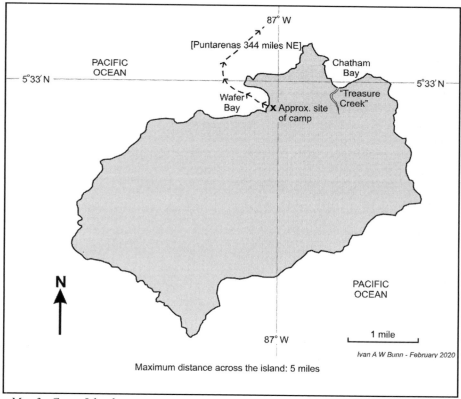

Map 3: Cocos Island

The Pacific island belonging to Costa Rica, where the mythical Lima Cathedral treasure was believed to be buried—and actually was! In this simplified map, lines of latitude and longitude are given to enable a precise location to be established (for anyone who is interested in such detail).

all were picked up in the West Indies.[4] From Low'stoft, there wuz Captain Arthur and his wife, Laughlin, Edwards and myself. And before we left, we tested the *compass* and did some *trials* out here. It wuz then we discovered that the cross-trees were not quite what we anticipated. They exaggerated the roll o' the ship, but it wasn't to a terribly dangerous extent, so we kept them up.

"I think we were looked upon as crazy and what-have-you, and there was one very interesting remark when we left. My wife was on the South Pier waving cheerio and bon voyage (we were engaged then), and near her were two fishermen. And one said to the other, 'Thass the last we shall see o' them silly buggers!' Not very encouraging. Anyway, we left Low'stoft on February 11, 1935. And we left in glorious sunshine, about four o' clock in the afternoon. The sea was like a lake and I thought, 'Well, this is great!' But we hadn't been at sea very long and, o' course, the normal thing happened at the time o' year—a very big mist came down, which slowed us up considerably. And after about four or five hours in that, we then ran into a force eight gale, which was with us all the way to Dover! And, putting into Dover, I was congratulating myself that I hadn't felt at all seasick. I thought, 'This is going to be great! I'm goin' to be O.K.'

"We spent just the one night in Dover and put to sea for Cocos the next morning with the rest of the crew. And it was a nice breeze when we left Dover, but we hadn't been at sea more than about an hour when things began to hot up a bit. And we eventually found ourselves off Berry Head [Brixham] in a force ten gale. We could do nothing but just put the mizzen up and *dodge* around until we could get into Poole Harbour. And we put into Poole Harbour and moored quite near the *King's Head*, and we spent two or three evenings in there. We just passed the time away until the gales eased. And when we thought they'd eased sufficiently (I think it was after about eight days), we set orf once again for Cocos.

"Well, we hadn't been at sea many hours and the same thing happened—but even worse. We lost the *dinghy*; we lost all our crockery; the wireless set was ruined; everything was awash. The sea was in the ship, yuh know. Everything was soaked. And I was really ill then. But there we are—I suppose one has to get one's sea legs! And, you know, I did think once or twice, 'Well, I don't know whether I've made the right decision.' However, I thought, 'Well, it's not always goin' to be bad weather.' And we put into Brixham and spent ten days there, because there was so much to do. We had repair work to do and a dinghy to get hold of and install. The radio we didn't bother about, but it took us two or three days just to dry out.

---

4   The *Veracity's* total party was as follows: Captain C.W.A. Arthur and wife, Commander F.A. Worsley (sailing master) and wife, Commander Finnis R.N. (master), Commander Edwards R.N.V.R. (chief engineer), Lieutenant-Commander Laughlin (second-in-command), Mr. Byrom (second engineer), Dr. Harris (geologist), Mr. Atkinson (wireless operator), Mr. Paynter (storekeeper), Alec Tucker (deckhand), Henry Leighton (cook), Johnny (Barbadian cabin boy) and Casey (Barbadian cook).

"But, once again, we managed to get to sea and things went better. We got into the Bay of Biscay and there was very little wind to speak of, thinking of what we had been through, but there was an enormous north-westerly *swell*—which I'm told is not very pleasant conditions in the Bay. But, after several hours, we eventually came into the sunshine, and the sea was calm and things were great. And I really began to enjoy being at sea. And I was cured of my sea-sickness by the *chief engineer*. He said, 'I can cure you!' I said, 'Well, I wish you could.' He said, 'Well, I will if you do what I tell yuh!' So I said, 'Well, I'll do anything.' You see. And he got some sea water and filled a tumbler half full. He said, 'Now, knock that back!' Which I did. And I didn't keep it long! But it did the trick. And, even in severe gales, afterwards I was never seasick again.

"Our next port of call was Casablanca. And we didn't stay there very long—just long enough to build up stores and take on water and fuel. And then we were off once again. I did all the buying of the stores on the trip and, actually, when we got to the island, I used to do the *catering*. I also did all the *cooking* on the voyage, which I'd agreed to do. I'd been trained in catering for eight years before I went out there. That's right, yes. My father was in the restaurant trade in Low'stoft. He originally started where the Odeon Cinema was (now W.H. Smith's) and then he had the restaurant further down London Road North.[5] And we got to sea from Casablanca and the storekeeper, Paynter, was taken ill with very sharp stomach pains. So we headed off to Santa Cruz and put in there and got a medical man aboard.[6] And he said the water was bad that we'd taken on in Casablanca, so we had to pump all that out and get fresh water, and set off once more.

"Then our troubles began again, because we hadn't only been two days out o' Santa Cruz and the *bearings* in the engine started hotting up. And we had to stop the engines. We found that the lubrication system wasn't working satisfactorily. But they stripped things down as best they could at sea and cleared them, and off we went again. And then we'd been going about, oh, another few hours (not more than twelve), and the engines just more or less blew up! They got red hot. It was terrible. It was about two o' clock in the morning, and they shut them all off and we said, 'Well, that's that.' So we set all the sails, the *square-riggeds* [on the two yards of the foremast] and the *mizzen*. And fair enough, because if we had the wind, we knew we'd be all right. But, as things happened, when we really wanted the wind, we didn't get it! Having had all that lot before, we were now becalmed! And this went on for two or three days. And then we had a little breeze and got under way. And then the same thing—becalmed again. We'd been at sea about twelve days and weren't even halfway to Barbados. Food supplies were definitely going to be a problem, and water. So I had a word with Captain Arthur and we

---

5 Near the junction with Suffolk Road.

6 This port was Santa Cruz de Tenerife, in the Canary Islands, which is usually referred to today simply as Tenerife. Horatio Nelson lost his right arm there in July 1797, in an action against the Spanish.

agreed that the water had got be rationed straight away. And I suggested, being a very keen angler, that we try and catch some of the *dolphin* which were around us.

"Now, these dolphin were not the breed of dolphin that they train to do tricks. They were a different type of fish altogether. And they were very edible, actually, though we didn't know this at the time. We didn't know whether they were edible or not. We tried all sorts of things to catch them and in the end, of all things, we tried a jar of *Bismarck Herrings* which we happened to have aboard (Mrs. Arthur was very fond of them). I bound some of this onto a hook, and this produced a result. We got a dolphin—which we used for bait to get more dolphin. And we had dolphin in our diet nearly every day, in some shape or form, until we got to Barbados. And another thing we did wuz hang lights on the *engine-room casin'* at night, and these *flyin' fish* would come out and hit the casin' and drop down on the deck—and we'd pick 'em up an' put 'em in a bucket and eat those for breakfast. And they were very similar to our herring. They were very, very nice. They were very rich, and so were the dolphin. Yes, and they both supplemented our food supply.

"As for the water—well, we all had a strict ration. We washed in sea water, and we took some special *sea-water soap*, which helped. But half an hour later, after you'd washed in the tropical heat and what have you, you were very sticky and uncomfortable. We set a sail, an old sail, in the hope of catching some water when it rained, but though we wanted the rain we didn't get it. Like the wind! However, we did get some eventually for about three or four days, and we got a good breeze and were doing six to eight knots with all the sails set—which was quite useful. We had the square-rigged big sail and then we had a square-rigged *tops'l* as well. Yes. And to the knowledgeable I suppose this is quite normal, but when we were under full sail the ship was much more steady. We didn't get that rolling, and it was very pleasant.

"We eventually got to Barbados, and I know we hadn't been there many minutes before there wuz a terrific downpour.[7] And we all got out into the rain and had a jolly good shower. This was when we were laying out in the bay before they towed us into harbour. We weren't kept out in the bay too long and they towed us into the harbour and we were made very welcome. And Cockburns, which are a very well-known wine and spirit people, they presented us with a case of rum, which was very acceptable. And, I can tell you, very much appreciated! We got the engineers aboard the following morning and they told us it would be quite a long job to fix the engine (at least a fortnight), so we said, 'Fair enough.' I think we were all glad to know that we had a fortnight to rest up. And I went ashore the following morning to various *shipping agents* and bought up supplies, and we took on fuel and what have you so we were ready to go when the engines were done. We picked up another *cook* and a *cabin boy*, and we had a new stove fitted

---

7 The *Veracity* left Santa Cruz de Tenerife on 28 March and arrived in Barbados on 23 April.

in the *galley* because the original one was a *diesel* one [i.e. heated by diesel fuel] which had the container of oil right over the stove. And, when you were in rough weather, it slopped over and the smell alone was enough to make you sick. And I honestly think that was what created my trouble in the first place.

"We actually arrived there on Easter Monday, in 1935. It was late April—the twenty-second or twenty-third, I think. Yes. And we were also there on the sixth o' May, I think I'm right in sayin', which was King George V's Silver Jubilee. And there were great celebrations there. Well, I mean, we all know how the West Indians celebrate! And we were invited to a party ashore in the evening, but we were not allowed to go unfortunately. The following morning we set sail, and the first night at sea the old engine started to heat up again.[8] And there was some feeling that the second engineer might be partly responsible, so he was withdrawn and I took his place in the engine-room. He must have neglected his lubricating, because I'm not an engineer (I never was an engineer, though I will say that the old chief did teach me quite a lot)—but we never did have any more trouble with the engines. We went into Curaçao one night and had the oil looked at [i.e. the lubricating oil], just in case it was dirty oil, but they said it was all right, so we put to sea again and went across the Caribbean to Colon and Christobal and through the old Panama Canal—which was a hectic experience.[9]

"You get in those *locks* in a little old drifter—well, we were like a rowing boat! The power of the water coming in there, it took us all our time to hold the ship in a position of safety, because we could have been dashed against the walls. You couldn't have your engines going, you see. They're vast locks and your engine wouldn't be powerful enough to do any good in that terrific current. We got *fenders* over one side and then we lined the deck with *quants* and poles.[10] And they had a mule the other side—you know, a *mechanical mule*, as they call it, for towing the boat through. And they were holding us off the side, you see, and this was how we got through the locks. There was a series of locks, I think I'm right in saying (it's a long while ago now): three at Gatun, one at Pedro Miguel and two at Miraflores. They lift you up quite some way in the time that you're in them. I could tell you the exact figures if I could look them up, but at the moment I just can't remember.

"Having got to the other side, we tied up in Balboa and got in touch with the powers-that-be in Costa Rica—in Puntarenas [main town of the province of that name]—because they had confiscated all the gear from a previous adventure to the island, belonging to the company when they had the chartered yacht, *Queen of Scots*. But they didn't get permission, or a licence, to search for treasure on the

8 The vessel actually left Barbados on the morning of 8 May.

9 Curaçao was an island off the coast of Venezuala (and a Dutch dependency); Colon and Christobal were towns on the Atlantic side of the Panama Canal.

10 The quants and poles were held ready by members of the crew to push the vessel away from the sides of the lock, should it be driven too close. The fenders had been put in place to reduce any impact.

island, so everyone was arrested and the gear was confiscated.[11] Captain Arthur was not involved in the actual arrest, but he wasn't allowed on the island on our expedition. The Costa Ricans wouldn't give him a visa. He wuz Mr. X in a court case [a financial scandal of some kind, in 1924] which concerned some eastern potentate [Rajah Sir Hari Singh, whose aide-de-camp he was] and they didn't think he was the right sort of person to go on Cocos Island. And the extraordinary thing was that they wouldn't let his wife land either! This all seemed a little bit petty, but there we are. They made the rules and one had to abide by them. Anyway, they said that they would authorise our party to land, with the exception of Captain Arthur and his wife. But there was a problem. The ship belonged to Mrs. Arthur. So then there was a big argument whether they were going to let us go any further or not. In the end, it was agreed that Captain Arthur would return to London and see if he could get some satisfaction through the Foreign Office and make arrangements, and then he would return.

"We went off to Puntarenas to pick up the gear. And the stuff was all there, ready, so we took a load on board and sailed for Cocos the next day. And we eventually arrived at the island—entirely uninhabited and very beautiful. A beautiful island! It's *volcanic*, and it's a series of ridges rising up above 600 feet, with a peak of over 2,000 feet. And it's very, very densely vegetated. All jungle, really, inland. And when you got among these trees, they were full of little red ants. And they dropped off, down yuh neck, and that wuz just like burnin' liquid on yuh, you know! More like as though you'd been thrashed with stinging nettles, or something like that. But we found a way of wearing our shirts outside our shorts, so that they dropped right through—otherwise, they'd take the skin right off yuh waist in no time at all. Oh, they were a problem.

"We landed the gear on the island, and I left the ship and helped with stowing the gear ashore. And the ship made two or three trips to the island to bring the stuff over, and they even brought some chickens over and landed those. And the camp, of course, was already built by the previous expedition. There was a large *bunkhouse*, probably eighty feet long I would think, with a *storehouse* at one end. Wood-built. Yes, all timber-built and it was very, very nice. You know, quite comfortable as things are, in the jungle like that. And the next morning, while *Veracity* was away collecting more goods and we had a sort of hour or two to spare, it was amazing the number of people who'd got hazel twigs (and one particular person had got an old gramophone spring), which they were using as *divining rods*![12] Wandering up and down the beach, looking for gold, you see! This was rather amusing, actually. And, I mean, some of them spent hours at it

---

11 Treasure Recovery Ltd. had sent an expedition to Cocos Island in August 1934. It had arrived in September and begun to search for valuables without the Costa Rican government's permission.

12 These were either hazel wands which had been taken out from England for divining purposes or twigs and small branches gathered on the island. Mr. Leighton could not remember which.

and they were quite surprised that they didn't turn up something. But it calmed down eventually and we went to bed. And next morning, about six o' clock, Dr. Harris (he was the *geologist* with us and he wuz a Scotchman), he was wandering up and down the bunkhouse with a stiff collar! Where he got this stiff collar from, goodness only knows, but he wuz walkin' up an' down with that just like it was a divining rod in his hand. I said, 'What's up, Jock?' He said, 'Shush, shush.' I said, 'what's up, Jock?' He said, 'Well, can't yuh see? I've lost my collar stud!' And it looked as if he was he was trying to divine for it with a stiff collar!

"There were reputedly several lots of treasure been on the island, but the particular one we were searching for was the Lima Cathedral treasure. There wuz a life-size statue of the Virgin Mary, in solid gold, and there wuz pieces-of-eight, gold ingots, diamonds, emeralds, rubies. Oh, it was valued in 1935 at £25 million! It was Benito who stole it. Benito. *Benito of the Bloody Sword.* The story goes that when there was plundering along the coast there, the people took all this treasure from the cathedral for safe-keeping and put it aboard a British ship, which wuz in the harbour at Lima at the time. But the temptation wuz too much and the crew murdered the guards and put to sea. But they, in turn, were attacked by Benito, and the treasure was believed to either have been transferred from one ship to the other or towed in the British ship into Cocos. Benito wuz a Spaniard [Portugese] and this all happened in the 1600s—about 1660 roughly, I believe.[13]

"It would appear that, after the treasure was landed, neither ship was heard of again, and neither was Benito. But they were pretty confident that he actually landed the treasure, and some people said that if you found the treasure you'd find the skeleton of Benito. But whether there's any truth in this, of course, we don't know. But there's very little doubt that there was treasure on the island. O yes, yes. And, having seen the island, there wuz numerous caves round the coastline and many a creek where you could have got a flat-bottomed boat up to bury stuff or hide it. And in the olden days, when these pirates were about, they quite often used to use Cocos to water the ships, because there was beautiful cold spring water come down from the mountains, you see. We watered our own ship with the water. We couldn't get water anywhere else like that. Lovely!

"There wasn't a lot of fruit on the island, but there were some limes and there was one orange tree. It was a very old one. And there were guava, and there were wild pigs, which we used to shoot. And they were a bit tough to what we get in this country, but they were quite edible. But the most edible thing around there, on the island, wuz the lobsters. *Langoustes*, they called them [Spiny Lobsters, or Rock Lobsters—members of the genus *Panulirus*]. And, at low tide, you'd walk among the coral and you'd just see one underneath and you'd put yuh hand in and

---

13 The whole story may seem to be fanciful (Lima, for instance, is situated inland—so if a vessel was lying in harbour, it would have been at Callao). However, the removal of the Lima Cathedral treasure actually did take place in 1820—a time of revolt against the ruling authorities in Peru's capital city.

drag him out. They'd got no nippers; they'd just got very rough, spiky heads. But if you got hold of 'em underneath and just dragged them out, and put 'em in a canvas bag, you could go out for an hour in the afternoon and have half-a-dozen beautiful lobsters. I suppose they weighed about two pound, and they were really good. Lovely. There wuz *rainbow runner* there [*Elagatis bipinnulata*], *sailfish* [*Istiophorus platypterus*]. Oh yes, there was plenty of food, if you spent the time looking for it.[14]

"The agreement was that the Costa Rican government should have 33⅓ per cent of whatever was found. They were protectin' their rights, more or less. But I don't think we worried too much about that, in any case. But they were very helpful, because the army sergeant who came onto the island with the Costa Ricans, we asked him if he would pick people who would be useful on the island. And these chaps were not all regulars [i.e. not military personnel]. They were picked from all walks of life. We had a hairdresser and an electrician and a carpenter, and they were a great help and we got on very well with them—though they kept to their own quarters. We were there from June to December—six months or so, yeah. We got there June 8th and left in the middle of December.[15]

"Now, one thing that wuz all very surprisin' wuz when we pulled into Chatham Bay, after we'd unloaded in Wafer Bay. We pulled into Chatham Bay and there wuz two chappies on the beach, frantically waving and shouting, and no sign of any ship or anything.[16] So we thought, 'Oh, these poor chaps have been shipwrecked or stranded in some way or other.' Anyway, we put a dinghy ashore and brought them aboard and gave them a meal and asked them if they'd like to move aboard, and we'd take them to Costa Rica on the next journey. But they said no, they were quite happy to remain ashore—though they hadn't got much food, and had only got very little of anything because the ship was wrecked and they'd just got ashore in what they were standing in, more or less. You see. Well, then one of them turns around and brings out a packet of cigarettes and offers us one! Well, if anyone gets cigarettes ashore—I mean, that seems a bit ridiculous, doesn't it? So, from that, we got suspicious—but we told them to come aboard the next day and have breakfast. And they said no, they didn't want to bother us like that, but they would like to be taken away when possible. Well, after about a couple of days, we were going to Costa Rica again, and we got these chappies aboard and said, 'Look, we'll drop you in Puntarenas and you can get yourselves up to San José, from where you can get to Panama.' Which is where they were supposed to

---

14 If parts of this paragraph remind the reader of *Lord of the Flies* (especially the references to wild pigs), it is worth remembering that Peter Brook shot his memorable black-and-white film version of the novel in Puerto Rico the early 1960s.

15 The expedition began to founder in mid-November because of a lack of funds. Mr. Leighton left Costa Rica for England on 9 December.

16 The expedition base was at Wafer Bay, but the *Veracity* usually anchored in Chatham Bay because it was more sheltered and had a greater depth of water.

have originated from.

"Well, now, they didn't want to do that. They'd rather wait till we went to Panama. Well, with this, we got more suspicious than ever. So we got them aboard the ship and kept them aboard, and the Costa Rican guards then had a good scout round and found a store. These chaps had got a radio and arms and what have you, and plenty of food, so we we knew that there was something not quite right. We contacted the authorities in Panama and they said, 'Well, keep them there and don't let them know you've informed us, and we'll deal with it. Just play it quiet.' And about three or four days afterwards, two American destroyers came into the bay, the USS *Taylor* and the USS *Claxton*, and said, 'Right. We've come to fetch these bods. We've picked up their boat, which wuz layin' offshore, and we'll take that back to Panama and them with it.' I think that they were people who knew Pete Bergman (who I will talk about a little later), and they knew he was coming back to the island and that he had taken treasure off and sold it in Chicago, when he wuz shipwrecked there previously. And they were not going to let him guide us to the treasure, whatever happened! I think this is what it was all about. But, anyway, the Americans took them off and, the same day they did that, Bergman wuz brought by *Veracity* to the island!

"Yes, Bergman had found treasure previously and sold it to a jeweller in Chicago for 11,000 dollars. And they [Treasure Recovery Ltd.—the company financing the expedition] found out through some various means where he was. I think he contacted the company to say he wuz in jail in Belgium and, if we liked to bail him out or get him out, he would come to the island and lead us to the treasure—with a contract that he should have ten per cent of whatever was found, you see. So this wuz agreed and they eventually got him out to Costa Rica (where he was attacked and his shoulder badly injured) and then to the island. And when he got to the island, he said, 'Well, I know roughly where it is, and I've got some buried on the beach, which I left there to take with me when I left before. But I couldn't get it all away.' So we said, 'Right.' I think *pieces-of-eight* wuz the main thing which he took with him, but he wuz supposed to have taken some *rubies* as well. It was late June when he came [27 June]; we hadn't been there long. No, no. And he wuz convinced that Wafer Bay wuz where the treasure wuz hidden, but he could never find it. I'll admit that he didn't try very hard! And after he'd been there about three or four weeks, he said that he wanted to get back to the mainland. His shoulder was playin' up and what have you. And I must admit that he wasn't fit, by any means—though that wuz partly from the life he'd led, I would think.

"After a few more weeks, we took him aboard ship. I'd now returned to the *Veracity*. I didn't have all the time on the island and I'd returned to the ship to do some buying of stores in Costa Rica. And Bergman had been aboard one night, and we should have sailed the following morning, and he said, 'Well, let me have one more look.' He said, 'I'd like to have a look ashore here, at Chatham Bay.' We used to anchor there; it was more sheltered. And he wuz put ashore about half-past eight in the morning and we could watch him when he wuz going over the high part of the hills. And we watched him as far as we could, and he eventually turned up about half-past three in the afternoon with a little canvas bag, and it was full up with stuff. I said, 'What have you got there, Pete?' He said, 'Oh, I've got some lovely shells.' I said, 'Oh, have yuh? Let's have a look.' Well, he just opened the top so I could peep in, and there were lots of shells in there. But I wouldn't like to say there were shells all the way through, for the simple reason that all the while I'd been on the island, right up to the time I came orf, I only found about four really nice shells. And for him to do that in three or four hours, to fill a canvas bag, wuz a bit of a tall story.

"However, we took him back to Costa Rica the following day and we left him in hospital to get treatment for his shoulder and general condition, and we said we would call in the next day and see how things were. Well, when we got there the next day, he'd flown to Panama! Where he got the money from, I don't know, but anyway he was in Panama.[17] And we did hear later that he was trying to get some people interested in financing a ship to go to Cocos Island when we left, to lift the treasure for himself. But this never came off and I did hear later that he had returned to his native country, Belgium. But I was never able to contact him any more.

"He was shipwrecked on the island originally with a mate called Lane, who also came to the island.[18] He didn't know as much. Ol' Pete had said, 'I'll give yuh some o' the stuff, but I'm not goin' to tell yuh where it comes from.' He used to go away each day and come back with a little, and he buried some of it on the beach where he was taken off. This was on his first trip, when he was shipwrecked. And he and Lane were picked up by a ship whose captain's name was Hunter, and we contacted this Hunter and he verified the story that he had picked them up from the island and also that some treasure had been sold in Chicago. We didn't do a terrific lot of digging ourselves. We did some digging in Chatham Bay and a bit of digging on the beach at Wafer Bay. We got down to six foot and then we were in trouble—the tide would come up and you'd be back to square one. We found a copper *lifeboat-tank* [a buoyancy aid] in one dig! See, we did a lot of *divining*. We took some electrical divining gear with us and this picked up the tank. But we didn't get much else from it!

"If you went on the island, you would realise that you were wasting your time digging, because there was so many natural places where they would obviously hide stuff for quickness. But we never thought the treasure wuz actually buried. We thought it was in a cave, or in some rocks. See, there were so many places. I mean, all the way round the coastline wuz no end of caves and we were always looking at what we thought was the easiest landing-places. There was one place,

17 Bergman left Costa Rica on 28 August.

18 This shipwreck had occurred in 1929.

called Treasure Creek, where a flat-bottomed boat could well get into—and we never did get to search that. And it was in that direction that Bergman went that morning.

"Now, these pirates were not mugs. I mean, they were crafty, and they were not going to bury that stuff where we would think it was most likely they would. I mean, they'd do just the opposite. And I feel that the people who searched on Cocos Island had all been going in the wrong area. There's been a lot of them— Captain Campbell among them. Malcolm Campbell, yes! Yeah, we came across his old camp, actually. And there wuz one expedition went about ten or twelve years ago, and they went from Felixstowe as a matter of fact.[19] I wrote to them and told 'em that I'd like to have a word with 'em, but they sailed before they got my letter. I didn't know they were going, but I read a little bit in the *Lowestoft Journal* and tried to contact them.

"There's a swamp on the island, between the camp and where you go inland from Wafer Bay, and then it's quite level for a little way—grassy soil—and this is where the lime trees and orange tree are. And the number of old diggings in there is fantastic! I mean, there must be thirty or forty of them. People have all dug in the same place. Oh yes, definitely. There wuz several rocks there with writing on. Quite a lot of 'em were just the names of ships and the dates they were there. Some had called for water and some, of course, had been treasure-hunting. We were unfortunate. We didn't find anything and funds ran out. The old *Veracity* did a fair mileage altogether. After we'd had the engines repaired in the West Indies, we didn't have any more real problems. The engine was marvellous. Yeah, we were getting twelve knots out of it. Oh, we had some wonderful runs to Panama and back.

"We met a hurricane once. When we came from Puntarenas one night, we got into the tail end of a hurricane—so we set sail and just went with it. We had the engine turning over, just to give us some sort of *steerage-way*, but we went with it for, oh, twenty-four hours. And that was really something! But when we came out of it—unfortunately, we had a replacement for the guards on board that night and, boy, were they ill! Yeah, they had a really rough journey, and the old commandant on the island was really worried. See, we didn't arrive when we should have done, and they knew this hurricane wuz in the vicinity. Yeah, they thought we'd probably been lost, but we turned up the next day, about twenty-four hours late.

"We were off the island one morning, about half-past ten, and there was two 10,000 ton American cruisers come into Chatham Bay. And we wondered what they were, obviously, and it wasn't long before a ship's *pinnace* came across and a naval captain came aboard and said that the President was on board and they would like to know, for security reasons, what we were doing there. So we told

19 The tape-recording session with Mr. Leighton, on which this chapter is based, took place on 15 February 1982.

them, and they were very interested, and then they went back to their ship. Then, in the afternoon, they returned and invited us aboard for a meal and a cinema show, on the *Houston*, with the President.[20] We had a very nice evening aboard and we were really royally treated. They even played the national anthem when we went into the cinema. Most of them, I think, only stood on one leg when they realised who we were! But, anyway, they really did treat us well. And I was talking to one or two of the sailors aboard and one of 'em said, 'Did you come over in that?' Meaning the *Veracity*, of course. And I said, 'Well, yes, of course we did.' He said, 'Well, you goddamn limeys are sure crazy!' I mean, people sail all over the place now, don't they? But, in those days, it just wasn't done, was it?[21]

"The following day, boats were going across from cruiser to cruiser—the *Houston* and the *Portland*—and the Americans came ashore with food and ice-cream, fruit, and everything you could think of. And they gave the whole of the shore-party a picnic. And Roosevelt himself went ashore, and they fixed up an awning for him and he sat there and chatted to us, and it was really marvellous. He was a marvellous man! To get where he'd got, with the handicap he had, was fantastic! He wuz there for about three days altogether and he'd come past in his boat, fishing.[22] Sitting in the back. They'd got a special seat for him and he was sitting in the back, fishing. *Sailfish*, mainly. Yes, and he caught one which was over 100 pounds—which pleased him a good deal.

"The last day the Americans were there, I took a party across the island from Chatham Bay to Wafer Bay, to the camp.[23] And the boys there had been out and got some of these lobsters I've been previously talking about. And they'd made a marvellous lobster mayonnaise and gave these chaps a jolly good feed. Two of them were on the staff of the *New York Times* and there wuz a big report all about it in the *New York Times* magazine. When we went back aboard the *Portland*, the Medical Officer said, 'I'm sure you must have got bitten by all those snakes, or one of them!' I said, 'What snakes?' And he said, 'There must be snakes over there in the undergrowth.' I said, 'Well, I didn't see any. Did you?' He said, 'Yes, I did, as a matter of fact. And you'd better come down to my office and let me just have a look.' And, o' course, we went down and (you know how American ships were *dry*!) he had a bottle of *snake-bite cure* in there—which was very nice! Whisky!

"We all had a shower aboard and, while we were there, they had a cablegram to say that Roosevelt's son had had a car accident on a railway crossing. He wasn't badly injured and Roosevelt said, 'Well, he's crazy enough, he is! He'll grow

---

20 The other cruiser was the *Portland*.

21 The cinema show on board the *Houston* took place on the evening of 9 October.

22 The two American cruisers anchored in Chatham Bay on 9, 10 and 11 October, before leaving for Pearl Harbour.

23 The party included the captain of the *Portland* and two journalists.

out of it!' Ha, ha, ha. He wasn't too concerned and, you know, the way he said it was marvellous. And that evening, they sailed. And, when they got out to sea, they flashed the signal lights: 'Good luck. Hope you find the treasure. Franklin D. Roosevelt.' It was done with Morse, which I thought wuz very nice.

"One o' the things that spoilt the expedition, in the end, was the Costa Ricans not letting the Arthurs come to the island. If they'd been able to, I think that might have made a difference. They had this Lane chappie [Peter Bergman's fellow-castaway] all sewed up and brought him out from England themselves, and I think we might have got somewhere with him. Yes, the Costa Ricans were a bit tough on us, though I spose that wuz only natural. Cash was running out, and they didn't want to be caught, and they wouldn't let the ship sail. And we said, 'Well, look, we've got to get back to the island, otherwise there'll be no food for them.' And they said, 'Right. We'll go in a Costa Rican ship.' So we bought the food and got it aboard their ship, and they were not going to let Finnis [the *Veracity's* commander] and myself go on the island. They said, 'No. No way!' So I said, 'Well, I've got to go.' And there was an argument, and they put to sea, and they had to come back because they'd sprung a leak. So they transferred the stuff onto another ship and took that over. But in no way would they let us off. This wuz late November time. There wuz no time-limit on my contract. Oh no. Just the clause that there was repatriation at the end of the expedition. I had the princely sum of £8 a month, which I didn't get half of![24] And I would have got a quarter of one per cent if the treasure was found. Which wouldn't have been bad in those days.

'O' course, we had some wonderful times in San José when we used to go there. Oh, we did! Yes, yes. Edwards and I were very friendly (he wuz chief engineer), and we would have like to have gone back to Cocos just once more to go and look at this Treasure Creek site, where we felt Bergman went that day. But there was no question of it; we never got back to the island. I mean, we were stuck in Costa Rica, and we were given the sack and told to leave the ship. The Costa Ricans, yuh see, they said it was their ship, and then the firm [Treasure Recovery Ltd.] came through and gave us the sack. So we said, 'Well, that's very clever! We've no intention of leaving *Veracity*, unless we're repatriated!' And I went up to San José with Finnis, and they'd arranged one ticket home—and I wuz the lucky one who got it. All the others came home as *D.B.S.* [Distressed British Seamen]. I came home on the *Cordilleras*—a 12,000 ton liner. I arrived in Plymouth without a penny! I hadn't got a penny in my pocket! Five o' clock in the morning! There wuz a schoolteacher on board who'd won a lottery and she kindly lent me a fiver to get to London. And I wuz met in London with a cheque to give her. You see, I'd got a sister who lived in London, and that was the way I got out of that.

---

24 Mr Leighton remarked about the irregularity of payment of the expedition members' wages as the weeks went by. He himself, as buyer of all food stores, was entitled to a 2½ per cent discount on purchases, which he used to create "a bit of beer money" for himself and his colleagues.

"I'd only got a small bag with me. Most of my stuff wuz left in Costa Rica. See, I had to fly from San José to Port Limon and they wouldn't allow much weight.[25] The weather was terrible. They wouldn't let us take off. We should have taken off at eight o' clock in the morning. It was eventually half-past ten before we took off! I picked the liner up at Port Limon, on the Atlantic coast. And we had to fly across the Cordilleras in terrible rainfall. And when we got to other side, I didn't know whether I wuz in an aeroplane or a submarine! You couldn't see anything but water. We got over Port Limon, and it wuz only a small plane with about eight passengers, and we went round and round and round. The ol' pilot said, 'Well, you know, things are a bit grim. We can't find the actual landing strip, but we're going to try and put you down anyway.' This was because of the fuel situation, you see. He said, 'Don't bother. We'll get down somehow.' So he gradually eased it down and we suddenly saw the sea under us, with about fifteen feet to spare! And he just glided in to the beach and put us down there. And I'd got about fifteen minutes to get from there to the pier to pick up the liner! And I just made it.

"When I got home, it was the middle of winter and I just had a suit! No coat or anything. It was December 28th, and I came back from London to Low'stoft the same day. Yes, and I had yours truly waiting for me! [His fiancée, later his wife.] Yes, and that wuz the end of my marvellous trip. My parents just thought I wuz a bit crazy. Oh yes, yes. I don't think they wholeheartedly agreed with the idea. Shall I put it that way? But you know how things were in 1935. The unemployment. This wuz it. And it's a thing which has stood me in good stead. It's something to talk about, something to think about. I met up with Edwards later. I met him just before the war, but I haven't been in touch with anyone since. O' course, a lot of 'em were ex-R.N. and probably one or two of 'em were lost in the war. Captain Arthur, I know, died—and Mrs. Arthur. So did Worsley. O' course, Laughlin [second-in-command] wuz a youngster and Tucker [deckhand], who came from Brixham, wuz a youngster. But most o' the others were older than me. I spose there could be one or two still knocking around.

"The *Veracity* was sold by the Costa Ricans to a coastal trading company, and she used to ply between the Orinoco and the Amazon with fruit, vegetables and light freight. And, unfortunately, in a fog, on the Orinoco, she came into collision with a merchant vessel and sunk. And that was rather an inglorious end! You know, I didn't hear till some time after that she'd been sunk—and I felt a bit sad. O' course, the beauty of it was that, once we got to Panama and took the cross-trees down, she behaved beautifully. No problems. She was a good sea ship. Yes, yes. Well, she had to be to get through what she did. She faced some really rough weather and I thought she served us jolly well. Yeah.

"The only reports of the expedition I saw in the English newspapers are what I wrote myself. I never heard of any of the others actually getting back, only from

---

25 This flight took place on 9 December.

Edwards when he came to see me in Low'stoft. And he told me that some of them came back about three months after I did. Byrom [second engineer] stayed out there and signed on with Macaya Airways; Harris [geologist] stayed out there; Tucker [deckhand] came home as a D.B.S. and so did Finnis [commander], I think—and Worsley [sailing master]. But it was an unfortunate thing, that break-up. If we could only have broken up so that we could all have returned together, it wold have been so much nicer. I often thought to myself how nice it would have been to sail back in *Veracity* and come into Low'stoft harbour after that voyage. That would have been something, wouldn't it? Yes, that would—but it wasn't to be. The whole thing wanted better organisation. You see, it's the same as everything else. It was dependent on an inflow of cash from shares on the *Stock Exchange*. It was floated with *five bob shares* [5s = 25p], you see, and of course if things had started to go well the money would have flocked in. But we just didn't get that good bit of news to boost it. When Bergman's story wuz put on to the market, by the press, the shares jumped and we sold several thousand. We got through a lot of money in the end. I've got the balance sheet somewhere. It's very interesting to look at.[26]

"On the first expedition, they even had a sea-plane. They used to come and land in Wafer Bay. The firm was called Treasure Recovery Ltd. and our telegraph address was *Pieces of Eight*.[27] Really! But, as I say having to rely on public funds like that, it was just a bit dodgy. Oh yes, I mean to feed, what, thirty to thirty-five people cost quite a bit. And then there was fuel for the ship and what have you. We used to buy quite a bit of oil fuel from Costa Rica, and I think probably what happened is that we got behind with the payments and the authorities there just jumped. I mean, they were very quick on jumping. They even slapped me in jail for doing nothing. I was just running to catch up with some friends after a cinema show in San José—but *running after dark* was against the law! Yes. And when we went ashore at Puntarenas, praps we'd take a load of washing with us. Well, they'd always check it over. It was the same when we loaded stores; they'd always go over the cases of food and other stuff. Oh, they were very watchful. But when you think about what we were doing, praps you couldn't really blame them."

As a postscript to this high-seas adventure, it is worth noting that a good deal of information relating to the Cocos Island treasure is available on the Internet. On 5 August 2012, *The Daily Telegraph* ran a story (so did *The Daily Mail*) about an

---

26 Treasure Recovery Ltd's two expeditions cost a combined total of £20,892 (£11,792 and £9,100 respectively). Other incidental expenditure brought the figure closer to £25,000. Overall, the whole venture cost nearly £64,000, about £30,000 of which was spent on purchasing the rights of an earlier company, Spanish Main Exploration Ltd.

27 *Pieces of eight* were Spanish silver coins first minted in 1497 and worth eight *reals*. They were also known as *Spanish dollars* and became synonymous with acts of piracy in South, and Central, American waters. Robert Louis Stevenson, in *Treasure Island*, has Long John Silver's parrot (Captain Flint) constantly squawk the name of these coins as its identifying catch-phrase.

expedition being planned to visit Cocos (now a UNESCO World Heritage Site)—though not solely for treasure-hunting. Scientific investigation was to have been a major part of the venture, with the area's natural history featuring prominently. The *Veracity's* voyage was not referred to in the article, but two earlier searchers for the Lima hoard were named: Franklin D. Roosevelt (with two friends) in 1910 and Malcolm Campbell during the 1920s. Henry Leighton, of course, met Roosevelt on the latter's fishing vacation described above, while Campbell was mentioned by him as a previous visitor to the island. The *Telegraph* piece also cited Errol Flynn, the Hollywood film actor, as looking for the treasure during the 1940s (as did that in *The Daily Mail*).

The Lima Cathedral treasure was reputedly removed by the Spanish ruling authorities in 1820, at a time of growing revolution in Peru, and put aboard a British ship (under guard) for safe transportation to Mexico. William Thompson, captain of the *Mary Dear*, had the escort murdered and then landed at Cocos to bury the treasure. He and his crew were later captured by the Spanish and all of them (with the exception of Thompson himself and the mate) were hanged for piracy. The two men were spared, on the promise of leading the Spanish to where they had hidden the treasure. On arriving at the island, they managed to escape into the jungle and evade capture. A year later, they were rescued by a ship putting in to take on fresh water. In her *The New Book of Days* (1941), a 365-piece anthology of mixed material for young readers, Eleanor Farjeon has as the entry for 18 February the story of *Veracity's* voyage to Cocos Island—though she names the commander of the expedition as Captain Arthur Macfarlane, not plain Captain Arthur as Henry Leighton refers to him.

In March 2015, there were reports from Costa Rica of six park-rangers (who were walking the seashore of Cocos Island to make assessments of the damage done to nesting seabirds by a recent storm) having found five buried wooden chests partly unearthed by tidal scour. The contents included 89,000 gold and silver coins, ingots of precious metal, thirty-six bejewelled crosses, three gold chalices and two life-size gold statues of the Virgin and Child. The whole hoard was given a preliminary estimated value of 200 million dollars. Was this the famed Lima Cathedral treasure come to light, at last?

Anyone wishing to take the story of Cocos Island and its buried wealth further can carry out his or her own treasure-hunting at the keyboard of a computer or the touch-screen of an iPad.

Glossary

Aft: the rear section of a vessel.

After: rearward (the word is formed directly from the one immediately above).

Allotment: a weekly payment made to drifter crew members (usually those with family dependents), which was deductable from their pay-off settlement at the end of a voyage.

Astern: towards the stern (rear) of a vessel, or actually behind it.

Back in/off: 1. To detach fish from the hooks on **longlines** (q.v.). 2. To place longlines back into their containers after any fish had been removed from the hooks, prior to baiting-up again.

Bag: 1.The **cod-end** (q.v.) of a trawl-net. 2. An individual catch of **trawlfish** (q.v.) taken in one tow.

Bait-box: a large wooden box in which the bait for longlines was kept.

Bait-net: a **drift-net** (q.v.) carried by longlining vessels, which was used to catch pelagic species for baiting the hooks.

Barmskin: a fisherman's oilskin apron.

Bass: a coarse vegetable fibre, used for making ropes.

Batings: the upper part of a **trawl-net** (q.v.), where tapering down to the **cod-end** (q.v.) occurred.

Beach (The): the community sometimes referred to as the *Beach Village*, which had developed below the cliff at Lowestoft as the town expanded during the nineteenth century. Its inhabitants customarily referred to it as *The Grit*.

Beach-net: a **draw-net** (q.v.).

Beam: the length of wood referred to immediately below.

Beam-trawl: trawling gear which used a long wooden spar to keep the mouth of the net open.

Beat: to sail against the wind.

Beet (or beat): to mend drift-nets.

Bellies: pieces of old net, which were fastened to the under-side of **cod-ends** (q.v.) to diminish the chafing effect of the seabed.

Belly: the under-part of a trawl, in contact with the seabed.

Bend: a method of joining two ropes, using knots instead of **splicing** (q.v.).

Berth: 1. A position, or job on board a fishing vessel. 2. A sleeping-place on board ship. 3. The position of a vessel at sea relative to other boats engaged in fishing. 4. A vessel's place at the quayside when moored.

Berthing master: a harbour official who showed vessels where to moor and generally tried to keep order in port—especially at busy times of year.

Big-boating: a term used by **longshoremen** (q.v.) for going on drifting or trawling voyages.

Big boats: a term used by **longshoremen** for steam drifters, steam trawlers and sailing smacks.

Bight: a loop (or curve) in a rope or chain.

Bismarck herring(s): fish which were marinated in white-wine vinegar and spices and named after the famous German chancellor.

Blinder: A piece of small-meshed net, which was fixed inside a cod-end in order to catch fish less than the permitted minimum size.

Bloater: a herring lightly salted and smoked overnight with the gut left in. As such, it was somewhat perishable and needed to be consumed within about a day of processing.

Block: 1. A trawler's **towing-block** (q.v.). 2. A wooden case containing a **sheave** (q.v.), which was used to facilitate the free passage of ropes and increase their pulling-power in lifting and lowering sails.

Block up: to secure a steam, or diesel, trawler's warps (q.v.), in the towing-block (q.v.) prior to fishing.

Blue skate: Skate (*Raja batis*).

Bobbins: wheel-like devices on a trawl's **ground-rope** (q.v.), which facilitated the gear's passage across the seabed.

Bogeyman: a fisheries patrol vessel.

Bollards: steel housings with integral **sheaves** (q.v.) strategically set into a trawler's deck between the winch and the **galluses** (q.v.)—through which the **warps** (q.v.) ran freely.

Borsprit (bowsprit): a spar projecting from a vessel's bow, which supported stays and sails. The second element of the word derives from the Old English *sprēot,* meaning "a pole".

Bosom: the curved mouth of a trawl-net, along the ground-rope.

Bosun: the rank below mate on a fishing vessel.

Bottles: spherical glass floats on a trawl-net's (or seine's) **head-line** (q.v.).

Bower anchor: a secondary anchor (usually one of a pair), which was carried on the bow of a vessel.

Bowl: 1. The curved part of a fishing-hook. 2. A wooden cask used as a float on drift-nets.

Box: to pack fish (notably herrings and soles) in wooden or metal cases on board ship—to create ease of handling in the case of the former species and to achieve maximum sale-value in the case of the latter.

Braid: to make trawl nets.

Bridles: lengths of rope or wire that joined the **doors** to the net on **otter trawls** (q.v.) and improved the fishing capacity of the gear.

Bring up: to anchor offshore.

Britch(es): the hard roe (eggs) of the female cod—so called because the shape resembled a pair of floppy, knee-length trousers.

Buffs: large canvas or plastic floats used to buoy up **drift-nets** (q.v.) and also to perform the same task on **otter-trawl** (q.v.) headlines.

Bunts: the parts of a trawl-net's **wings** (q.v.) nearest the **quarters** (q.v.).

Buster: a strong gale.

Cabin: the crew's quarters on board a fishing vessel, usually located aft-side of the engine-room.

Cable: 1. a distance of 100 fathoms (600 feet). 2. The mooring-rope or chain attached to an anchor.

Cans: metal containers of a gallon capacity, or more, used as floats on **longshore** (q.v.) drift-nets.

Capstan: a vertical, steam-powered winch used to haul in the **warp** (q.v.) on steam drifters and smacks. Many of those in use in England and Scotland were made by Elliott & Garrood Ltd. of Beccles.

Casing: the steel housing above a fishing vessel's engine-room.

Cast-off: a crew member on a steam drifter who untied the **seizings** (q.v.) from the warp and regulated the speed of the capstan when the nets were being hauled. He was usually a young man working his way up from cook.

Chafing-pieces: see **Bellies** above.

Chance: occasional.

Chance-time: occasionally.

Chief: the chief engineer on board a vessel.

Chittle(d): the term used to describe **drift-nets** (q.v.) that had rolled up on themselves.

Clinker: an overlapping plank in the hull of a boat.

Clinker-built: the term used to describe the construction of a boat, with its outer planks on the hull overlapping from the top downwards and secured by *clinched* (or *clenched*) nails, the outwards ends of which were flattened over a conical **rove** (q.v.).

Close: evening-time; dusk.

Coal (to): to take coal on board as fuel for the engine.

Cock mackerel: a half-sized mackerel.

Cod-end: the bag at the end of a trawl or seine-net.

Coils: the warps of a **Danish seine-net** (q.v.), after they had been looped ready for use by a mechanical process.

Combination fishing-line: a length of steel cable and fibre rope twisted together for use as the **ground-rope** (q.v.) on a trawl.

Come fast: the term used of fishing-gear becoming fouled on an underwater obstruction.

Compound (engine): a two-cylinder steam engine, having the high-pressure cylinder exhausting into the low-pressure one.

Cooking: a joint of meat.

Cooper's rusks: hard-tack biscuits, made at the Cooper Bros. bread and steam-biscuit bakery in Compass Street, Lowestoft.

Cop: an old English dialect word for a heap or pile, dating from the mid-seventeenth century.

Cran: a measure of 37½ Imperial gallons; 28 stones of herring by weight.

Cran-hook: a steel bar, fixed in the middle to a running-line and with hooks at either end which engaged with the handles of the quarter-cran baskets used in landing herring. This device helped to run the catches ashore, with the steam capstan's pulley-wheel providing motive power and the foremast's boom serving as a derrick.

Creepers: grapnels.

Crow's foot: two strands of a drift-net's mesh broken.

Crushed ice: blocks of manufactured ice, which had been put through a machine to break them up and reduce their mass for easy use on board fishing-vessels.

Cutch: a substance used to preserve **drift-nets** (q.v.) against the rotting effect of bacteria and salt water. It was the gum taken from a tropical tree, *Acacia catechu*, and the name is a corruption of the second element.

Dan: a vertical marker-buoy for fishing nets or **longlines** (q.v.), which has either a light or a flag on its upright in order to create maximum visibility. It was sometimes spelled as *dhan* and was an English dialect word of unknown origin, dating from the late seventeenth century.

Dan leno: a device that keeps the **head-line** (q.v.) and **ground-rope** (q.v.) apart on either side of a **trawl** (q.v.). The original type was a wooden post, developed in France—the two of which were known as *guindineaux*. During adoption of the development in England during the 1920s, the French term became corrupted (because of a similarity of sound) to the name of a popular, late Victorian music hall entertainer.

Dan-tow: the length of rope which joined the **dan** (q.v.) buoy to its anchor.

Dangles: metal rings linked to short lengths of chain threaded along a trawl's **ground-rope** (q.v.) to weight it down and aid the sanding-up process.

Danish seine-net: light trawling gear which operated by barely touching the seabed beneath.

Dead-reckoning: estimating a vessel's position from the distance travelled and recorded on the **log** (q.v.) and the direction of the course set on the compass, with allowances made (if applicable) for wind-strength and tidal drift. No astronomical calculations were applied.

Deckie: deckhand—a term usually applied to a fisherman who worked on a trawler.

Demersal: species of fish which lived on, or near, the seabed.

Derrick: a crane of some description. In a fishing context, it often refers to the boom of a steam drifter's foremast, which was an essential part of the landing process.

Didall: a tapering, rounded, triangular net on a long pole, rather like a giant butterfly net. It was often used for catching herrings that were falling from the meshes of a net during hauling.

Dirty: the term used of any vessel which shipped a lot of water in bad weather.

Dodge: to keep a boat head to wind during a gale.

Dodger: a canvas shelter under which a sailing smack's helmsman stood.

Dogs: dogfish. The term was usually reserved by fishermen for the Spur Dogfish (*Squalus acanthias*).

Dollop: 1. a moderate or large quantity of herrings taken in any one haul. 2.

The term used of a large wave striking a vessel (usually broadside on) in rough weather.

Don: a top skipper—one who earnt a lot of money for himself and his crew. The term must, presumably, have derived from the word used for a Spanish *grandee*.

Door: a large, heavy, rectangular, wooden paravane on either side of an **otter trawl's** (q.v.) mouth which served to keep the net open.

Double swim: the term used for when herrings were enmeshed on either side of the nets—an occasional occurrence which made hauling difficult.

Down: northwards (the direction of the ebb tide in the North Sea).

Draw-net: a beach-net—a type of **seine** (q.v.) which was shot from a rowing boat that followed a semi-circular course out from the shore and back again, and which was then hauled in from the land.

Dress: to treat fishing nets with a preservative agent.

Driers: paint thinners, which were often used to preserve longshore drift-nets.

Drifter: a fishing vessel which drifted along on the tide, attached to its nets, with herring or mackerel as the usual species sought.

Drifter-trawler: a dual-purpose fishing vessel (powered either by steam or diesel engine), which was able to keeep working all year round

Drift-net: a long, rectangular net which (with others attached to it) floated on the tide, in the upper reaches of the sea, to catch pelagic species such as herrings, mackerel and sprats.

Drive: to drift on the tide.

Driver: the chief engineer on a steam drifter.

Drum: one of two moving cylinders on either side of a trawler's winch, which were the means of winding in the **warps** (q.v.) and whose speed of rotation could be independently controlled if needed.

Duck-lamp: a flat-bottomed oil-lamp with projecting wick.

Duffel: thick woollen cloth, with a heavy nap, which took its name from the town in Belgium where it was first made.

Dump: to discard catches of herring that had either not sold or reached rock-bottom prices on the market. This was done quite a lot in the 1920s and 30s, when surpluses of fish and unpredictable demand led to a fluctuating and unpredictable trade.

Dust: a smacksman's term for **stocker bait** or **stockie** (q.v.), usually referring to the small sums of money made from the sale of under-sized fish (or species that had no great commercial value)—which were then shared out among crew members.

Dutchman's bowls: large wooden casks, used as floats to assist with salvage work.

East-and-west boats: cargo vessels plying between England and Holland, with processed fish being conveyed on the outward run and with butter carried on the return journey.

Elliott pot: a small marine, two-cylinder, **compound engine** (q.v.), of about 15 h.p., made by Elliott & Garrood Ltd. of Beccles.

Elliott monkey-triple: a triple-expansion engine, with the high-pressure cylinder set above the intermediate-pressure cylinder and working the same crank—the low-pressure cylinder being set at the side and working a second crank. These most reliable engines which were designed to fit into a restricted engine-room owed their nickname to their somewhat strange appearance, which the fishermen likened to a monkey sitting on a barrel organ. They were very economical in the use of the coal required to heat the boiler.

Eye: a loop in the end of a rope.

False bellies: see **Bellies**.

Fantails: squid. The term usually refers to the Northern Squid (*Loligo forbesi*).

Fastener: an obstruction on the seabed that causes trawling gear to come fast when towing is under way.

Fathom: a measure of six feet depth of water.

Fiddle-fish: Angel Ray or Monkfish (*Squatina squatina*)—a small member of the shark family whose shape roughly resembles that of a violin.

Fiddley: a grating above the engine-room on a drifter or drifter-trawler. It was a favourite place for crew members to sit in cold weather, because of the heat rising from below.

Figure-eight knot: a knot in a single length of rope, formed by two interlocking loops. Its main use was to prevent a rope unreeving through a block.

Fireman: 1. In Lowestoft, the second engineer on a steam trawler or a longliner. 2. In Great Yarmouth, the second engineer on a steam drifter.   3. The stoker on a steam railway locomotive.

Fish-room: the main fish-hold on board a vessel.

Fish-trawl: a beam trawl used by **longshore** fishermen to catch flatfish of various kinds.

Fisherman's knot: a means of joining two cords or narrow-diameter ropes. An overhand knot was tied in the end of one of the cords or ropes around the other one, and a similar knot was then tied in the second cord around the first. When both free ends were pulled, the two knots slid towards each other, tightened and made a neat join which would not loosen under strain.

Fishing (the): another term for the so-called **Home fishing** (q.v.)—the East Anglian autumn herring season in Lowestoft and Great Yarmouth.

Five-fingers: starfish (any species).

Flake(d) ice: ice which had been manufactured in sheets, by freezing the water on the surfaces of vertical or horizontal drums and then cracking it for use. It was of finer quality than the earlier **crushed ice** and easier to handle on board ship.

Flats: inshore areas of the seabed where the bottom levelled out after the sloping down from the heach itself.

Fleet: the term used either of a full complement of **drift-nets** (q.v.) or of a set of **longlines** (q.v.).

Fleeter: a vessel belonging to a company, which worked the same fishing-ground in conjunction with other craft owned by the firm, making the trawling a combined operation. The term was applied particularly to steam trawlers from

Hull and Grimsby during the early years of the twentieth century.

Fleeting: the practice of collective trawling, on the same ground, by vessels owned by a particular company (or companies). This became customary with sailing craft from Hull and Grimsby working the Dogger Bank during the second half of the nineteenth century, and it continued into the steam era of the early 1900s.

Floats: glass spheres used to keep the **head-line** (q.v.) of a trawl buoyed up.

Flopper: a net flap that prevented fish from getting out of the **cod-end** (q.v.).

Flow: the slack deliberately created in a **trawl-net** (q.v.) or **seine** (q.v.) in order for the gear to move correctly through the water.

Fluke(s): the spaded ends of an anchor's arms, which dug into the seabed.

Fly-shoot: to shoot a **seine-net** (q.v.) without anchoring the gear to start with, but merely buoying the end of the warp. This was sometimes done for the sake of quickness, when a new piece of ground was being assessed by the skipper.

Foc'sle: living quarters in a vessel's bow section.

Foot-rope: 1. The double rope at the bottom of a **drift-net** (q.v.). 2. The weighted rope at the bottom of a **draw-net** (q.v.).

Fore-peak: a small storage-space in the bows of a fishing vessel.

Fore-room: a fish-hold for'ad of the main one.

Foresail: a triangular sail set on the foremast's stay.

Fouling: the term used of fishing gear (of any kind) becoming entangled by one means or another.

Frame: the rectangular structure of rope(s) to which the meshes of a **drift-net** (q.v.) were fixed, or the combination of head-line and ground-rope on a seine or trawl.

Freeboard: the distance between the surface of the sea and the top of the **gunwale** (q.v.).

Fresh o' wind: a sudden stiff breeze.

Fry: a small quantity of fish for eating by crewmen or members of their families.

Full: the term used of mature herrings containing milt or roe.

Gaff: 1. The spar on the head of a fore-and-aft sail. 2. A stick or pole with a metal hook at the end, used to bring fish (usually large ones) inboard from longlines.

Galley: the area in which the food was cooked on board a vessel.

Gallus: the curved metal frame on which the door of an **otter-trawl** (q.v.) hung when the gear was not in use. Most trawlers and drifter-trawlers had a pair on each side, though it was mainly the starboard side ones which were used. The word is a corruption of *gallows*.

Gat: a gap between coastal sandbanks, which offered vessels a navigable channel.

Gimbal: a universal joint used at sea, which allowed a suspended object to remain horizontal, in spite of the pitch and roll of the vessel.

Go about: to turn a vessel at sea, to face or move in the opposite direction.

Gobstick: a wooden disgorger, used to remove longline hooks from fishes' mouths.

Grandfather: a fish of large size and age. The term was usually applied to soles.

Gripe: a lashing used to secure a vessel's **little boat** (q.v.) to the after-deck.

Gripe (up): to secure a vessel's lifeboat to its station on deck (the word is a variant of *grip*—in reference to the *lashings* used).

Grog: cheap gin sold to fishing craft by (mainly) Dutch vessels, which followed the North Sea trawling fleets (especially during the last quarter of the nineteenth century) strictly for that purpose.

Gross hundred: the sum of £100 earned by a fishing vessel before expenses had been paid.

Ground-rope: the thick bottom rope on the mouth of a **trawl** (q.v.).

Gulley: a channel in the seabed, which often seemed to attract fish because of the feed located there.

Gunboat: a fisheries patrol vessel.

Gunwale: the upper edge of the side of a boat or ship.

Haberdines: Good-quality cod and ling (and also haddock and hake), which had been salted and dried. The term derives from the Middle Dutch *abberdaen*, itself a variant of *laberdaen*, which represents either the Basque district of Labourd or the old name for the French town of Bayonne (Lapurdum). The fish were a staple item in European diet of the Early Modern period.

Half-quarter: an eighth part of a full share in the profits of a fishing **voyage** (q.v.) –applied mainly to herring-catching and longlining). *Eighths* were never referred to; the term *half-quarters* was always used.

Halyard: a rope used for raising and lowering a sail.

Handkerchief: a **storm-jib** (q.v.)—the smallest of all the sails used on board a smack.

Handlines: hand-held fishing-lines with varying kinds of hook attachments able to be used, which were worked over the side of a drifter by crew members as the vessel lay to its nets. Common demersal species were caught in this way and sold for pocket-money when the boat reached port.

Hank: a length of rope or line, often doubled over and secured.

Haven: a sheltered area on a coastline, which offers safe anchorage close to land. In East Anglia, it often refers to the stretch of water between the beach and any outlying sandbanks.

Hawkers: fish-sellers who travelled from inland village to village, peddling a variety of species that they had acquired as cheaply as possible at the point of landing.

Hawseman: the crew member of a **steam-drifter** (q.v.) who was next in rank down from the mate. He was paid a full share and the name suggests that he was originally in charge of the vessel's ropes (and perhaps the nets as well).

Headings: the cords which ran down the sides of a **drift-net** (q.v.).

Head-line: the top rope on the mouth of a **trawl** (q.v.).

Heft: any obstacle which prevented the free passage of fishing gear or caused it to come fast.

Herring trawl: specialised gear which caught herrings near the seabed rather than in the upper levels of the water.

Hob mittens: fishermen's mittens made from white, oiled wool.

Hoddy: the thicker, guarding meshes at the top and bottom of a drift-net. The word is also found rendered as *oddie* or *oddy*.

Home fishing: the North Sea autumn herring season—the busiest time of year in both Lowestoft and Great Yarmouth.

Hoodway: the entrance to the **cabin** (q.v.) on a fishing vessel.

Hook: 1. An anchor. 2. A gaff used for bringing large fish inboard from longlines.

Horse mackerel: the Scad (*Trachurus trachurus*).

Hot-bulb engine: an early type of internal combustion engine fuelled by paraffin.

Hunch: hunk (a variant pronunciation usually applied to bread).

Husky: Larger Spotted Dogfish (*Scyliorhinus stellaris*). The term is obviously a variant of the word *Huss*, which was sometimes used for the species.

Ice-locker: a storage-space below decks on a fishing vessel, in which ice was kept for the preservation of catches.

Inboard: on board a vessel; within its **gunwale** (q.v.). The term was used particularly of fishing gear being hauled over the side.

Indenture money: the premium paid to an employer by a parent or sponsor to have a boy (or girl) apprenticed to a traditional craft or trade.

Inshore: close to land. The term was used of any kind of fishing which took place within easy reach of the shoreline.

Inside: Close to land. The term has a particular association with illegal fishing that was carried out within a country's three-mile exclusion zone.

Jenny/Jinny henniven: a term generally applied to small rays of various kinds, but best reserved for the Starry Ray (*Raja radiata*).

Jenny/Jinny rooker: see **Jenny henniven** immediately above.

Jib: a triangular sail (of varying size according to wind-strength), set on a **stay** (q.v.) running from the top of the foremast to the outer end of the **bowsprit** (q.v.). It was an important and steadying influence in the handling qualities of a **smack** (q.v.).

Jinny hanniver: a variant of **Jenny henniven** above.

Kedge anchor: a small, portable anchor, which was sometimes used (in conjunction with the capstan) in **warping** (q.v.) a vessel out of a dock.

Kid: the space on a steam drifter's deck between the gunwale and the edge of the hold.

Kipper: a herring that is gutted, split along the backbone, soaked in brine for half an hour or so, then smoked overnight. This particular type of cure was first practised in Scotland, using salmon, and was applied to herrings by John Woodger of Newcastle, in 1843, when he produced the first kippers at Seahouses, on the Northumbrian coast.

Kit: 1. Ten stones weight of trawlfish. 2. The cylindrical wooden or metal container which held the quantity of fish previously defined.

Kite(s): 1. Small wooden paravanes which were attached to the head-line of a **herring trawl** (q.v.) and helped to keep the mouth of the net open. 2. Paravanes of wood or metal that were fixed to a minesweeping wire and helped to control the depth it worked at.

Klondyker: a fish merchant who was involved in the export trade to Germany of fresh herrings packed in salt and ice. The term was also applied to market hands involved in the enterprise.

Kneel: the term used to describe a sailing vessel heeling over in a breeze and adopting a particular angle in the water.

Labour (went on the): a term used of going on the dole when out of work—originating from having to report to local Labour Exchange offices, to sign on for unemployment pay.

Laid in: moored up in a harbour.

Laid up: the expression used for a vessel which had been withdrawn from fishing operations by its owners and taken to a long-term mooring. The southern shore of Lowestoft's inner harbour was a favourite location.

Larnch: 1. Launch (used as a verb). 2. The word of command given to the cast-off, on board a steam drifter, to stop the **capstan** (q.v.) when hauling nets was in progress. It was also the order given to stop a **line-hauler** (q.v.) on vessels engaged in longlining.

Lashing: a rope used to keep something (or someone) stable and in place on board ship—especially in bad weather.

Latchet: Tub Gurnard (*Trigla lucerna*).

Lay: the term used of a vessel when it was anchored up and stationary.

Lay up: to keep a vessel head on to the wind and ride out a storm.

Lazy fish: the term used for bottom-dwelling marine species which moved slowly over the seabed.

Lead(line): a device used to measure the depth of water and assess the quality or type of seabed. It consisted of a long, cylindrical lead weight fastened to a length of rope or cord. The other end of the weight was hollowed out. Fat or tallow (or even soap, on some occasions) was pressed into the hollow, which would cause particles from the seabed to adhere when the weight reached the bottom. This would enable fishermen to tell what kind of ground they were on. The depth calculation was made possible by the line itself having ties attached to it at one-fathom (six feet) intervals.

Lee: The sheltered side, opposite to that against which the wind blows.

Lee shore: a shore onto which the wind was blowing—a dangerous place to be, in a gale of any proportions.

Lee tide: a tide running in the same direction as the wind.

Legs: wire strops (two on each side) which connected the **doors** (q.v.) with the net on an **otter trawl** (q.v.).

Lemon: Lemon Sole (*Microstomus kitt*).

Light duff: dumplings made with flour and water only.

Lighthouse hauler: a steam-driven line-hauler for longlines, of columnar form, which was supposed to resemble a lighthouse in shape.

Limit-line: the twelve-mile, territorial waters, exclusion zone agreed at the International Fisheries Convention of May 1882. By this agreement, all those

European nations with a coastline bordering on the North Sea had exclusive right of fishery for their own native industry within a twelve-mile distance from shore. The term also applied to any variations of this agreement and any local bye-laws in Great Britain and Ireland which prohibited fishing of one kind or another in certain stipulated areas, as well as to the three-mile limit also imposed by some countries.

Line-hauler: a small winch, fixed to the side of a vessel, which facilitated the hauling of longlines. The earlier models were driven by steam power to start with, but were later succeeded by hydraulic and electrical ones.

Lint: the meshes of a drift-net, exclusive of the rope frame. The word is a throwback to the time when fishing nets were often made from linen fibre.

Little boat: a fishing vessel's lifeboat or dinghy.

Liver-jar: a wooden cask, of thirty-six gallons capacity, in which cod livers were kept (after gutting), for processing into oil when the boat returned to port.

Living (a): the term used by fishermen to describe profitable **trips** (q.v.).

Locked harbour: a harbour having lock-gates to control tidal movement and flow, such as Milford Haven and Fleetwood.

Locker: the term always used at sea for a built-in cupboard of some kind.

Lock-pit: a lock basin.

Log: 1. An instrument for measuring the speed of a vessel. 2. A daily, written record of activity on board a ship. 3. A fishing skipper's personal notebook, containing details of fishing grounds, catches made and details of weather and tide.

Logie swell: a heavy ground-swell at sea.

Longboat: a ship's lifeboat.

Long fish: demersal species such as cod, haddock and whiting, as opposed to flatfish and rays.

Long hundred: a measure of 132 herrings and 120 mackerel.

Longline: a varying length of twine or cord, of different thickness and strength according to particular requirements, on to which hooks were affixed at periodic intervals (again, this varied). These hooks were baited with whatever was deemed to be suitable (whelk, squid, etc.) and the line paid overboard, to rest upon the seabed and catch demersal species.

Longline(r)man's knot: an alternative term for **fisherman's knot** (q.v.).

Longshore: a contraction of "along the shore", which referred to fishing activity relatively close to the beach rather than further out to sea in deeper water.

Longshoreman: a man who practised longshore fishing.

Longshoring: fishing close in to land, in small rowing-vessels which were sometimes equipped with a mast and sail.

Lump: a quantity of fish waiting to be gutted.

Lumpers: fish market workers who landed catches from vessels—especially trawlfish.

Main(sail): the largest sail on a vessel, set on its mainmast.

Make up: to tidy up a fishing vessel and check through the gear at the end of a voyage.

Making round: a term used of the tide changing from flood to ebb, or vice versa.

Mand: 1. A wicker basket that held about two and a half stones of herring. 2. A basket of similar size used for handling sprats, which was often used as the official measure for the species.

Manil(l)a: a vegetable fibre (*Musa textilis*) used for making high-quality rope.

Margarine boxes: wooden (and later alumimium) boxes used on board drifters which held about three and a half stones of fish.

Markings/Marks: prominent natural or built features on (or near) the shoreline, which were used by **longshore** (q.v.) fishermen as navigational aids.

Maroons: large fireworks which were used as call-out signals for lifeboat crews.

Mash(es): meshes. The word is a dialect variant of the original one.

Messenger: a steel cable which was used to draw both warps into the **towing-block** (q.v.).

Midwater trawl: a trawl-net that was rigged to operate above the seabed, but at some distance down from the surface.

Ministry (The): the Ministry of Agriculture and Fisheries (as it was, at the time). This arm of government is currently known as DEFRA (Department for Environment, Food and Rural Affairs).

Mission boats: sailing trawlers or (later) steam vessels belonging to the Royal National Mission to Deep Sea Fishermen, which carried out a limited amount of fishing and also ministered to the physical and spiritual needs of men working in the North Sea.

Mizzen: 1. the mast nearest the stern of a vessel. 2. The sail that was set on this mast. The term was used particularly of the steadying sail fitted to steam drifters.

Muddly: mild, damp, foggy weather.

Mull: a fleshy area on either side of a ray's mouth.

Muzzle: the term used of a **snood** (q.v.) becoming wrapped round the mouth of a fish caught on longlines. This occurred particularly with conger eels.

Needle: a hand-bobbin made from wood or bone, used to make or mend fishing nets.

Net-barrow: a wooden platform, like a small litter, with handles at either end and four short legs, used to transport **longshore** (q.v.) fishing gear.

Net(t) hundred: the sum of £100 earned by a fishing vessel after expenses had been paid.

Net-rope: the double rope on the top of a **drift-net** (q.v.), to which the corks were attached.

Nip: a tight turn, to port or starboard, made by a vessel towing a trawl.

Norsels: lengths of twine which joined the meshes to the **net-rope** (q.v.) on a drift-net and held the corks in position. The original form of the word was **ossel** (q.v.). In East Anglian dialect, "an ossel" (spoken) became "a norsel"—and the variant then became an accepted term.

Nurse: Larger Spotted Dogfish (*Scyliorhinus stellaris*). The species was given this particular name because its skin was believed to secrete a healing substance.

Ossel: the original form of **norsel** (q.v.).

Oddie/oddy: See **Hoddy**.

Oily/oily frock: an oilskin smock, an essential part of a fisherman's working apparel on board ship.

Ollabut: Halibut (*Hippoglossus hippoglossus*).

On-the-door gear: an **otter-trawl** (q.v.) whose doors were secured directly on to the net without the use of **dan lenos** (q.v.) or **bridles** (q.v.).

Ossel: the original word for a **norsel** (q.v.).

Otter-doors: heavy, rectangular, wooden paravanes (one on each side of the net), which helped to keep the mouth of a trawl open when towing was in progress.

Otter-trawl: trawl gear which had the mouth of the net kept open by large wooden doors acting as paravanes.

Outboard: a term used to describe anything that was situated on the outside of a vessel, beyond the physical barrier of its hull.

Overtail/-tale: the specific number of twelve herrings, by which the long hundred increased from 120 to 132. *Tail/tale* could have the sense either of an imposed payment or be a variant of *tally*.

Owners: the commonly-used abbreviated form of boatowners.

Paralysed: the word used to describe trawl gear which had been badly damaged by rough ground or by under-water obstructions.

Part(ed): the term used to describe the severing of a **warp** (q.v.) on either drifting or trawling gear.

Pay off: 1. To take up the money due to crew members (if there was any!) at the end of a drifting **voyage** (q.v.). 2. The term used of a vessel when it veered either to port or starboard.

Peck: 1. An Imperial measure of dry volume equalling two gallons. It was used particularly for shrimps. 2. A 420-fathom length of longlines coiled into a wooden chute. The word is a variant of *pack*.

Ped: a general term for a wicker fishing basket. Originally, the ped had been a tall basket, with a lid, carried from place to place by itinerant hawkers (*pedlars*).

Peg anchor: a small anchor used in **seine-netting** (q.v.), whose function was to hold the main anchor in place on the seabed.

Pelagic: fish which lived (or spent some of their time) in the upper levels of the sea.

Pennant: a long, tapering streamer flown at a vessel's mast-head.

Pennants: see **Reef pennants** below.

Perks: 1. Stout wooden boards slotted into a steam drifter's hold opening, on which the nets were stacked when not in use and on which crew members sometimes stood when hauling was in progress. 2. Extra money, in addition to what was earned or expected—an abbreviated form of *perquisite*.

Pickle: to gut herrings and pack them, layered, in wooden casks with a sprinkling of salt on each tier of fish.

Pilot: 1. A suitably qualified Trinity House employee, with appropriate local knowledge, who was responsible for steering vessels into, and out of, harbour.

2. An old, retired fisherman who joined a fishing vessel's crew to give them the benefit of his experience when new grounds or methods were being tried out.

Pleasure trip: a casual fishing-trip undertaken by a boy before he left school, usually during holiday periods or at the weekend. He was given his food on board, but was expected to do some useful work to earn his keep.

Poaching: fishing illegally inside **limit-lines** (q.v.).

Pockets: compartments on the sides of a trawl-net, above the **cod-end** (q.v.), which acted as fish-traps (especially for soles).

Poke: the cod-end of a trawl-net.

Pollards: bollards. The word is simply a variant pronunciation.

Poop one: to take a heavy sea over the stern of a vessel.

Pots: basket-traps of varying size and shape, made from cane and wicker, which were baited and placed on the seabed to catch crabs and lobsters. Later models used plastic mesh stretched over wooden or metal frames.

Pounds: compartments on deck, or down in the fish-hold, for the storage of fish.

Prime fish: valuable flatfish species such as halibut, sole, turbot and brill.

Pud: term used in ports outside Lowestoft (especially Hull, Grimsby and Fleetwood) for fishermen from the Suffolk town.

Puddly water: oily water at sea, which indicated the presence of herring. There is an obvious connection here with *puddle*, in the sense of the water being less than clear.

Punch: to steam against the wind and tide.

Purse-seine: a wall of netting in which the foot-rope and head-line are drawn together by **reeving lines** (q.v.) to form a large, cup-shaped enclosure in which a shoal of pelagic fish (usually, herrings, mackerel or pilchards) is trapped.

Push net: a single, triangular-shaped, bag-net, or one that was divided into two compartments, which was set across a spar of wood and pushed by the operator (by means of a pole set at right-angles to the spar) through shallow water to catch shrimps.

Quant: a punting pole. The word is particularly associated with the *Norfolk wherry*.

Quarter (port or starboard): the side of a vessel (to left or right) between the stern and the mainmast.

Quarter-cran basket: a stout wicker basket containing seven stones weight of herring.

Quarters: those areas of an **otter-trawl** (q.v.) where the upper wings meet the head-line and where the lower wings meet the ground-rope at either end of the bosom.

Rail: the top part of a vessel's **gunwale** (q.v.).

Reef: to shorten sail in rough weather by the process described immediately below.

Reef pennants: short lengths of cord fixed in rows along the bottom of a sail which were threaded through eyes in the canvas, to allow the sail to be shortened in rough weather.

Reeve: to thread a cord or rope through an eye or hole.

Reeving-lines: the master-lines at the top of a **purse-seine** (q.v.), which are drawn together by the winch and serve to close the net—thereby trapping the fish contained within.

Reining: a length of old drift-net which was fixed along the bottom of a **longshore** (q.v.) herring or sprat net to weight it down and make it hang better in the water.

Relieving tackle: a rope made fast to the tiller-bar of a **smack** (q.v.), which could be led to a block set on the gunwale to either side of it and then used by the helmsman to apply greater leverage to the rudder when steering in heavy weather.

Ride: to face the wind head on, with the anchor down.

Rippers: handlines which had two or three hooks attached to the lead sinker.

Roads: 1. The inshore sea approaches to a port. 2. Areas between outlying sandbanks and the beach itself, where vessels could find safe anchorage. The word was used especially in association with Great Yarmouth and Lowestoft.

Rolls: the roes, or eggs, of a female fish.

Ro(o)ker: 1. Various species of ray. 2. The Thornback Ray (*Raja clavata*).

Ross: hard, sandy deposits on the seabed, resembling coral in shape, built up from the casts of polychaetes (marine worms).

Roves: small metal washers on to which the end of clencher-nails are beaten over when a boat's hull is built.

Rough stuff: 1. The less valuable species of trawlfish, such as gurnards and weevers. 2. Any trawlfish that wasn't classed as **prime** (q.v.).

Rows: 1. The number of meshes per yard in a **drift-net** (q.v.). 2. The roes of a female fish (the word is a simple variant pronunciation).

Run: to sail or steam before the wind, when the weather was stormy.

Sand ray: Shagreen Ray (*Raja fullonica*).

Sansom post: the section of a sailing smack's mizzen mast which passed down through the cabin.

Score: the depth of **drift-nets** (q.v.) was reckoned in scores (twenties) of meshes. Hence, with a mesh being roughly an inch in length, a net of six-score size would have been ten feet in depth.

Scotch nets: herring drift-nets made of cotton—the fibre which superseded linen or hemp and which was first put into production at Mussleburgh amd Leith.

Scratchers: small trawlers which worked fairly close to the home port. The word is a reference to the lightness of the gear they used and its effect on the seabed.

Scruff ground: an area of the seabed where there is a lot of shell debris.

Scuppers: holes at the bottom of a vessel's gunwale which drained excess water off the deck.

Sea biscuit: a hard-tack biscuit made from flour and water and intensively baked to create long-lasting qualities at sea.

Sea louse: a general term used to describe any kind of parasite afflicting fish.

Second: second engineer, on a steam trawler.

Seine(-net): 1. A generic term for any kind of bag-net used in fishing. 2. The term used for the **Danish seine** (q.v.)—a specific type of gear used to catch demersal species.

Shank: 1. The straight length of a fishing hook. 2. An individual length of **longline** (q.v.), measuring sixty fathoms, which was tied to others to make up the overall length required. The longlines used in **longshore** (q.v.) fishing had shanks of about thirty fathoms' length.

Shannocking: longlining for cod in the North Sea.

Shannocks: The nickname given to inhabitants of the Norfolk coastal town of Sheringham.

Share system: the method of remuneration used to pay fishermen engaged in herring fishing or longlining. If a vessel was in profit at the end of a **voyage** (q.v.), the crew members were rewarded according to their respective status on board, starting with the skipper and working down to the cook.

Sheave: a grooved wheel set in a wooden block, which allowed a rope to run freely.

Sheer: 1. To veer to port or starboard. 2. The upward curvature of a vessel towards bow and stern. 3. A word used to describe clear water at sea.

Shimmer: a quantity of herrings or sprats taken in one haul—the term deriving from the species' silver colour.

Ship up: 1. To provide crew for a vessel. 2. To join the crew of a vessel.

Ship's husband: the man on shore in charge of crewing arrangements and a fishing vessel's general well-being.

Ship's papers: official documents relating to the construction and ownership of a vessel.

Shoal: 1. An assembly of fish swimming together. 2. A sandbank.

Shoe (-kettle): a metal container, shaped something like a shoe, which was designed for heating water and making tea in a sailing smack's capstan boiler. It was shaped to fit in the stoke-hole of the boiler.

Shoot: to cast fishing nets.

Shore net: see **Draw-net**.

Shoulder(s): the area(s) of netting in a Danish seine which joined the wings to the main body of the net.

Shrimp-trawl: a fine-meshed beam-trawl used by **longshore** (q.v.) fishermen to catch shrimps only.

Sidelights: the lamps carried by all ships at sea (one on either side of each vessel) for visibility at night: green for starboard and red for port.

Skipper-owner: a man who both owned and commanded a fishing-vessel.

Skipper's log: a record kept by individual masters of their fishing activities, year on year, as an attempted means of maximising a vessel's earnings.

Slack tide: 1. The turn of the tide between low and high water. 2. A tidal current of no great strength.

Slink: a mature cod with very little flesh on it.

Slips: small soles, which have not grown to maturity.

Smack: in the case of Great Yarmouth and Lowestoft, a term that refers specifically to gaff-rigged sailing trawlers.

Smokehouse: a building of varying size (depending on the scale of the enterprise) in which herrings were hung to cure above slow-burning sawdust fires. Vents or louvers in the roof-ridge, or the upper part of the walls, allowed a current of air to circulate and the smoke to escape. Brick was the customary material used to construct smokehouses, but wooden ones were not unknown.

Snotch: to score herrings with about six transverse cuts across the backbone, prior to frying them. This made the flesh easier to remove. The word is obviously a variant of *notch*.

Snood/Snud: a length of twine which joined a hook to a longline.

Spent: a herring that had spawned.

Splice: to join two lengths of rope by unravelling and re-plaiting the individual strands. The origin of the word is probably the Middle Dutch *splissen*.

Sprag: a half-grown cod.

Spronk/sprunk: one strand of a drift-net's mesh broken.

Spunyarn: rope strands that were twisted together to make line for use in rigging.

Square: the top part of a trawl net between the **head-line** (qv.) and the **batings** (q.v.).

Stanchions: H-section vertical supports in the hull of a vessel.

Standard boat: a steam drifter or trawler built during World War I to Admiralty specifications and intended for patrolling or minesweeping duties.

Standard trawl: trawl-gear that had a **head-line** (q.v.) of sixty-five feet length and a net fitted directly onto the **otter-doors** (q.v.).

Stay: a rope or wire guy used to support a mast and give it stability.

Stocker bait: the money allowed trawlermen (on top of their wages) from the sale of under-sized fish and species of no great commercial value.

Stockie: an abbreviated form of **stocker bait**.

Stockfish: The coarsest variety of processed cod, which had been decapitated, gutted, split along the backbone (which was usually removed) and dried in the open air—the low fat content preventing deterioration. The origin of the term is to be found in the Dutch *stok*, meaning "pole" because, in Iceland, the fish were traditionally dried in pairs by being secured by the tail to poles.

Store: a net-store—the two-storey building in which fishing gear was rigged, repaired and kept.

Storm-jib: a small triangular sail set on mainmast stay and bowsprit, to help keep a smack steady in bad weather. It was the smallest of all the **jibs** (q.v.) carried.

Strike: to catch fish—a term used especially of taking pelagic species in **drift-nets** (q.v.).

Swing: a term sometimes used to describe the curve (caused by the effect of tidal flow) on a set of inshore **longlines** (q.v.), if these had not been sufficiently weighted down to the seabed and buoyed up on the surface.

Taffrail: the top section of the gunwale which ran around the stern of a vessel. The word is a variant of *tafferel*, which was the one used during the seventeenth century.

Takle: a variant pronunciation of *tackle*: a pulley-block, with its accompanying sheet or rope.

Tally: a paper label with a fish merchant's name printed on it, which was placed on containers of fish (after an auction had finished) to denote ownership.

Tan: to preserve **drift-nets** (q.v.) from the rotting effect of bacteria and sea water, which was done by boiling them in **cutch** (q.v.). The word is a hang-over from the time when nets were preserved by being soaked in a leather-tanning solution made from either ash or oak bark.

Tender: a general-purpose vessel belonging to Trinity House, which was used for repair and supply work connected with buoys and lightships around the British coasts.

Thick: 1. a term used to describe foggy weather. 2. Sea water that was discoloured with a combination of herring oil and zoo plankton.

Third hand: the rank below mate on a trawler.

Thole(-pin): one of a pair of wooden pegs set in the top of a boat's gunwale to act as rowlocks.

Thortcher-board: see **Thwartship board**.

Thrush: the coupling which connected the engine to the propeller shaft on a marine steam-reciprocating engine.

Thwarts: the seats of a rowing boat or dinghy.

Thwartship-board: a plank which ran the width of a steam drifter, fore and aft of the hold, thereby acting as the end of the **kids** (q.v.).

Ticket: a certificate of navigational competence, verifying the ability of a man to serve as mate or skipper of a vessel (depending on which certificate he held).

Ticklers: see **Titlers** below.

Tiller: a stout wooden bar attached to the rudder, which was used to steer a sailing vessel.

Tired voyage: a fishing season that involved a lot of hard work and little sleep. It was a term mainly applied to seine-netting for haddock on the Dogger Bank, to the Milford Haven lining voyage for conger and to trawling for soles out of Padstow.

Titlers: light chains stretched across the mouth of a trawl, which stirred up sediment and caused flatfish to rise from the seabed, prior to their being caught in the net. The word is a variant form of *ticklers*.

Tittle: to trawl lightly over a piece of ground. The word is a variant of *tickle*.

Tongue: an immature sole of lesser size than a **slip** (q.v.).

Top-weight: a term used to describe a vessel which had too much construction and mast-height above decks, relative to the size and depth of the hull. This made a craft unwieldy and difficult to handle—especially in bad weather.

Tosher: a small sailing smack, crewed by three men in the summer and four in the winter.

Tow: To pull a trawl along the seabed.

Towing (along): working a trawl to catch demersal species of fish.

Towing-block: a steel box which held both trawl **warps** (q.v.) together while towing otter gear was in progress.

Train-oil: A generic term for any kind of fish oil (the origin is the Middle Dutch *traen*, meaning *oil*). This product was used mainly to fuel lamps or dress leather.

Trawl(-net): a triangular-shaped bag-net, with its **beam** (q.v.) or **otter doors** (q.v.) which was dragged along the seabed to catch demersal species.

Trawler: a fishing vessel which operated a trawl.

Trawlfish: demersal species (bottom-dwelling) caught by trawlers.

Trawl-head: a large, forged, iron, stirrup-shaped hoop (one of a pair) on a beam trawl, which supported the beam at either end and helped to keep the mouth of the net open.

Trimmer: a crew member on a steam trawler who prepared coal for the furnace.

Trip: a single fishing expedition.

Trip o' fish: a successful single fishing expedition, with a good catch.

Triple-expansion (engine): a marine steam-reciprocating engine which had three cylinders (high-presure, intermediate and low-pressure), through which the steam was successively exhausted.

Truck: the top of a mast—or, more precisely, the circular cap fixed there, with holes bored for halyards to run through.

Trunk: a wooden case in which trawlfish were packed, later superseded by metal boxes.

Tubes: the fire-tubes in a ship's boiler (or a railway locomotive's), which enabled flame from the furnace to heat the water surrounding them and thus produce the steam required to power the engine.

Underfoots: see **Perks**.

Under-run: the term used for a **longshore** (q.v.) vessel being rowed up and down a fleet of drift-nets, while the other crew member inspected the nets and removed fish from the meshes.

Up (and) Along: a trawling area off the Suffolk and Essex coast, in the area of the Gabbard and Galloper banks. It was popular with smacks and drifter-trawlers in the early months of the year, to provide good fishing, with a variety of species being caught. *Up* derives from the southerly direction taken by the vessels (that being the direction of the flood-tide); *along* refers to the grounds being relatively close to land (about twenty miles out).

Vacuum fishing: drawing fish up from the seabed by a vacuum pump.

Voyage: a fishing season, conducted out of the home port or further afield. It consisted of a number of individual trips which constituted the whole.

Waleman: one of the threequarter and half-quarter sharemen in a steam drifter's crew (there were two).

Walings: the double-stepped landing-stage structure which once existed on the Lowestoft fish market below the top level.

Walking about: the term used by fishermen for being out of work. It reflects the difficulty of getting a job during the 1920s and 30s, at a time of uncertainty in the fishing industry and of economic difficulty in the country generally.

Warp: 1. The master-rope which holds and supports a fleet of **drift-nets** (q.v.). 2. The rope or wire cable used to tow a **trawl** (q.v.). 3. A count of four herrings or mackerel (two held in each hand), used to tally up the fish in **long hundreds** (q.v).

Warping round/out: working a sailing (or steam) vessel around a harbour's quays, using a rope and capstan, as a means of moving it from one place to another—the rope being fixed (usually) to a bollard on the quayside and wound in by the capstan.

Washing: a quantity of whelks used as longline bait.

Watch: a turn of duty in the wheelhouse of a steam drifter or trawler, or at the tiller of a smack.

Watchman: a man employed to keep an eye on vessels overnight (and sometimes at the weekend) after they had landed their catches.

Weather shore: a shore from which the wind was blowing outwards.

Weather side: the side of a vessel nearest the wind.

Weather tide: a tide running against the direction of the wind, which could create a good deal of turbulence (depending on the strength of the wind).

Went through: became bankrupt.

West'ard: the name used for fishing **voyages** (q.v.) undertaken in Devon and Cornish waters. A simple variant of *Westward*.

Whale-deck: deck space which is roofed over (usually for'ad), to afford protection from the elements. Its rounded upper profile bore comparison with the cetacean's back.

Wheelhouse: a superstructure raised above the level of the decks containing the steering gear and other equipment necessary for navigating the vessel. It was integral with the engine-room casing and, in the earlier vessels, often located aft-side of the funnel. Later models always had it in front.

Whiffler: a device which regulated the draught on a steam engine's furnace.

Whip: a young conger eel (*Conger conger*).

White fish: trawlfish.

White horses: broken water and foaming waves, caused by extreme weather conditions at sea or by the presence of sandbanks close to the surface.

Wing: 1. A space below deck between the main hold and the side of the vessel. 2. That part of the trawl-net (there was one on either side) which was nearest the otter door or the beam. 3. The section of a seine-net (again, there were two) between the warp and the cod-end.

Wolded: the word used to describe a trawl's **ground-rope** (q.v.) which had lengths of old net fastened round it, to cause a more effective sanding-up process.

Wolding: lengths of old netting used in the manner described immediately above.

Workhouse ships: Dutch fishing vessels which had a number of young lads among the crew. The term is probably a throwback to the second half of the nineteenth century, when the Hull and Grimsby smacks particularly often had apprentices on board supplied by English workhouses.

Wrapper/wropper: a fisherman's neckerchief. Black silk was very fashionable during the 1920s and 30s.

Yowler: an immature herring.

Select Bibliography

Benham, H., *The Cod Bangers* (Colchester, 1979).

Butcher, D., *The Driftermen* (Reading, 1979).

        The Trawlermen (Reading, 1980).

        Living from the Sea (Reading, 1982).

        Following the Fishing (Newton Abbot, 1987).

        The Ocean's Gift (Norwich, 1995).

        Lowestoft 1550-1750 (Woodbridge, 2008).

        Rigged For River and Sea (Hull, 2008)

        Fishing Talk (Cromer, 2014).

        Medieval Lowestoft (Woodbridge, 2016).

Campbell, A.C., *The Hamlyn Guide to the Seashore and Shallow Seas of Britain and Europe* (London, 1976).

Cherry, P. & Westgate, T., *The Roaring Boys of Suffolk* (Hadleigh, 1970).

Claxton, A.O.D., *The Suffolk Dialect of the Twentieth Century* (Ipswich, 1954).

Curtis, A.J., *Lowestoft Fishermen's War 1914-1918* (Lowestoft, 2018).

Davis, F.M., *An Account of the Fishing Gear of England and Wales*, 4th ed. (London, 1928).

De Caux, J.W., *The Herring and the Herring Fishery* (London, 1881).

D'Enno, D., *Fishermen Against the Kaiser*, vol. 1 (Barnsley, 2010).

Dyson, J., *Business in Great Waters* (London. 1977).

Elliott, C., *Sailing Fishermen in Old Photographs* (Reading, 1978).

        Steam fishermen in Old Photographs (Reading, 1979).

Evans, G.E., *The Days That We Have Seen* (London, 1975).

Festing, S., *Fishermen* (Newton Abbot, 1977; Stamford, 1999).

Finch, W., *The Sea in My Blood* (Weybread, 1992).

Forby, R., *The Vocabulary of East Anglia*, 2 vols. (London, 1830; Newton Abbot, 1970).

Frost. T., *From Tree to Sea* (Lavenham, 1985).

Higgins, D., *The Beachmen* (Lavenham, 1987).

Hodgson, W.C., *The Herring and its Fishery* (London, 1957).

Kurlansky, M., *Cod* (London, 1998).

Lee, A.J., *The Directorate of Fisheries Research* (Lowestoft, 1992).

Lund, P. & Ludlam, H., *Trawlers Go to War* (London, 1971).

Malster, R.,   *Saved from the Sea* (Lavenham, 1974).

        Lowestoft, East Coast Port (Lavenham, 1982).

        Lowestoft, a Pictorial History (Chichester, 1991).

        The Mardler's Companion (Ipswich, 1999).

        Maritime Norfolk, Part One (Cromer, 2012).

        Maritime Norfolk, Part Two (Cromer, 2013).

        North Sea War 1914-1919 (Cromer, 2015).

        Maritime Suffolk (Cromer, 2017).

March, E.J., *Sailing Drifters* (London, 1952; Newton Abbot, 1969).

        Sailing Trawlers (London, 1953; Newton Abbot, 1970).

Mather, E.J., *Nor'ad of the Dogger* (London, 1887).

Moor, E.,   *Suffolk Words and Phrases* (Woodbridge, 1823; Newton Abbot, 1970).

Muus, B.J. & Dahlstrøm, P., *Collins Guide to the Sea Fishes of Britain and North-Western Europe* (London, 1974).

Nall, J.G.,   *Great Yarmouth and Lowestoft* (London, 1866).

        Etymological and Comparative Glossary of the Dialect and Provincialisms of East Anglia (London, 1866).

Oliver, R.C., *Trawlermen's Handbook* (London, 1965).

Parkin, D, & Rose J., *The Grit: the Story of Lowestoft's Beach Village* (Halesworth, 2019)—updated version of the original work of 1997.

Richards, L.E. *Eighty Years of Shipbuilding* (Lowestoft, 1956).

Robb, I.,   *Memories of the East Anglian Fishing Industry* (Newbury, 2010).

Rose, J. & Parkin, D.,*The Grit: the Story of Lowestoft's Beach Village* (Lowestoft, 1997).

Smylie, M.,   *Herring* (Stroud, 2004).

Starkey, D. et al. (eds.), *England's Sea Fisheries* (London, 2000).

Thompson, P.,   *Living the Fishing* (London, 1983).

Wheeler, A., *The Fishes of the British Isles and North-west Europe* (London, 1969).

Wren, W.J., *Ports of the Eastern Counties* (Lavenham, 1976).

Wright, J.,   *The English Dialect Dictionary*, 6 vols. (Oxford, 1898 & 1970).

Index

Index of People Referred to In-text

A majority of the names recorded are those of fishermen from the Lowestoft area (including Kessingland) who worked on steam drifters and drifter-trawlers, with no account being taken here of their status on board ship—which is often made clear in-text. Further information is given on people of different occupation and experience, as well as those from places beyond the Lowestoft locality.

Lowestoft-area Place Names

Other UK Place-names & Mainland Locations

Foreign Place-names and Mainland Locations

Sandbanks, Channels & Associated Fishing-grounds

Rivers & Areas of the Oceans

You may also like

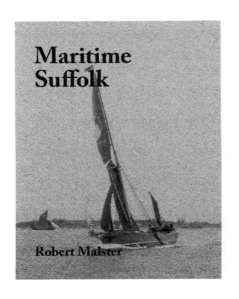

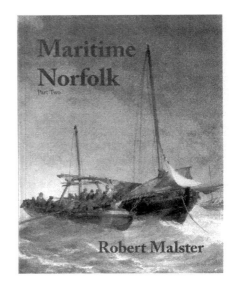

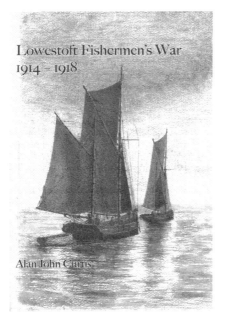

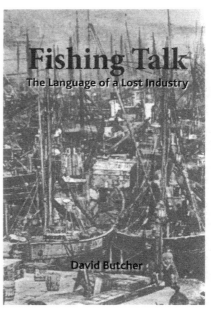

available from local bookshops and www.poppyland.co.uk

Printed in Great Britain
by Amazon

44621305R00154